The Teutonic Knights in the Holy Land
1190–1291

The Teutonic Knights
in the Holy Land
1190–1291

NICHOLAS EDWARD MORTON

THE BOYDELL PRESS

First published 2009
The Boydell Press, Woodbridge
Paperback edition 2017

ISBN 978 1 84383 477 9 hardback
ISBN 978 1 78327 181 8 paperback

The Boydell Press is an imprint of Boydell & Brewer Ltd
PO Box 9, Woodbridge, Suffolk IP12 3DF, UK
and of Boydell & Brewer Inc.
668 Mt Hope Avenue, Rochester, NY 14620–2731, USA
website: www.boydellandbrewer.com

The publisher has no responsibility for the continued existence or accuracy
of URLs for external or third-party internet websites referred to in this book,
and does not guarantee that any content on such websites is,
or will remain, accurate or appropriate

A CIP catalogue record for this book is available
from the British Library

For my parents,
Andrew and Juliet

Contents

List of Illustrations and Tables

This book is produced with the generous assistance
of a grant from Isobel Thornley's Bequest
to the University of London

Acknowledgements

About six years ago, I was a BA student at Royal Holloway and I took a course on the crusades with Jonathan Phillips; looking back on the intervening years, I haven't really looked back since. I owe Professor Phillips an enormous debt of gratitude for his kindness, his enthusiasm and for putting up with me for so long! He has been an inspiration.

I would also like to express my profound gratitude to the Arts and Humanities Research Council for their support. I would also like to thank William Urban, Guy Perry, Paul Crawford, Adrian Boas, Denys Pringle and Jonathan Riley-Smith for their kindness and advice. I am also grateful to Alison Phelan, Randa Haddad, Andrew Morton, Mary Morton and most particularly Reena Shenton for their help with my linguistic studies.

For my parents, it is difficult to know where to begin. From childhood bedtime stories about King Arthur through to their support in the preparation of this work they have always been a rock of support and encouragement. To my beloved wife Dina, I would like to express my great appreciation for her loving kindness and support; a Jonathan Phillips student herself, her ongoing enthusiasm and interest have been of such value.

Nicholas Morton
December 2008

Abbreviations and Editorial Note

The following abbreviations are used throughout the book.

AOL   *Archives de l'Orient Latin*, ed. P. Riant, 2 vols (Paris, 1881–1884)

AZM   K. Militzer, *Von Akkon zur Marienburg: Verfassung, Verwaltung und Sozialstruktur des Deutschen Ordens 1190–1309*, QuStDO, 56 (Marburg, 1999).

BEFAR   Bibliothéque des écoles françaises d'Athènes et de Rome.

CDOT   *Codex Diplomaticus Ordinis Sanctae Mariae Theutonicorum*, ed. J. H. Hennes (Mainz, 1845).

CGJJ   *Cartulaire Général de l'Ordre des Hospitaliers de S. Jean de Jérusalem: 1100–1310*, ed. J. Delaville Le Roulx, 4 vols (Paris, 1894–1905).

Eracles   *L'Estoire de Eracles Empereur et la Conqueste de la Terre d'Outremer*, in *RHC. Oc.*, vol. 2 (Paris, 1859).

HB   *Historia Diplomatica Friderici Secundi*, ed. J. L. A. Huillard-Bréholles, 6 vols (Paris, 1852–1861).

HOC   *A History of the Crusades*, ed. K. M. Setton, 6 vols (Philadelphia, PA, 1955–1989).

HU   *Hohenlohisches Urkundenbuch*, ed. K. Weller, 3 vols (Stuttgart, 1899–1912)

KSJJC   J. S. C. Riley-Smith, *The Knights of St John in Jerusalem and Cyprus c.1050–1310* (London, 1967).

MGH Epis. Saec. XIII   *Monumenta Germaniae Historica: Epistolae Saeculi XIII e Regestis Pontificum Romanorum selectae.*

MGH Leges Const.   *Monumenta Germaniae Historica Leges: Constitutiones et Acta Publica Imperatorum et Regum.*

MGH SRG   *Monumenta Germaniae Historica: Scriptores rerum Germanicarum*

MGH SRGNS   *Monumenta Germaniae Historica: Scriptores rerum Germanicarum, Nova Series*

MGH SS   *Monumenta Germaniae Historica: Scriptores*

MGH SVL   *Monumenta Germaniae Historica: Scriptorum qui Vernacula Lingua usi sunt*

MO   *The Military Orders: Fighting for the Faith and Caring for the Sick*, ed. M. Barber, 2 vols (Aldershot, 1994)

PL   *Patrologia Latina*, ed. J.-P. Migne, 221 vols (Paris, 1844–1865).

Potthast   *Regesta Pontificum Romanorum*, ed. A. Potthast, 2 vols (Berlin, 1873–1875)

PU   *Preussisches Urkundenbuch*, ed. A. Seraphim, M. Hein,
E. Maschke et al., 6 vols (Königsberg, 1961–2000).

QuStDO   Quellen und Studien zur Geschichte des Deutschen Ordens

R. Reg.   *Regesta Regni Hierosolymitani: 1097–1291*, ed. R. Röhricht,
2 vols (Innsbruck, 1893. *Additamentum*, 1904).

Reg. Alexandre IV *Les Registres de Alexandre IV*, ed. C. Bourel de la
Roncière, BEFAR, 3 vols (Paris, 1895–1953).

Reg. Clément IV   *Les Registres de Clément IV*, ed. É. Jordan, BEFAR,
4 vols (Paris, 1893–1904).

Reg. Grégoire IX   *Les Registres de Grégoire IX*, ed. L. Auvray, BEFAR,
4 vols (Paris, 1896–1955).

Reg. Grégoire X   *Les Registres de Grégoire X*, ed. J. Guiraud, BEFAR
(Paris, 1892).

Reg. Innocent IV   *Les Registres d'Innocent IV*, ed. É. Berger, BEFAR,
4 vols (Paris, 1884–1921).

Reg. Martin IV   *Les Registres de Martin IV*, ed. O. Martin, BEFAR
(Paris, 1901).

Reg. Nicolas IV   *Les Registres de Nicolas IV*, ed. E. Langlois, BEFAR
(Paris, 1886–1891).

Reg. Urbain IV   *Les Registres D'Urbain IV*, ed. J. Guiraud, BEFAR,
4 vols (Paris, 1899–1906).

Regesta Imperii IV *Regesta Imperii IV: Ältere Staufer*, ed. J. F. Böhmer,
3 vols (Cologne, 1972–2001).

Regesta Imperii V *Regesta Imperii V: Die Regesten des Kaiserreichs:
unter Philipp, Otto IV, Friedrich II, Heinrich (VII), Conrad IV,
Heinrich Raspe, Wilhelm und Richard, 1198–1272*, ed. J. F.
Böhmer, 4 vols (Innsbruck, 1881–1983).

RHC. Arm.   *Recueil des Historiens des Croisades: Documents Arméniens*,
2 vols (Paris, 1869–1906).

RHC. Oc.   *Recueil des Historiens des Croisades: Historiens Occidentaux*,
5 vols (Paris, 1844–95).

RHP   *Regesta Honorii Papae III*, ed. P. Pressutti, 2 vols (Hildesheim,
1978).

Rothelin   *Continuation de Guillaume de Tyr de 1229 à 1261, dite du
manuscript de Rothelin*, in *RHC. Oc.*, vol. 2, pp. 489–639.

RS   Rolls Series

Sanuto   Marino Sanuto, *Liber Secretorum Fidelium Crucis: Super
Terre Sancte Recuperatione et Consevatione*, in *Gesta Dei Per
Francos*, ed. J. Bongars (Jerusalem, 1972).

SDO   *Die Statuten des Deutschen Ordens nach Ältesten
Handschriften*, ed. M. Perlbach (Hildesheim, 1975).

TOT   *Tabulae Ordinis Theutonici: Ex Tabularii Regii Berolinensis
Codice Potissimum*, ed. E. Strelke (Berlin, 1869; reprint ed.
H. Mayer, Jerusalem and Toronto, 1975).

Editorial Note

Many of the locations discussed in this work can be identified with different names. For example, the Teutonic Order's fortress to the north of Acre is referred to as 'Montfort' in French, 'Starkenburg' in German (which naturally carries the same meaning) and Qal'at al-Quarain in Arabic. In situations such as this I have used the most common name for ease of comprehension, so, in the case above, the name Montfort has been employed.

Personal names, in many instances, have been given in their modern English form. In this way, for example, Petrus de Confluentia is shown as Peter of Koblenz. Accordingly, toponyms have largely been updated in accordance with their modern equivalents. Furthermore, the French and German prepositions 'de' or 'von' have generally been replaced with 'of'. There are a number of exceptions to this, including the Teutonic Order's masters, such as Herman von Salza or Poppo von Osterna, who are commonly referred to with the German preposition 'von'. In these cases the preposition has been left unaltered. Arabic place and personal names are, as far as possible, given in their correct form.[1] Despite this, modern naming conventions concerning well-known names such as Saladin are used throughout.

With regard to the regulations of the Teutonic Knights, it is customary to describe them as the 'rule'. This work, however, will refer to them as the 'statutes'. This is because the statutes were divided into three main sections: the rule, the laws and the customs.[2] As a result, the term 'rule' would be inappropriate because it would be unclear as to whether reference was being made to the document as a whole or simply to this subsection. Consequently when reference is made to the 'rule' of the Order it will refer only to that particular section.

---

[1] Many of these names have been drawn from P. M. Holt, *The Age of the Crusades: The Near East from the Eleventh Century to 1517* (London, 1987), pp. xi–xii.

[2] I. Sterns, 'The Statutes of the Teutonic Knights: A Study of Religious Chivalry' (unpublished doctoral thesis, University of Pennsylvania, 1969), pp. 48–49.

Introduction

In 1190, while the forces of the Third Crusade laid siege to the city of Acre, a group of crusaders from Bremen and Lübeck established a small field hospital under a ship's sail to care for some of the many sick and wounded among the Christian forces.[1] In time this organisation grew into a major military order that would command vast resources, great estates and shape the history of the Western world. Its members became known collectively as the Teutonic Knights.

As with every military order, the foundation of the Teutonic Hospital was a response to a specific need. The Templars were formed to help address the kingdom of Jerusalem's perennial shortfall of troops.[2] The Hospitallers originated as a medical institution providing assistance for pilgrims visiting the city of Jerusalem.[3] Over time, as such institutions grew in military and financial power, they were able to broaden the range of 'needs' to which they could respond. By the mid-twelfth century the Templars' military power had evolved to the point where they were able to contribute a major contingent to the field armies of the Latin East and to provide garrisons for a number of strongholds.[4] The Hospitallers also developed a military arm and, in time, as both institutions received appeals from other realms, they provided warriors for many of Christendom's embattled frontiers.

The development of institutions of this type was not unique and certainly not confined to Christendom. In the Islamic world, for example, there developed organisations called *ribats*. A *ribat* was a 'fortified convent whose inmates combined a religious way of life with fighting against the enemies of Islam'.[5] Previously, some have argued that these Islamic communes were so similar in nature to the Christian military orders that they must have provided

---

[1]   U. Arnold has pointed out that the field hospital could have been founded at any point between 29 August 1189 and the middle of September 1190 although he acknowledges that there is no reason to doubt the traditional contention that it was founded in 1190; U. Arnold, 'Entstehung und Frühzeit des Deutschen Ordens', in *Die Geistlichen Ritterorden Europas*, ed. J. Fleckenstein and M. Hellman (Sigmaringen, 1980), p. 83. In reality, it seems that the former of these two dates should be amended to September 1189 because this was the time when the fleet from Bremen and Lübeck arrived.

[2]   A. Luttrell, 'The Earliest Templars', in *Autour de la Première Croisade*, ed. M. Balard (Paris, 1996), pp. 193–202.

[3]   A. Luttrell, 'The Earliest Hospitallers', in *Montjoie: Studies in Crusade History in Honour of Hans Eberhard Mayer*, ed. B. Z. Kedar, J. Riley-Smith and R. Hiestand (Aldershot, 1997), pp. 37–54.

[4]   M. Barber, *The New Knighthood: A History of the Order of the Temple* (Cambridge, 1995), pp. 93–95; A. J. Forey, *The Military Orders: From the Twelfth to the Early Fourteenth Centuries* (London, 1992), pp. 58–77.

[5]   Forey, *The Military Orders*, p. 8.

1

a template for them. This view has since been rejected on strong grounds; however, such establishments do share the common characteristic that they were all established to respond to a military/religious necessity.[6]

This quintessential characteristic, which lay at the core of each military order's identity, was also the reason – in many cases – why the idea prospered. Founded in 1170, the Order of Santiago flourished through the gifts of magnates, who could see the value of its work in the *Reconquista*.[7] The Swordbrethren, established in 1202, expanded through the support of nobles and churchmen who wished to support the Order as it drove back the pagan frontier in Livonia.[8] By contrast, once the necessity for a military order had evaporated, its future could be placed in jeopardy. In thirteenth-century Aragon, when the border with Moorish territory disappeared, the Hospitallers' retention of their local properties became contested as rulers such as King Jaume II began to try to recover control of the Order's lands and powers.[9]

The origins, development and decline of the Teutonic Knights were based on precisely the same principles. The brotherhood's first vocation was to provide support for the many sick at the siege of Acre. As the Order grew it began to assume greater obligations and to respond to wider needs. In 1198 a group of German princes on crusade in the Holy Land requested that the Teutonic Hospital should become a military order so that it could continue their struggle to retake Jerusalem after their return to the West. In time, as the brethren's labours attracted praise from across Christendom, they felt able to respond to the needs of other regions. In 1211, they answered a cry for help from the king of Hungary, who was suffering from the raids of his Cuman neighbours. In *c*.1225 the Order was granted the region of Kulmerland (the area around today's Chełmno in Poland) to help to protect the kingdom of Poland from the incursions of the Prussians. In 1237 it took over the defence of Livonia from the defeated and corrupt Swordbrethren. In time, the Teutonic Knights created semi-autonomous realms in both Livonia and Prussia. For all these tasks they were richly rewarded by benefactors who could see the importance of their labours.

This study (one of only a very few works on the Order in English) provides a comprehensive analysis of the role played by the Teutonic Knights in the Holy Land during the period 1190–1291. These terminal dates have been chosen because they cover the history of the institution from its original foundation to the final collapse of the kingdom of Jerusalem. The brethren maintained a presence in the eastern Mediterranean after 1291, but after this date their role took a very different form. To this end, the first part of this

---

6   For discussion of the different views on this subject see Forey, *The Military Orders*, pp. 7–10.
7   J. F. O'Callaghan, *Reconquest and Crusade in Medieval Spain* (Philadelphia, PA, 2003), pp. 54–55.
8   Forey, *The Military Orders*, p. 33.
9   A. Luttrell, 'The Aragonese Crown and the Knights Hospitallers of Rhodes: 1291–1350', *English Historical Review*, 76 (1961), pp. 1–19.

work offers a chronological study of the political, economic and diplomatic development of the Order in the Latin East and seeks to place its actions in the context of wider events taking place in the Orient and the Occident. The second part explores the institutional infrastructure and organisational framework which implemented these policies. The objective of this section is to depict the evolution of the Teutonic Knights as an organic progression and to demonstrate how the defining features of their identity were sculpted over time through the opportunities and threats they encountered.

Previously historians have tended to concentrate their research on the Teutonic Knights' policies in Prussia and Livonia. Certainly, it was in this region that they conducted their most famous campaigns and today they are generally remembered for their wars on these northern frontiers. Nevertheless, for 101 years the brethren worked to support the Holy Land, and their actions in this area form a vital part both in their own history and also that of the Latin East.

Given that the Teutonic Knights' position in the Latin East represented only one sector in their international deployments, this work analyses the division of the Order's resources between its frontier territories. With heavy military commitments in both the eastern Mediterranean and the Baltic, representatives from both areas stressed the importance of their region in an attempt to gain a greater share of the available materials. Each had compelling arguments to support their cause. On the one hand, the defence of the Holy Land and the struggle to regain Jerusalem was the Teutonic Knights' founding purpose. Prussia and Livonia, however, were bulwarks protecting Christendom against eastern invaders. They also gave the brethren considerable independence and power whilst providing supplies of manpower and resources.

Tensions between these battlefronts form an ongoing dialogue within the Order during the thirteenth century and the intensity of the disputes they engendered fluctuated in response to the evolving situation on both fronts. In the eastern Mediterranean, after the defeat of La Forbie in 1244, the outlook became increasingly bleak as the Christian position declined in the face of rising Muslim consolidation and power. In the Baltic, by contrast, although the brethren faced two serious rebellions in Prussia, the long-term trend was one of expansion and growth. The precedence given to the needs of any one area seems to have altered according to the character of each master and can occasionally be glimpsed in their allocation of resources at times when two fronts were in crisis simultaneously.

In the Latin East itself, the Teutonic Knights inhabited a world which contained many natural predators even among the Christian leadership. Within its first thirty years, both the Templars and Hospitallers attempted to gain control over this nascent institution. Despite the inevitable tension this caused, the brethren remained tied to these older institutions by their shared objectives and vocation. The Templars and Hospitallers were still the best institutional templates for an aspiring military order and so the Teutonic

3

Knights' uneasy relations with these formidable organisations formed a vital element in their early growth. Other Levantine rulers also saw potential in the German Order, including the rulers of Jerusalem, Cyprus and Antioch. For some, the Order presented an opportunity to tap the crusading resources of the German empire; for others it was a potential ally in regional disputes.

Certainly, the founding of the Teutonic Order was a symptom of a rising tide of German enthusiasm for crusading to the Holy Land and, in its early years at least, the brethren's main function was to supply and support German *milites* in the Latin East. These *milites* frequently expressed their gratitude to the brotherhood with grants of agricultural land and property in Germany. Through such gifts a cycle of goodwill formed in which the brethren's development became fuelled by investment whilst, in return, the nobility could feel they were supporting the work of reconquest. This symbiotic relationship formed the primary engine which drove the Teutonic Knights' growth and tied them closely to the German elite.

The Teutonic Knights' two greatest patrons were the papacy and the German emperor. As a religious institution, the Order was subordinate to the pope. Although its relationship with Rome was not one of equals, it was based on the mutually beneficial principle that service to the pontiff would be rewarded with privileges and patronage. The same was true of the emperor; he expected obedience from the Order as an institution of the empire, but was prepared to reward service with land, taxation rights and income. These arrangements lay at the heart of the Order's material and institutional advancement, but – crucially – they could also restrict the brethren's ability to frame an independent policy. As far as the imperial princes, the papacy and the emperor were concerned, the Teutonic Knights were useful but not indispensable; the brethren, however, were almost entirely dependent upon these patrons. If they were to alienate any one of these groups or individuals then their very future could be threatened, through either censure or military action. During the course of the thirteenth century such punishments became an occupational hazard for a German religious order that trod a dangerous path between the Hohenstaufen emperors and the papacy. The interplay between all the above factors forms the core of the first part of this work.

These are areas which have not been entirely neglected by previous historians; however, there are still many questions which have not been answered. Previous studies on the Order in the Mediterranean, such as those by Prutz and Hubatsch, have tended to focus upon two contentious issues: its origins and its landholdings.[10] The problem of the Teutonic Knights' origins centres upon the question of whether the Order (founded in 1190) was an entirely new organisation or whether it was simply a continuation of a previous

---

[10] H. Prutz, *Die Besitzungen des Deutschen Ordens* (Leipzig, 1871). W. Hubatsch, 'Montfort und die Bildung des Deutscheordensstaates im Heiligen Lande', *Nachrichten der Akademie der Wissenschaften in Göttingen: Philologisch-Historische Klasse* (Göttingen, 1966), pp. 161–199.

German hospice, established in Jerusalem *c.*1118.[11] This was a crucial issue for contemporaries because the earlier hospice had been subject to the authority of the Hospitallers who, believing the Teutonic Order to be a later incarnation of this older institution, demanded that it submit to their control. The Teutonic Order energetically repudiated these allegations and insisted that it had been formed as an entirely new organisation which was not bound to the Hospitallers in any way. The accuracy of these claims has consumed a sizeable proportion of both the abovementioned studies and many other works devoted to this subject.[12] The present consensus – one supported in this study – appears to be that there was no connection between the Teutonic Order and the earlier German hospice. Nonetheless, there are two strands of this debate which are of great relevance for this present work. The first is that the Hospitallers believed that they had rights of authority over the Teutonic Knights. The second is that the Knights denied their claims.

A further topic that has attracted a number of studies concerns the Order's landholdings in the Holy Land. Interest in this area has seemingly been driven by the quantity and availability of the brethren's Levantine property transactions, which can be found chiefly in the cartulary *Tabulae Ordinis Theutonici*. This source has been extensively mined on a number of occasions.[13] Other historians to comment on these and other issues include Forstreuter, whose work covers some aspects of the Levantine branch of the Order, including the two abovementioned matters, although it also examines the brethren's role in regions as diverse as Spain, Greece, Italy and Sicily.[14] In 1985 Sterns contributed a chapter on this subject to Setton's *A History of the Crusades*. This covers the Teutonic Knights' origins, landholdings, political policy and international relations; being only a single chapter, however, it is necessarily brief on each of these matters.[15] These studies form the greater part of the

---

[11] A good overview of the different theories on this subject is G. Müller, *Jerusalem oder Akkon: Über den Anfang des Deutschen Ordens nach dem gegenwärtigen Stand der Forschung* (Bad Münstereifel, 1989), *passim.*

[12] See, for example, M. Favreau, *Studien zur Frühgeschichte des Deutschen Ordens* (Stuttgart, 1974), *passim*; Arnold, 'Entstehung und Frühzeit des Deutschen Ordens', pp. 81–107; H. Prutz, *Die Besitzungen des Deutschen Ordens*, pp. 10–22.

[13] For a selection of further works on the Order's landholdings see M. Favreau, 'Die Kreuzfahrerherrschaft Scandalion (Iskanderūne)', *Zeitschrift des Deutschen Palästina-Vereins*, 93 (1977), pp. 12–29; H. E. Mayer, 'Die Seigneurie de Joscelin und der Deutsche Orden', in *Die Geistlichen Ritterorden Europas* (Sigmaringen, 1980), pp. 171–216; P. Hilsch, 'Der Deutsche Ritterorden im Südlichen Libanon: Zur Topographie der Kreuzfahrerherrschaften Sidon und Beirut', *Zeitschrift des Deutschen Palästina-Vereins*, 96 (1980), pp. 174–189. For the Teutonic Order in Armenia see J. S. C. Riley-Smith, 'The Templars and the Teutonic Knights in Cilician Armenia', in *The Cilician Kingdom of Armenia*, ed. T. S. R. Boase (Edinburgh, 1978), pp. 92–117; M. Chevalier, 'Les Chevaliers teutoniques en Cilicie: "les maccabées" du royaume arménien', *Bizantinistica*, 6 (2004), pp. 137–153.

[14] K. Forstreuter, *Der Deutsche Orden am Mittelmeer*, QuStDO, 2 (Bonn, 1967).

[15] I. Sterns, 'The Teutonic Knights in the Crusader States', in *HOC*, vol. 5, pp. 315–378. In 2004 the first of a new series of essay collections entitled *l'Ordine Teutonico nel Mediterraneo* was launched and these included an article by Favreau-Lilie which, in a similar way to Stern's work, provides a concise summary of the Order's actions in the Holy Land. M. Favreau-Lilie, 'L'Ordine

existing historiography that is focused specifically on the Order in the Holy Land.

A number of further monographs discuss a specific theme that concerns the Order as a whole, but has relevance for its Levantine branch. Of these, the nature of the brethren's relations with the Hohenstaufen emperors is an area which has attracted particular attention. Historians such as Cohn, Kluger and Arnold have provided extensive studies on this subject, generally with particular emphasis upon the relationship between Herman von Salza (master, *c*.1210–1239) and Emperor Frederick II.[16] These have tended to take the general view that, when conflict between the papacy and the empire placed the Order in a conflict of interests, Herman's loyalties lay more with the empire than with the Church. This work will address this contention and argue instead that Herman attempted to maintain a position of neutrality. The wider ramifications of this stance are not confined merely to this particular issue but, given the importance of the Hohenstaufen family in the politics of the Levant, they significantly re-cast the policy of the Order in this region until the late 1250s.

The second part of this book comprises of a series of thematic chapters which explore the extent to which the Order's hierarchy and administration were able to meet the demands posed by its political actions and dispersed territorial responsibilities. This will reveal the interrelationships between the brethren in the Levant and their wider support facilities across Western Christendom. In recent years there have been a number of similar studies on this subject conducted for the Templars and the Hospitallers by authors such as Selwood, Barber, Burgtorf and Bronstein.[17] For the Teutonic Knights, aspects of these issues have been explored in Toomaspoeg's work on the Order in Sicily and also in Militzer's general organisational survey of the institution.[18] This work will provide a new study of the Order's rural and urban infrastructure in the Latin East; it will examine the level of control exerted by the ruling chapter in the kingdom of Jerusalem and question the extent to

Teutonico in Terrasanta (1198–1291)', in *L'Ordine Teutonico nel Mediterraneo*, ed. H. Houben (Galatina, 2004), pp. 55–72.

16 H. Kluger, *Hochmeister Hermann von Salza und Kaiser Friedrich II: Ein Beitrag zur Frühgeschichte des Deutschen Ordens*, QuStDO, 37 (Marburg, 1987); U. Arnold, 'Der Deutsche Orden zwischen Kaiser und Papst im 13. Jahrhundert', in *Die Ritterordern zwischen geistlicher und weltlicher Macht im Mittelalter*, ed. Z. H. Nowak (Torun, 1990), pp. 57–70; W. Cohn, *Herman von Salza* (Breslau, 1930). A more detailed commentary on the historiography on this subject can be found in chapter 4.

17 D. Selwood, *Knights of the Cloister: Templars and Hospitallers in Central-Southern Occitania c.1100–c.1300* (Woodbridge, 1999); M. Barber, 'Supplying the Crusader States: The Role of the Templars', in *The Horns of Hattin*, ed. B. Z. Kedar (Jerusalem, 1992), pp. 314–326; J. Bronstein, *The Hospitallers and the Holy Land: Financing the Latin East 1187–1274* (Woodbridge, 2005). J. Burgtorf, *The Central Convent of Hospitallers and Templars: History, Organisation and Personnel, 1099–1310*, History of Warfare, L (Leiden, 2008).

18 K. Toomaspoeg, *Les Teutoniques en Sicilie: 1197–1492* (Rome, 2003); *AZM*; A further valuable article which concerns these matters is Arnold, 'Entstehung und Frühzeit des Deutschen Ordens', pp. 81–107.

which the statutes of the Order were actually implemented in the day-to-day running of the organisation.

One further area of note, although not one which will be covered in detail, is the brethren's medical role. When the Teutonic Order was created it was as a medical institution and this always remained an important function. Nevertheless, the military wing swiftly achieved a dominance that overtook its initial vocation. Perhaps in consequence of this, little evidence remains for the Order's hospital in the Holy Land beyond the regulations of the Order's statutes and a number of papal privileges. Such evidence as there is will be discussed in connection with the brethren's support of pilgrims.[19]

In comparison to the material available on the Templars and Hospitallers, there are comparatively few primary materials which describe the Teutonic Knights' actions in the eastern Mediterranean. Indeed, as Nicholson has noted, 'the Teutonic Order was unable to attract much attention from European writers for its deeds in the Holy Land'.[20] Perhaps the best known source on this subject is the aforementioned *Tabulae Ordinis Theutonici* which contains many of the Order's property transactions in this region as well as a comprehensive collection of early papal privileges. These documents are supplemented by a number of further cartularies for the Order as well as collections covering areas of the Levant and Latin East such as the *Regesta Regni Hierosolymitani*.[21] In many cases it is only possible to learn about the Knights' deeds through the records of other establishments such as the Hospitallers and the Templars. Accordingly, sources such as the *Cartulaire général des Hospitaliers de S. Jean de Jérusalem* have been employed to provide material for the Teutonic Knights' actions and their relations with these other military orders.[22]

The brethren's actions in the Baltic are outlined in a number of narratives and cartularies. Chief amongst these are the accounts of Peter von Dusburg, Nicolaus von Jeroschin and the *Livländische Reimchronik*.[23] Peter von Dusburg's chronicle provides a wealth of material, not merely about

---

[19] For a comprehensive analysis of the Order's medical role in Prussia see C. Probst, *Der Deutsche Orden und sein Medizinalwesen in Preussen: Hospital, Firmarie und Arzt bis 1525*, QuStDO, 29 (Bad Godesberg, 1969).

[20] H. Nicholson, *Templars, Hospitallers and Teutonic Knights: Images of the Military Orders 1128–1291* (Leicester, 1993), p. 107.

[21] For the general cartularies which contain material concerning the Teutonic Order in the Holy Land see *TOT*; M. Perlbach, 'Die Reste des Deutschordensarchives in Venedig', *Altpreussische Monatsschrift*, 19 (1882), pp. 630–650; H. Prutz, 'Eilf Deutschordensurkunden aus Venedig und Malta', *Altpreussische Monatsschrift*, 20 (1883), pp. 385–400; R. Predelli, 'Le Reliquie dell'Archivio dell'Ordine Teutonico in Venezia', *Atti del Reale Istituto Veneto di Scienze, Lettere ed Arti*, 64 (1905), pp. 1379–1463; *Historia Ordinis Equitum Teutonicorum: Hospitalis S. Mariae V. Hierosolymitani*, ed. R. Duellius (Vienna, 1727); *CDOT*; *R. Reg.*

[22] *CGJJ*.

[23] Peter von Dusburg, *Chronicon Terrae Prussie*, in *Scriptores Rerum Prussicarum: Des Geschichtsquellen der Preussischen Vorzeit*, ed. T. Hirsch, M. Töppen and E. Strehlke, vol. 1 (Leipzig, 1861); Nicolaus von Jeroschin, *Di Kronike von Pruzinlant*, in *Scriptores Rerum Prussicarum: Des Geschichtsquellen der Preussischen Vorzeit*, ed. T. Hirsch, M. Töppen and E. Strehlke, vol. 1 (Leipzig, 1861); *Livländische Reimchronik*, ed. L. Mayer (Paderborn, 1876).

the history of the Prussian frontier, but also concerning the brethren's sense of self-identity and purpose. Peter was a Teutonic Knight who wrote his narrative in the early fourteenth century at the request of Werner von Orseln (master, 1324–1330). This was written in the knowledge that Acre had fallen and Peter dedicates a section of his account to an explanation for the decline of the Holy Land, which is highly suggestive for the attitude of the Order towards this event. To supplement these accounts, the *Preussisches Urkunden-buch* and the cartularies of the Order's regional commanders and the major German cities supply a large body of charters and legislative evidence for the Order's actions in this theatre and across Western Christendom.[24]

In short, this book will discuss the rise of one of the most powerful religious orders in the history of the Catholic Church. It will explore the influences which fuelled the Teutonic Knights' development and discuss how these compared to the earlier examples set by Templars and Hospitallers. These questions will be assessed in the light of modern historiography concerning the crusades and the military orders, but this study will also offer a significant reappraisal of a number of major areas whilst examining a range of new topics concerning the Order in the Holy Land. It will combine evidence concerning the Order from across Christendom including the Holy Land, Germany, Prussia and Livonia, as well as further material from the Muslim world. Overall it is hoped that this study will help to develop our knowledge of the military orders as institutions, revealing their inherent advantages, flaws and dependencies.

---

[24] *PU*. For a sample see: *Urkundenbuch der Deutschordens-Ballei Hessen, Hessisches Urkunden-buch*, vol. 1 (Osnabrück, 1965); *Urkundenbuch der Deutschordensballei Thüringen*, ed. K. H. Lampe (Jena, 1936), no. 26; *Württembergisches Urkundenbuch*, 11 vols (Stuttgart, 1972–1978). *Chartes de la Commanderie de Beauvoir de l'Ordre Teutonique*, in *Collection des Principaux Cartulaires du Diocèse de Troyes*, vol. 3 (Paris, 1878).

CHAPTER 1

The Foundation of the Order, 1190–1215

In 1187, the forces of the kingdom of Jerusalem suffered a crushing defeat on the slopes of an Iron Age fort called the Horns of Hattin, above Lake Tiberias. With the destruction of the Christian field army, the path was open for the Muslim forces under Saladin to seize control of Jerusalem and the other cities of the kingdom. Within months, only the city of Tyre remained in Christian hands.

In the West, the arrival of this news provoked outrage and disbelief. Pope Urban III is said to have died from the shock.[1] Nine days later his successor, Pope Gregory VIII, proclaimed a new crusade with a single objective: the reconquest of Jerusalem.[2] The response to this appeal was vast. Major armies were raised in Germany, the Angevin Empire and Capetian France. Several further contingents departed from other provinces such as Sicily and Hungary and travelled independently. Among these great expeditions was a smaller naval force that had been raised from the cities of Bremen and Lübeck.[3] The intentions of this contingent are outlined in the chronicle *Narratio Itineris Navalis ad Terram Sanctam*:

> In the year of our Lord 1187 when the Promised Land had been laid waste by Saladin, king of Egypt, when the cities had been captured, when their inhabitants had been imprisoned or killed, a trumpet call, [which] spread widely over the boundaries of the Christians with the indulgence of apostolic authority, moved countless people to the recovery of the lamentable disaster.[4]

Armed with this intent, these forces departed from Bremen on 23 April 1189

---

[1] *La Continuation de Guillaume de Tyr: 1187–1197*, ed. M. R. Morgan (Paris, 1982), p. 55.
[2] Gregory VIII, *PL*, vol. 202, col. 1539D–1542D; J. S. C. Riley-Smith, *The Crusades: A History*, 2nd edn (London, 2005), p. 137.
[3] For an account of their journey see *Narratio Itineris Navalis ad Terram Sanctam*, in *MGH SRGNS*, vol. 5, pp. 179–196.
[4] 'Anno siquidem dominice incarnationis MCLXXXVII a Salahadino rege Egypti destructa terra promissionis, captis urbibus captivatis vel necatis incolis predicationis tuba cum indulgencia apostolice auctoritatis late per Christianorum terminos evagata ad restaurationem miserabilis cladis innumerabilem movit populum'; *Narratio Itineris Navalis ad Terram Sanctam*, p. 179.

and arrived at the siege of Acre in September of the same year.[5] According to the chronicle quoted above, this fleet included 12,000 men and 50 ships (referred to as cogs), which Saladin is said to have described as 'towers on the sea'.[6] The kings of England and France arrived subsequently as did the remnants of the German crusading army, which had broken up after the death of its leader, Emperor Frederick I, in Armenia.[7] At Acre, the Christian armies were opposed by both the defenders of the city and Saladin's field army, which was situated at 'Toron de Saladin'.[8] Amidst the turmoil of the siege, the crusaders from Bremen and Lübeck established the small hospital which was to become the Teutonic Order.[9]

The Order was therefore a child of the Third Crusade and, like a child, it drew its identity from the ideas and influences that were present during its childhood. The most pervasive and enduring of these was the determination to retake Jerusalem. This overriding imperative became a major feature of the brethren's policy and this is reflected in the source *De Primordiis Ordinis Theutonici Narratio*, which details the foundation of the first hospital. This brief chronicle was written *c*.1244 by a brother of the Order and states that:[10]

> They were called by the principal name of the Hospital of St Mary of the Teutons in Jerusalem with the hope and faith that with the return of the land to the Christian faith, the principal house of the same Order might be made in the city of Jerusalem.[11]

Similar sentiments can be found in the prologue to the Order's statutes, which was composed *c*.1264, probably by the chapter of leading brethren in the Levant:

> This Order, signifying both the heavenly and the earthly knighthood, is the foremost for it has promised to avenge the dishonouring of God and his cross and to fight so that the Holy Land, which the infidels subjected to their rule, shall belong to the Christians.[12]

---

5   *Narratio Itineris Navalis ad Terram Sanctam*, p. 179; *La Continuation de Guillaume de Tyr*, pp. 90–91.
6   *La Continuation de Guillaume de Tyr*, p. 90; *Itinerarium Peregrinorum et Gesta Regis Ricardi*, in *Chronicles and Memorials of the Reign of Richard I*, ed. W. Stubbs, RS, 38, vol. 1 (London, 1864), pp. 64–65.
7   Frederick I died on 10 June 1190.
8   *La Continuation de Guillaume de Tyr*, pp. 90–91.
9   The use of the cogs' sails as the material with which the German Hospital was created can be found in *De Primordiis Ordinis Theutonici Narratio*, in *Scriptores Rerum Prussicarum: Des Geschichtsquellen der Preussischen Vorzeit*, ed. T. Hirsch, M. Töppen and E. Strehlke, vol. 1 (Leipzig, 1861), p. 220.
10 For discussion of this chronicle see Arnold, 'Entstehung und Frühzeit des Deutschen Ordens', p. 89.
11 'Principali nomine hospitale sancte Marie Theutonicorum in Jerusalem nuncuparunt ea spe et fiducia, ut terra christiano cultui restituta in civitate Jerusalem domus fieret eiusdem ordinis principalis, mater caput pariter et magistra'; *De Primordiis Ordinis Theutonici Narratio*, p. 221.
12 'Dise ritterschaft ist ouch bezeichent bie der himelischen unde irdischen ritterschaft unde ist die

This passage was repeated in later editions of the statutes that were created in the fourteenth century, demonstrating the persistence of this idea.[13] Moreover, each member of the Order was expected to make a personal commitment to this goal at the time of his admission to the brotherhood because his vow contained a promise to defend the Holy Land.[14] This common theme, which can be found in these fundamental statements of intent, serves as a recurring echo of the Third Crusade's determination to retake the Holy Land.[15]

The impact of these ideas can also be seen in the imagery employed by the Teutonic Knights and their supporters. Throughout their sojourn in the Holy Land and for long afterwards the brethren drew comparisons between their own struggles and those of the Old Testament warriors who had fought to protect the Promised Land. Like the Templars and Hospitallers, the Teutonic Knights compared their endeavours to those of the Israelites and the Maccabees.[16] With such allusions the brethren could style themselves as a new generation of defenders of the Holy Land. The Third Crusade itself was imbued with such ideas and the crusade encyclical *Audita Tremendi* stated that Christians should imitate the Maccabees in their quest to regain the city of Jerusalem.[17] In the wake of the expedition a number of warriors, including Richard I of England and the Count of Flanders, were depicted in these terms.[18] Given that the Teutonic Knights were a creation of the Third Crusade it is not surprising that they adopted the same role models, just as they had accepted the same vocation. Accordingly, in 1212 the king of Armenia described them as, 'successors of the Maccabees'.[19] The papacy

vorderste, wande sie gelobet hat, daz sie Gotes versmênisse unde sînes crûces wollen rechen unde vehten umbe daz heilige lant, daz der christen sîn sal, daz die heidene under sich hânt betwungen'; *SDO*, p. 24. Translation taken from Sterns, 'The Statutes of the Teutonic Knights', p. 203.

13 *SDO*, p. 24.
14 *SDO*, p. 127.
15 See also U. Arnold, 'Eight Hundred Years of the Teutonic Order', in *MO*, vol. 1, p. 224.
16 The Maccabees were a Jewish family whose deeds are recorded in the Apocrypha to the Bible. In the medieval period contemporaries considered the books of the Maccabees to be fully canonical and they were included in the Bible under the title *Libri Historici Novissimi*. The Maccabean realm was established in the second century BC around the city of Jerusalem, which the Maccabees defended against a range of foes. For a history of the Maccabean struggle see B. Bar-Kochva, *Judas Maccabaeus: The Jewish Struggle against the Seleucids* (Cambridge, 1989). For an example of comparisons between the military orders and Maccabees see *Papsturkunden für Templer und Johanniter*, ed. R. Hiestand (Göttingen, 1972), p. 215.
17 Gregory VIII, *PL*, vol. 202, cols. 1539D–1542D.
18 *Historia de Expeditione Friderici Imperatoris*, in *MGH SRGNS*, vol. 5, p. 86; *Itinerarium Peregrinorum et Gesta Regis Ricardi*, pp. 251, 422; *Genealogiae Comitum Flandriae, PL*, vol. 209, col. 976.
19 'Vicem Machabeorum', *TOT*, no. 46. Fischer has argued that the earliest comparison between the Order and the Maccabees was made in 1221 by Pope Honorius; however this charter demonstrates that this was not the case. See M. Fischer, 'Biblical Heroes and the Uses of Literature', in *Crusade and Conversion on the Baltic Frontier: 1150–1500*, ed. A. V. Murray (Aldershot, 2001), p. 270. See also M. Fischer, 'The Books of the Maccabees and the Teutonic Order', *Crusades*, 4 (2005), pp. 59–71.

subsequently made similar comparisons in a number of charters issued in the 1220s.[20] The Order began to present itself in this way and the prologue to the Order's statutes contains an allusion to the Maccabees.[21] Later historians of the Order such as Peter von Dusburg – described by Forstreuter as a 'semi-official chronicler of the Order' – continually made allusions to the Maccabees in his *Cronica Terre Prussie*.[22] Fischer claims that he mentions the Maccabees twenty-five times in his work.[23] Thus his chronicle, although it is focused on the wars of the Baltic, contains much of the imagery of the crusades to the Holy Land. Ideas of this kind provide a mere handful of examples of the ways in which Jerusalem became both the political goal and the ideological talisman of the Order throughout the early years of its existence and even into the fourteenth century.

The events of 1190 witnessed the creation of the Teutonic Hospital and clearly had a profound effect on the character of the subsequent order; even so it was many years before it would acquire its military function. This transformation occurred during the crusade launched by Emperor Frederick I's son and successor, Henry VI. Henry took the cross on Good Friday 1195 and funded his expedition with vast sums of money extracted from the Greeks.[24] He actively promoted the recruitment of the crusade although he was unable to embark for the East in person. The army's objective, like those that had gone before it, was to continue the work of reconquest that had been begun by the armies of the Third Crusade.[25]

The main imperial army landed at Acre on 22 September 1197 and proceeded north to capture the city of Beirut. It then began to besiege the castle of Toron – situated to the east of Tyre – but this operation was abandoned when news arrived of the death of Henry VI on 28 September 1197 and the leaders were forced to return home.[26] In March 1198, prior to the departure of the army from the Levant, the crusade commanders suggested that the Teutonic Hospital should be militarised.[27] They then sought the approval of the barons of the kingdom of Jerusalem, who concurred with this decision. In this way the Teutonic Hospital became a military order. To give this new institution a viable organisational framework and to support this new vocation these magnates decided that the brethren should be given

---

20 Pope Honorius III, 1221: *TOT*, no. 321. Pope Honorius III, 1223: *TOT*, no. 389. Pope Gregory IX, 1230: *TOT*, no. 72.

21 *SDO*, p. 25.

22 'Halbamtliche Chronist des Ordens', in Forstreuter, *Der Deutsche Orden am Mittelmeer*, p. 51.

23 Fischer, 'Biblical Heroes', p. 270.

24 Much of the following account of Henry VI's crusade has been derived from E. N. Johnson, 'The Crusades of Frederick Barbarossa and Henry VI', in *HOC*, vol. 2, pp. 118–122.

25 *MGH Leges Const.*, vol. 1, no. 365.

26 For discussion of the fall of Toron see M. Piana, *Burgen und Städte der Kreuzzugszeit* (Petersburg, 2008), pp. 398–407.

27 *De Primordiis Ordinis Theutonici Narratio*, p. 223; Johnson, 'The Crusades of Frederick Barbarossa and Henry VI', pp. 87–122. For further discussion of the militarisation see Favreau, *Studien zur Frühgeschichte des Deutschen Ordens*, pp. 61–62.

the rule of the Templars for matters concerning its military personnel and the rule of the Hospitallers for the care of the sick and poor. Seemingly, the intention was to incorporate the most efficacious elements from the regulations of these older establishments.[28] This ceremony was then performed in the palace of the Templars in Acre and Pope Innocent III confirmed the act in 1199.[29]

Through this process, the Order acquired a mandate to wage holy warfare but it still lacked the strength to pursue this objective on any significant scale. Fortunately for the Teutonic Order, the same patrons who had advocated its creation and militarisation were prepared to fund the growth of its infrastructure. In this way, the Order owed its material and institutional development chiefly to three groups: the German empire, the papacy and the magnates of the Holy Land.

The Empire

The assistance offered to the Order from the German empire came from all levels of society and each group brought their own advantages and agendas. For the Hohenstaufen emperors, the support given to the Teutonic Knights seems to have been one element in a wider effort to increase their influence over the eastern Mediterranean. As has been shown, in the space of seven years, the emperors launched two major crusades into the eastern Mediterranean. They coupled this military assistance with a determined effort to gain authority in this region and during Henry VI's campaign the imperial chancellor endowed the rulers of Cilician Armenia and Cyprus with imperial crowns.[30] The Armenians had requested this coronation in May 1194 when Leon II sent messengers to meet Henry in Lombardy. The Cypriots had similarly sent emissaries to Henry VI in the same year. Their acceptance of these crowns signified their vassal status to the German empire. Significantly, King Aimery of Cyprus was also the king of Jerusalem and although, as Mayer has shown, he ruled the two kingdoms separately, it is not likely that he could have pursued imperial policy in Cyprus whilst completely ignoring it in Jerusalem.[31] For the Christians in the Levant, the patronage of the emperor connected them to the most powerful political and military institution in Christendom. Certainly, they would have been aware of the potential benefits of such a benefactor because in previous decades the Latin East had flourished

---

[28] *De Primordiis Ordinis Theutonici Narratio*, p. 223. Previously the Order had been regulated through reasonable customs (*racionabiles consuetudines*). See *TOT*, no. 296. For discussion see *AZM*, p. 48.

[29] *TOT*, no. 297; *Die Register Innocenz' III*, ed. O. Hageneder and A. Haidaher, vol. 1 (1964), p. 823; *CDOT*, no. 4; Potthast, vol. 1, no. 606.

[30] *La Continuation de Guillaume de Tyr*, p. 195.

[31] Aimery was king of Cyprus 1194–1205; king of Jerusalem 1197–1205. H. E. Mayer, *The Crusades*, trans. J. Gillingham, 2nd edn (Oxford, 1990), p. 240; Forstreuter, *Der Deutsche Orden am Mittelmeer*, p. 59.

through the support of the Byzantine Empire. Nevertheless this assistance had come to an end with the rise of Andronicus Comnenus in 1182.[32] Whether the rulers of the Latin East sought imperial patronage specifically to replace that of the Byzantine empire is not stated; however, there were obvious advantages to be gained from such a connection.

For the rulers of Germany the development of political influence over the Latin East held a number of advantages. Firstly, as Ross has illustrated, by supporting the Holy Land an emperor could imitate the mythical example of Charlemagne by becoming a defender of Jerusalem.[33] Munz has outlined the importance of this factor to Frederick I: 'All through his life, Frederick had realised that the ultimate and most formidable task of the emperor of Christendom was to protect the Church and to defend the holy places in Palestine against the infidels.'[34]

Correspondingly, it is not surprising that when his son Henry VI wrote to the prelates of the Church concerning his expedition, his stated motivation for taking the crusading oath was his desire to alleviate the suffering of the Latin East, just as one might expect from a ruler who was attempting to style himself as the protector of the Holy Land.[35] When examining the motives for imperial expansion into this region, it seems likely that there was a genuine and pious desire to support this work and possibly in doing so to adopt the mantle of Charlemagne.

The relationship between the Hohenstaufen family and the Teutonic Hospital began at the time of its creation. One of its earliest patrons was Duke Frederick of Swabia, son of Frederick I. After his father's death in Armenia on 10 June 1190 he travelled to the siege of Acre with the remnants of the crusading army. On 7 October he joined the assembled armies of Christendom, which were entrenched outside the walls, but within four months he died of the illness which is thought to have become endemic at about the time of his arrival.[36] During this brief sojourn Fredrick was evidently so impressed by the medical care offered by the Teutonic Hospital that he gave it responsibility for his burial.[37] The interment of such an exalted personage

---

32   J. Harris, *Byzantium and the Crusades* (London, 2003), pp. 93–125; J. Phillips, *Defenders of the Holy Land: Relations between the Latin East and the West: 1119–1187* (Oxford, 1996), pp. 100–139, 225–266; R. Lilie, *Byzantium and the Crusader States: 1096–1204* (Oxford, 1993), pp. 246–258.

33   This paragraph has drawn on L. Ross, 'Relations between the Latin East and Western Europe, 1187–1291' (unpublished doctoral thesis, Royal Holloway University, 2003), p. 140; L. Ross, 'Frederick II: Tyrant or Benefactor of the Latin East?', *Al-Masāq*, 15 (2003), pp. 149–150.

34   P. Munz, *Frederick Barbarossa: A Study in Medieval Politics* (London, 1969), p. 372.

35   *MGH Leges: Const.* vol. 1, no. 365.

36   *La Continuation de Guillaume de Tyr*, p. 99; *De Primordiis Ordinis Theutonici Narratio*, p. 223; M. Perlbach, 'Deutsch-Ordens Necrologe', *Forschungen zur Deutschen Geschichte*, 17 (1877), p. 363; C. Tyerman, *God's War: A New History of the Crusades* (London, 2006), p. 429.

37   *La Continuation de Guillaume de Tyr*, p. 99; *De Primordiis Ordinis Theutonici Narratio*, p. 222; *Gesta Episcoporum Halberstadensium*, in *MGH SS*, vol. 23, p. 110; *Annales Marbacenses*, in *MGH SRG*, vol. 9, p. 62; *Chronicon Breve Fratris, ut videtur, Ordinis Theutonicorum*, in *MGH SS*, vol. 24, p. 153.

would have added to the hospital's prestige and the importance of this event is highlighted by the resistance shown by the Hospitallers, who insisted that they alone should have the right to bury a man of his rank.[38]

Frederick's most significant act was to write to his brother Emperor Henry VI, asking him both to confirm the hospital's establishment and to seek recognition for it from the papacy.[39] According to *De Primordiis Ordinis Theutonici Narratio*, Henry acted upon both these requests and became a notable patron. Over succeeding years he granted the brethren properties in Apulia and trading privileges in Messina (Sicily) and Calabria (Apulia).[40] Material enrichment in Western Christendom was an important factor for any religious institution in the Levant. Landholdings could channel supplies to the Latin East, providing additional manpower and resources. Certainly, it is not hard to imagine that Henry would have enthusiastically supported a German order in the Holy Land at a time when he was seeking to extend his influence in the eastern Mediterranean.

Combining the known political goals of the Hohenstaufen family at this time and its advocacy of the Teutonic Knights, historians have tended to characterise the development of the Order as an extension of Hohenstaufen power in the Holy Land during this period. Richard argues, 'It [The Teutonic Order] introduced into the Holy Land a presence indissolubly linked to the Hohenstaufen Empire.'[41] The only challenge offered to this belief can be found in a brief comment made by Forey who argues:

> The transformation of the German hospital has been interpreted as an attempt to maintain and strengthen German influence in the Holy Land and even to further imperialist plans; but the reality of the latter may be questioned, and arguments concerning political considerations can be no more than hypotheses.[42]

Whilst neither the Hohenstaufen family's patronage nor its wider policies can

---

[38] *La Continuation de Guillaume de Tyr*, p. 99.

[39] *De Primordiis Ordinis Theutonici Narratio*, p. 221.

[40] *Regesta Imperii IV*, vol. 3, nos. 709, 727. Confirmed in 1219 by Frederick II, *Nürnberger Urkundenbuch*, Quellen und Forschungen zur Geschichte der Stadt Nürnberg, I (Nürnberg, 1959), no. 169. Henry VI acquired his Sicilian and Apulian territories in 1194 from Tancred of Lecce. It seems that the Teutonic Order had already gained a foothold in Brindisi before Henry's invasion; see *Codice Diplomatico Brindisino*, ed. G. Maria Monti, vol. 1 (Trani, 1940), no. 26. See also Toomaspoeg, *Les Teutoniques en Sicilie*, pp. 30–33.

[41] J. Richard, *The Crusades: 1071–1291* (Cambridge, 2001), p. 237. For comparable views concerning the Order in the twelfth and early thirteenth centuries see Arnold, 'Der Deutsche Orden zwischen Kaiser und Papst im 13. Jahrhundert', p. 59; Hilsch, 'Der Deutsche Ritterorden im Südlichen Libanon', p. 176; Favreau, *Studien zur Frühgeschichte des Deutschen Ordens*, p. 62; K. Militzer, 'From the Holy Land to Prussia: the Teutonic Knights between Emperors and Popes and their Policies until 1309', in *Mendicants, Military Orders and Regionalism in Medieval Europe*, ed. J. Sarnowsky (Aldershot, 1999), p. 72; Mayer, *The Crusades*, p. 156. Furthermore, the term 'staufischen Hausorden' or 'thüringisch-staufischen Hausorden' has been used frequently in connection to the Order at this time; see *AZM*, p. 34; Arnold, 'Der Deutsche Orden zwischen Kaiser und Papst', p. 62.

[42] Forey, *The Military Orders*, p. 21.

be denied, it does not follow that this was the defining influence which shaped the character or policies of the young order. The bestowal and acceptance of aid is not conclusive proof that the beneficiary holds precisely the same objectives as a the donor; nor is it clear in this case that Hohenstaufen policy was the main influence in the formation of the Order's policy at this time. Although the objectives of Order and ruler seem to have overlapped in many points – particularly where they concerned the recovery of the Holy Land – it is also important to note that there were many other groups from whom the Teutonic Knights received aid, which had at least as great an influence.

Perhaps the most important of these was the rising tide of German pilgrims who travelled to the Holy Land to support the reconquest. At the time of its establishment the Teutonic Hospital's primary function was to provide a hospice for pilgrims. It evidently performed this service with some skill because, within a year of its establishment, the Order received support from Frederick of Swabia and from the king of Jerusalem. King Guy's approbation took the form of a promise, made in September 1190, that if the city of Acre fell to the Christian forces then the German Hospital would be given sufficient property within the city to continue its vocation. After the collapse of Muslim resistance on 12 July 1191, Guy kept his word and assigned some buildings to the Hospital near to the gate of St Nicolas.[43]

From this establishment the German Order offered medical care and accommodation to later crusaders and pilgrims in the Latin East. Through these roles it earned the gratitude and admiration of many who enjoyed its hospitality. The material consequence of this praise was a stream of donations and bequests. The importance attached to this function is reflected in the Order's statutes, which state that there should always be a hospital in the main house of the Order.[44] Accordingly, like the Hospitallers, the Teutonic Hospital's initial purpose lay in its care for the poor of Christ through the maintenance of a *xenodocium* (a hospice) which attended to the spiritual and medical needs of pilgrims.[45] In Acre itself, the brethren's initial foundation seems to have grown to become a major complex. There are also reports that they supplied a field hospital during the Fifth Crusade.[46] Subsequently, the brethren's medical wing expanded and Militzer has demonstrated that 'by 1230 the Order had received at least twenty-six hospitals across Christendom'.[47] Such a rate of expansion stands as testimony to the popularity of the Order's work. Nevertheless, in time, the Teutonic Knights evidently became wary about the creation of too many hospitals and their rule, composed *c.*1264,

43 *R. Reg.*, vol. 1, no. 696; *TOT*, no. 25.
44 'In dem obersten hûs, oder dâ der meister mit dem capitele ze râte wirdet, spitâle habe zu allen cîten'; *SDO*, p. 31. Translation taken from Sterns, 'The Statutes of the Teutonic Knights', p. 209.
45 *TOT*, no. 362; Luttrell, 'The Earliest Hospitallers', pp. 37–54.
46 *CDOT*, no. 35; *Oorkondenboek van het Sticht Utrecht: tot 1301*, ed. K. Heeringa, vol. 2 (The Hague, 1940), no. 668.
47 K. Militzer, 'The Role of Hospitals in the Teutonic Order', in *MO*, vol. 2, p. 54.

stated that no hospital should be created without the specific consent of the master and the senior brethren.[48]

Organisationally, hospitals generally fell under the authority of the grand commander, whilst the hospital in Acre was run by the hospitaller.[49] When pilgrims were admitted they were expected first to confess their sins and to receive Eucharist. Any personal property was then stored and a receipt was issued.[50] Afterwards, the hospitaller, along with other physicians, decided upon the method of treatment.[51] Every day, the patients ate their meals before the brethren, demonstrating how they, like the Hospitallers, symbolically placed their patients' needs before their own.[52] Riley-Smith has shown that the Hospitallers cared for each individual as though he or she was Christ and because the Teutonic Order's statutes were based on their rule – at least with regard to the care of the sick – it seems probable that they took a similar view.[53] The hospital was to be lit at all times and those who died within the house were to be buried as soon as possible.[54] Like the Hospitallers, the brethren gave their patients sugar and other expensive commodities that were deemed to assist in a swift recovery.[55] In 1198 Aimery II gave the Order an allowance of sugar for the support of the infirmary along with a source of income and pasturage for its animals.[56] In these ways, it may well be imagined how the assurance of professional care would have encouraged the faithful in Western Christendom to embark upon a pilgrimage or crusade.

Women were permitted to work in these infirmaries and even to be admitted as sisters of the Order. It is not entirely clear whether such women were present in the Holy Land – although it seems likely – but there are several pieces of evidence that support this conclusion. Abū l-Mahāsin, when describing the surrender of the Teutonic Knights at Acre in 1291, reports, 'on the same day the Teutonic Hospitallers asked for amnesty and this was granted to them and their women'.[57] These 'women' could well have been sisters of the Order who worked in the infirmary. A second piece of evidence that may both support this hypothesis and also solve an archaeological dilemma is a building which lies below the ramparts of the Teutonic Knights' fortress of Montfort on the floor of Wadi Keziv. Although this two-storey structure has been identified

[48] *SDO*, p. 31.
[49] *SDO*, pp. 32, 69. For further discussion of the Order's hospitals see *AZM*, pp. 123–125; P. Mitchell, *Medicine in the Crusades: Warfare, Wounds and the Medieval Surgeon* (Cambridge, 2004), pp. 90–93. For a list of Grand Commanders see appendix E.2.
[50] *SDO*, pp. 31–32. S. Edgington, 'Administrative Regulations for the Hospital of St John in Jerusalem dating from the 1180s', *Crusades*, 4 (2005), p. 29.
[51] *SDO*, p. 32.
[52] *SDO*, pp. 32–33.
[53] J. S. C. Riley-Smith, 'The Death and Burial of Latin Christian Pilgrims to Jerusalem and Acre: 1099–1291' (unpublished paper, 2006), p. 7.
[54] *SDO*, p. 32.
[55] Edgington, 'Administrative Regulations for the Hospital of St John', p. 25.
[56] *TOT*, no. 34.
[57] Abū l-Mahāsin, *Arab Historians of the Crusades*, ed. and trans. F. Gabrieli and E. J. Costello (London, 1984), p. 348.

as a mill on its lower level, the purpose of the upper storey has provoked much discussion among historians.[58] Current debate has been summarised by Pringle who has suggested that it may have been a guesthouse, although he does not come to a definite conclusion.[59] One possible solution may be that this was a dormitory for the sisters of the Order or perhaps for female pilgrims. This contention is supported by the statutes which stipulate that female members of the order should always be housed away from the male brethren.[60]

Consequently, this building may have been constructed sufficiently close to the fortress for protection, yet outside the walls to preserve the moral integrity of the brethren. Furthermore, the castle may have received female guests from within the Levant, perhaps the wives of soldiers or visiting landowners. Additional evidence can be drawn from a description of the ruins of the German hospice in Jerusalem (acquired by the Order in 1229) by a fifteenth-century pilgrim called Brother Felix Fabr. He commented that this institution consisted of two separate buildings for the accommodation of the male and female pilgrims.[61] As a result, it seems possible that this hall in Montfort was designed to perform a similar function.

Alongside its medical vocation the Teutonic Order also provided burial for the dead. The brethren offered this service from the first days of their establishment at the siege of Acre. Certainly, Ralph of Diceto mentioned that the German Hospital managed a cemetery at this time.[62] Moreover, in 1196 Pope Celestine III confirmed the Order's right to bury any Christian provided that he or she was not under sentence of excommunication or interdict.[63] In 1216 Honorius III developed these rights by granting the Order the ability to build its own cemeteries.[64] There are several later references to German pilgrims and settlers seeking burial in the Teutonic Knights' cemeteries. Among these were Gerald Magnus Alemannus, who donated property to the Order in exchange for the promise that he would be buried with the same funeral rites as a brother knight.[65] Barzella Merxadrus, a pilgrim of the Fifth Crusade, similarly stipulated in his will that he wished to be interred in the hospital.[66]

---

[58] D. Pringle, 'A Thirteenth-Century Hall at Montfort Castle in Western Galilee', *Antiquaries Journal*, 66 (1986), p. 75.

[59] Pringle, 'A Thirteenth-Century Hall at Montfort Castle in Western Galilee', pp. 75–76.

[60] 'Dieselben sal man doch niht wenne mit des lantcommendûres urlobe entphâhen, unde sô sî entphangen sint, sô sal man in ir wonunge ûswendich der wonunge der brûdere bereiten'; *SDO*, p. 52.

[61] Brother Felix Fabri, *Fratris Felicis Fabri Evanatorium in Terrae Sanctae, Arabiae et Egypti Peregrinationem*, ed. C. D. Hassler, Bibliothek des Literarischen Vereins in Stuttgart, 18, vol. 1 (Stuttgart 1843), p. 322.

[62] Ralph of Diceto, *Radulfi de Diceto Decani Londoniensis Opera Historica*, ed. W. Stubbs, RS, 68, vol. 2 (London, 1876), p. 81.

[63] *TOT*, no. 296. The Teutonic Order broke this condition in 1247 see *Reg. Innocent IV*, vol. 1, no. 2781.

[64] *TOT*, no. 303; *CDOT*, no. 25.

[65] *TOT*, no. 92.

[66] *Annali Bolognesi*, ed. L. V. Savioli, vol. 2, pt 2 (Bassano, 1789), no. 480.

In return for their care, the Teutonic Knights received many gifts and donations.[67] Their benefactors can be grouped into two main categories. The first were those who had actually travelled to the Latin East and experienced the Order's work at first hand. Swederus of Dingede, a pilgrim of the Fifth Crusade, for example, made a gift of land to the brothers citing explicitly the importance of their medical role.[68] Similarly Walter of Brabant, whilst ill at the siege of Damietta, made a gift to the Order.[69] It should be remembered that a pilgrimage to Jerusalem was a penitential act in which the bestowal of alms was an integral part and an indication of an individual's renunciation of the material in favour of the spiritual. To reflect the pious nature of these gifts it appears that a specific ceremony developed in which a pilgrim could make a donation, presumably to provide a proper context for such an act of pious charity. In 1228, Conrad of Grüningen, whilst on pilgrimage, granted the Order some property in Konstanz (then in Swabia [Germany]), specifically for the good of his soul and those of his predecessors.[70] The charter which outlines the gift specifies that it was made in Acre, upon the altar of St Mary, within the house of the Order and in the presence of the master. These circumstances seem to suggest that a set formula was followed during the process of bestowing alms.

As returning pilgrims brought news of the work of the Teutonic Knights to the West, noblemen began to offer alms to the brethren even though they had not embarked for the East themselves. Examples of these gifts can be found in many of the principalities of the empire as well as in France and elsewhere (these will be discussed below). By the late thirteenth century, the fame of the Order's hospitality towards pilgrims in the Holy Land was reflected in song and verse including the epics *Wolfdietrich*[71] and *Die Kreuzfahrt des Landgrafen Ludwigs des Frommen von Thüringen*.[72] Both these works affirm the care and solicitude of the Levantine brethren.

In some cases, the relationships formed between pilgrims and the Teutonic Knights in the Holy Land continued for years or even generations after an individual's expedition. Swederus of Dingede, having made the abovementioned gift to the Order during the Fifth Crusade, continued to offer patronage after his return. In 1231 he took a second crusading oath, along with his wife,

---

67 M. Favreau-Lilie, 'The German Empire and Palestine: German pilgrimages to Jerusalem between the 12th and 16th century', *Journal of Medieval History*, 21 (1995), p. 339.
68 *Oorkondenboek van het Sticht Utrecht*, vol. 2, no. 668.
69 *Regesta Imperii V*, vol. 2, no. 10851.
70 *Regesta Imperii V*, vol. 1, no. 1734; *Württembergisches Urkundenbuch*, vol. 3, no. 749.
71 Written *c.*1280–1300, see *Ortnit und die WolfDietriche*, in *Deutsches Heldenbuch*, vol. 4 (Berlin, 1873), pp. 56–62; H. Nicholson, *Love, War and the Grail: Templars, Hospitallers and Teutonic Knights in Medieval Epic and Romance* (Boston, 2004), p. 79.
72 Written in Germany in the early fourteenth century, see *Die Kreuzfahrt des Landgrafen Ludwigs des Frommen von Thüringen*, in *MGH SVL*, vol. 4, p. 215; Nicholson, *Love, War and the Grail*, p. 80.

which he redeemed with a cash payment to the brethren.[73] It seems likely that his enthusiasm for both the crusade and the Order was such that he took this second oath without any real intention of travelling to the East but specifically to render aid to the institution for the remission of his sins. In 1205 Count Bertold II of Katzenellenbogen, whilst on a diplomatic mission to the Holy Land, travelled to Acre where he confirmed a number of charters issued for the Order.[74] He later became regent for the kingdom of Thessalonica and is thought to have been instrumental in the concession of land to the Order (totalling four knights' fees) in the Peloponnese in 1209.[75] Subsequently, the lords of Katzenellenbogen were to continue to support both the crusades to the Holy Land and the Teutonic Order. Dieter of Katzenellenbogen fought in the Fifth Crusade and Gerhard of Katzenellenbogen became a brother of the Order and rose to become the marshal of Livonia.[76]

The papacy strongly advocated these donations and issued many charters detailing the significance of the brethren's work in the East and their ongoing support of pilgrims and the poor.[77] One of the best examples of this can be found in a charter of Pope Honorius III (9 February 1221) addressed to all the prelates of the Church which makes the following statement:

> There is a place so pleasing to God, so venerable to men and so welcoming and convenient a *xenodochium* (a hospice for the care of strangers) for pilgrims and the poor, providing the hospitality of the Hospital of Saint Mary of the Teutons of Jerusalem to those who constantly recall it to mind traversing the many dangers of the sea to visit, with the intention of pious devotion, the holy city of Jerusalem and the sepulchre of the Lord. For there the needy and the poor are refreshed, many forms of healthcare are dispensed to the weak and those worn out by various labours and dangers are invigorated with strength renewed; thus they may be able to set forth more confidently to the sacred places consecrated by the bodily presence of our Lord Jesus Christ, servants, whom the brothers of the same house engage at their own expense when the occasion requires and appoint specially for this duty, act devoutly and diligently.[78]

---

[73] *Oorkondenboek van het Sticht Utrecht*, vol. 2, no. 814.

[74] This example has been drawn from H. Houben 'Wie und wann kam der Deutsche Orden nach Griechenland?' in *Néa 'Ρώμη: Rivista di ricerche bizantinistiche*, vol. 1 (Rome, 2004), pp. 243–253; *TOT*, nos. 41,42.

[75] Houben 'Wie und wann kam der Deutsche Orden nach Griechenland?' p. 253; *The Crusaders as Conquerors: The Chronicle of Morea*, trans. H. Lurier (New York and London, 1964), p. 127.

[76] Houben 'Wie und wann kam der Deutsche Orden nach Griechenland?' p. 253.

[77] *TOT*, nos. 346, 353, 358.

[78] 'Quam amabilis deo et quam venerandus hominibus locus existat, quam eciam iocundum et utile receptaculum peregrinis et pauperibus prebeat xenodochium hospitalis sancte Marie Theutonicorum Ierosolimitani, hii, qui per diversa maris pericula pie devocionis intuitu sanctam civitatem Ierusalem et sepulchrum domini visitant, assidue recognoscunt. Ibi enim indigentes et pauperes reficiuntur, infirmis multimoda sanitatis obsequia adhibentur et diversis laboribus et periculis fatigati resumptis viribus recreantur atque, ut ipsi ad sacrosancta loca domini nostri Ihesu Christi corporali presencia dedicata securius valeant proficisci, servientes, quos fratres eiusdem domus

This passage is interesting because it demonstrates the papacy's readiness to act as an advocate for the Order and to disseminate news of its services across Christendom. This in turn would have provided reassurance to those planning a pilgrimage to the Holy Land and encouragement for others to offer alms.

Pope Honorius III enhanced these positive reports with further privileges designed to persuade the people of Western Christendom to make benefactions to the Order. He issued charters to some prelates encouraging them to donate alms and to others commanding them not to interfere with the Knights' collection of these gifts.[79] He subsequently granted special privileges to agents of the Order who were sent across Western Christendom to collect these donations. Perhaps most significantly, on 3 February 1223 he granted these agents the ability to offer remission of sins in return for alms. This inducement could be granted in proportion to the size of an alms donation.[80] Such concessions had been made before for other purposes and in 1215 Pope Innocent III granted remission of sins to those who bestowed alms to the Fifth Crusade.[81] It seems that Honorius's gift was an expansion on this theme. In 1224 Henry of Weida made a gift to the Order expressly for the remission of his sins, seemingly a practical example of this new privilege in operation.[82] It is notable in these charters that the pope generally stipulated that any alms should be used in support of pilgrims, thus illustrating the significance of the Order as an institution dedicated to this vocation.[83] In 1257, the papacy granted the brethren authority to offer forgiveness of sins to those who planned to travel to the Holy Land and had confessed their sins.[84] These papal charters are mirrored in the Order's rule which states that alms collectors should be appointed by the master or provincial master and should make specific reference to the papal indulgence when gathering donations from the laity.[85]

It is clear that a strong symbiotic relationship developed between pilgrims travelling to the Latin East and the Teutonic Order. Pilgrims received medical care and accommodation and showed their gratitude by becoming patrons of the Order. Reviewing the enormous level of support that the brethren received from such travellers, it seems likely that the bulk of the funds and lands which drove the Order's initial expansion came from this quarter. Relating this evidence back to the question of the Order's connection to the Hohenstaufen family, it seems that, although the emperors were important patrons,

---

ad hoc officium specialiter deputatos proprios sumptibus retinent, cum opportunitas exigat, devote ac diligenter efficient'; *TOT*, no. 362.

[79] *TOT*, nos. 314, 357.

[80] *TOT*, no. 389. Frederick II also supported the collection of alms and in 1216 he permitted the Order to maintain two brothers at his court to collect alms. *TOT*, no. 254.

[81] *Decrees of the Ecumenical Councils*, ed. N. P. Tanner, vol. 1 (Georgetown, 1990), pp. 228–271.

[82] *Urkundenbuch der Deutschordensballei Thüringen*, no. 26.

[83] *TOT*, no. 362.

[84] *TOT*, no. 539.

[85] *SDO*, p. 34.

the brethren's early development was supported more by German pilgrim traffic to the East.

One further group within the German empire that requires independent analysis is the imperial princes. The relationships forged between the Teutonic Knights and these noble families were to support them for decades, both in the Holy Land and later in the Baltic. These magnates occupied the social level directly below that of the emperor and enjoyed a notable level of autonomy. The connection between this group and the Order may have begun during the Third Crusade; however, a more permanent bond seems to have been formed during Henry VI's expedition when a large group of these princes advocated the militarisation of the Teutonic Hospital. This decision seems to have been driven in part by the desire of a number of these men to remain in the East after the return of the main crusader army and Humbert of Romans commented upon this, writing, 'And thither at length noble men devoted themselves to the Lord in order that thereafter they might fight against the Saracens and thus three military orders, like a three-ply rope, which is difficult to break, were created'.[86]

If this was the case, then it was not the only time that a group of crusaders founded a military order to provide themselves with a base to continue to fight in the Holy Land, because Edward I of England is thought to have formed the Order of St Edward of Acre for those 'few men left by Edward in the east to continue the struggle against the infidels'.[87] After the Teutonic Order's militarisation, these imperial noblemen became some of the staunchest supporters of the brotherhood and their patronage became a crucial factor its development. In 1254 the Order's marshal in the Holy Land wrote an appeal for assistance to the king of Castile (who was considered to be an imperial prince through his grandfather Philip of Swabia[88]) and commented upon the importance of this connection, writing, 'Since we are linked by a certain special faith and bond of nature to return in our need to you and the other princes and nobles of Germany whose ancestors and predecessors specially founded our Order'.[89]

---

86 'Et illuc tandem viri nobiles se domino vouerunt, qui postea contra saracenos pugnarent. Et sic factae sunt tres religiones quasi triplex funiculus qui difficile rumpetur'; Humbert of Romans, 'De Modo Prompte Cudendi Sermones', in *Maxima Bibliotheca Veterum Patrum*, ed. M. de la Bigne, vol. 25 (Lyon, 1677), p. 473.

87 M. Prestwich, *Edward I* (New Haven, CT, 1997), p. 79.

88 King Alfonso of Castile's mother was Beatrice of Swabia, who was the daughter of Phillip of Swabia. See J. M. R. García, 'Alfonso X and the Teutonic Order: An Example of the Role of the International Military Orders in Mid Thirteenth-Century Castile', in *MO*, vol. 2, pp. 319–320. Interestingly, Alfonso X was also a candidate for the imperial throne so this letter may have been an attempt to gain favour with a future emperor.

89 'Cum exquadam spetiali fidutia et naturae vinculo astringamur ut ad vos et ceteros principes ac nobiles Alemaniae quorum progenitores ac predecessores nostrum ordinem specialiter fundaverunt in nostris necessitatibus recurramus.' The transcription of this letter was drawn from J. M. R., García, 'Alfonso X, la Orden Teutónica y Tierra Santa: una nueva fuente para su estudio', in *Las Órdenes Militares en la Península Ibérica*, ed. R. I. Benito and F. R. Gómez, vol. 1 (Cuenca, 2000), pp. 489–509. García believes this letter to have been written in 1254, before

Clearly the link between the Teutonic Knights and these noble families was a major influence in their evolution. In many cases these relationships lasted for generations and two excellent examples of this can be found with the dukes of Austria and the landgraves of Thuringia.

The Babenburg family would have first learnt of the Teutonic Hospital during the Third Crusade when Leopold V (duke of Austria, 1177–1194) took part in the siege of Acre. His sojourn in the East was relatively short – he is said to have arrived in the spring of 1191 and to have left the same winter – but the Teutonic Hospital was in existence by this time. A few years later, his successor Frederick I (duke of Austria, 1195–1198) joined Henry VI's expedition and advocated the militarisation of the Order.[90] He then remained in the Latin East after the death of the emperor and died of illness on 16 April 1198 – possibly less than a month after the militarisation.[91] His brother, Leopold VI (duke of Austria, 1198–1230), perhaps in memory of his sibling, continued to patronise the brethren with grants of property in Styria, possibly as early as 1200.[92] He subsequently gave the brethren property in Austria in 1210.[93] The following year, the Order's master accompanied Austrian envoys in an embassy to Armenia and Cyprus.[94] After 1214, Leopold witnessed various charters made by Emperor Frederick II and his son, King Henry VII, for the benefit of the Order.[95] More significantly, Leopold subsequently joined the Fifth Crusade where he served at Damietta. Prior to his return, he gave the Order the considerable sum of 6,000 marks, which is said to have provided much of the capital for the purchase of its first estate in the kingdom of Jerusalem.[96] Leopold's support was evidently so great that the day of his death was remembered in a number of the Teutonic Order's necrologies where he was labelled as a *benefactor domus Theutonicorum*.[97] After the Fifth Crusade, the association continued to flourish and further grants

---

the end of May. García, 'Alfonso X and the Teutonic Order', pp. 319–327. This hypothetical date seems likely not least because a similar letter of appeal was written to Henry III in 1254 from the Holy Land, which was countersigned by the same marshal, *Foedera, Conventiones, Litterae et cuiuscunque generis Acta Publica inter Reges Angliae et alios quosvis Imperatores, Reges, Pontifices, Principes, vel Communitates*, ed. T. Rymer, vol. 1 (London, 1816), p. 308. The manuscript source can be found in Madrid: Biblioteca de la Real Academia de la Historia, Colección Salazar, 'Carta de la Orden Teutónica a Alfonso X' (G49, fol. 453, Sig. 9/946. Index Number 33005).

90 *De Primordiis Ordinis Theutonici Narratio*, p. 224.
91 A. W. A. Leeper, *A History of Medieval Austria* (Oxford, 1941), p. 286.
92 Arnold, 'Eight Hundred Years of the Teutonic Order', p. 224.
93 *CDOT*, no. 10.
94 Wilbrand of Oldenburg, *Peregrinatio*, in *Peregrinatores Medii Aevi Quatuor*, ed. J. C. Laurent (Leipzig, 1864), p. 162.
95 1214: *CDOT*, no. 15; 1214: HB, vol. 1, pp. 313–315; 1217: HB, vol. 1, pp. 510–511; 1227: HB, vol. 3, pp. 309–311.
96 Oliveri Scholastici, *Historia Damiatina*, in *Die Schriften des Kölner Domscholasters, Späteren Bischofs von Paderborn und Kardinal-Bischofs von S. Sabina*, Bibliothek des Litterarischen Vereins in Stuttgart, 202 (Tübingen, 1894), p. 207. See also *TOT*, no. 72.
97 Perlbach, 'Deutsch-Ordens Necrologe', p. 359. Leopold's successor Frederick is also mentioned in this same document.

were made.[98] In 1230 the Order's master, Herman von Salza, and Leopold worked together to bring about a peace agreement between the emperor and the papacy. On 9 September Pope Gregory IX exhorted Leopold's son and successor, Duke Frederick II (1230–1246), to follow in his father's footsteps and to render aid to the brethren.[99] However, Gregory asked Frederick to lead troops to the support the Order in Prussia, rather than the Holy Land.

A similar trend can be found with the landgraves of Thuringia. Ludwig III (landgrave, 1172–1190) took part in the Third Crusade. His successor, Herman I of Thuringia (landgrave, 1190–1217), then participated in the crusade of Henry VI and advocated the militarisation of the Teutonic Knights.[100] By 1200, the Order is said to have gained property in Thuringia.[101] In subsequent years the landgraves acted frequently on the brethren's behalf and made a number of further concessions to them. They also represented the brethren's interests to the papacy and acted as witnesses to charters issued for the institution. Documents to this effect were issued in in 1203, 1207, 1213, 1214, 1215, 1218, 1223, 1227 and 1234.[102] Herman von Salza (master, c.1210–1239) came from a Thuringian *ministerialis* family and it has been suggested that he came to the Holy Land in the entourage of Landgrave Herman I in 1196. Certainly this expedition would have been one of the few opportunities available to the son of a Thuringian *ministerialis* family to travel to the Holy Land at this time.[103] There were a number of further thirteenth-century masters who were of Thuringian descent, including Conrad von Thüringen, Anno von Sangershausen and Hartman von Heldrungen.[104] Conrad was a younger son of Landgrave Herman I.

Herman I's successor, Ludwig, offered the Order his protection in Thur-

---

[98] For examples see *Urkundenbuch zur Geschichte der Babenberger in Österreich*, ed. H. Fichtenau and E. Zöllner et al., vol. 2 (Vienna, 1955), nos. 227, 313, 344, 450.

[99]   *MGH Epis. Saec. XIII*, vol. 1, no. 596.

[100] *De Primordiis Ordinis Theutonici Narratio*, p. 224.

[101] Arnold, 'Eight Hundred Years of the Teutonic Order', p. 224.

[102] 1203: *Urkundenbuch der Deutschordensballei Thüringen*, no. 3; *Regesta Diplomatica necnon Epistolaria Historiae Thuringiae*, ed. O. Dobenecker, vol. 2 (Jena, 1900), no. 1245. 1207: Charter 1: *Regesta Imperii V*, vol. 1, no. 159; Charter 2: *Regesta Thuringiae*, vol. 2, no. 1346. 1213: *CDOT*, no. 14. 1214: HB, vol. 1, pp. 299–301. 1215: Charter 1: HB, vol. 1, pp. 355–356; Charter 2: *Regesta Imperii V*, vol. 1, no. 782; *Regesta Thuringiae*, vol. 2, no. 1612. 1218: *Regesta Thuringiae*, vol. 2, no. 1796. 1223: *Regesta Thuringiae*, vol. 2, no. 2062. 1227: HB, vol. 3, pp. 309–311. 1234: *Reg. Grégoire IX*, vol. 1, no. 1998.

[103] Cohn, *Herman von Salza*, p. 2. A possible parallel case might be seen in the election of Robert of Burgundy as master of the Templars. Like Herman von Salza, Robert had formerly been under the authority of a major crusading lord (Fulk, count of Anjou, who later became king of Jerusalem). Nevertheless, the extent to which these noble dynasties played a role in the elevation of their followers is unknown, see H. E. Mayer, 'Angevins versus Normans: The New Men of King Fulk of Jerusalem', *Proceedings of the American Philosophical Society*, 133 (1989), pp. 6–7.

[104] See U. Arnold, 'Hartmann von Heldrungen', in *Die Hochmeister des Deutschen Ordens 1190–1994*, QuStDO, 40 (Marburg, 1998), pp. 36–38. For discussion of Thuringian influence in the Order see D. Wojtecki, 'Der Deutsche Orden unter Friedrich II', in *Probleme um Friedrich II*, Voträge und Forschungen, 16 (Sigmaringen, 1974), pp. 219–213.

ingia as well as further property.[105] This was followed with further concessions in 1225.[106] It seems likely that Herman von Salza drew upon this relationship subsequently when he persuaded Ludwig to participate in the crusade of Frederick II. Ludwig brought a large contingent of knights to this expedition but died of illness shortly after his departure for the Latin East.[107] In the 1230s, the brothers of Landgrave Ludwig, acting as regent for his son, granted the brethren further rights and properties. Interestingly in the epic poem *Die Kreuzfahrt des Landgrafen Ludwigs des Frommen von Thüringen* both the Teutonic Knights and Conrad von Thüringen are described as accompanying Ludwig during the Third Crusade.[108] Although this anecdote is historically inaccurate, it does reflect the perceived connection between the Order and the Landgraves. In this way it can be seen how the relationship, formed between this imperial prince and the brethren at the time of the Third Crusade, continued to sustain the institution well into the thirteenth century.

Drawing together the three social groups discussed above, it can be seen that the Teutonic Knights' early growth was driven by the support it received from all levels of German society. The brotherhood *did* build a strong relationship with the emperors of Germany; however, this was only one source of patronage among many. Rather, at the heart of the Order's expansion can be found the numerous pious benefactions it received either from the many pilgrims who travelled to the Holy Land or from admirers in the West. Admittedly, the advocacy of the emperor may have encouraged the German nobility to imitate his example. Even so, donations generally seem to have been made in the wake of a pilgrimage or a crusade, not in reaction to an act of imperial benevolence.

The Church

As a primarily German order, it was natural for the Teutonic Knights to look to the empire for patronage and support; however, as an institution of the Church, it also needed the advocacy of the papacy to endorse and encourage its growth. According to *De Primordiis Ordinis Theutonici Narratio*, the papacy first learnt of the German Hospital from Emperor Henry VI, who had been asked to seek its official confirmation by his late brother.[109] If it occurred in precisely this way then Henry must have acted swiftly upon his brother's request because Frederick of Swabia was only present at the siege of

---

[105] *Urkundenbuch der Deutschordensballei Thüringen*, no. 23.
[106] *CDOT*, no. 68; *Urkundenbuch der Deutschordensballei Thüringen*, no. 35.
[107] See chapter 3.
[108] *Die Kreuzfahrt des Landgrafen Ludwigs des Frommen von Thüringen*, p. 249; Nicholson, *Love, War and the Grail*, p. 81.
[109] *De Primordiis Ordinis Theutonici Narratio*, p. 221.

Acre between 7 October 1190 and 20 January 1191 and yet Pope Clement III confirmed the establishment of the Order on 6 February 1191.[110]

In 1196 Celestine III granted the brethren a number of basic privileges, including the right to appoint their own master and to conduct burials for any Christian who was not under sentence of excommunication or interdict.[111] He also confirmed their initial landholdings.[112] The privileges granted by Celestine would have been useful to the brethren, but they were hardly effusive. It is possible that his rather lukewarm reception of the Order may have been connected to his conflict with Emperor Henry VI, which manifested itself in 1197 in the Tuscan League. The papacy may have been reluctant at this time to promote an Order which had originally come to its attention through a Hohenstaufen advocate.

Innocent III's major contribution to the Teutonic Knights was to confirm their use of the rule of the Templars and Hospitallers in 1199.[113] This concession acknowledged their status as a military order and is particularly significant because Innocent III was generally resistant to the development of new orders.[114] Certainly, as Powell has shown, the Franciscans had difficulty acquiring Innocent's official confirmation of their Order at this time.[115] Some further support was offered to the Teutonic Knights in 1198, 1207, 1209 and 1214 when the papacy confirmed their privileges and the possessions.[116] Despite this, Innocent was not a great patron and, although his confirmation of the Teutonic Knights' new rule was important, he did not significantly extend their privileges. Nevertheless, it must be acknowledged that these grants gave the Order legitimacy and licence to pursue its vocation.

The Magnates of the Latin East

The support of the papacy and the magnates of the empire helped to lay the foundations for the Order's support structure in Western Christendom, but this was also an institution that was centred initially in the Holy Land. As such, the local nobility's attitude towards this new military order was naturally of the greatest moment. These magnates were generally prepared to encourage this fledging order and it may well be imagined how readily such men – conscious of their need for troops and money – would have promoted

---

110 *TOT*, no. 295.
111 *TOT*, no. 296; 'Bulle des Pabstes Cölestin III für den Deutschen Orden vom 22. December 1196', in *Scriptores Rerum Prussicarum: Des Geschichtsquellen der Preussischen Vorzeit*, ed. T. Hirsch, M. Töppen and E. Strehlke, vol. 1 (Leipzig, 1861), pp. 225–227.
112 *TOT*, no. 33.
113 *TOT*, no. 297; *Die Register Innocenz' III*, vol. 1, p. 823; *CDOT*, no. 4; Potthast, vol. 1, no. 606.
114 *Decrees of the Ecumenical Councils*, vol. 1, p. 242; J. M. Powell, 'The Papacy and the Early Franciscans' *Franciscan Studies*, 36 (1976), pp. 249–254.
115 Powell, 'The Papacy and the Early Franciscans', pp. 249–257.
116 (1198) *CDOT*, no. 3. (1207) *Codex Diplomaticus et Epistolarius Regni Bohemiae*, vol. 2 (Prague, 1912), no. 67. (1209) *TOT*, no. 298; (repeated in 1215) *TOT*, no. 302. (1214) HB, vol. 1, p. 299.

an institution that would encourage the flow of pilgrims and warriors to the Latin East. They may also have viewed their patronage of the Order as an opportunity to strengthen their ties to the German empire. Even so, although these motives may have played their part, the first grant to the Order by King Guy of Jerusalem seems to have been driven purely by his admiration for their care of the sick at the siege of Acre.[117] Subsequently, monarchs such as Henry of Champagne[118] and Aimery continued to support the Order with further grants of lands and privileges.[119] Henry gave the brethren a house in Jaffa and vineyards outside the city – although these would presumably have been lost soon afterwards because the city fell to Sultan Al-Adil in September 1197.[120] Henry also granted the brethren a section of walls, towers, ditches and a barbican in the defences of Acre.[121] This action seems to have been part of a wider policy of entrusting the upkeep of the walls of Acre to the military orders because he made a similar concession to the Hospitallers in the same year.[122] These endowments reflect the goodwill of the rulers of Jerusalem and their desire to involve the religious orders in the rebuilding of the Latin East. Furthermore, these properties gave the Order sufficient wealth to pursue, at least on a modest scale, its medical function. Through these small concessions the brethren acquired a degree of financial independence and under Aimery they were even able to make a number of purchases. In 1198, they spent 3,000 Saracen bezants on their purchase of the village of Aguille.[123] Further acquisitions were made in 1200 and 1206.[124] These provided an early nucleus

[117] *R. Reg.*, vol. 1, no. 696; *TOT*, no. 25.
[118] Henry of Champagne arrived in the Latin East in the summer of 1190, prior to the arrival of his master King Philip II of France. After Phillip's departure, Henry of Champagne remained and became ruler of Jerusalem after marrying Isabella, widow of Conrad of Montferrat. He died in 1197 when he fell from a high window. He made several gifts to the brethren: gift 1: February 1193, village of Cafresi and property in Acre (*TOT*, no. 29; *R. Reg.*, vol. 1, no. 710); gift 2: 1193, further property in Acre (*R. Reg.*, vol. 1, no. 716; *TOT*, no. 28; *CGJJ*, vol. 1, no. 939); gift 3: April 1195, property in Tyre (*TOT*, no. 31); gift 4: a house in Jaffa and vineyard outside the city (*R. Reg.*, vol. 1, no. 727; *TOT*, no. 32); gift 5: trading privileges in the kingdom of Jerusalem (see chapter 7; *TOT*, no. 30).
[119] Aimery made the following gifts to the Order: gift 1: 8 February 1198, the village of Aguille and various further privileges on Cyprus (*TOT*, no. 34);. gift 2: August 1198, One tower in Acre (*TOT*, no. 35). He also sold various properties to the Order: sale 1: the village of Lebassa along with the *gastina* of Missop (*R. Reg.*, vol. 1, no. 776; *TOT*, no. 38); sale 2: 8 February 1198, the village of Aguille (*TOT*, no. 34).
[120] *TOT*, no. 32. For accounts of the fall of Jaffa see *La Continuation de Guillaume de Tyr*, pp. 191–193; *Chronique D'Ernoul et de Bernard Le Trésorier*, trans. M. L. de Mas Latrie (Paris, 1871), p. 305.
[121] *TOT*, no. 28; *CGJJ*, vol. 1, no. 939.
[122] Bronstein, *The Hospitallers and the Holy Land*, p. 14; *CGJJ*, vol. 1, nos. 938, 972. It has been argued by some historians that these gifts carried defensive responsibilities which – if true – would then suggest that the Teutonic Knights had adopted a military role prior to their militarisation, see Forstreuter, *Der Deutsche Orden am Mittelmeer*, p. 35. Forey has convincingly argued that these gifts carried no such requirement, *The Military Orders*, pp. 19–21. See also Arnold, 'Entstehung und Frühzeit des Deutschen Ordens', p. 96; Favreau, *Studien zur Frühgeschichte des Deutschen Ordens*, pp. 57–58.
[123] *TOT*, no. 34.
[124] 1200: *R. Reg.*, vol. 1, no. 774; *TOT*, no. 36. 1206: *R. Reg.*, vol. 1, no. 812; *TOT*, no. 41.

of properties from which the Teutonic Order could operate its military and medical functions. They gave the brethren a foothold in the eastern Mediterranean and a focus for the support structure emerging in the West. Reviewing the Order's position in the first decades of its existence it is possible to see how it began to form an international network spanning a range of families across the empire, the papacy and the barons of the Holy Land. Although this gave the Order the ability to draw upon the resources of all these groups it was still a highly fragile framework because it relied on the continued goodwill of each.

Welf and Hohenstaufen

The first major test of this system of patronage came in the first decades of the thirteenth century. On 28 September 1197 Henry VI died leaving one son, Frederick, who was a child of two.[125] As Frederick was unable to assume his father's imperial title, a number of contenders emerged to claim power for themselves. In Germany, Philip of Swabia (Frederick's uncle) and Otto of Brunswick (from the Welf family) attempted to take the throne. For Pope Innocent III there were natural dangers in a long interregnum and the papacy's agenda at this time was to break the union of Sicily and the empire which had been achieved by Henry VI. To this end, Innocent endorsed Otto as king of Germany in 1201 and accepted Frederick as king of Sicily when he came of age in 1208. Nevertheless, Frederick was not content with Sicily alone and determined to challenge Otto's authority. As a result, there arose three major contenders for the imperial throne. In 1208, the field narrowed to two claimants when Philip of Swabia was assassinated. After Philip's death, Otto was crowned as emperor on 4 October 1209 in Rome by Innocent III. In 1210 Otto's fortunes changed when, disregarding papal orders, he invaded Sicily and was excommunicated. Papal support then shifted to Frederick, who marched north in 1211 to join his ally Philip II of France. Frederick was crowned king of Germany in Mainz on 9 December 1212. Otto marched out to meet him but was defeated at Bouvines in July 1214. Frederick then organised a second coronation, which took place in Aachen in July 1215. He was later crowned as emperor in Rome in 1220 by Pope Honorius III.

These turbulent events are extremely illuminating for the Teutonic Knights' political position at this time, with the most salient fact being that they received patronage from all three of these claimants. Firstly, they received concessions from Frederick during his minority. In 1206 they were placed

---

[125] This section has drawn on M. Barber, *The Two Cities: Medieval Europe 1050–1320* (London, 2000), pp. 212–217; T. C. Van Cleve, *The Emperor Frederick II of Hohenstaufen: Immutator Mundi* (Oxford, 1972), pp. 28–113; D. Abulafia, *Frederick II: A Medieval Emperor* (London, 2002), pp. 94–131.

under imperial protection by Philip of Swabia.[126] Philip seems to have made a number of further gifts to the Order although these are only mentioned in Frederick II's subsequent confirmations.[127] In 1210, Otto IV also offered his support, granting full imperial protection, trading privileges and also a church in Nuremberg.[128] In return, the Order's master, Herman von Salza, assisted a delegation of Otto's representatives, led by Wilbrand of Oldenburg, who travelled to the Levant to offer a new crown to the king of Armenia in 1211.[129] It seems that Herman's presence with the imperial envoys was fortuitous because, soon after his coronation, King Leon II of Armenia gave the brethren the castle of Amudain with its estate specifically 'for the love of God and the Roman Empire'.[130] Shortly afterwards, as Otto's fortunes started to wane, Frederick of Sicily bestowed further patronage upon the Knights and in 1214 and 1216 he granted them lands around Altenburg and Nenewitz, which were to form the nucleus of two commanderies.[131]

Regarding the brethren's general political position at this time and the question of their loyalties to the Hohenstaufen these events are highly illuminating. First, it can be seen that if the Order was really little more than a Hohenstaufen satellite then it would not have received patronage from Otto IV or supported his envoys. It is evident, therefore, that, at this early stage, the Knights did not consider themselves to be bound politically to the Staufen. It is also tempting to interpret these events as evidence that the Order switched its allegiances repeatedly throughout this period to align itself with whichever faction was in the ascendancy.[132] *Prima facie* this idea seems to be supported by the evidence. Despite this it is important to consider both the brethren's vocation and the way in which these political rivals offered their gifts. As already shown, the Teutonic Hospital was created through the piety and dedication of the German people to serve the needs of the Holy Land. The Order's fulfilment of this objective was not compatible with taking sides in an imperial civil war. Furthermore, the benefactions of Philip, Otto and Frederick all reflect their dedication to the Latin East. On 20 May 1206 Philip of Swabia placed the Order under his protection specifically to support the Holy Land.[133] In August 1207 he advocated a further gift whilst holding court in Nordhausen.[134] Notably, the patriarch of Jerusalem along with the masters of the Templars and Hospitallers were present at the same time to seek assistance for the kingdom of Jerusalem.[135] From this, it seems likely

---

126 *CDOT*, no. 7; *Regesta Thuringiae*, vol. 2, no. 1307.
127 *Codex Diplomaticus et Epistolaris Regni Bohemiae*, vol. 2, nos. 108, 165.
128 For Otto IV's protection see: *TOT*, no. 252; *CDOT*, no. 12. For his gift of the church in Nuremberg see *CDOT*, no. 13.
129 Wilbrand of Oldenburg, *Peregrinatio*, pp. 162–163, 174.
130 'Pro amore dei et imperii Romani'; *TOT*, no. 46.
131 *AZM*, pp. 31–32.
132 For discussion see Kluger, *Hochmeister Hermann*, pp. 6–7.
133 *CDOT*, no. 7; *Regesta Imperii V*, vol. 1, no. 132.
134 *Regesta Imperii V*, vol. 1, no. 159.
135 *MGH Leges: Const.* vol. 2, no. 13.

that Philip supported this gift in the context of the needs of the Holy Land. Likewise, the charters which detail Otto's concessions describe the same motivations.[136] Otto himself had taken a crusading oath in 1210 and was generally well disposed towards the military orders; in 1211 he confirmed the Hospitallers' privileges in his realms.[137] It seems likely that these gifts, as well as the embassy of Wilbrand of Oldenburg, were viewed as preparatory steps for Otto's departure on crusade. If this was the case then the Teutonic Knights' readiness both to receive aid from Otto and to support Wilbrand may merely indicate their desire to encourage the work of the Holy Land. Frederick II similarly took a crusading oath in 1215 and, as we shall see in the next two chapters, he worked closely with Herman von Salza to prepare his expedition. It seems, therefore, that these rulers' concessions to the brethren were more concerned with their personal piety and the rebuilding of the Latin East than with any idea of political affiliation. As a German military order, the Teutonic Knights were well placed to support these German rulers' crusading objectives and it seems likely that it was in this context that these alms were given. The Order, for its part, demonstrated a readiness to receive aid from any who were prepared to offer it, a stance that was fully compatible with a politically non-aligned institution that was focused specifically towards the defence of the Levant.

By 1215, the Teutonic Knights had established an institution which represented the combined commitment of the German people to the recovery of the Holy Land. The Order also enjoyed the support of the nobility of the Holy Land and the approbation of the pope. Territorially, the brethren had acquired property across much of the eastern Mediterranean, including frontier regions such as Armenia, the kingdom of Jerusalem and the Peloponnese. They had also obtained territories in Italy, Sicily and across the German empire, which could supply materials for the Order's medical and military undertakings. In 1211, Herman von Salza also began operations in the kingdom of Hungary when King Andrew granted the Order the province of Burzenland, which had been subjected to repeated Cuman raids. Twenty-five years after its establishment, therefore, the Teutonic Knights had begun to carve a niche for themselves in the ongoing defence of Christendom.

---

[136] Charter 1: *CDOT*, no. 12. Charter 2: *Archieven der Ridderlijke Duitsche Orde: Balie van Utrecht*, vol. 1, no. 2.
[137] *CGJJ*, vol. 2, no. 1368.

CHAPTER 2

The Fifth Crusade and the Development of the Teutonic Knights, 1216–1223

> These men however, having their origin as it were from a small and sparse spring, have swelled into a great river. The Blessed Virgin Mary their patroness, whom they serve with all piety and humility, advances them both in matters temporal and spiritual and bestows prosperity.
>
> (James of Vitry, bishop of Acre)[1]

Building upon their early foundations the Teutonic Knights grew rapidly during the thirteenth century and enhanced their ability to conduct their military vocation. The Fifth Crusade specifically was the event which heralded an almost meteoric rise in their fortunes.[2] Although this venture was ultimately a failure, it provided the brethren with the opportunity to demonstrate their abilities under the watching eyes of Western Christendom.

In the aftermath of Henry VI's crusade, Pope Innocent III attempted to raise new forces for the defence of the East. Accordingly, he proclaimed a new crusade, which is now known as the Fourth Crusade.[3] This crusade became diverted from its objectives in the Levant and conquered the city of Constantinople in 1204. Some contingents did reach the Holy Land, but they suffered heavy losses from disease. The Fifth Crusade was the next major expedition that was intended to retake Jerusalem. Pope Innocent launched this campaign in 1213 but died in 1216, before it could be realised, and thus it is was his successor Honorius III who carried this campaign to fruition.[4]

---

[1] 'Hi autem quasi a modico et tenui fonte principium habentes in magnum fluuium excreuerut, beata virgine Maria eorum advocata, cui cum omni devotione et humilitate serviunt, eos tam in bonis spiritualibus quam temporalibus subsidiis promovente, et incrementum largiente'; James of Vitry, *Historia Hierosolimitani*, in *Gesta Dei per Francos*, vol. 1 (Hanover, 1611), p. 1085. The translation of this passage has been made with reference to James of Vitry, *The History of Jerusalem*, trans. A. Stewart, Palestine Pilgrims' Text Society 11 (London, 1896), p. 55.

[2] Favreau-Lilie, 'L'Ordine Teutonico in Terrasanta (1198–1291)', p. 61; Favreau, *Studien zur Frühgeschichte des Deutschen Ordens*, p. 82; *AZM*, p. 34; W. Urban, *The Teutonic Knights: A Military History* (London, 2003), pp. 24–25.

[3] Previously it has been suggested that the Order played a part in the Fourth Crusade; however Houben has demonstrated that this was almost certainly not the case, see Houben 'Wie und wann kam der Deutsche Orden nach Griechenland?' p. 253.

[4] This section has drawn on Riley-Smith, *The Crusades*, pp. 173–180; Richard, *The Crusades*, pp. 296–307; J. M. Powell, *Anatomy of a Crusade: 1213–1221* (Philadelphia, PA, 1990).

In the summer of 1217 the crusading contingents assembled at Acre. Their first venture was to launch an attack into Muslim territory during which they assaulted Mount Tabor, which posed a threat to Acre. In a further engagement the army raided the territory around Sidon. In May 1218, the army set sail for Egypt where it disembarked, meeting only limited resistance. The Christian forces then initiated a siege of the city of Damietta, which fell after a prolonged defence on 5 November 1219. Prior to the fall of the city, the Egyptian Sultan al-Kāmil offered to return the lost territories of the kingdom of Jerusalem (with the exception of the fortresses of Kerak and Shaubak) in exchange for the removal of the crusading army. His offer was rejected. The army then remained idle at Damietta, although several contingents engaged in some raiding activity. In the spring of 1221, after the arrival of Duke Louis of Bavaria, the leadership decided to advance south along the Nile towards Cairo. Initially the Christian forces won a victory at Fariskur; however, they had not accounted for the rising waters of the Nile, which hindered the army, bringing hunger and disease. Under relentless attack from the land and with their supply lines cut by Egyptian warships patrolling the Nile, the army surrendered on 29 August 1221. The Egyptian sultan demanded – and was granted – hostages from among the crusade's leaders and the return of Damietta.

Within these events, the Teutonic Knights had been extremely active. Prior to the Fifth Crusade, the Order had remained a relatively small institution that supported pilgrims in the Latin East. Peter von Dusburg described its military strength at the time of Herman von Salza's election (*c.*1210) as follows: 'It was able to have ten brother knights prepared in arms and no more'.[5] This estimate concerning the size of the Order roughly twelve years after its militarisation is reminiscent of William of Tyre's comment on the position of the Templars in the early twelfth century: 'although they had been in existence for nine years, they were still only nine in number'.[6] Despite this, just as the Council of Troyes in 1129 and the advocacy of Bernard of Clairvaux drew attention to the Templars, so too did the work of Herman von Salza during the Fifth Crusade raise awareness of the Teutonic Knights.[7]

This was achieved largely during the campaign itself because the Knights do not appear to have played a significant role in the crusade's recruitment or preparation. The brethren are first mentioned in 1217 when Herman is said to have been present at the first major council of crusading leaders in Acre.[8]

---

5 'Posset habere in armis paratos decem fratres milites et non plures'; Peter von Dusburg, *Chronicon Terrae Prussie*, p. 31.

6 'Cumque iam annis novem in eo fuissent proposito, non nisi novem erant, extunc vero cepit eorum numerus augeri et possessiones multiplicari'; William of Tyre, *Chronicon*, ed. R. Huygens, Corpus Christianorum: Continuatio Mediaeualis 63, vol. 1 (Turnhout, 1986), p. 554. The translation was taken from *The Templars: Selected Sources*, ed. M. Barber and K. Bate (Manchester, 2002), p. 26.

7 Forey, *The Military Orders*, p. 15.

8 Eracles, p. 323.

Subsequently, the Order participated in the construction of the Templar fortress of Atlīt.[9] The brethren took part in much of the fighting at Damietta and they seem to have distinguished themselves on several occasions. Various chronicles contain references to their contributions to the defence of the army's camp, an attack on the Muslim camp outside Damietta on 29 August 1219, and also in a raiding expedition.[10] The remarks of these chroniclers chime well with the comments of participants who indicate the importance of the Teutonic Knights' military actions during the crusade.[11] It appears that the Orders' casualties during the Fifth Crusade were significant because subsequent papal charters frequently mentioned their suffering as a result of the campaign. Even if one makes allowance for hyperbole, it seems likely that the Order's limited military resources were significantly depleted.[12]

Despite the accounts of their valour, the Knights' most significant contribution was not in arms but in diplomacy. Herman attended the crucial councils which decided the course of the campaign. He is known to have been present at the first major assembly in Acre in 1217.[13] He subsequently advocated the acceptance of al-Kāmil's offer to return the Holy Land in exchange for the removal of the crusading army from Egypt.[14] He also supported the fateful decision to advance along the Nile towards Cairo.[15] Herman's presence at these gatherings and the fact that chroniclers felt it necessary to record his opinions demonstrates his perceived importance.

After the surrender of the army, Herman was chosen along with the masters of the Temple and the Hospital to be among the twenty-four hostages who acted as surety for the peace settlement with the sultan.[16] To be selected as a hostage, Herman – only a minor contributor of manpower to the operation – must have been viewed by both the Christian and Muslim forces to be a man of considerable ability and consequence; otherwise he would have had little

---

9   *Annales Sancti Rudberti Salisburgenses*, in *MGH SS*, vol. 9, p. 780; *Chronica Regia Coloniensis*, in *MGH SRG*, vol. 18, p. 243; *Cronica Reinhardsbrunnensis*, in *MGH SS*, vol. 30, p. 591; *Cronica S. Petri Erfordensis Moderna*, in *MGH SS*, vol. 30, p. 386; Matthew Paris, *Chronica Majora*, ed. H. R. Luard, RS, 57, vol. 3 (London, 1876), p. 14.

10 See Oliveri Scholastici, *Historia Damiatina*, p. 210; Matthew Paris, *Chronica Majora*, vol. 3, pp. 48–50. One source suggests that during one action the Order lost 30 knights; see Alberti Milioli Notarii Regini, *Liber de Temporibus et Aetatibus et Cronica Imperatorum*, in *MGH SS*, vol. 31, p. 490; *AZM*, p. 34. See also, Oliveri Scholastici, *Historia Damiatina*, p. 207. The Teutonic Knights also participated in a raiding expedition towards Burlus, see Oliveri Scholastici, *Historia Damiatina*, p. 252. For a further description of this raid see Jamal ad-din Muhammed be Salim bin Wasil, *Moufarraj al-Kurub*, ed. H. M. Rabiah and S. Abed ad Fatah Ashour, vol. 4 (Cairo, 1972), p. 16.

11 The Order received much praise from Oliver of Paderborn and it is interesting to note that the brethren had links to the bishop of Paderborn who, between 1214 and 1220, confirmed a number of pilgrims' gifts to the Order: *Urkundenbuch der Deutschordens-Ballei Hessen*, vol. 1, no. 4; *CDOT*, no. 35; *Oorkondenboek van het Sticht Utrecht*, vol. 2, no. 668; *AZM*, p. 35.

12 *TOT*, no. 357.

13 Eracles, p. 323.

14 Eracles, p. 342.

15 Matthew Paris, *Chronica Majora*, vol. 3, p. 69.

16 Oliveri Scholastici, *Historia Damiatina*, p. 276.

value as security for the treaty. Later, he and the master of the Temple were chosen to surrender Damietta to the Sultan.[17] This appointment required men of sensitivity and diplomatic skill because new crusading contingents had arrived at Damietta during the crusaders' advance towards Cairo which were unwilling to return the city to the sultan.[18]

Herman's prestige is also reflected through the correspondence which passed between the crusading army and Western Christendom. Herman countersigned major letters sent by the crusade leadership to Frederick II and Honorius on 15 June 1218 and again to Honorius on 11 November 1219.[19] Only senior dignitaries such as the papal legate, the king of Jerusalem, major nobles and the masters of the Templars and Hospitallers were among these signatories. Other counts and lords were not allotted an individual signature and therefore Herman's presence among these exalted personages demonstrates his perceived importance. Additionally, Herman wrote about the progress of the expedition to Leo, cardinal of Holy Cross in Jerusalem, and part of this letter was copied into the *Cronica de Mailros*.[20]

Honorius acknowledged Herman's growing prestige when he replied to these letters by including him among the intended recipients of the letters despatched to the crusading army.[21] Once again, only the most important crusading leaders enjoyed such a distinction. Furthermore, when Honorius related the events of the crusade to the rulers of Christendom, he included the brethren's exploits in his account.[22] The significance that the papacy attached to the Teutonic Knights at this time stands in stark contrast to papal correspondence issued before the crusade where the Teutonic Knights were never mentioned. For example, in 1216 Honorius wrote to the magnates of the Latin East to inform them of the death of Innocent III and to assure them of his continued support; yet he did not include the Teutonic Knights among the addressees of this document.[23] A similar trend can be seen with his subsequent correspondence to the Latin East prior to the Fifth Crusade. Accordingly, it appears that the inclusion of the Order during the Fifth Crusade into this exalted inner circle of recipients stands as testimony to the sudden growth in their perceived significance.

A further role played by the brethren was in the supply of the army. This

17 Oliveri Scholastici, *Historia Damiatina*, p. 277.
18 Richard, *The Crusades*, p. 306; Kluger, *Hochmeister Hermann*, p. 33.
19 15 June 1218: *Studien zur Geschichte des Fünften Kreuzzuges*, ed. R. Röhricht (Innsbruck, 1891), pp. 39–40; *R. Reg.*, vol. 1, no. 911. 11 November 1219: *R. Reg.*, vol. 1, no. 925.
20 *R. Reg.*, vol. 1, no. 926; *Chronica de Mailros*, ed. J. Stevenson (Edinburgh, 1835), pp. 135–137.
21 Letter 1 (13 August 1218) *RHP*, vol. 1, no. 1580. Letter 2 (24 Feb 1220) *RHP*, vol. 1, no. 2338. Letter 3 (20 June 1221) *RHP*, vol. 1, no. 3478.
22 *PL*, vol. 207, cols. 479D–481D.
23 *RHP*, vo l. 1, no. 1. M. Pacifico has noted that the Order's master was not mentioned in this early correspondence: 'I Teutonici tra papato e impero nel Mediterraneo al tempo di Federico II, 1215–1250', in *I Cavalieri teutonici tra Sicilia e Mediterraneo*, ed. A. Giuffrida, H. Houben and K, Toomaspoeg, Acta Theutonica, 4 (Galatina, 2007), p. 96.

took a number of forms including the provision of shipping. Oliver of Paderborn reports that corsairs sank a ship carrying barley to the army which belonged to the Order off the Egyptian coast.[24] More significantly, agents of the Order helped to convey wealth to the crusade leadership from the papacy. In a letter dated 24 July 1220 Pope Honorius mentioned that he had sent a Teutonic Knight to transmit funds to the army. In this same letter he granted 5,000 ounces of gold (through the offices of the papal legate) to both the bishop of Bethlehem and the Teutonic Knights for distribution. Significantly, he allotted the same sum to the Templars and Hospitallers.[25] In this case, therefore, it appears that the Teutonic Order received the same level of funding as the Templars and Hospitallers, institutions which are each believed to have deployed around 700 horsemen and 2,000 infantry for this expedition.[26] The parity of this financial support serves as a clear recognition of how far the Teutonic Order had grown in repute.[27] Herman seems to have built upon his Order's profile by making two journeys to Western Christendom during and directly after the campaign. On both occasions he visited both the emperor and the papacy.[28] In general, the Fifth Crusade can be seen as the moment when Herman von Salza used his diplomatic skill to manoeuvre both himself and his Order into the decision-making circles in the crusader leadership.

Herman's personal abilities were clearly important in the development of the Order's international profile; however, another crucial area was the Order's support of pilgrims during the expedition. The care of pilgrims was the primary vocation of the Teutonic Order at this time and the development of its military role gave it the opportunity to offer a new range of services to pilgrims in the Latin East. Before the Fifth Crusade, it seems likely that the Order used its troops to escort groups of pilgrims to the holy sites in the Levant and Pope Honorius mentioned this service in two papal charters issued in 1221 and 1230.[29] During the Fifth Crusade, the opportunity to render aid to pilgrims grew enormously. The crusade contained tens of thousands of troops, a large number of whom came from the German empire.

Herman von Salza seems to have risen to this challenge by offering a range of opportunities to crusading knights during the campaign. The first was the option to become a brother knight of the Order. The chronicle of Eracles contains a reference to this in an account of the siege of Damietta. Appar-

---

[24] Oliveri Scholastici, *Historia Damiatina*, p. 253.

[25] *MGH Epis. Saec. XIII*, vol. 1, no. 124; Powell, *Anatomy of a Crusade*, pp. 97–103.

[26] Bronstein, *The Hospitallers and the Holy Land*, p. 20; *CGJJ*, vol. 2, no. 1633.

[27] Incidentally, there is a further letter written in 1219 which also reflects the Order's role in the employment of such funds, *RHP*, vol. 1, no. 2195.

[28] Herman travelled to the imperial court and was present to sign several charters in the autumn of 1220 see HB, vol. 2, pp. 40–41. Frederick then sent Herman to the papacy in October 1220, HB, vol. 1, p. 863. Herman's second journey to Western Christendom occurred in late 1221, Eracles, pp. 352, 355. For discussion of the timing of this second journey see Kluger, *Hochmeister Herman*, pp. 34–35.

[29] *TOT*, nos. 72, 321, 362.

ently a knight named Litot, who stormed the chain tower at Damietta, chose to become a member of the house.[30] Indeed it appears that the Order had acquired a sufficiently high level of recruits during this expedition for it to be necessary for Honorius to grant them a privilege stating, 'It is lawful for you to receive whosoever is marked by the sign of the cross as a brother unless some canonical impediment stands in the way'.[31] Certainly, it is possible that a large number of knights may have welcomed the opportunity to continue to fight in the Holy Land, perhaps as a result of their experiences during the operation; perhaps out of a sense of shame for the failure of the crusader army. For Herman, it may well be imagined that the chance to recruit large numbers of trained knights, who were already present in the Latin East, would have been a valuable opportunity for his fledgling order.

Other *milites* decided to become *confratres*. *Confratres* were secular men and women who chose to become affiliated with an Order (although they did not take a monastic vow). Many of these *confratres* were soldiers who fought with the Teutonic Knights' host and bolstered the Order's strength during military ventures. The presence of numerous *confratres* during the Fifth Crusade is indicated by the large number of papal privileges concerning these men, which were issued during and shortly after the campaign. It is possible that impoverished knights may have affiliated themselves to the Order at this time as an expedient measure to remain with the army. An example of a privilege issued to support such soldiers can be found in 1221 when Honorius protected the Order's right to bury *confratres* in the Holy Land.[32] The interment of *confratres* by a military order was a controversial issue at that time because it denied the local parish revenues that would otherwise have been collected from the funerary arrangements and subsequent masses for the dead.[33]

In 1223 Honorius encouraged knights who were departing for the East to become *confratres* of the Order by allowing them to claim remission of one seventh of penance.[34] The ability to offer this incentive was a customary privilege granted by the papacy for the encouragement of patrons and supporters of military orders. In 1230 Gregory IX offered the same inducement for those who assisted in the building of the Teutonic Order's fortress of Montfort in the Galilean hills.[35] Previously, Pope Celestine II in his bull *Milites Templi* (1144) had permitted the Templars to offer the same incentive to *confratres*,[36] and in 1256 Alexander IV granted a similar privilege to the Order of St

---

[30] Eracles, p. 328.
[31] 'Liceat vobis quemlibet sancte crucis signaculo signatum in fratrem recipere, si impedimentum aliquod canonicum non obsistat'; *TOT*, no. 320.
[32] Charter 1: *TOT*, no. 315. Charter 2: *TOT*, no. 348.
[33] Selwood, *Knights of the Cloister*, pp. 128–129.
[34] *TOT*, no. 370.
[35] *TOT*, no. 72.
[36] *Papsturkunden für Templer und Johanniter*, no. 8; Selwood, *Knights of the Cloister*, p. 77.

Thomas of Acre.[37] In general, given both the level of encouragement shown to *confratres* by the papacy and the references to pilgrims becoming brothers of the Teutonic Knights, it is possible that the military forces at the disposal of the Order rose dramatically during the course of the operation.

In addition to these new recruits, many other pilgrims – including a number of highly placed imperial nobles and princes – were sufficiently impressed by the brethren to make donations to support their work. These included Duke Leopold VI of Austria,[38] Frederick of Baden,[39] Walter of Brabant,[40] Count Adolf of Berg,[41] William of Gurcenich,[42] the Count of Bar,[43] Lord Albert of Tirol[44] and Swederus of Dingede.[45] Another pilgrim, Barzella Merxadrus, when writing his will in Damietta, left his arms and armour to the Knights.[46] The overall impression left by this evidence is that the Teutonic Order became a central hub for German crusaders in the Damietta campaign, offering considerable support and being rewarded in turn by those with funds to spare.

In the wake of the expedition, news of the Order's exploits provoked a storm of approbation in Western Christendom, particularly from the papacy.[47] Many of the most important charters that the brethren were ever to receive were granted at this time and, shortly afterwards, Honorius issued a total of fifty-seven privileges.[48] As noted earlier, the papacy had only offered a limited amount of support previously, so these concessions marked a dramatic rise in its patronage. Admittedly, Honorius also granted new liberties and privileges to other institutions – particularly to the Hospitallers – during the preparations for the expedition; however, these were not on the same scale.[49] Among the most striking elements of these documents are the repeated eulogies of the Order's virtues to the people of Christendom. In 1221 alone, statements of this kind were issued repeatedly in papal bulls.[50] A good example can be seen in a document issued on 16 January 1221,

---

[37] *Reg. Alexandre IV*, vol. 1, no. 1553; A. J. Forey, 'The Military Order of St Thomas of Acre', *English Historical Review*, 92 (1977), p. 491.

[38] *Gesta Crucigerorum Rhenanorum*, in *Quinti Belli Sacri: Scriptores Minores*, ed. R. Rohricht (Geneva, 1879), p. 49; Oliveri Scholastici, *Historia Damiatina*, p. 207.

[39] *Württembergisches Urkundenbuch*, vol. 3, no. 630.

[40] *Studien zur Geschichte des Fünften Kreuzzuges*, p. 70.

[41] *Urkundenbuch für die Geschichte des Niederrheins*, ed. T. Lacomblet, vol. 2 (Aalen, 1960), no. 72.

[42] *Studien zur Geschichte des Fünften Kreuzzuges*, p. 64.

[43] *Chartes de la Commanderie de Beauvoir de l'Ordre Teutonique*, no. 28.

[44] *Tiroler Urkundenbuch*, vol. 2 (Innsbruck, 1949), no. 742.

[45] *CDOT*, no. 35; *Oorkondenboek van het Sticht Utrecht*, vol. 2, no. 668. See also *AZM*, p. 35.

[46] *Annali Bolognesi*, vol. 2, pt 2, no. 480.

[47] *AZM*, p. 36.

[48] This figure has been suggested by Militzer in *AZM*, p. 33. Pacifico has suggested the figure of 109 privileges during the period 1220–1227, Pacifico, 'I Teutonici tra papato e impero nel Mediterraneo al tempo di Federico II, 1215–1250', p. 104.

[49] Bronstein, *The Hospitallers and the Holy Land*, pp. 108–110.

[50] See *TOT*, nos. 311, 312, 321, 322, 326, 327, 340, 345, 358.

Knights of the hospital of St Mary of the Teutons of Jerusalem, new favoured Maccabees of this time, scorning secular desires and their own goods, taking up their cross, have followed the Lord; they themselves are [the ones] through whom God frees the Eastern Church from the filth of the pagans.[51]

Within these and further charters, Honorius conferred a wide variety of powers upon the brethren. These included the right to exact one third of a vassal's property in the event of his death and further liberties concerning their exemption from the payment of tithes.[52] Arguably the most important concession, however, was the grant of the same privileges as those enjoyed by the Templars and Hospitallers.[53] This gift alone (on an institutional level) raised the Order to the same position as these older military orders. Among the remaining documents, a large number protected the Teutonic Order from the attacks of other churchmen. There were several which prohibited clerics from exacting the crusading tax of one-twentieth of all clerical incomes. This had been levied by the papacy for the support of the crusade.[54] Other charters prohibited clerics from preventing the Teutonic Knights from collecting alms, using financial punishments against members of the Order, or abusing the brethren's exemptions from various ecclesiastical tithes.[55] When examining these documents it is necessary to establish whether these disputes took place in the Latin East or in Western Christendom. This question is complicated by the fact that the papacy addressed most of these charters to the prelates of the Church in general rather than to an individual region or cleric.[56] In some cases it is possible to suggest tentatively that abuses were not committed in the Levant. For example, it seems unlikely that the papal charter which prohibited the illegal exaction of tithes was applicable to the Holy Land. Admittedly, the Order subsequently became involved in a dispute over tithes with the bishop of Acre in 1257; however, at the time of the Fifth Crusade there appears to

---

51 'Milites hospitalis sancte Marie Theutonicorum Ierosolimitani novi sub tempore gratie Machabei, abnegantes secularia desideria et propria relinquentes, tollentes crucem suam, dominum sunt secuti; ipsi sunt, per quos deus orientalem ecclesiam a paganorum spurcitiis liberat'; *TOT*, no. 321.

52 Property: *TOT*, no. 335. Tithes: *TOT*, no. 314, confirmed in following documents: *TOT*, nos. 375, 453, 478, 482, 487, 489, 491, 492, 493, 498, 499, 502, 544, 572, 587, 598, 606, 626, 642, 645, 646. *R. Reg.*, vol. 1, no. 1419. Tithes: *TOT*, no, 319.

53 *TOT*, no. 309 (granted 9 January 1221), confirmed in the following documents issued between 1223 and 1277: *TOT*, nos. 373, 398, 416, 545, 551, 553, 555–557; *R. Reg.*, vol. 1, nos. 1415, 1417.

54 See Powell, *Anatomy of a Crusade*, p. 92. For the charters prohibiting the collection of the twentieth (19 January 1221) see *TOT*, no. 332, confirmed in the following documents issued in 1227, 1244, 1247 and 1248: *TOT*, nos. 425, 473, 514, 519.

55 For a sample of charters protecting the Order's right to collect alms (15 January 1221) see *TOT*, no. 312; (16 January 1221) *TOT*, no. 315. For the charter protecting the Order from financial punishments (20 January 1221) see *TOT*, no. 339. Confirmed in the following documents issued in 1248, 1257: *TOT*, nos. 520, 554. For charters regarding the tithes collected from the Order (8 February 1221) see *TOT*, no. 356. For the charter which freed the Order from paying tithes upon its lands (1216) see *TOT*, no. 303.

56 Kluger, *Hochmeister Hermann*, p. 25.

have been a strong accord between this prelate and the brethren.[57] Indeed, James of Vitry (bishop of Acre, 1216–1228), writing after the Fifth Crusade, commented explicitly upon the Order's readiness to pay its tithes.[58]

One controversy, which does appear to have taken place in the Levant, concerned the Order's cemeteries. In 1221, Honorius repeatedly forbade members of the Church from withholding the brethren's right to bury the dead, whilst confirming the Order's ability to perform this function.[59] This dispute appears to have occurred in the Levant and there are a number of reasons for this conclusion. Firstly, although the brethren owned many cemeteries across Western Europe (they may have owned one in Brindisi as early as 1191), the burial of the dead was a particularly lucrative service in the Latin East.[60] It was there that many wealthy Christians chose to be buried and they were prepared to pay for the privilege. This issue had caused trouble for the Order from the time of its inception and, as shown above, in 1190 its right to bury Frederick of Swabia was contested by the Hospitallers.[61] Further proof can be derived from the existence of a parallel dispute between the Hospitallers and the prelates of the kingdom of Jerusalem which occurred at roughly the same time as the Teutonic Knights' controversy.[62] The fact that both Orders were in dispute with the clergy at the same time over the same issues suggests that firstly the two cases were linked and secondly that they both occurred in the Latin East. Incidentally, this seems to have been a prolonged issue for the Hospitallers and, as Riley-Smith has shown, they continued to encounter difficulties on this subject until 1228.[63]

Not all of Honorius's charters sought to address external issues. There are several documents which concern the internal problem of desertion. In 1216, the pontiff issued a charter censuring those who had deserted from the Order.[64] On 1 February 1223 the papacy issued a further document, which referred to members of the Teutonic Knights who had travelled to Egypt and become diverted by sinful practices. It states that these brethren had left the Order and either tried to resume a secular life or joined another religious institution without licence. The charter then insists that such deserters should return to the Order and obtain permission.[65] It is interesting to note that this was obviously a serious problem during the Damietta campaign and naturally, for Herman, a cause for concern. One factor that may be of significance here is that in 1220 the Order's marshal and grand commander were captured

[57] *R. Reg.*, vol. 1, no. 1260; *TOT*, no. 112.
[58] James of Vitry, *Historia Hierosolimitani*, p. 1085.
[59] Charter 1 (5 February 1221): *TOT*, nos. 348, 349. Charter 2 (16 January 1221): *TOT*, no. 314, confirmed: *TOT*, no. 375. Charter 3 (1221): *TOT*, no. 324. Charter 4 (18 January 1221): *TOT*, no. 329.
[60] *Codice Diplomatico Brindisino*, vol. 1, no. 26.
[61] *La Continuation de Guillaume de Tyr*, p. 99.
[62] *CGJJ*, vol. 2, nos. 1543, 1716, 1729.
[63] *KSJJC*, pp. 407–408.
[64] *TOT*, no. 304.
[65] *TOT*, no. 385.

during a raiding expedition (see Appendices E.1 and E.2).[66] Later that same year, Herman was sent to Western Christendom. Although Herman would presumably have appointed deputies, it is possible that the sudden removal of the Teutonic Knights' command structure may have encouraged lax behaviour or provided an opportunity to desert. Honorius issued a further charter on this matter in 1227, reinforcing the penalties against those who deserted.[67] After this time the matter was rarely mentioned, although rumours circulated during the siege of Acre in 1291 that a deserter named Bertold had joined the forces of Islam.[68]

These factors reflect Honorius's goodwill towards the Order and his willingness to endow them with important privileges. Indeed, his patronage takes on even greater significance when it is remembered that the Templars and Hospitallers had been criticised during the Third Lateran Council 1179 for abusing these same privileges.[69] Consequently, his readiness to make the same concessions for a new order is all the more remarkable. Incidentally, recent historians have begun to show that Honorius did not merely pursue the policies of his predecessor Innocent III but was responsible for some innovations. Certainly the unprecedented level of support he offered to the Teutonic Order accords well with this conclusion.[70]

There is a contention, however, that these papal charters were not issued entirely through the initiative of the papacy, but rather at the request of the emperor. This is stated in several chronicles and also in a papal charter issued on 17 April 1222.[71] In this document the pope explicitly stated that it was Frederick, 'who on the day of his coronation requested this from us as a special gift'.[72] Given Frederick's request that the Order should be supported by the papacy, an argument could be created to claim that these papal charters were the result of the emperor's insistence rather than Honorius's free choice. Certainly the fact that the majority of these charters were issued within three months of Frederick's coronation (22 November 1220) appears to support this idea. On the other hand, the knights had already performed some major services for the papacy, long before the coronation, and had received recognition for them. As mentioned, certain brethren had been entrusted with large sums of money that were conveyed to Egypt. Additionally, many of the papal privileges specified that they had been issued as a direct consequence of the Order's work in the Holy Land. It is clear therefore that, even before

---

[66] Oliveri Scholastici, *Historia Damiatina*, p. 252.
[67] *TOT*, no. 428.
[68] Iohannis Abbatis Victoriensis, *Liber Certarum Historiarum: Liber Secundus*, in *MGH SRG*, vol. 36, pt 1, p. 303.
[69] *Decrees of the Ecumenical Councils*, vol. 1, p. 216.
[70] For discussion see J. M. Powell, 'Honorius III and the Leadership of the Crusade', *Catholic Historical Review*, 63 (1977), pp. 521–523.
[71] *Continuatio Itala*, in *MGH SS*, vol. 26, pp. 85–86; *TOT*, no. 368; *Chronicon Breve Fratris*, pp. 151–154.
[72] 'Qui in die coronationis sue id a nobis pro speciali munere postulavit'; *TOT*, no. 368.

Frederick's advocacy, a strong bond had developed between Honorius and the Teutonic Knights. It may be that Frederick's request at his coronation spurred the pope into granting these particular concessions, but this would only have strengthened their mutual accord, not created it. Like Honorius, Frederick also made several notable concessions in the wake of the Fifth Crusade. Before the campaign, he permitted the Order to draw a regular income from the taxation receipts of several southern Italian and Sicilian ports (see chapter 7).[73] This income was payable in ounces of silver or gold. Frederick's gifts are all the more notable because he sought to restrict the development of the other military orders on Sicily at this time.[74] After his coronation, Frederick made additional grants which included further land-holdings and taxation rights.[75]

By 1221, flourishing under the praise of the papacy, Empire and much of Christendom, the general standing of the Teutonic Knights had developed considerably from their position before the crusade. A consequence of this approbation seems to have been a change in their perceived status in relation to the Templars and Hospitallers. Previously historians have drawn attention to the charter which granted the brethren the same privileges as these older orders and they have also discussed the Order's legal equality to these institutions; yet these developments appear to be symptoms of a far wider change.[76]

For much of the thirteenth century many chroniclers, who described the events in the Holy Land, used a concise way of identifying the three major military orders in their narratives. Instead of listing the Templars, Hospitallers and Teutonic Knights individually they frequently used the terms 'the three houses' or 'the three masters'. It is clear that they included only the most powerful military orders in this triumvirate because other institutions such as the Order of St Lazarus and that of St Thomas of Acre were evidently excluded. A description of this kind implies a level of parity between such establishments and raises the question as to when the Teutonic Knights possessed sufficient strength to be included in this select grouping. The first chroniclers to include a description of this kind were Oliver of Paderborn and James of Vitry. Both these men were participants in the Fifth Crusade and wrote their accounts shortly afterwards. They both use these abbreviates references and – more explicitly – James of Vitry wrote of the Teutonic Knights:

---

[73] Toomaspoeg, *Les Teutoniques en Sicilie*, pp. 51–52.

[74] Barber, *The New Knighthood*, pp. 238–239.

[75] This list of concessions is not intended to be exhaustive but for further details see the following charters: Charter 1: HB, vol. 2, pp. 165–166. Charter 2: *TOT*, no. 255; *CDOT*, no. 56. Charter 3: HB, vol. 2, pp. 163–165. Charter 4: HB, vol. 2, pp. 157–159. Charter 5: HB, vol. 2, pp. 160–163. Charter 6: *TOT*, no. 256. HB, vol. 2, p. 156–157.

[76] Kluger, *Hochmeister Hermann*, pp. 22–23, 50–51. See also H. Houben, 'I Cavalieri Teutonici nel Mediterraneo Orientale (secoli XII–XV)', in *I Cavalieri teutonici tra Siclia e Mediterraneo*, ed. A. Giuffrida, H. Houben and K. Toomaspoeg (Galatina, 2007), p. 56.

Now, since a threefold cord is not easily broken, it hath pleased divine providence to add a third to the two aforesaid houses, one which is very needful to the Holy Land and is, as it were, compounded from the other two.[77]

A similar sentiment can also be found in James of Vitry's sermons and later in the writings of Humbert of Romans.[78] It seems that writers began to link the Teutonic Order to the Templars and Hospitallers with such terminology during or shortly after the Fifth Crusade. This is not to argue that Teutonic Knights had become equally wealthy or powerful; only that they were now perceived to be among the ranks of the greatest institutions of Christendom.

In summary, Herman von Salza squeezed every possible drop of advantage out of the Fifth Crusade. His diplomatic exploits earned him a place in the councils of the crusade leadership, whilst his embassies to the West drew attention to the Order's capabilities. Although the Order itself could initially deploy only a small force of knights, its military strength seems to have increased dramatically with the recruitment of new brothers and the affiliation of new *confratres*. The crusade itself may have been a failure, but Herman returned to the West to be greeted by a pope and emperor who were prepared to shower benefactions on the Order. Perhaps Honorius hoped that his praise for the Teutonic Knights' achievements might ease the sense of general outrage provoked by the crushing defeats in Egypt. Likewise, Frederick may have hoped that his public support for this military order might divert attention away from his conspicuous failure to fulfil his crusading vow. Whatever their motives, the result was the elevation of the Order from a position of relative obscurity to a state where it began to be associated with the Templars and Hospitallers.

---

[77] 'Et quoniam funiculus triplex difficile rumpitur, placuit divinae providentiae praedictis duabus domibus addere tertiam, sancte Terrae admodum necessariam, quasi ex praedictis duabus compositam'; James of Vitry, *Historia Hierosolimitani*, p. 1084. Translated in James of Vitry, *The History of Jerusalem*, p. 54. Oliveri Scholastici, *Historia Damiatina*, pp. 176, 276.

[78] *Analecta Novissima*, ed. J. Pitra, vol. 2 (Paris, 1888), p. 405; Humbert of Romans, 'De Modo Prompte Cudendi Sermones', p. 473.

CHAPTER 3

The Preparations for the Expedition of Frederick II

The failure of the Fifth Crusade's Egyptian campaign caused many to demand a scapegoat. According to the evidence of several accounts, the responsibility lay with Frederick II because he had not fulfilled the crusading vow he had made at his coronation. Writers described how the crusaders at Damietta had anticipated his arrival in vain.[1] In his defence, Frederick had offered some support by sending contingents to Egypt under nobles such as Henry of Malta and the duke of Bavaria.[2] Despite these efforts, the simple fact remained that by 1221 the crusade had failed and Frederick's vow lay unfulfilled. In the years that followed, pressure increased upon the emperor, particularly from the papacy, to depart for the East. Herman von Salza contributed to this by travelling twice to visit Frederick, once during the expedition and once shortly afterwards, to acquaint him of events. Perhaps as a consequence of these factors, Frederick renewed his vow at his imperial coronation in 1220 and promised to depart by March 1222.[3] Nevertheless, March 1222 came but Frederick had still not set out. In 1223, further pressure was applied by Herman, Ralph of Merencourt (patriarch of Jerusalem, 1215–1224), John of Brienne (king of Jerusalem, 1210–1225) and other representatives from the Holy Land, who travelled to Italy where they secured an undertaking from Frederick that he would set sail for the east by June 1225.[4] Seemingly to bind Frederick's interests tightly to those of the Holy Land, they reached an agreement with Frederick that he would marry the daughter of John of Brienne.[5]

Nevertheless, by 1225 Frederick was still not ready to leave and he asked Honorius to grant him a delay of two years. Honorius agreed to this proposal, although he injected clauses into the ensuing agreement (known as the Treaty of San Germano) that were designed to ensure that the emperor would not delay any further.[6] This treaty stipulated that Frederick should depart within

---

[1] Oliveri Scholastici, *Historia Damiatina*, p. 257; Matthew Paris, *Chronica Majora*, vol. 3, p. 66.
[2] Oliveri Scholastici, *Historia Damiatina*, p. 256; Matthew Paris, *Chronica Majora*, vol. 3, p. 70.
[3] *MGH Epis. Saec. XIII*, vol. 1, no. 176; *RHP*, vol. 1, no. 3478.
[4] HB, vol. 2, pp. 375–377. Much of this narrative has been drawn from T. C. Van Cleve, 'The Crusade of Frederick II', in *HOC*, vol. 2, pp. 429–462.
[5] For discussion of the motives which lay behind Frederick's betrothal to Isabella of Brienne see Ross, 'Relations between the Latin East and Western Europe', p. 128.
[6] HB, vol. 2, pp. 501–503.

two years with 1,000 knights (along with shipping for a further 1,000) and 100 transport vessels escorted by 50 galleys. Frederick promised that he would remain in the East himself with these knights for two years and swore that if, during this two-year sojourn, the number of knights he maintained should fall below 1,000 then he would offer a cash sum in their place. He agreed to send 100,000 ounces of gold in advance to the Holy Land where it would be held by the patriarch, Herman and John of Brienne, who would also arbitrate on whether he had fulfilled his promises. Frederick swore that if he failed to carry out his duties he would forfeit the gold and accept voluntary excommunication.[7] The final date for his departure was set as August 1227. This was not the first time that such measures had been introduced to induce recalcitrant crusaders to fulfil their vows; in 1123 Pope Calixtus II had threatened Iberian crusaders with similar sanctions if they had not completed their vows by the following Easter.[8] It was the first time, however, that such clauses had been deployed against an emperor.

For Herman von Salza, these events offered an excellent opportunity to develop his institution's international position through the organisation of a crusade for two of his order's greatest patrons: Honorius and Frederick. In the pursuit of this work, Herman and agents of the Order travelled across Christendom to generate the enthusiasm and materials that would be necessary for this undertaking. One of the prerequisites for this – or indeed any – recruitment drive for a crusading venture was the settlement of any disputes which might prevent the departure of a nobleman or ruler. Previously, in 1146, King Conrad III of Germany had stated that he would only take the cross if Bernard, abbot of Clairvaux, was able to solve the internal controversies of his kingdom.[9] During the preparations for the Fourth Crusade, Innocent III sent a monk called Rainerius to make peace among the rulers of the Iberian Peninsula.[10] Likewise, in the 1220s, Herman worked continually to end dissent across the imperial territories. In the early stages of the preparations, Herman helped the emperor to conclude internal disputes with his barons in Italy. In one case, during the peace settlement between Frederick and Thomas of Salerno in 1223, he agreed to hold the hostages yielded by Thomas as surety of good behaviour.[11] In 1224, Frederick wished to recruit forces in Germany, but was prevented from travelling north in person by internal strife in Sicily. Herman therefore volunteered to travel in Frederick's place so that the emperor might resolve this matter.[12] On this journey,

7 HB, vol. 2, pp. 501–503.
8 W. J. Purkis, *Crusading Spirituality in the Holy Land and Iberia, c.1095–c.1187* (Woodbridge, 2008), p. 73; Calixtus II, *Bullaire*, ed. U. Robert, vol. 2 (Paris, 1891), pp. 266–267.
9 J. Phillips, 'Papacy, Empire and the Second Crusade', in *The Second Crusade: Scope and Consequences*, ed. J. Phillips and M. Hoch (Manchester, 2001), pp. 25–27.
10 J. C. Moore, *Pope Innocent III (1160/61–1216): To Root Up and To Plant*, The Medieval Mediterranean, 48 (Boston, 2003), pp. 44–45.
11 HB, vol. 2, pp. 357–360.
12 HB, vol. 2, pp. 409–413; *Regesta Imperii V*, vol. 1, no. 1516. Herman was in Germany in late 1223 at Nordhausen possibly to help preach the cross; he must have travelled there rapidly

Herman also visited Denmark where he created a treaty with King Valdemar over the disputed territories of Schleswig and Holstein. He also persuaded Valdemar to take an oath stating he would travel on crusade with 100 ships.[13] Subsequently in 1226, when conflict occurred between Frederick and the Lombards, Herman travelled by imperial command to the papacy where he and other papal negotiators helped to resolve the dispute.[14]

Herman also worked to recruit troops for the expedition and to this end he made two major journeys to Germany. In the first, he travelled north from Catania in Italy, between March and April 1224.[15] He then crossed the Alps to the court of Frederick's son, Henry, in Frankfurt where he arrived in May 1224.[16] In front of the nobility of Germany, Herman made a speech encouraging participation in the crusade. He then travelled north to Denmark as we have seen.[17] Despite Herman's efforts, however, he recruited very few warriors. At Frankfurt, the princes were interested in the venture but were not prepared to take part. Also, the Danish king did not fulfil his vow to travel to the Holy Land. Herman's experience in 1224 was not unique. Other agents of the crusade including John of Brienne met with similar results.[18] Indeed Frederick later claimed that John and Herman had managed to recruit only the poor and sick.[19] It is possible that the defeats of the Fifth Crusade had blunted Christendom's appetite for further ventures in the Levant and Van Cleve describes 'a feeling of indifference, if not of positive aversion, to the crusade', at this time.[20] Once again a precedent for such apathy can be found during the Second Crusade when King Louis VII of France attempted unsuccessfully to raise a second expedition in 1149, after the failure of his first campaign.[21] In 1226 Pope Honorius sent Herman to Germany for a second time to gather recruits.[22] On this occasion he was more successful because he is reported to have returned with 700 knights.[23] Herman also persuaded the Landgrave of Thuringia to take part and it seems likely that many of these *milites* were part of his contingent. These troops appear to have formed the greater part of the expedition which finally departed for the Latin East and

---

because he had been in Catania in Sicily in April 1223, see Kluger, *Hochmeister Hermann*, pp. 39, 41. See also Appendix A.

[13] *Diplomatarium Danicum (Raekke 1)*, ed. N. Skyum-Nielsen, vol. 6 (Copenhagen, 1979), no. 16; *Chronica Regia Coloniensis*, p. 254. For discussion of the Danish king's oath see Kluger, *Hochmeister Hermann*, p. 43.

[14] *CDOT*, no. 71; HB, vol. 2, pp. 675–677; Richard of San Germano, *Chronica*, in *MGH SS*, vol. 19, p. 346. See also HB, vol. 2, pp. 691–692; Kluger, *Hochmeister Hermann*, pp. 66–68.

[15] HB, vol. 2, pp. 409–413; *Regesta Imperii V*, vol. 1, no. 1516.

[16] *Chronica Regia Coloniensis*, pp. 253–254.

[17] *Diplomatarium Danicum*, vol. 6, no. 16.

[18] Van Cleve, 'The Crusade of Frederick II', p. 439; Cohn, *Herman von Salza*, pp. 53–57.

[19] HB, vol. 3, pp. 36–48.

[20] Van Cleve, 'The Crusade of Frederick II', p. 439; Kluger, *Hochmeister Hermann*, p. 39.

[21] T. Reuter, 'The "Non-Crusade" of 1149–50', in *The Second Crusade: Scope and Consequences*, ed. J. Phillips and M. Hoch (Manchester, 2001), pp. 150–163. Mayer, *The Crusades*, pp. 104–105.

[22] *RHP*, vol. 2, no. 6156.

[23] HB, vol. 3, pp. 36–48.

thus Herman can be seen as one of the most important recruitment agents for the campaign. Soon after his arrival with these men, Herman embarked himself for the east.

One of the interesting aspects of Herman's second journey to Germany was the type of troops he sought to recruit. Commenting upon this subsequently, Frederick wrote: 'We sent away the master of the Teutonic House for [the purpose of] recruiting soldiers, but it was his opinion to choose vigorous men and those of personal merit and to offer pay according to his wisdom.'[24] It can be seen, therefore, that Herman envisaged a highly professional and paid army to conduct the crusade. It should be added that these were not necessarily mercenaries. Krieger has shown that the Hohenstaufen emperors 'increasingly supported vassals who took part in military campaigns by granting them *stipendia*'. He also demonstrates how this practice was used particularly in wars fought outside the empire to which German vassals were not necessarily obliged to contribute.[25] The advantages of hiring forces of this kind are obvious because they would have encouraged the formation of a highly trained army without the inherent problems attached to non-combatants or under-trained levies. It seems likely that these soldiers still took a crusading vow because in a papal letter issued in April 1227, Gregory referred to them as 'crucesignatos Theutonie'.[26]

Another element of the preparations was the construction of ships which would ferry the army to the Latin East. Members of the Teutonic Order assumed part of the responsibility for this task and they oversaw the manufacture of ships which would be suitable for operations in the Nile delta, the crusade's initial destination.[27] Herman described these vessels and the advantages of their purpose-built construction in his speech to the imperial princes at Frankfurt. They were built so that a knight might arm and mount his warhorse whilst still within the ship before emerging and attacking the enemy. This would allow a knight to be deployed directly into battle, which would have conferred greater tactical flexibility for manoeuvres in the Nile.[28] Admittedly, this was not the first time that ships had been specifically designed for use in Egypt. Pryor has demonstrated how the ships of the Byzantine fleet launched against Damietta in 1169 contained horse trans-

---

24 'Misimus magistrum domus Theotonicorum pro militibus solidandis, sed in optione sua potentem viros eligere strenuous et pro meritis personarum ad suam prudentiam stipendia polliceri'; HB, vol. 3, pp. 36–48.
25 K. F. Krieger, 'Obligatory Military Service and the Use of Mercenaries in Imperial Military Campaigns under the Hohenstaufen Emperors', in *England and Germany in the High Middle Ages*, ed. A. Haverkamp and H. Volrath (Oxford, 1996), pp. 158–159.
26 *MGH Epis. Saec. XIII*, vol. 1, no. 354.
27 HB, vol. 2, pp. 409–413.
28 *Chronica Regia Coloniensis*, p. 254. For discussion of the ship types used during this operation see J. H. Pryor, 'The Crusade of Emperor Frederick II, 1220–29: The Implications of the Maritime Evidence', *American Neptune*, 52 (1992), pp. 113–132.

ports equipped with stern doors and landing ramps.[29] The Sicilians also used similar technology during the Third Crusade.[30]

Reviewing these factors, it can be seen that Herman was one of the major organisers of this expedition, performing a role comparable to that of Bernard of Clairvaux for the Second Crusade or Hugh of Payns, first master of the Templars, for the crusade in 1127–1129. In many ways, his work in the recruitment and shipping of such large numbers of pilgrims can be seen as the next level in the Order's support of the pilgrim traffic to the Holy Land. It is also interesting to note how both Herman and Hugh of Payns used this role to gain international recognition for their respective orders.

The successful realisation of the crusade, however, required more than just recruitment and ship-building. Frederick's continual procrastination linked to the delicate relations between the papacy and the empire meant that Herman's diplomatic skills were needed to ensure that relations between these powers remained cordial. His role as an intermediary between Honorius and Fredrick began during the Fifth Crusade when he travelled twice to Western Christendom during the campaign to inform both parties of the progress of the expedition.[31] Herman was also present in 1223 when Frederick made his promise to embark for the East within two years.[32] In 1224, when he travelled to Germany on Frederick's command, he travelled first to the papacy where he informed Honorius of the emperor's plans.[33] For much of his subsequent journey Herman was accompanied by a papal legate, Conrad, cardinal bishop of Porto. In 1225, when Frederick sought Honorius's permission to postpone the crusade, he sent Herman and John of Brienne to Rome on his behalf.[34] Furthermore, both Herman and John were appointed as recipients of the 100,000 ounces of gold specified in the San Germano agreement.[35] Powell has shown that Honorius continually sought to co-operate with Frederick in the business of the crusade and likewise it can be seen that Herman also worked with both men to maintain this accord.[36]

Throughout these operations, Herman became so indispensable to Honorius that he was required to compromise his Order's interests in Hungary. In 1211 King Andrew II of Hungary granted a sizeable area of land to the Teutonic Knights in the province of Burzenland, specifically to guard against

---

[29] J. H Pryor, 'Transportation of Horses by Sea during the era of the Crusades: Eighth Century to 1285 AD: Part 1: to *c.*1225', *Mariner's Mirror*, 68 (1982), p. 18. For further information concerning the creation and design of crusader transport ships see J. H. Pryor, 'The Naval Architecture of Crusader Transport Ships: A Reconstruction of some Archetypes for Round-hulled Sailing Ships: Part I', *Mariner's Mirror*, 70 (1984), pp. 171–219.

[30] Pryor, 'Transportation of Horses', pp. 20–27.

[31] See above, p. 35.

[32] HB, vol. 2, pp. 375–377.

[33] HB, vol. 2, pp. 409–413.

[34] HB, vol. 2, p. 500.

[35] HB, vol. 2, pp. 501–503.

[36] Powell, 'Honorius III and the Leadership of the Crusade', p. 531.

the attacks of the Cumans.[37] In time, the Knights established a series of fortresses in this territory, coining the name Siebenbürgen. Nevertheless, by 1224 the relationship between King Andrew and the local commander had deteriorated to a point where the Order turned to the papacy for protection.[38] The brethren may have provoked this discord themselves by trying to take too much power and certainly Forey has argued that the 'Order appears to have been seeking to withdraw itself from the authority of the Hungarian king'.[39] Honorius responded by placing the Order's lands under his protection, but this seems only to have inflamed Andrew's fear that the Order might try to establish itself as an independent power in Siebenbürgen and so he expelled them in 1225.[40] Herman seems to have wanted to travel to Hungary to resolve this matter with the king in person; however, in January 1226, Honorius informed Andrew that the master could not make this journey because he had been detained by 'certain business of the Church and Empire'.[41] It appears self-evident that this 'business' was the matter of the crusade. Evidently, Honorius's need for Herman's assistance was sufficiently acute to compel him to prevent the master from managing a serious crisis in his own affairs. In the event, the pope sent letters to the queen of Hungary and also to Bishop Robert of Veszprém, who were both instructed to compel the king to restore these lands.[42] Neither of them was successful.

Through the preparations for this crusade, Herman's desire to build a successful expedition is self-evident; however these actions are also sugges-tive about his relative loyalties to the papacy and the empire. Reviewing his actions, one possible conclusion could be that he was merely an imperial agent recruiting on Frederick's behalf and communicating with the papacy on his command. Certainly there is evidence that could support this conclusion. After all, Frederick sent Herman to Germany in 1224 to recruit troops for his campaign. Also much of the master's peacemaking in Sicily, Lombardy and Denmark was in Frederick's service and its generally favourable results were to his advantage. On the other hand, Herman also carried out the instructions of the papacy. Herman's second journey to Germany was made on the pope's express command; indeed in 1227 Honorius's successor, Pope Gregory IX, wrote a letter to Herman containing the following passage,

---

37 *TOT*, no. 158. It seems likely that the decision to make this grant may have been connected to the engagement between the son of Herman, landgrave of Thuringia, and the daughter of Andrew of Hungary, which took place in the same year. As we have seen the landgraves were keen supporters of the Order and, if this was the case, then these events serve as an example of the importance of the patronage of the major imperial families. See Forey, *The Military Orders*, p. 35.

38 This commander may have been called Theodoric; certainly this was the name of the Order's Hungarian commander in 1212. *TOT*, no. 159.

39 Forey, *The Military Orders*, p. 35.

40 *TOT*, nos. 164, 166; Urban, *The Teutonic Knights*, p. 36.

41 'Quedam negotia ecclesie ac imperii', *Monumenta Historica Hungariae*, ed. A. Theiner, vol. 1 (Rome, 1859), no. 136.

42 *RHP*, vol. 2, nos. 5832–5833.

Therefore, for the aid of the Holy Land, for which the same emperor nobly arms himself, you may seek to gather crusaders from the Teutons and others, whomsoever you are able, according to the wisdom given to you by God.[43]

Moreover, the papacy had equipped Herman with a host of privileges that would support his efforts at recruitment. In general, it could be said that the Order was acting as the servant of two masters in his attempts to prepare the new crusade and indeed, this is generally the opinion of Kluger, Cohn and many other historians who detail the history of the Order to this point.[44]

With regard to the Order's motivation during this period there is a further factor that needs to be added to these wider diplomatic considerations. There has previously been some useful debate about the Teutonic Knights' attempts to acquire an *ordensstaat* during this period.[45] Historians have pointed to their actions in Hungary and suggested that the rapid growth of their power in this region is indicative of a desire to found an independent state.[46] After their ejection from this land, the brethren sought and were granted the right to colonise Prussia by the emperor through the Golden Bull of Rimini in 1226.[47] This is presented as a further expression of this trend. Hubatsch has even viewed the Teutonic Knights' expansion in the hills of Galilee in the kingdom of Jerusalem as a further example of state-building.[48] Certainly, the close-knit distribution of the Order's villages appears to support this conclusion (see appendix B). The brethren purchased villages that were either within, or on the edge of, their domains, suggesting that they wished to build a tightly cohesive territorial unit. This idea has been nuanced slightly by Kluger, who has rightly suggested that the Montfort estate never enjoyed the same degree of independence that the Hospitallers experienced in the county of Tripoli, although he agrees with the general principle that the Order was seeking autonomy.[49]

Whilst this discussion has added a valuable dimension to our understanding of the Teutonic Knights at this time, it is also vital to recognise that while the

---

[43] 'Tu ergo ad Terre Sancte subsidium, ad quod idem imperator magnifice se accingit, crucesignatos Theutonice ac alios, quoscumque potes, studeas secundum datam tibi a Deo prudentiam animare'; *MGH Epis. Saec. XIII*, vol. 1, no. 354.

[44] Arnold, 'Der Deutsche Orden zwischen Kaiser und Papst', p. 61; Kluger, *Hochmeister Hermann*, pp. 41, 50; W. Hubatsch, 'Der Deutsche Orden und die Reichlehnschaft über Cypern', *Nachrichten der Akademie der Wissenschaften in Göttingen: Phil.-hist. Klasse* (Göttingen, 1955), p. 259; Favreau, *Studien zur Frühgeschichte des Deutschen Ordens*, p. 86; Cohn, *Herman von Salza*, pp. 44–49; Pacifico, 'I Teutonici tra papato e impero nel Mediterraneo al tempo di Federico II, 1215–1250', p. 107.

[45] This paragraph has drawn on Kluger, *Hochmeister Hermann*, pp. 51–54.

[46] W. Hubatsch, 'Montfort und die Bildung des Deutschordensstates im Heiligen Lande', *Nachrichten der Akademie der Wissenschaften in Göttingen: Philologisch-Historische Klasse* (Göttingen, 1966), pp. 177–178; Favreau-Lilie, 'L'Ordine Teutonico in Terrasanta (1198–1291)', p. 62; Favreau, *Studien zur Frühgeschichte des Deutschen Ordens*, p. 84.

[47] *PU*, vol. 1.1, no. 56.

[48] Hubatsch, 'Montfort und die Bildung des Deutschordensstates', pp. 180, 186. See also *AZM*, p. 38; Favreau-Lilie, 'L'Ordine Teutonico in Terrasanta (1198–1291)', p. 62.

[49] Kluger, *Hochmeister Hermann*, p. 54.

Order may have been engaged in a search for independence, *in practice* it was actually becoming more dependent on its patrons over this period. The vast bulk of the institution's estates were located either among Frederick II's personal landholdings or within the empire as a whole.[50] Consequently, although these lands granted power to the Order, they hardly granted independence from Frederick or from the major imperial princes. Indeed, with every acquisition in imperial territory the brethren grew ever more dependent upon the emperor's goodwill, a consideration of which Frederick would have been well aware. The Teutonic Knights were not like the Hospitallers or Templars, who had extensive properties in many realms; they were reliant upon the empire. Admittedly, the subsequent successful realisation of an expansion into Prussia was to confer some autonomy; but in the mid-1220s that dream was far off.

Furthermore, the Order was always reliant upon the goodwill of the pontiff. As an institution of the Church, the Teutonic Knights needed papal support to maintain their growing privileges and liberties. As these papal concessions multiplied and – crucially – as the brethren came to rely on them, their dependency increased dramatically. To speak of the Teutonic Order's drive for independence at this time is therefore perhaps a little misleading. It is right to suggest that Herman wished to create an autonomous state but that conclusion should not obscure the fact that the Order was still fundamentally and increasingly dependent upon the support of the Church and the empire. This weakness was to play a critical and damaging role in the Knights' policy in later years.

The Marriage of Frederick II and the Promise of Herman Von Salza

In 1223 Frederick promised that he would marry the daughter of King John of Jerusalem. The match initially seems to have been suggested by Honorius III, presumably in an attempt to encourage Frederick to embark for the East.[51] In 1225 a marriage ceremony was performed in Acre with Isabella in attendance even though Frederick was still in Italy. Isabella was crowned queen of Jerusalem and conveyed to Italy under escort. A second ceremony took place in Italy in November 1225.[52] Some time before this, John of Brienne had expressed a fear that by marrying his daughter to Frederick he might lose

---

[50] Militzer, 'From the Holy Land to Prussia', p. 72; Wojtecki, 'Der Deutsche Orden unter Friedrich II', pp. 188–197; Hubatsch, 'Montfort und die Bildung des Deutschordensstates', p. 180.

[51] Ross has shown that, although a number of historians have suggested that it was Herman von Salza who instigated this match, it was in fact Honorius III. The suggestion that it was Herman's idea comes from a comment in the chronicle of Eracles, which states that he supported the match. The argument that it was Honorius's idea comes from a contemporary letter to the king of France. The latter evidence is both the more contemporary and the more explicit. See Ross, 'Relations between the Latin East and Western Europe', pp. 118–119.

[52] HB, vol. 2, pp. 921–924.

his throne. John himself was only king through his wife Maria (daughter of Queen Isabella I of Jerusalem and Conrad of Montferrat), who had died in 1212. John's concern was that the husband of his daughter, who was of the royal bloodline, would claim the throne. Significantly, John's concerns had been silenced by Herman von Salza, who had assured John that Frederick would allow him to remain king for the remainder of his life.[53] It is not known when this guarantee was given although it is highly likely that an arrangement of such fundamental importance would have been discussed during the early negotiations, perhaps even in 1223. Despite this, after marrying John's daughter, Frederick immediately seized the throne.[54]

Within these events, the Teutonic Knights had played a major part. Herman had not only offered John this vital assurance but he had also been present when the marriage had been arranged.[55] Sanuto described him as the 'mediator of the business'.[56] Furthermore a Teutonic Knight had been sent to Acre to serve as a personal escort for Isabella on her journey to Italy.[57] This evidence demonstrates that Herman strongly supported the match and this chimes with his ongoing efforts to support Frederick's crusade. The question that arises from these dealings, however, is whether Herman's promise that John could retain his throne for life had been made in good faith and then been broken by Frederick, or whether Herman and Frederick had worked in partnership to trick John into yielding his throne.

Historians have rarely discussed this issue and yet it is a vital matter when assessing Herman's relationship to both John and Fredrick. Virtually all those who have explored these events have characterised Herman as the emperor's man and perhaps have considered the evidence of Herman's collusion with Frederick to be so overwhelming that it requires little further examination. Despite this, it seems plausible that Herman had not been deliberately deceitful but had actually acted in good faith.[58] Certainly this conclusion is compatible with the chain of events between 1223 and 1225. It is likely that Frederick permitted Herman to assure John of a lifetime's interest in the throne of Jerusalem in 1223, when the marriage was arranged. Naturally, the preservation of his own power would have been one of John's primary interests in the agreement and so it would have been logical to cover such matters at this time. In 1225, Herman, Frederick and John then arranged the San Germano treaty. Given that Frederick agreed to sign this pact, which contained clauses stipulating that John would have control over large quanti-

---

[53] Eracles, p. 358.
[54] HB, vol. 2, pp. 921–924.
[55] HB, vol. 2, pp. 375–377.
[56] 'Mediator negotii', Sanuto, p. 211.
[57] HB, vol. 2, pp. 921–924. It has been suggested that it was Heinrich von Hohenlohe (later master, see appendix C) who acted as escort for Isabella, but given that only the first name of the escorting brother is supplied, this can only be accepted as conjecture. U. Arnold, 'Heinrich von Hohenlohe', in *Die Hochmeister des Deutschen Ordens 1190–1994*, QuStDO, 40 (Marburg, 1998), p. 24.
[58] A historian who also expresses this view is Cohn, *Herman von Salza*, p. 84.

ties of imperial bullion (see above), it is hard to believe that at this point he had any intention of taking John's throne. If this hypothesis is correct then Frederick's decision to take the throne would have been made at some point between the treaty (July 1225) and the wedding (November 1225) and not at the outset. If this was the case then it is possible that *initially* Frederick intended to allow John to keep his throne and therefore that Herman acted in good faith. This hypothetical scenario does fit the events but it gains further credibility when a number of additional factors are considered.

By 1225, John and Herman had fought together in the Fifth Crusade and worked together during the preparations for Frederick's crusade; they were united by their desire to bring aid to the Holy Land. One of the crowning achievements of their combined labour was the San Germano treaty, which compelled Frederick to travel to the Holy Land. Both men were intrinsic elements in the formation and the future execution of this pact. Should Herman have knowingly risked this agreement by causing such a major rift between Frederick and John then he would have jeopardised one of the cornerstones of the impending expedition for which he had worked so hard. Depriving the king of Jerusalem of his throne was also a serious act that had the potential both to deter nobles from travelling to the Holy Land and to anger the papacy – potentially opening a rift between Church and empire. In the event, Honorius did not officially censure Frederick but this could probably not have been predicted beforehand and, even so, public opinion was beginning to turn against the emperor.[59] Accordingly, it is stretching credulity to believe that Herman could have been knowingly complicit in an act that had the potential to damage his main objectives and waste years of work.

Another significant factor is the ongoing relationship between the Brienne family and the Teutonic Knights after the marriage. John's nephew, Count Walter IV of Brienne, – a man whom Frederick hated and whom he had attempted to assassinate – continued to make concessions to the Order after 1225 and charters of this kind can be found in 1231 and in 1237, while he was in the Holy Land.[60] It is hardly plausible that Walter would have continued to patronise the brethren if he believed them to be in collusion with a man who was responsible for both attempting his own assassination and seizing his uncle's kingdom. It seems therefore that the Brienne family did not blame Herman for the breach of his promise and that they at least did not believe him to be complicit. In summary, the evidence demonstrates that it is very likely that Herman made his promise in good faith and, therefore, that he should not be viewed as complicit in the emperor's attempt to take the throne of Jerusalem.

---

[59] Abulafia, *Frederick II*, p. 153.
[60] Charter 1 (January, 1231): *Catalogue d'Actes des Comtes de Brienne: 950–1356*, ed. H. d'Arbois de Jubainville (Paris, 1872), no. 163. Charter 2 (June, 1231): ibid., no. 165. Charter 3 (January, 1237): ibid., no. 170. HB, vol. 2, p. 923. I am indebted to Guy Perry for his advice concerning the background of Walter of Brienne.

If we accept Herman's innocence therefore, Frederick's seizure of the throne should be seen as a serious insult to the Teutonic Knights because he had publicly broken Herman's promise. Frederick appears to have been aware of this because shortly after his wedding he made a series of donations to the Order. The background to this compensation dates back to an agreement made during the Fifth Crusade. In 1220 the Teutonic Order bought the entire inheritance of Joscelin III of Courtney from his son-in-law Otto, count of Henneburg. Otto and his wife Beatrix, Joscelin's daughter, wished to leave the Holy Land and return to Franconia.[61] Many of the lands included in this transaction were in Muslim hands and the only remaining castle was Castellum Regis (now the modern village of Mil'ilya in northern Israel). This was the Order's first major estate in the kingdom of Jerusalem. The purchase of these lands had been witnessed by John of Brienne to whom the Teutonic Knights had paid 500 bezants for this confirmation. They had also signed away their rights to John for all the lands pertaining to this patrimony that were under Muslim control and also an income of 2,266.66 bezants per annum from the *cathena* and *fundaq* of Acre (see chapter 10).[62] The motives or manoeuvres which provoked such a large consideration for the king are not specified; however, it is possible that this agreement was linked to other lucrative negotiations in which John gave the Order a portion of the plunder which had been acquired during the Fifth Crusade.[63] Another related factor may be that Beatrix (Otto's wife) was the elder of two sisters who were joint heirs to Joscelin's lands, and yet Beatrix and Otto sold the entire inheritance themselves to the Order without reference to the other sister. Although there was some, albeit dubious, legal basis for this action, it can be seen that through purchasing this estate the Teutonic Knights were vulnerable to legal action from the younger sister (as indeed occurred over subsequent years). It seems therefore, that the large income granted to John of Brienne may have been intended to ease the legal situation and to give him a vested interest in the suppression of any further lawsuits.[64]

Frederick's gift to the Order in 1226 was partially the return of some of the concessions that had been ceded to John in 1220. He permitted the brethren to claim ownership over the elements of Joscelin's patrimony that were under Muslim control. The most important part of these was the estate

---

[61] *R. Reg.*, vol. 1, no. 933; *TOT*, no. 52; R. Ellenblum, 'Colonization Activities in the Frankish East: The Example of Castellum Regis (Mil'ilya)', *English Historical Review*, 111 (1996), pp. 115. The counts of Henneburg did not offer much more support to the Order during the thirteenth century because they were engaged in an ongoing dispute with bishops of Würzburg, see B. Arnold, *Princes and Territories in Medieval Germany* (Cambridge, 2003), p. 84.

[62] *R. Reg.*, vol. 1, no. 934; *TOT*, no. 53.

[63] For the charters which discuss the division of plunder see *AOL*, vol. 2, p. 166 (documents); *TOT*, no. 55.

[64] The above section has drawn on Mayer, 'Die Seigneurie de Joscelin und der Deutsche Orden', pp. 189–204.

Plate 1. Castellum Regis ©N. Morton

of Toron.[65] Frederick may also have promised to restore the estate to Christian hands himself at this time because during his later crusade he concluded an agreement with the Egyptian sultan in 1229 which returned the estate of Toron to the kingdom of Jerusalem.[66] Later in 1229, prompted by the Order, he attempted to transfer ownership of this property to the brethren; however, this was blocked by Alice of Armenia who proved conclusively that she had a stronger claim.[67] Prevented from restoring Toron to the Order, Frederick, still obliged to the brethren for the events of 1225, then attempted to compensate them with other lands and privileges within the kingdom of Jerusalem.[68]

Within these clauses and sub-clauses a narrative forms which shows that in 1226 Frederick, seemingly in recompense for the humiliation he caused by breaking Herman's promise, made a number of concessions to the Teutonic Knights and undertook to grant them the fief of Toron. In the event this promise was not realised, through Alice's intervention; nevertheless Frederick's subsequent compensation to the Order carries with it the suggestion that he was beholden to them on this account.

---

[65] Frederick's charter, *TOT*, no. 58. Isabella's charter, *TOT*, no. 59; Kluger, *Hochmeister Hermann*, pp. 48–49; Mayer, 'Die Seigneurie de Joscelin und der Deutsche Orden', p. 196.

[66] HB, vol. 3, pp. 90–93; *CDOT*, no. 75.

[67] HB, vol. 3. pp. 123–125; Abulafia, *Frederick II*, p. 191; J. S. C. Riley-Smith, *The Feudal Nobility and the Kingdom of Jerusalem: 1174–1277* (London, 1973), pp. 171–172.

[68] HB, vol. 3, pp. 123–125; John of Ibelin, *Le Livre des Assises*, ed. P. W. Edbury, The Medieval Mediterranean, 50 (Boston, 2003), pp. 453–454.

Relations with Armenia and the Templars

Two vital elements in the Teutonic Knights' work in the Levant were their relationships with the kings of Armenia and the Templars. The Order's connection to the Armenian kingdom may date back as far as 1190. In this year King Guy of Jerusalem referred to the brethren's care of Armenians in their hospital at the siege of Acre.[69] Certainly, King Leon II sent troops to the siege of Acre.[70] The next reference to the brethren's role in this area occurred in 1209 when Pope Innocent III mentioned that the king of Armenia had sent a Teutonic Knight as an envoy to the papal court.[71] The fact that the Teutonic Knights were already in a position where they were chosen to be royal envoys suggests that they had achieved a high level of trust in the king's estimation. Furthermore, in a papal charter of this year, Innocent confirmed the Order's possession of several villages in Armenia.[72] The causes of the institution's initial expansion into Armenia are not specified in any document; however, it seems likely that, as Riley-Smith has suggested, its establishment was linked to the emerging bond between Armenia and the empire.[73] In 1198, during the crusade launched by Henry VI, Archbishop Conrad of Mainz travelled to Armenia to present Leon with an imperial crown. In this way Armenia passed under imperial suzerainty.[74] In 1205, Bertold II of Katzenellenbogen travelled to Armenia as an emissary of the papacy and Houben has suggested that he supported the cause of the Order in this region; certainly he acted on the Order's behalf during his later sojourns in Acre and Greece.[75] By 1211 it became apparent that the Teutonic Order had become an expression of this bond between the empire and the kingdom of Armenia when Herman von Salza accompanied an imperial emissary on a mission to bestow a new crown upon Leon. Shortly after this embassy, the Order was granted the castle of Amudain explicitly because of the love Leon held for the empire, thus reinforcing the argument that the brethren's development in this region originated from this cause.[76] This same pattern has been identified by Houben, who has drawn attention to a later letter issued by Conrad, son of Frederick II, which mentioned that his father 'used to keep the crown of Armenia either in the

---

[69] *R. Reg.*, vol. 1, no. 696; *TOT*, no. 25; Chevalier, 'Les Chevaliers teutoniques en Cilicie', p. 139.
[70] S. Der Nersessian, 'The Kingdom of Cilician Armenia', in *HOC*, vol. 2, p. 646.
[71] *PL*, vol. 216, col. 54D–56C.
[72] *TOT*, no. 298; Chevalier, 'Les Chevaliers teutoniques en Cilicie', p. 143.
[73] Riley-Smith, 'The Templars and the Teutonic Knights in Cilician Armenia', p. 111; Forstreuter, *Der Deutsche Orden am Mittelmeer*, p. 59; Chevalier, 'Les Chevaliers teutoniques en Cilicie', pp. 140, 142–143, 153.
[74] Riley-Smith, 'Templars and the Teutonic Knights in Cilician Armenia', p. 111.
[75] See Houben 'Wie und wann kam der Deutsche Orden nach Griechenland?' pp. 250–253.
[76] *R. Reg.*, vol. 1, no. 859; *TOT*, no. 46; Riley-Smith, 'Templars and the Teutonic Knights in Cilician Armenia', p. 111. For further discussion of the timing of this gift see Forstreuter, *Der Deutsche Orden am Mittelmeer*, p. 60. For the ground plans and archaeological details of the fortifications of Amudain see R. W. Edwards, *The Fortifications of Cilician Armenia*, Dumbarton Oaks Studies, 23 (Washington DC, 1987), pp. 59–62.

house of the Grand Master of the Teutonic Order in Acre or in the castle of Montfort'.[77] It is also likely that the growing connection between the kings of Armenia and the papacy encouraged this relationship. Towards the end of the twelfth century relations between the Catholic and Armenian churches became increasingly cordial. One example of this can be seen in 1184 when the Armenian *catholicus* Gregory IV issued a document to the papacy that was interpreted as a submission to the Catholic Church.[78] Consequently it is possible that the concessions to the Teutonic Knights were designed to encourage this relationship. This is implied by Leon's use of a Teutonic Knight as an envoy to the papal curia in 1209.[79] From this point, relations continued to flourish between the Order and the Armenians.

The association between Armenia and the Teutonic Order would have been generally advantageous for both parties; however, it did place the brethren on the Armenian side in its war with Antioch.[80] One of the early causes of this conflict was a dispute between the Templars and Leon of Armenia over Baghras. This fortress had been taken from the Templars by Saladin in the wake of the battle of Hattin, but was then recaptured by Leon. Leon refused to return the fortress to the Templars, thus creating a conflict between these two protagonists which also drew in the prince of Antioch on the Templar side. A further problem arose after the death of Prince Bohemond III in 1201 when the succession to the throne of Antioch became contested between Raymond Roupen (grandson of Bohemond III and great-nephew of Leon) and Bohemond IV (second son of Bohemond III).[81] Hostilities continued for many years between Armenia and Antioch, drawing in the Hospitallers and the Teutonic Knights on the Armenian side.

Although by 1211 it seems that the Teutonic Knights had aligned themselves with the Armenian party, in 1200 their loyalties were evidently undecided. In this year, Bohemond granted them trading privileges in Antioch, including the right to buy and sell in the principality.[82] Clearly the Order had yet to affiliate itself to either party. Even so, by 1219, they appear to have become firm supporters of the Armenians and their trading privileges were extended by Raymond Roupen when he claimed the throne of Anti-

---

77 H. Houben, 'Intercultural Communication: the Teutonic Knights in Palestine, Armenia and Cyprus', *Diplomatics in the Eastern Mediterranean: 1000–1500*, ed. A. D. Beihammer, M. G. Parani and C. D. Schabel (Leiden, 2008), p. 150; J. Riedmann, 'Unbekannte Schreiben Kaiser Friedrichs II. und Konrads IV. In einer Handschrift der Universitäts-bibliothek Innsbruck', *Deutsches Archiv für Erforschung des Mittelalters*, ed. J. Fried and R. Schieffer, 62 (2006), p. 167; H. Houben, 'I Cavalieri Teutonici nel Mediterraneo Orientale (secoli XII–XV)', p. 52. Incidentally, the masters of the Hospitallers and Templars, along with the patriarch of Jerusalem, kept the keys to the crown jewels of the kingdom of Jerusalem, *KSJJC*, p. 79.

78 B. Hamilton, *The Latin Church in the Crusader States: The Secular Church* (London, 1980), pp. 204–207.

79 *PL*, vol. 216, cols. 54D–56C.

80 Chevalier, 'Les Chevaliers teutoniques en Cilicie', p. 143.

81 Der Nersessian, 'The Kingdom of Cilician Armenia', p. 649.

82 *R. Reg.*, vol. 1, no. 772; Perlbach, 'Die Reste des Deutschordensarchives in Venedig', pp. 647–648.

och.[83] More significantly, in 1225 the brethren imprisoned Philip (the fourth son of Bohemond IV) in their fortress of Amudain.[84] He was subsequently poisoned whilst in their custody.[85] Naturally, by connecting themselves to the kingdom of Armenia, the Order put itself on the opposing side to the Templars. Possibly as a result of this, the Templars began to exert their influence over the far smaller German institution. The early relationship between these two orders will now be outlined.

The first contact between these institutions dates back to 1190 when the Hospitallers attempted to prevent the brethren from burying the corpse of Frederick of Swabia. The account known as *Tractatus de locis et statu sancte terre Ierosolimitane* goes further, suggesting that the Hospitallers wished to deprive them of their goods.[86] It seems that the independence of the Teutonic Order was in such doubt after this time that, as Forstreuter points out, King Aimery even placed a clause in his gift of property to the brethren in 1198 stipulating that they could hold the specified land only while they retained their religious identity.[87] According to *Tractatus de locis et statu sancte terre Ierosolimitane*, faced with this threat from the Hospital, the Teutonic Order turned to the Templars for protection. This was granted and the Templars permitted the Order to use the symbol of a black circle and a half black cross.[88] In exchange, the brethren are said to have agreed to come under Templar authority.[89] Templar influence at this time is certainly evident because the Teutonic Order's militarisation was carried out in the palace of the Templars in Acre and a Templar, Henry Walpot, was appointed as master.[90] Furthermore, at the militarisation, the brothers were permitted to use the Templars' white mantles.[91] This seems to have been another symbol of submission to the Templars and certainly in the late thirteenth century the use of these white

---

[83] *R. Reg.*, vol. 1, no. 921; *TOT*, no. 51.

[84] Bar Hebraeus, *The Chronography of Gregory Abû'l Faraj: The Son of Aaron, the Hebrew Physician commonly known as Bar Hebraeus*, trans. E. Wallis Budge, vol. 1 (Oxford, 1932), p. 381; Riley-Smith, 'Templars and the Teutonic Knights in Cilician Armenia', p. 113.

[85] Der Nersessian, 'The Kingdom of Cilician Armenia', p. 651; Chevalier, 'Les Chevaliers teutoniques en Cilicie', p. 143.

[86] B. Z. Kedar, 'The *Tractatus de locis et statu sancte terre Ierosolimitane*', in *The Crusades and their Sources: Essays Presented to Bernard Hamilton*, ed. J. France and W. Zajac (Aldershot, 1998), p. 132.

[87] *TOT*, no. 35; Forstreuter, *Der Deutsche Orden am Mittelmeer*, pp. 35–36; Prutz, *Die Besitzungen des Deutschen Ordens*, p. 23.

[88] *La Continuation de Guillaume de Tyr*, p. 99; Kedar, 'The *Tractatus de locis*', p. 132. The symbol of the circle and the cross may reflect the north German influence in the Order's establishment. Notably during the Second Crusade, Otto of Freising noted that the Saxons used the device of a cross surmounting a wheel. See Otto of Freising, *The Deeds of Frederick Barbarossa*, ed. and trans. C. Mierow (Toronto, 1994), p. 76.

[89] Kedar, 'The *Tractatus de locis*', p. 132.

[90] Kedar, 'The *Tractatus de locis*', p. 132. It seems that Heinrich Walpot was not a knight but rather was of burgher origins. See Favreau, *Studien zur Frühgeschichte des Deutschen Ordens*, p. 67.

[91] *De Primordiis Ordinis Theutonici Narratio*, p. 225. Favreau claims that the brethren did not receive the white mantles at this time because a later charter of 1210 claims that they had only recently begun to use them. Despite this, it is possible that the Order had been granted the power to wear these mantles at the militarisation but only acted upon this right some time afterwards.

mantles by the Order of St Thomas of Acre became an important point in its proposed union with the Templars.[92]

Despite this early bond, relations between these two institutions deteriorated in the early thirteenth century. The first indication of this can be found in 1210 when the Templars complained to Pope Innocent III that the Teutonic Knights were wearing their white mantles illegally. This might be an indication that the Teutonic Knights had renounced Templar authority and were deemed, consequently, to be ineligible to wear their mantles. Innocent supported their claim and forbade the Order to wear these robes.[93] Evidently the argument with the Templars persisted for many years and the author of *La Continuation de Guillaume de Tyr* explicitly stated that:

> The device that they wore on their mantles was a wheel with a half cross in black. The brother knights had mantles of Stamford cloth. They did not dare wear white mantles because of the Templars. But since the Damietta campaign they have had their white mantles with the cross without the wheel.[94]

Seemingly, by the end of the Fifth Crusade, the Teutonic Knights were in a better position to defend their interests and had the strength to defy the Templars. Furthermore, in 1221 Pope Honorius III confirmed their right to use these white mantles.[95] Despite this, Honorius's confirmation was evidently contested because in the following year he wrote a far more strongly worded letter to the Templars, reinforcing the Teutonic Knights' rights on this matter.[96] In addition, it appears that Frederick II became involved because in 1217 and 1221 he permitted the Knights to draw an income from the taxation receipts of Sicilian and Apulian ports explicitly to cover the purchase of these white mantles.[97] These gifts may well have been designed to offer tacit support to the Order's rights in this matter.

So it can be seen that the breach in relations between the Templars and Teutonic Knights took place at some point before 1210 and persisted for many years. It is possible that it occurred in *c.*1209 because in this year Innocent III reported that the king of Armenia had sent a Teutonic Knight to

---

Certainly this piece of evidence ties in well with the Templars' seeming authority over the Order. Favreau, *Studien zur Frühgeschichte des Deutschen Ordens*, p. 67.

92 Forey, 'The Military Order of St Thomas of Acre', p. 494.

93 *TOT*, no. 299; *CDOT*, no. 9; Potthast, vol. 1, no. 4068; *AZM*, pp. 31, 33; Sterns, 'The Statutes of the Teutonic Knights', pp. 42–43.

94 'L'abit que il porteient en lor mantiaus si esteit une roe a une demie crois neire. Les freres chevaliers avoient mantiaus d'estanfort. Mantiaus blans n'oseient il porter, por les Templiers. De l'ost de Damiate en ça ont il eu les mantiaus blans et la crois sans roe'; *La Continuation de Guillaume de Tyr*, p. 99. Translation taken from *The Conquest of Jerusalem and the Third Crusade*, trans. P. W. Edbury, Crusade Texts in Translation, I (Aldershot, 1996), p. 90.

95 *TOT*, no. 308.

96 *TOT*, no. 368.

97 (1217) *CDOT*, no. 28; HB, vol. 1, pp. 510–511. (1221) HB, vol. 2, p. 224. Kluger, *Hochmeister Hermann*, pp. 22–23; *AZM*, p. 33.

the curia to represent his interests concerning the principality of Antioch.[98] Certainly, from this point the Order seems to have become an overt supporter of the Armenians whilst the Templars remained allied to Antioch. In these ways, the early accord between these institutions was ruptured and relations became hostile.

[98] *PL*, vol. 216, col. 54D–56C.

CHAPTER 4

From the Crusade of Emperor Frederick II to the Death of Herman von Salza, 1227–1239

In 1227 Frederick II sailed for the Latin East as had been agreed in 1225, but shortly afterwards he became ill and returned to Italy. Having recovered, he re-embarked, yet the delay created by his convalescence caused him to miss the deadline for departure which he had accepted in 1225. The new pope, Gregory IX, was not inclined to overlook this fact and in September 1227 he excommunicated the emperor. Shortly afterwards, Gregory began to prepare an invasion against Fredrick's kingdom of Sicily. Consequently, Frederick departed for the Levant in the full knowledge that war was brewing against him in the West. This fact overshadowed much of his subsequent expedition. Frederick landed at Limassol (northern Cyprus) on 21 July 1228. He was not the first excommunicate to travel on crusade; during the Fourth Crusade Conrad, bishop of Halberstadt, set off for the East in a similar predicament, seemingly in an attempt to gain absolution. Perhaps Frederick hoped that his departure would similarly cause Gregory to relent; if so, he was to be disappointed.[1] Ironically, as Brundage has demonstrated, it was during the pontificate of Gregory IX that release from excommunication became 'part of the bundle of privileges which crusaders regularly received'.[2]

After his arrival in Cyprus, the emperor proceeded to impose his will upon the local nobility and arbitrarily demanded both the bailliage of Cyprus and possession of the city of Beirut from the influential baron John of Ibelin.[3] These demands caused outrage and provoked the hostility of many of the local magnates. The emperor then took ship for Acre where, on 7 September 1228, he joined the main crusading army.[4] In November he marched south to Jaffa, which he began to refortify.[5] During this time, emissaries were dispatched to negotiate a treaty with the sultan of Egypt, which they final-

---

[1] M. Angold, *The Fourth Crusade: Event and Context* (Harlow, 2003), p. 17.
[2] J. A. Brundage, *Medieval Canon Law and the Crusader* (Madison, WI, 1969), p. 155.
[3] For details of these demands see Filippo da Novara, *Guerra di Federico II in Oriente (1223–1242)*, ed. S. Melani (Naples, 1994), p. 88.
[4] Eracles, p. 369.
[5] HB, vol. 3, pp. 90–93; *CDOT*, no. 75.

ised on 18 February 1229.[6] The main clause of this treaty was the return of the city of Jerusalem and the towns of Bethlehem and Nazareth.[7] At a stroke, therefore, the emperor had returned arguably the three most important locations in Jesus Christ's life to Christian control. Frederick then set out for Jerusalem where he arrived on 17 March. The following day he performed a crown-wearing ceremony in the Church of the Holy Sepulchre.[8] The prelates of the kingdom of Jerusalem perceived this act to be an insult to the papacy because Frederick was an excommunicate and they responded by placing Jerusalem under interdict.[9]

Frederick then returned to Acre by way of Jaffa on 25 March.[10] After his arrival, he ordered his troops to attack the properties of the patriarch and the Templars, who he believed were opposing him.[11] These actions, once they were relayed to the papacy by Patriarch Gerold, caused great anger at the curia.[12] Gregory was not mollified by the return of Jerusalem and he declared the peace settlement to be inadequate.[13] Frederick, concerned by news from the West, then took ship for Italy to make peace.[14] By this time Gregory was also prepared to end his conflict with the emperor. He had attempted to invade Frederick's kingdom of Sicily, but his armies, under the leadership of an aggrieved John of Brienne, had suffered reverses and he himself had been evicted from Rome by an angry mob.[15] Pope and emperor concluded a treaty on 23 July 1230 at San Germano and for some time afterwards there was a degree of co-operation between the two rulers. In 1231 Gregory even acknowledged Frederick as king of Jerusalem and the nobleman Richard Filangieri as his bailli in the Holy Land.[16]

This struggle between the pontiff and emperor posed a serious problem for the Teutonic Knights because it involved their major benefactors and placed them in a conflict of interests. As shown in the previous chapter, the brethren had received considerable patronage from both; however, by accepting support from these sources they had become dangerously dependent upon two patrons who, by late 1227, were at war. Historians have stressed the importance of this period for the Teutonic Knights and indeed Kluger has described it as the '*Hohepunkt*' (climax) of Herman's role between Empire

---

6   Filippo da Novara, *Guerra di Federico II*, p. 100; Jamal ad-din Muhammed be Salim bin Wasil, *Moufarraj al-Kurub*, p. 234; Rothelin, p. 525.
7   Matthew Paris, *Chronica Majora*, vol. 3, pp. 173–176.
8   HB. vol. 3, pp. 99–102; *CDOT*, no. 76. For discussion of the nature of this ceremony see Mayer, *The Crusades*, p. 254; Abulafia, *Frederick II*, p. 187; Kluger, *Hochmeister Hermann*, pp. 95–102.
9   HB. vol. 3, pp. 99–102; *CDOT*, no. 76.
10 Matthew Paris, *Chronica Majora*, vol. 3, p. 181.
11 Matthew Paris, *Chronica Majora*, vol. 3, pp. 179–184.
12 There are two letters from Patriarch Gerold: Matthew Paris, *Chronica Majora*, vol. 3, pp. 179–184; HB, vol. 3, pp. 102–110.
13 Matthew Paris, *Chronica Majora*, vol. 3, pp. 184–185.
14 Filippo da Novara, *Guerra di Federico II*, p. 104.
15 Matthew Paris, *Chronica Majora*, vol. 3, p. 156.
16 HB, vol. 3, pp. 297–299; *KSJJC*, p. 171.

and papacy.[17] This subject has drawn the attention of many historians who have attempted to define the political stance taken by the Order. The conclusion drawn by these studies is almost exclusively that the Teutonic Knights were either general supporters or militant partisans of the emperor. Statements of this kind can be found in most general surveys of the crusades as well as some specific works on the Teutonic Order and Frederick II.[18] A more nuanced standpoint has been adopted by Cohn and Favreau, who have similarly emphasised the Order's support of the emperor but have accepted that Herman wished to act as a peacemaker between these factions and perceived the need to take responsibility for his actions with the papacy.[19] Cohn also argues that Herman exerted considerable influence over the emperor at this time.[20] More recently this subject has been discussed in detail by Kluger and Arnold, who have also stressed the Order's work of mediation and its commitment to the crusade, but are emphatic in their belief that Herman was both an advocate and supporter of the emperor.[21] Kluger makes the following statement, 'In this situation, which permitted only an either/or, not a more conciliatory position, Herman von Salza decided for Frederick against the unambiguous orders of Gregory.'[22] In general, the Teutonic Knights are defined as imperial partisans who carried out peacemaking on Frederick's behalf whilst attempting to avoid papal censure. Most of these arguments are predicated on the belief that the Order was an expression of Hohenstaufen influence in the Mediterranean.

This chapter will nuance or alter a number of these conclusions. It will show that the Teutonic Knights by 1228 were driven by three key policy priorities: the work of the crusade, the preservation of their relationship with both the empire and the papacy and the continued survival of their own institution. During the preparations for the crusade the political environment had been conducive to the realisation of each of these objectives; nevertheless the excommunication of the emperor had shattered this balance. Herman's eminent position in the crusading army meant that he could not disassociate himself from the conflict to the same degree as the Templars and Hospitallers

---

17 Kluger, *Hochmeister Hermann*, p. 163.
18 A sample: Sterns, 'The Teutonic Knights in the Crusader States', pp. 364–365; Abulafia, *Frederick II*, p. 181; Riley-Smith, *The Crusades*, pp. 235–236; Van Cleve, 'The Crusade of Frederick II', p. 452; B. Hamilton, 'King Consorts of Jerusalem and their Entourages from the West from 1186 to 1250', in *Crusaders, Cathars and the Holy Places* (Aldershot, 1999), p. 23; Richard, *The Crusades*, p. 309; S. Runciman, *A History of the Crusades*, vol. 3 (Cambridge, 1954), p. 183; Nicholson, *Templars, Hospitallers and Teutonic Knights*, p. 5; C. Marshall, *Warfare in the Latin East: 1192–1291* (Cambridge, 1994), p. 61.
19 Cohn, *Herman von Salza*, pp. 121–123; Favreau, *Studien zur Frühgeschichte des Deutschen Ordens*, pp. 86–87. See also, Pacifico, 'I Teutonici tra papato e impero nel Mediterraneo al tempo di Federico II, 1215–1250', pp. 115–120.
20 Cohn, *Herman von Salza*, p. 121.
21 Arnold, 'Der Deutsche Orden zwischen Kaiser und Papst', pp. 61–62; *AZM*, p. 37.
22 'In dieser Situation, die nur ein Entweder-Oder, aber keine vermittelnde Position mehr zuließ, entschied sich Herman von Salza für Friedrich und gegen die unmißverständliche Anweisung Gregors'; Kluger, *Hochmeister Hermann*, p. 79.

and so he was forced to plot a course between his desire to support the Holy Land and his divided loyalties. To serve these needs he *attempted* to remain overtly neutral.

When Herman had embarked for the East in early 1227 it had been on an expedition that still represented the combined efforts of the papacy and the empire. After his arrival, he participated in the army's first ventures: the re-conquest of Sidon and the fortification of Caesarea and Montfort.[23] It was only then that reports of Frederick's excommunication reached the army. Coupled with this news were instructions from the papacy that the military orders should defend themselves against the emperor.[24] Frederick landed at Acre soon afterwards and seemingly demanded the co-operation of the Templars, Teutonic Knights and Hospitallers. All three military orders, therefore, were forced to decide how they would respond to these conflicting instructions.

In the light of these demands, the situation of the Teutonic Order was delicate. From Gregory's perspective, Herman had embarked for the East in command of crusading forces and in company with the papal legate; he was subject to orders of the papacy.[25] From Frederick's perspective, Herman was in charge of imperial troops on an imperial expedition; he was bound to the emperor. Caught between these duties, Herman's close affiliation to the crusade placed him in an exposed position.

Herman was not alone in his predicament and magnates across the German empire found themselves under pressure to take sides. Louis, duke of Bavaria, for example, resolved this dilemma by supporting the papal cause. This provoked an invasion led by Frederick's son Henry who inflicted a crushing defeat on the Bavarian forces. Other nobles chose to remain neutral. Leopold VI, duke of Austria, received demands of support from both parties, but he chose to ally himself with neither and acted instead as a peacemaker.[26] Consequently he travelled between Frederick and Gregory and helped to negotiate the Treaty of San Germano in 1230.[27] Leeper has shown that, through these actions, Leopold managed to remain 'a loyal son of the Church and a loyal vassal of the emperor and in spite of the growing difficulties between these two masters he succeeded in serving both'.[28] These examples demonstrate both the dangers of taking sides in this conflict and the prudence of adopting a neutral stance. The conduct of the duke of Austria provides a useful precedent for the behaviour of another imperial prince: the Teutonic Knights.[29]

---

[23] Sanuto, p. 211. Kluger believes this building work continued until March of this year, see Kluger, *Hochmeister Hermann*, p. 78.

[24] Eracles, p. 370.

[25] Eracles, p. 370; Sanuto, p. 213.

[26] This paragraph has drawn extensively upon Leeper, *A History of Medieval Austria*, pp. 301–305.

[27] Richard of San Germano, *Chronica*, p. 359. Note that there were two treaties signed at San Germano – in 1225 and in 1230.

[28] Leeper, *A History of Medieval Austria*, p. 301.

[29] The Teutonic Knights had become an imperial prince in 1226 through the Golden Bull of Rimini. This will be discussed in greater detail below.

An Order of the Church

From a papal perspective, the Teutonic Knights owed their allegiance to Rome. After his excommunication of the emperor, Gregory does not seem to have doubted that he could rely on them because he continued to issue and confirm privileges in their favour for over a year.[30] Certainly, every religious order was bound to serve the papacy at a time of conflict; Maier has written, with regard to the Franciscans, that 'supporting the papacy against the excommunicate emperor was, in any case, not only a matter of honour and gratitude. As faithful followers of the Roman Church, it was the Franciscans' duty.'[31] Moreover, such institutions risked severe reprimands if they failed in this responsibility because the papacy had the power to strip them of their privileges or even to dissolve them entirely. Dissolution was a very real threat and it was only a short while after these events that the papacy ended the disobedient Order of the Swordbrethren.

Aside from fear of such general punishments, the Teutonic Knights had a number of specific reasons to preserve their relationship with the papacy at this time. As shown in chapter 3, they had been stripped of their landholdings in Hungary in 1225. Since this time, Honorius III and then Gregory IX had applied considerable pressure upon the king to restore these properties. Admittedly, by 1228, these diplomatic efforts had not been successful but the papacy's goodwill was still necessary to ensure that the diplomatic pressure would be maintained.[32] Additionally, in late 1225, the Teutonic Order had been granted a foothold in Prussia by Duke Conrad of Masovia.[33] This concession gave the brethren the opportunity to carve out an independent territory for themselves in this region, but such an expansion required the acquiescence of the pontiff and the emperor.[34] Frederick II gave his confirmation in the Golden Bull of Rimini in 1226, thus elevating the Order to the status of an imperial prince.[35] By 1228 however, Gregory IX had yet to give his full support. Not only was the pontiff's basic approval necessary for this endeavour, but the brethren also needed him to license the preaching tours which would gather pilgrim forces to assist them in this scheme.[36] Herman

[30] 25 November 1227–28 October 1228: *TOT*, nos, 440–446, 200.
[31] C. T. Maier, *Preaching the Crusades: Mendicant Friars and the Cross in the Thirteenth Century* (Cambridge, 1998), p. 28.
[32] For a sample of the papal letters written on the Teutonic Knights' behalf concerning their lands in Hungary see: *RHP*, vol. 2, no. 5531 (12 June 1225); *RHP*, vol. 2, no. 5532 (12 June 1225); *RHP*, vol. 2, no. 5702 (27 October 1225); *RHP*, vol. 2, no. 5832 (17 February 1226); *RHP*, vol. 2, no. 5833 (17 February 1226).
[33] Peter von Dusburg, *Chronicon Terrae Prussie*, p. 36; Urban, *The Teutonic Knights*, pp. 51–52; L. Pósán, 'Prussian Missions and the Invitation of the Teutonic Order into Kulmerland', in *The Crusades and the Military Orders: Expanding the Frontiers of Medieval Latin Christianity*, ed. Z. Hunyadi and J. Laszlovsky (Budapest, 2001), pp. 429–448.
[34] Peter von Dusburg, *Chronicon Terrae Prussie*, p. 36.
[35] *PU*, vol. 1.1, no. 56.
[36] For discussion see G. Labuda, 'Die Urkunden über die Anfänge des Deutschen Ordens im Kulmerland und in Preußen in den Jahren 1226–1235', *Die Geistlichen Ritterorden Europas*, ed. J.

clearly realised the importance of such preaching because in September 1230 he and Gregory asked the Dominicans for their support.[37] In short, failure to comply with Gregory's demand for loyalty had the potential to result in censure, the removal of the Order's privileged status, the destruction of its ambitions in both Prussia and Hungary or even dissolution.

An Order of the Empire

From the imperial perspective, Frederick was a major patron and the Order maintained a permanent presence at the imperial court.[38] The vast majority of the brethren's lands were located in the empire and were only retained at his pleasure. Indeed, Frederick had sponsored the development of many of their regional commanderies in areas under his direct control.[39] Should Herman have followed Gregory's commands and opposed Frederick, he could have expected the confiscation of these lands along with the trading privileges, exemptions, alms donations and supply facilities which supported the Order's administrative network. Shortly after these events, Frederick confiscated the properties of the Templars and Hospitallers in Sicily, demonstrating the consequences of disobedience.[40] Furthermore, Frederick was now king of Jerusalem and held an imperial army in that land. Herman and the Teutonic Knights were present in the same army and, if we take the subjugation of the duke of Bavaria as a precedent, it is possible that the consequences of disobedience would have been brutal.

Additionally, in 1226 Frederick had promised that the brethren could take control of all the lands belonging to the Seigneurie of Joscelin which were in Muslim hands (see chapter 3).[41] Of these, the most important was the estate of Toron.[42] As a result, the Order needed to maintain Frederick's support because they stood to gain considerable landholdings in the Levant during the course of his crusade. To conclude, just as it would have been unthinkable for the Order to have opposed Gregory, so too would it have been illogical for them to have antagonised Frederick. The Teutonic Knights needed to support both parties in this conflict and they were not in a position to withhold their assistance from either.

Fleckenstein and M. Hellman (Sigmaringen, 1980), pp. 299–317; Maier, *Preaching the Crusades*, pp. 49–52.
[37] *PU*, vol. 1.1, no. 81. See also *Pommersches Urkundenbuch*, ed. K. Conrad and R. Prümers et al., vol. 1 (Cologne, 1970), no. 274.
[38] *CDOT*, no. 20.
[39] For the development of these commanderies see Wojtecki, 'Der Deutsche Orden unter Friedrich II', pp. 188–197.
[40] Matthew Paris, *Chronica Majora*, vol. 3, pp. 154–5.
[41] *TOT*, nos. 58, 59, 66; *R. Reg.*, vol. 1, no. 1003; HB. vol. 3. pp. 123–125.
[42] Toron was a sizeable fortress which in *c.*1185 owed fifteen knights' service, see John of Ibelin, *Le Livre des Assises*, pp. 453–454.

The Balancing Act

In these circumstances, the only sensible course available to Herman was to act as a peacemaker. In this capacity he – like Leopold – might have hoped to serve both factions without failing in his duty to either. To this end, Herman wrote two letters to the papacy whilst in the Holy Land. In the first of these, he relayed the importance of the crusade's work to the business of the Holy Land; dwelling upon the refortification of Jaffa and the return of Jerusalem. He also emphasised to Gregory how the expedition was inhibited by the war between the papacy and the empire, writing:[43] 'For truly it is perceived that if the lord emperor had crossed [the sea] in grace and concord with the Roman Church, the business of the Holy Land would have prospered far more effectively and advantageously.'[44] The general import of this letter was to persuade Gregory to make peace with the emperor so that greater aid might be brought to the Holy Land. Herman also took steps to end the emerging rift between Frederick and the patriarch.[45] Perhaps Herman's most significant act of diplomacy, however, was his work, some time later, towards the formation of the 1230 peace treaty between Gregory and Frederick.[46] Within these talks, Herman and the Teutonic Knights were evidently deemed to be sufficiently impartial to take temporary custody over a large number of fortresses across Apulia for both the emperor and papacy until a peace settlement could be reached.[47] This act is reminiscent of the compromise made in October 1190, during the Third Crusade, between Philip II of France and Richard I of England over the Sicilian city of Messina. Both monarchs, whilst wintering on Sicily, claimed a right to the city (which had been wrested from the control of the Norman ruler, Tancred of Lecce) and the ensuing argument was only resolved when control was handed over to the Templars and Hospitallers who were prepared to act as neutral parties.[48] Likewise, Herman seems to have hoped that by publicly styling himself as a mediator and intermediary he might weather the crisis. Even so, there was a still a period before the formation of the San Germano Treaty in 1230 when his actions attracted severe censure from the papacy.

The circumstances which gave rise to this criticism were centred upon the problems posed by the Teutonic Knights' desire to support the business of the crusade whilst remaining in favour with both their patrons. As has been shown, the defence of the Holy Land was ingrained into the brethren's identity and, for them, Frederick's crusade was the bitter fruit of over ten

---

[43] Kluger, *Hochmeister Hermann*, pp. 81–82.
[44] 'Verisimile enim videtur quod si dominus imperator in gratia et concordia Ecclesie Romane transivisset, longe efficacius et utilius prosperatum fuisset negotium terre sancta'; HB, vol. 3, pp. 90–93.
[45] HB, vol. 3, pp. 102–108; Van Cleve, 'The Crusade of Frederick II', p. 457.
[46] Richard of San Germano, *Chronica*, pp. 355–365.
[47] *CDOT*, nos. 78–81.
[48] J. Gillingham, *Richard I* (New Haven, CT, 2002), p. 135.

years of labour.[49] During the Fifth Crusade and for many years afterwards they – and indeed all those who cared about the defence of the East – had waited in vain for his arrival. For these men therefore, even though Frederick was an excommunicate, his was the much needed expedition that would help them to recover the Holy Land.[50] It is said that when Frederick finally arrived, 'the Templars and Hospitallers worshipped him on his arrival with bended knees kissing his knees'.[51] Similarly, John of Ibelin, even though he had been so badly abused by Frederick on Cyprus, was prepared to remain with the emperor through much of the expedition because he did not want it said that he had prevented the work of the Holy Land.[52] As a result, although the inhabitants of the Latin East may have objected to Frederick's position as an excommunicate, they were equally aware of their need of his troops, money and influence. Consequently, although Herman had every reason to remain neutral in the conflict between the Church and the empire, he was inextricably linked to the crusade for which he had had worked for so long. The problem was that if Herman aided Frederick's crusade, he would lay himself open to allegations that he had taken sides against Gregory. Conversely, if he followed papal instructions then he would be jeopardising the venture and alienating Frederick.

All three military orders were in a similar predicament and each found a separate position of compromise. As Nicholson has explained, 'The Templars, Hospitallers and other religious and secular leaders in the Holy Land then faced the dilemma of working alongside an excommunicate crusader without offending the pope.'[53] In this climate, the Templars and Hospitallers decided to offer Frederick's expedition a measure of support in its early stages. To this end, they followed the emperor to Jaffa but marched one day behind the main army. They also made an agreement with the emperor concerning any future co-operation which, as Barber has demonstrated, 'avoided the appearance that they were under the emperor's command'.[54] Through these precautions the Templars and Hospitallers trod a fine line between observing the papal instructions and supporting the crusade. After the return of Jerusalem, the Teutonic Knights, Templars and Hospitallers also discussed the refortification of the city.[55]

Herman von Salza seems to have attempted to balance his actions in a similar way to the other military orders. The Teutonic Knights' position,

---

49 Kluger, *Hochmeister Hermann*, p. 92.
50 Ross, 'Frederick II: Tyrant or Benefactor?' p. 159.
51 'Templarii vero et Hospitalarii in adventu eius flexis genibus adoraverunt eum, genua eius deosculantes'; Matthew Paris, *Chronica Majora*, vol. 3, p. 159.
52 Filippo da Novara, *Guerra di Federico II*, p. 90.
53 Nicholson, *Templars, Hospitallers and Teutonic Knights*, p. 5. Incidentally, Nicholson does not seem to think that this issue pertained to the Teutonic Knights because she goes on to argue, 'The Teutonic Order had no such problem: the Order supported the emperor, even when this meant estrangement from the pope';
54 Barber, *The New Knighthood*, p. 133.
55 HB, vol. 3, pp. 102–110.

however, was more complicated than that of the Templars or Hospitallers because they were intrinsically linked to the expedition in a way that the others were not. Consequently, the Teutonic Knights played a greater role. They helped in the refortification of Jaffa and Herman travelled as an emissary to the Egyptian sultan.[56] He also organised the debates concerning the reconstruction of Jerusalem.[57] Notably, all these actions were concerned with the work of re-conquest and the crusade and none of them reflected any partisanship in the war against the papacy. As a consequence of their actions Frederick rewarded the Teutonic Knights by fulfilling many of the obligations of the 1226 charter as well as a few additional concessions. Frederick's first act was to insert clauses into his treaty with the Egyptian sultan which returned Toron and allowed the Order to fortify its major stronghold of Montfort.[58] Frederick also granted the Order: the buildings of the old German hospital that existed in Jerusalem before 1187, the royal palace on the *ruga Armeniorum* and trading privileges in Western Christendom.[59] As we have seen, the return of Toron proved more problematic than expected and the Order's rights were contested successfully by Alice of Armenia.[60] Consequently, Frederick compensated the brethren with other properties and incomes.[61]

Through these acts, Herman had both supported the crusade and preserved his relationship with the emperor. Despite this, he was clearly concerned that his actions might be misconstrued by Gregory and he wrote the following to emphasise his continued fidelity:[62]

> Moreover, the Lord Archbishop Reginus, who has been sent to the feet of your holiness, fully acknowledged [that it is] your privilege to determine how and in what manner we should remain with the lord emperor and, while you are not hindered by him, with what intent we should act and who should be advantaged; whatever your holiness orders us concerning these things, we are ready to obey in future and any other matters.[63]

---

[56] *R, Reg*, vol. 1, no. 999; HB, vol. 3, pp. 90–93; *CDOT*, no. 75; HB, vol. 3, pp. 102–108.

[57] HB, vol. 3, pp. 102–108.

[58] Matthew Paris, *Chronica Majora*, vol. 3, p. 175; HB, vol. 3, pp. 90–93; *CDOT*, no. 75.

[59] *R. Reg.*, vol. 1, no. 1010; *TOT*, no, 69; HB, vol. 3, pp. 126–127; *Chronique D'Ernoul et de Bernard Le Trésorier*, p. 465; D. Pringle, *The Churches of the Crusader Kingdom of Jerusalem*, vol. 3 (Cambridge, 2007), pp. 228–229. These were confirmed by Conrad in 1243 see HB, vol. 6, pp. 852–853. For discussion see Kluger, *Hochmeister Hermann*, pp. 132–140.

[60] HB, vol. 3, pp. 90–93; *CDOT*, no. 75; Sanuto, p. 213.

[61] See chapter 3. Kluger, *Hochmeister Hermann*, p. 125.

[62] Kluger, by contrast, seems to believe that Herman's letters were written to serve the needs of the emperor and his crusade although he allows that there may be some other influences; *Hochmeister Hermann*, pp. 86–95.

[63] 'Ceterum dominus archiepiscopus Reginus qui ad pedes vestre dignationis missus est, discretionem vestram plene novit expedire qualiter et in quem modum circa dominum imperatorem remanserimus, et dum per eum fueritis expeditus qua intentione fecerimus et quis fuerit profectus, quicquid super hiis vestra nobis preceperit dignatio et de futuris et de ceteris parati sumus obedire'; HB, vol. 3, pp. 90–93.

The phrase 'while you are not hindered by him' is particularly worthy of notice because it seems to make the argument that whilst Frederick was in the Holy Land he was not a threat to the papacy and – by implication – any support shown to his crusade by the Order was not an inherently hostile act against the papacy. As Kluger has pointed out, Herman also described the actions of the army, ascribing their success to divine intervention.[64] In his account of the rebuilding of Jaffa, he claimed that the army's position had been imperilled by a storm at sea which had prevented supply ships reaching them from Acre. Apparently, just as their position became hopeless, the tempest ended through God's intervention and the crusade was saved.[65] Through explanations of this kind Herman may have hoped to convince Gregory that the crusade was carrying out God's work. If successful, Herman's continued presence with the army could be justified, even though it contravened papal orders. Significantly, this letter was not the first time that a crusader had sought to explain potentially damaging facts to the papacy with such a description. Notably in 1204 Baldwin of Flanders used a similar device when he wrote to Innocent III to explain why the Fourth Crusade had breached papal instructions and sacked Constantinople.[66] Moore has argued that this letter was 'designed to make the unexpected events seem as both the work of God and the inevitable and necessary consequences of the treachery of the Greeks'.[67] It does appear that contemporaries were aware that when approaching the papacy with unwelcome news it was necessary to portray their more controversial deeds as the result of God's intervention. Consequently, reviewing Herman's letter as a whole, it can be seen that it was a highly skilful piece of literary craftsmanship that was intended to appease the papacy and provide licence for Herman's continued support of the crusade.

The problem came, however, when the business of the crusade overlapped with the war between the papacy and the empire. When Frederick secured the return of Jerusalem he declared a wish to receive mass and perform a crown-wearing ceremony in the Church of the Holy Sepulchre.[68] These actions, unlike the fortification of Jaffa, the return of Nazareth, Bethlehem, Toron, Jerusalem, etc., held enormous significance in the context of Frederick's conflict with Gregory. As an excommunicate Frederick could not receive mass and to do so was an act of defiance against the papacy. Furthermore, he wished to receive mass in the most important church of the Christian faith. This placed even more pressure on the fragile support offered to Frederick by the Levantine prelates. Where many clergymen had been prepared to support Frederick on occasions when his actions might be of benefit to the Holy Land, they were not inclined to countenance such a flagrant abuse of

---

[64] Kluger, *Hochmeister Hermann*, pp. 93–94, 118.
[65] HB, vol. 3, pp. 90–93.
[66] *Die Regesta Innocenz' III*, vol. 7, pp. 253–262.
[67] Moore, *Pope Innocent*, p. 133; J. Phillips, *The Fourth Crusade and the Sack of Constantinople* (London, 2005), p. 276.
[68] HB, vol. 3, pp. 99–102; *CDOT*, no. 76.

the Church. Through Herman's intervention, Frederick was dissuaded from receiving mass, but he was still determined to conduct a crown-wearing ceremony and this provoked the archbishop of Caesarea to place Jerusalem under interdict.[69] The Templars and Hospitallers, partly as a result of this deed and partly as a result of certain clauses in the treaty with the sultan, began to change their wary support of Frederick for overt defiance. For the Teutonic Knights these events added a further level of complication to an already dangerous situation. Frederick demanded that Herman both attend this event and translate a speech in which he specifically outlined his relations with the papacy.[70] In short, Frederick wished Herman to perform a service which could not be justified as the act of a legitimate crusader but which had direct relevance to his war with the papacy: to accept would have been an act of betrayal to the papacy; to refuse would have alienated Frederick. In this crisis of loyalties, Herman's actions represent a desperate and makeshift attempt to preserve his relationship with both.

In the event, Herman did translate this speech; indeed, it would have been very difficult to refuse a direct imperial command whilst situated within an imperial army, yet he appears to have been deeply concerned about the way this action might be interpreted by the papacy.[71] Seemingly in an attempt to counterbalance this deed, he persuaded Frederick not to receive mass in the Church of the Holy Sepulchre and also to keep the ceremony a simple affair.[72] It seems likely that he hoped that these actions might convince others of his continued support for the interests of the Church. He also wrote a lengthy letter to Gregory, describing his actions in detail in an effort to explain himself. He gave a full account of the speech he had given on behalf of the emperor and he tried to present it as an attempt to make peace.[73] Despite this, his fear that his loyalties might be questioned becomes clear in the final paragraph where he wrote:

> We write to you of these things not because it pleases the lord emperor or to say matters occurred that were otherwise. But, in the same way that God renews, it would not be possible in any another way to establish peace and a truce.[74]

---

[69] HB, vol. 3, pp. 102–108. Cohn and Kluger also show how Herman took steps to prevent Frederick from widening the rift between emperor and papacy; Cohn, *Herman von Salza*, p. 129; Kluger, *Hochmeister Hermann*, pp. 103–108.

[70] HB, vol. 3, pp. 99–102; *CDOT*, no. 76.

[71] Kluger believes that the fact that Herman gave this speech is compelling evidence of his loyalty to the emperor; it would seem rather that Herman was caught in an extremely difficult position; Kluger, *Hochmeister Hermann*, p. 115.

[72] HB, vol. 3, pp. 99–102; *CDOT*, no. 76; Pacifico, 'I Teutonici tra papato e impero nel Mediterraneo al tempo di Federico II, 1215–1250', p. 115.

[73] Kluger, *Hochmeister Hermann*, pp. 95–96; Cohn, *Herman von Salza*, p. 141.

[74] 'Hec vero non ideo vobis scribimus quod idem placeat domino imperatori et quod non libenter si potuisset aliter ordinasset. Sed, sicut Deus novit, pacem et treuguas non potuit aliter stabilire'; HB, vol. 3, pp, 99–102; *CDOT*, no. 76.

In this same letter Herman appealed to Gregory to understand the predicament he was in and to stress:

> For we, just as he who holds dear the honour of the Church and Empire and strives for the exaltation of both, stand apart by well known council and take care not to remove [ourselves] either from the Church or from him [the emperor].[75]

Subsequently, according to the report of Patriarch Gerold, Frederick asked the Teutonic Knights to travel back with him to Italy but they demurred. Gerold claimed that their refusal was provoked by a fear of excommunication and also by the adverse sailing conditions at that time.[76] Even so, Herman seems to have overcome these navigational objections fairly swiftly because he was in Italy soon after Frederick. It seems likely that his refusal to return with the imperial party was more concerned with his desire to distance himself from Frederick in an attempt to maintain the impression that he was a loyal servant of both parties.

Despite these protestations and manoeuvres, Herman's attempts to exonerate himself were not successful. The problem was that he was not the only person writing to Gregory at this time. In a stinging denunciation of Frederick's actions, Patriarch Gerold wrote to the papacy on 26 March.[77] He described the Teutonic Knights' exploits and claimed that Herman's translation of Frederick's speech was proof that he was in league with the emperor.[78] Evidently, the patriarch's account of events was accepted because on 13 June 1229 Gregory wrote to the archbishop of Milan describing Herman's testimony as false. On 17 August he stripped the Teutonic Knights of their independence and placed them under the authority of the Hospitallers through the agency of Patriarch Gerold.[79] The Templars also chose this moment to renew their demands about the Order's use of the white mantles to the papacy.[80] This demonstrates how quickly the brethren could become vulnerable without papal protection. Indeed, hostility towards the Order seems to have developed so swiftly that in 1231 Gregory issued a document which explicitly prevented both the laity and clergy from assaulting the Order.[81] Reflecting on these events, Herman's attempt to juggle his Order's relationship to the emperor and the papacy with his desire to support the crusade had failed. It had proved an impossible balancing act.

---

[75] 'Nos vero, sicut ille qui honorem Ecclesie et imperii diligit et utriusque exaltationi intendit, restitimus consilio memorato quia nec ecclesie nec sibi vidimus expedire'; HB. vol. 3, pp, 99–102.
[76] HB, vol. 3, p. 110.
[77] Kluger, *Hochmeister Hermann*, p. 92.
[78] HB, vol. 3, pp. 102–110; Cohn, *Herman von Salza*, p. 136.
[79] *MGH Epis. Saec. XIII*, vol. 1, pp. 308–310; *CGJJ*, vol. 2, no. 1944; *AZM*, p. 39; Kluger, *Hochmeister Hermann*, p. 84; Pacifico, 'I Teutonici tra papato e impero nel Mediterraneo al tempo di Federico II, 1215–1250', pp. 118–119.
[80] *TOT*, no. 449; Potthast, vol. 1, no. 8606.
[81] *Archieven der Ridderlijke Duitsche Orde*, vol. 1, no. 57.

Gregory's wrath did not last for long. Through his work of mediation between Frederick and Gregory in 1230, Herman was soon able to repair much of the damage. Long before the Treaty of San Germano, Herman had restored relations with the pope. Gregory issued his first charter in favour of the Order after their estrangement on 12 January 1230, six months before the final peace settlement with the emperor.[82] After this time, as shown above, the Teutonic Knights seem to have enjoyed the confidence of both parties.[83] Furthermore Gregory subsequently endorsed their expansion into Prussia and continued to demand that the king of Hungary should return their lands in Burzenland.[84] The Hospitallers do not seem to have enforced their rights over the Teutonic Order.[85] In the long term, therefore, the Order had made a fortunate escape.

Empire, Papacy and the Ibelins 1229–1239

After Frederick departed for Italy in 1229, the magnates of the Holy Land attempted to rid themselves of his yoke. Although the Ibelins had remained with Frederick whilst he could be of benefit to the Holy Land, they were quick to oppose his representatives after his departure. They had been outraged by his assumption of the bailliage of Cyprus and also by his demand for control of the city of Beirut.[86] Whilst on Cyprus, Frederick had also insisted that John of Ibelin should yield hostages to the imperial forces, including his sons Balian and Baldwin. These sons were apparently maltreated during their imprisonment.[87] Frederick subsequently sold the bailliage of Cyprus to a group of nobles known as the Five Baillis, who were politically opposed to the Ibelins.[88] The Templars were angered by Frederick's inability or disinclination to negotiate the return of the Temple in Jerusalem. The patriarch had been outraged by Frederick's actions in Jerusalem and violence broke out between these men after they returned to Acre. These events polarised the Latin East and laid the foundations for the ensuing civil war. This began

---

82 *Reg. Grégoire IX*, vol. 1, no. 387; *MGH Epis. Saec. XIII*, vol. 1, no. 411; Potthast, vol. 1, no. 8480. For Herman's actions and itinerary see Cohn, *Herman von Salza*, p. 146–171.

83 *CDOT*, nos. 78–81. Cohn, *Herman von Salza*, p. 170.

84 *Reg. Grégoire IX*, vol. 1, nos. 387, 643; Potthast, vol. 1, no. 8728. Hubatsch has suggested that Gregory encouraged the Prussian expedition so that the Order might be distanced from the emperor and there may be some truth in that suggestion. Hubatsch, 'Montfort und die Bildung des Deutschordensstates', p. 181.

85 Favreau-Lilie, 'L'Ordine Teutonico in Terrasanta (1198–1291)', p. 64.

86 Sanuto, p. 212. The need for a bailli in Cyprus began in 1218 after the death of King Hugh of Cyprus. Phillip of Ibelin, who was related to King Hugh's wife Alice, was appointed bailli for the young king, Henry. Frederick, however, felt that because Emperor Henry VI had conferred Cyprus with an imperial crown in 1198 he should hold the bailliage. For details of Frederick's previous demands for the bailliage see Filippo da Novara, *Guerra di Federico II*, p. 88.

87 For Frederick's maltreatment of John's sons Baldwin and Balian see Eracles, p. 367.

88 For Frederick's assumption of power see Eracles, pp. 368–369. For the sale of the island of Cyprus see Eracles, p. 375.

in late 1229 when reports were received that Frederick's baillis had plundered Cyprus. The Ibelins responded by invading the island and defeating the baillis.[89] In 1231 the emperor sent re-enforcements to the Levant under Richard Filangieri, who instituted a siege of Beirut before turning south and defeating the Ibelin forces at the battle of Casal Imbert in 1232.[90] The imperial troops then travelled to Cyprus where they were later defeated at the battle of Agridi.[91] Richard Filangieri was finally expelled from the island after the fall of the last imperial stronghold in Cerines in 1232 and the remnants of the imperial army took refuge in Tyre.[92]

In a similar way to the imperial/papal conflict, many historians have argued, to differing degrees, that the Teutonic Knights were staunch supporters of the imperial party against the Ibelins.[93] A slightly more nuanced stance has been taken by Urban who confirms the Order's imperial loyalties but he notes that Herman 'avoided antagonising the local nobles'.[94] For many of these historians, it is the brethren's actions during Frederick's crusade which seem to have generated this conclusion. Even so, a more detailed analysis of the available sources will show how these pieces of evidence have given an incomplete picture of the actions of the Teutonic Knights. In reality, the brethren appear to have pursued a policy of mediation in which they attempted to give all factions the impression that they were quietly sympathetic.

Between 1229 and 1239 the policy of the Teutonic Knights can be broken into two phases. The first, 1229–1233, is the period in which the major military operations of the Ibelin–Lombard war took place. The second, 1234–1239, can be defined, at least in part, by ongoing attempts to establish a peaceful settlement in the Latin East. These will now be examined in turn.

1229–1233

After 1229, Herman von Salza was absent from the Holy Land until *c.*1234 and command of the Order's forces in the eastern Mediterranean fell to his deputy. This was firstly a brother named Haymo and later Grand Commander Luttold (see appendix E.2).

A vital predicate for discussion of the Order's policy at this time lies in the fact that the sources, which contain detailed descriptions of the deeds of the other military orders in this conflict, do not contain any references to the participation of the Teutonic Knights in any military operations during the

---

89 For the plundering of Cyprus see Filippo da Novara, *Guerra di Federico II*, p. 106. For the defeat of the imperial forces see Filippo da Novara, *Guerra di Federico II*, p. 116–120.

90 Filippo da Novara, *Guerra di Federico II*, pp. 166–168.

91 Filippo da Novara, *Guerra di Federico II*, pp. 182–188.

92 Filippo da Novara, *Guerra di Federico II*, p. 194.

93 See Mayer *The Crusades*, p. 255; Richard, *The Crusades*, p. 309; J. Richard, *The Latin Kingdom of Jerusalem*, trans. J. Shirley, ed. R. Vaughan, vol. 2 (Amsterdam, 1979), p. 315; N. Coureas, *The Latin Church in Cyprus: 1195–1312* (Aldershot, 1997), p. 176; Hubatsch, 'Der Deutsche Orden und die Reichlehnschaft über Cypern', pp. 269, 278; Favreau-Lilie, 'L'Ordine Teutonico in Terrasanta (1198–1291)', pp. 65–66.

94 W. Urban, *The Prussian Crusade* (Lanham, MD, 1980), p. 47.

Ibelin–Lombard war between 1230 and 1239.[95] This is all the more notable because they would have been in a strong position to influence the outcome of several of the campaigns and especially the battle of Casal Imbert in 1232, which was conducted within five miles of the Order's fortress at Montfort.[96] This factor can partially be explained by the fact that during the period 1230–1239 the Teutonic Knights began a series of wars of expansion in Prussia. These endeavours required a considerable initial military commitment and, as the Order expanded along the Vistula, further reinforcements were sent to this battlefront. In 1237, the papacy granted Herman's representatives, including Hartmann von Heldrungen (master, 1273–1283), the ability to absorb the defeated and allegedly corrupt Order of the Swordbrothers in Livonia and to assume control of their embattled territories. Accordingly, on 12 May 1237, Ludwig of Oettingen led a well-equipped force of sixty brother knights to this region. Shortly afterwards, the Prussian master, Herman Balk, took office as the first Livonian master. Both these ongoing campaigns required the dedication of huge quantities of men, finance and equipment. A non-military policy in the Holy Land would have permitted the Order to concentrate its resources in Prussia.

Linking the advantages of neutrality in a conflict of patrons (Frederick and the barons of the kingdom of Jerusalem) to the pressing need for a concentration of military resources to the north, it was in the Order's interests to remain in favour with both factions in the Levant. With the imperial faction, the brethren enjoyed considerable success. Charter evidence reveals a number of gifts received from the imperial party and their allies during and shortly after this period. Richard Filangieri, deputy of the emperor, evidently held the Order in high esteem and in 1234 he issued a document in which he thanked Luttold and the Teutonic Knights for their loyal service to the emperor.[97] Several of Frederick's other Levantine allies also made concessions to the brethren including the Five Baillis, who granted them a house in Nicosia and a village on Cyprus in 1229.[98] In 1236, King Hetoum I of Armenia, who had offered Filangieri a place of refuge after the siege of Cerines, met with Luttold and granted the Order the important city of Harunia with an estate of nineteen villages and several religious houses.[99] Reviewing these endowments from the emperor and his satellites there can be little doubt that the

---

[95] Coureas has made a similar statement regarding the Ibelin–Lombard war on Cyprus; *The Latin Church in Cyprus* p. 176.

[96] For a description of the battle of Casal Imbert see Filippo da Novara, *Guerra di Federico II*, pp. 166–168.

[97] *TOT*, no. 78.

[98] *R. Reg.*, vol. 1, no. 1017; *TOT*, no. 71. These gifts were technically made by King Henry of Cyprus, but at this time Henry was both a minor and a prisoner of the Baillis.

[99] Filippo da Novara, *Guerra di Federico II*, p. 194; *TOT*, no. 83. For the ground plans and archaeological details of the fortifications of Harunia see Edwards, *The Fortifications of Cilician Armenia*, pp. 143–146. For discussion of the Order's rights in Harunia see Chevalier, 'Les Chevaliers teutoniques en Cilicie', pp. 145–147.

Teutonic Knights were highly regarded by the imperial forces during this conflict.

Conversely, the brothers also maintained their relationship with the Ibelin family and its allies. The Order's relationship with the Ibelin family dated back to the end of the twelfth century when in 1198 John of Ibelin witnessed two charters issued to the Order by King Aimery and a further three charters in 1200.[100] Subsequently, in 1206, John of Ibelin, lord of Beirut, issued a special confirmation for the Order's purchase of a house in Acre. This act was witnessed by his brother Philip.[101] John witnessed further grants made to the brethren in 1207, 1208, 1217, 1228 and 1229.[102] Admittedly, the Ibelins had not been great patrons of the Order, but it would seem that they had viewed the institution favourably and, much more importantly, they were a major power in the eastern Mediterranean. Any opposition to this dynasty would not merely have been an act of ingratitude and political folly but it would have raised the possibility of reprisals. The Teutonic Order may have owned a major castle in the kingdom of Jerusalem but this was still under construction and would have offered little defence against the combined wrath of the local barons.

During the civil war, these positive relations between the Ibelins and the Order seem to have continued and this was demonstrated by the Order's actions in Acre. At this time, a special commune was founded in Acre which Edbury has described as follows: 'The commune brought together military and commercial interests, and, as an alliance of Ibelin sympathizers, its essential purpose appears to have been to prevent Filangieri taking control in Acre.'[103] Given this decidedly anti-imperial agenda one might expect that the local property of any imperial ally would have been placed in jeopardy. It seems highly suggestive, therefore, that the Teutonic Knights' considerable establishment in Acre not only remained intact but actually increased, even at the height of the fighting. This was demonstrated in 1230, 1231 and 1235, when the brethren either rented or purchased a number of properties in Acre and its environs.[104] Furthermore, they clearly retained their commercial interests in the port of Acre because there is evidence for the arrival of their ships at this time.[105] Even the properties which had been granted to the Order by Frederick in 1229 (shortly before his departure for Italy) were retained.[106] In these ways, it appears that, despite the continuation of the Teutonic Knights' relations with the empire, they remained sufficiently secure in their accord

---

[100] *TOT*, nos. 34–38.
[101] *TOT*, no. 41; *R. Reg.*, vol. 1, no. 812.
[102] *R. Reg.*, vol. 1, nos. 821, 828, 900, 1002, 1003, 1004, 1009, 1010, 1011, 1013.
[103] P. W. Edbury, *John of Ibelin and the Kingdom of Jerusalem* (Woodbridge, 1997), p. 45.
[104] *TOT*, nos. 73, 74, 76, 80.
[105] Filippo da Novara, *Guerra di Federico II*, p. 146; *Chroniques de Chypre d'Amadi et de Strambaldi*, ed. R. de Mas Latrie, vol. 1 (Paris, 1891), p. 147.
[106] Urban, *The Teutonic Knights*, p. 27; Hubatsch, 'Der Deutsche Orden und die Reichlehnschaft über Cypern', p. 271.

with the Ibelins between 1229 and 1233 to strengthen their position in Acre, a pro-Ibelin city.

More explicitly, Ibelin chroniclers, describing the civil war, continued to present the Teutonic Knights in a favourable light. Perhaps the best known chronicler of the Ibelin faction was Philip of Novara. Philip was a contemporary who played his part in the Ibelin–Lombard war and Edbury has described the purpose of his chronicle as follows:

> His unashamed intention was to entertain his readers by extolling the family's achievements. The Ibelins, their relatives and dependents all behave with the utmost propriety; they are honourable, gracious, wise and magnanimous. Their opponents are correspondingly cowardly, irrational, prone to illegality and ridiculous.[107]

Given such a perspective, it is naturally of the foremost importance to examine the way in which he portrayed the Teutonic Knights. To begin, it must be stated that the brethren are barely mentioned; however, there is one highly important passage in a section describing the latter stages of Frederick's crusade:

> L'emperor fu maintenant mau de toute la gent d'Acre; espesciaument dou Temple fu trop mau; et au jor avoit mout vaillans freres au Temple, frere Piere de Montagu, quy mout estoit vaillant et noble, estoit aucy le maistre des Alemans; et ceaus de vau la terre n'estoient mie bien de l'empereour.[108]

This passage is suggestive for two reasons. Firstly, it seems to be a list of those men who Philip of Novara believed were opposed to Frederick. Herman's presence in this list is, therefore, highly significant. Furthermore, it appears that he was also describing Herman, like Peter of Montague, as valiant and noble. Given that Novara's chronicle was intended as a work of flattery for the Ibelin family, the positive representation of Herman in this way surely suggests that the Order was in favour with the Ibelins at this time.[109]

---

[107] Edbury, *John of Ibelin and the Kingdom of Jerusalem*, pp. 34–35.

[108] Filippo da Novara, *Guerra di Federico II*, p. 102.

[109] There is a problem here in that it is not quite clear whether Novara intended to extend the description of 'valiant and noble' to Herman or confine it to Peter of Montague. La Monte, in his translation of Novara's work believed that this description applied to Herman because the chronicle of Amadi, which was partially derived from Novara's work, states the following: 'L'imperator per queste operation era mal voluto de tutti et specialmente da quelli del Tempio, onde alhora haveva molti frati valentissimi, et era suo maestro fra Piero de Monteagu; et parimente haveva ne la casa di Alemani uno maestro valentissimo et savio' (*Chroniques de Chypre d'Amadi et de Strambaldi*, vol. 1, p. 134.)

J. La Monte, *The Wars of Frederick II against the Ibelins in Syria and Cyprus* (New York, 1936), p. 90. This is replicated in C. Tyerman, *The Fourth Crusade and the End of Outremer: 1192–1291* (London, 2004), p. 220. Similarly Kohler in his compilation of *Les Gestes des Chiprois*, actually injects the bracketed phrase '[et mout vaillant et noble]' to assure a reader that this description applied to Herman, *Les Gestes des Chiprois*, *RHC. Arm.*, vol. 2 (Paris, 1896), p. 683. A different interpretation has been made more recently by Melani who does not believe that

Another group that had vehemently opposed Frederick during his crusade was led by Gerold, patriarch of Jerusalem. As shown above, he had denounced both Frederick and Herman, but his hostility towards the Teutonic Knights, at least, did not last. It is significant that both before and after the crusade, the Order enjoyed a positive relationship with this prelate. Gerold was a Burgundian who was appointed as patriarch of Jerusalem in 1225. Previously he had been the abbot of Cluny and the bishop of Valence.[110] In the early years of his patriarchate, he and Herman had worked together to prepare Frederick's crusade. Gerold, like Herman, was one of the appointed representatives in the 1225 San Germano agreement.[111] The two men appear to have developed a bond of friendship and in 1226 Gerold witnessed a charter pertaining to the Order in Mantua.[112] Gerold also embarked upon crusade in company with Herman von Salza in September 1227.[113] More significantly, during Frederick's crusade, Gerold, along with the bishop of Winchester, was prepared to endorse the employment of the Teutonic Order's rule by the Order of St Thomas of Acre – an event that would have enhanced the brethren's prestige.[114]

It seems to have been at some point after this event (probably through Herman's translation of the emperor's speech) that Gerold came to believe that Herman had taken sides against the papacy and he wrote a letter vigorously condemning both Frederick and Herman on 26 March 1229.[115] On 17 August 1229 Gregory ordered Gerold to enforce his instructions that the Teutonic Knights be placed under the authority of the Hospitallers.[116] By the end of Frederick's crusade, relations between Frederick and Gerold had deteriorated to a point where fighting had broken out in Acre between their followers. Reporting on these armed clashes Gerold wrote a second letter which again vigorously denounced Frederick, although it did not mention Herman.[117] Whether this omission reflects a change in Gerold's attitude towards the Order is impossible to say; however, it seems that by October 1230 the relationship between Gerold and the brothers had been rebuilt. At this time, the Order made two purchases from the abbot of St Mary's of

---

this statement can have applied to Herman. He claims that because Herman is generally considered to have been a partisan of the emperor that such an appellation would be highly unlikely; Filippo da Novara, *Guerra di Federico II*, pp. 275–276. Melani's argument is understandable because modern historiography to this point has deemed Herman to be an imperial ally; however, the former interpretation fits better with the context of this passage in Novara's work.

110 Hamilton, *The Latin Church in the Crusader States*, p. 257.
111 HB, vol. 2, p. 501–503.
112 *Urkundenbuch der Deutschordensballei Thüringen*, no. 40.
113 HB, vol. 3, pp. 36–48.
114 *Reg. Grégoire IX*, vol. 2, no. 2944.
115 HB, vol. 3, pp. 102–108.
116 *CGJJ*, vol. 2, no. 1944.
117 Matthew Paris, *Chronica Majora*, vol. 3, pp. 179–184. Powell has cast doubt on the authenticity of this letter see J. M. Powell, 'Patriarch Gerold and Frederick II: The Matthew Paris Letter', *Journal of Medieval History*, 25 (1999), pp. 19–26.

Josephat.[118] Gerold not only confirmed both these purchases but became personally accountable on behalf of the Teutonic Knights as security for these agreements. Peter of Limoges, archbishop of Caesarea and the same man who had placed Jerusalem under interdict, also witnessed these documents. Given these men's outspoken hostility towards Frederick it is highly suggestive that they were prepared to act so positively in support of the Teutonic Order. Admittedly, Hamilton has convincingly argued that after the Treaty of San Germano in 1230 Gerold and Peter's role in the Levant became one of mediation rather than pro-Ibelin partisanship; however, it is unlikely that news of this peace would have reached the Levant by October 1230.[119] Furthermore, the emperor continued to view the patriarch as an enemy and in 1232 he compelled the pope to recall him to Rome.[120] As a result, the renewal of the association between the patriarch and the Teutonic Knights in 1230 appears to offer further evidence for the contention that the Teutonic Knights were viewed favourably by those who opposed the emperor.

In short, it can be seen that the brethren had nothing to gain by taking sides in the Ibelin–Lombard war and a great deal to lose. The 1230s was a time of enormous growth for them in the Baltic, an expansion that could only be stunted by war in the Holy Land. Urban has argued that the treaty with the Egyptians in 1229 would have reduced the Order's defensive responsibilities in the Holy Land, allowing them to focus on Prussia.[121] A policy of mediation in the subsequent civil war in the Latin East would have helped them to achieve this end. This strategy would have been implemented by Luttold and Haymo and their success suggests a high level of diplomatic ability. Indeed, the Order's achievements of this time (the military victories in Prussia under Herman Balk, the acquisition of the Swordbrethren and the maintenance of peace in the Holy Land) bear witness to Herman's ability to surround himself with lieutenants of the highest calibre.

1234–1239

During the civil war in the Latin East, events took place in Western Christendom which were to have enormous significance for both the kingdom of Jerusalem and the Teutonic Order. Shortly after the Treaty of San Germano in 1230, King Henry of Germany, Frederick's son, began to assert his independence. He had become increasingly estranged from his father in previous years and an outward sign of his defiance was his refusal to attend the Diet of Ravenna in January 1232.[122] The events surrounding this Diet were also symptomatic of a second problem facing Frederick – the Lombard communes.

---

118 *TOT*, nos. 73, 74.
119 Hamilton, *The Latin Church in the Crusader States*, p. 259.
120 Hamilton, *The Latin Church in the Crusader States*, p. 259.
121 Urban, *Teutonic Knights*, p. 55.
122 This section has drawn on the work of Van Cleve, *The Emperor Frederick II*, pp. 349–419.

These communes began to unite against imperial authority and barred the Alpine passes against the imperial princes, who were travelling south to attend this meeting. At the Diet, the Italian cities were heavily censured and a ban was placed upon the Lombard League. Frederick then ordered a further Diet in Aquileia later that year. Henry attended this meeting and Frederick compelled him to take a comprehensive oath of loyalty. By 1234 matters had deteriorated still further and Gregory IX, seemingly upon Frederick's instructions, placed Henry under sentence of excommunication. In May 1235, Frederick marched against Henry in Germany and resistance collapsed. Henry was imprisoned.

At the same time, Gregory began to organise a new crusade and was keen for the emperor to take part. By 1235, however, Frederick was more concerned with the issue of the Lombard communes. In this year he demanded 30,000 marks from those cities under threat of invasion. The pope, desiring peace, wrote to the emperor and princes encouraging them not to become involved in military operations. His main objective seems to have been to end this matter by mediation so that they might participate in the crusade. Nevertheless, the Lombards declared themselves to be ready to resist and Gregory's policy of mediation failed. Frederick, by return, declared that he wished to travel to the Holy Land but was only prepared to do so after matters in Lombardy had been settled.

Over succeeding months doubt was cast over the Church's relationship with Frederick when James, cardinal-bishop of Palestrina, provoked Piacenza into revolt against the imperial forces. Frederick's army then advanced and captured Vicenza. In the aftermath of this victory several further cities surrendered. Still keen to promote peace, the pope ordered a new conference in Mantua. He sent Herman von Salza as his representative to discuss terms with the Lombards. This conference did not satisfy the emperor because it did not conclude with any punishment of the Lombards but only specified that they should travel on crusade. Shortly after this event, the Lombard forces were compelled to give battle and were heavily defeated by Frederick at Cortenuova in 1237. With the growth of imperial influence in this area, relations between Gregory and Frederick began to decline rapidly. Gregory is said to have been deeply saddened by Cortenuova and Frederick's growing strength in Lombardy posed a threat to the pope's political authority in the Papal States. The final diplomatic breach occurred shortly afterwards when Frederick invaded Sardinia. This island had previously sworn to serve the papacy, thus Frederick's actions provoked both a bull of excommunication and the outbreak of war in 1239.

These events in Western Christendom had long-term implications for the Teutonic Knights' interests in the Holy Land. Initially, both the papacy and emperor encouraged the Order to help resolve the civil war in the Latin East. Certainly peace served the brethren's interests, just as peacemaking gave them the opportunity to gain favour with all the factions concerned. Efforts at mediation began in 1232 when the patriarch of Antioch endeavoured to negotiate a settlement.[123] Frederick then sought to achieve a reconciliation but his efforts were thwarted. At this point, Gregory intervened and despatched Herman von Salza and Albert of Rizzato, patriarch of Antioch, to the Levant.[124] By 1234 these emissaries appear to have had some success because, in a letter written on 8 August, Gregory IX referred to an agreement concluded by them.[125] He asked the Ibelins to observe this peace and he informed them that he was sending the archbishop of Ravenna as a papal legate to the Holy Land to preserve the agreement.[126] On the same day he also wrote to the commanders of the Hospitallers, Templars and Teutonic Knights in the Holy Land requiring them to offer their assistance.[127] The legate seems to have arrived to find that this peace settlement was not being upheld and his response was to excommunicate the leaders of the Acre commune and to put the city itself under interdict. These heavy-handed actions appear to have upset the political balance of the East and, in a later letter to Herman von Salza dated 22 September 1235, the pope explained that he had removed this interdict because of the damage it had caused to the business of the Holy Land.[128] By this time, therefore, the process of mediation was in chaos partly through the imprudent actions of the papal legate. Gregory then sent Herman to the Latin East for a second time to ask the Ibelins to send representatives to Rome.[129] Given the previous actions of the archbishop of Ravenna, it is a testament to Herman's enormous skill that the Ibelins agreed to this request. Indeed, Herman's success at this time may add further evidence to the contention that the Teutonic Order had successfully maintained a strong relationship with the Ibelins during the civil war.

Philip of Troyes and Henry of Nazareth travelled to Rome to represent the Ibelins' interests where they negotiated a treaty with Herman, who had been empowered to act on behalf of the emperor. We are informed of this treaty's main stipulations through a papal letter dated 21 February 1236. These include the dissolution of the commune of Acre and the removal of its appointed consuls. The barons were all to take oaths of loyalty to the emperor and Richard Filangieri was to be restored to office, although a separate bailli would be appointed for the kingdom of Jerusalem. The Teutonic Knights were to take control of the citadel of Tyre from the imperial forces, but to hold it in the name of the emperor. John of Ibelin's life was protected, but Frederick retained the option of legal action against him.[130] Nevertheless, when the emissaries returned to the Levant they were received with

---

123 This section has drawn on Riley-Smith, *Feudal Nobility*, p. 200; Edbury, *John of Ibelin and the Kingdom of Jerusalem*, pp. 24–56; Kluger, *Hochmeister Hermann*, pp. 177–185.
124 For background to this journey see Cohn, *Herman von Salza*, pp. 196–197.
125 *MGH Epis. Saec. XIII*, vol. 1, no. 578; Riley-Smith, *Feudal Nobility*, p. 204.
126 *MGH Epis. Saec. XIII*, vol. 1, no. 594.
127 *MGH Epis. Saec. XIII*, vol. 1, no. 594.
128 *MGH Epis. Saec. XIII*, vol. 1, no. 657; HB, vol. 4, p. 776.
129 Eracles, p. 406.
130 *MGH Epis. Saec. XIII*, vol. 1, no. 674; Riley Smith, *Feudal Nobility*, pp. 205–206.

outrage and were almost attacked.[131] The Ibelins appear to have objected to two clauses in particular: the dissolution of the commune of Acre and the clauses relating to John of Ibelin.[132] As relations between the empire and the papacy in Western Christendom began to crumble, all further talk of peace was abandoned and the treaty was not implemented.[133]

This history of negotiations conducted by Herman is highly suggestive for the political position of the Teutonic Knights at this time. Firstly, the Order's interest in the establishment of peace seems self-evident; civil war did not serve any of the Order's objectives. In this endeavour Herman acted both as an agent of the papacy and as a representative of the emperor. He also seems to have enjoyed the confidence of the Ibelins, although this may have been damaged by the treaty of 1236. It is perhaps indicative of his overall role that, just as the brethren had acted as a neutral third party and garrisoned contested fortresses in 1230–1231, so too were they required to garrison Tyre in 1236.[134] An indication of the esteem felt by Gregory towards the Teutonic Knights at this time can be seen in the support he offered for their acquisition of the Swordbrethren in 1237.[135] Herman's actions also seem to have been guided by his desire to support the preparations for Gregory's new crusading venture.[136] One of the main elements of this process was to establish peace across Western Christendom so that noblemen would be able to travel abroad for a prolonged period. Gregory himself had gained some experience as a peacemaker during the Fifth Crusade when, while still a cardinal, he had negotiated peace settlements for the Genoese.[137] As pope, he pursued a similar policy during the preparations for the Barons' Crusade and in 1234 he attempted to create a four-year truce between Louis IX of France and Henry III of England.[138] To settle other disputes, he relied heavily on Herman, who had distinguished himself in this role during Frederick's crusade. According to Gregory, Herman was to be 'making provisions that the discords of the world might be forced into truce and harmony'.[139] This sentiment was repeated in 1236 when the pope accused Frederick of inhibiting Herman's work of mediation. In this same letter, he also outlined Herman's fundamental importance to this expedition stating:

---

131   Eracles, p. 406.
132   Edbury, *John of Ibelin and the Kingdom of Jerusalem*, pp. 49–50.
133   Edbury, *John of Ibelin and the Kingdom of Jerusalem*, p. 50.
134   *CDOT*, no. 78–81; *MGH Epis. Saec. XIII*, vol. 1, no. 674.
135   For details over the Order's acquisition of the Swordbrethren see *AZM*, pp. 362–366; Urban, *The Teutonic Knights*, pp. 90–91.
136   Tyerman, *God's War*, p. 620.
137   Powell, *Anatomy of a Crusade*, pp. 67–68.
138   M. Lower, *The Barons' Crusade: A Call to Arms and its Consequences* (Philadelphia, PA, 2005), pp. 19–20.
139   'Providentes ut orbis terre discordes ad treuguas vel concordiam cogerentur'; *MGH Epis. Saec. XIII*, vol. 1, no. 657.

We saw to it that the aforementioned master Herman should be assisted [in] providing that the discords of the world be forced into truce and harmony and that already some of the great princes of the earth have been compelled to do this, indeed some kings, many nobles and powerful men have received the sign of the cross by the grace of God.[140]

This vital passage demonstrates the importance of Herman's role and places his peacemaking in the Latin East in a wider context. In the West, he worked to establish peace between the Hohenstaufen family and its adversaries. In 1234, when Gregory promulgated the crusade bull *Rachel suum videns*, the emperor was deeply involved in a dispute with his son which threatened to become an open rebellion. Should such a conflict have taken place, it would have drawn warriors away both from the Holy Land and from the Teutonic Order's wars in the Baltic. To prevent these consequences, Herman travelled to Germany in 1235 where he confronted Henry and persuaded him to yield to his father.[141] In later years Herman also sought to end the disputes between Frederick and the Lombard communes.[142] In 1235 he was sent to Rome to negotiate peace on behalf of the emperor and in 1237 he acted as an imperial representative in further talks concerning the Lombards.[143] As relations deteriorated between pope and emperor, Herman attempted to reconcile both protagonists. In 1236, the pope specifically asked that Herman might be sent to him so that he might mediate between them.[144] In response, the emperor declared himself to be unwilling to allow Herman to travel to the papacy, but claimed that the Order's master had persuaded him otherwise.[145] His stated reason for his eventual agreement was given as follows, 'Because he [Herman] has always thus far been zealous for the mutual good of the Church and Empire, we have assigned him to the Apostolic See'.[146] This passage can be seen as a significant echo of Herman's own statement made eight years before when he described himself as a man who 'who holds dear the honour of the Church and Empire and strives for the exaltation of both'[147] and it provides useful evidence for the continuation of Herman's work of intercession between Frederick and

---

[140] 'Duximus assumendum, providentes ut orbis terre discordes ad treugam vel concordiam cogerentur, et quod iam ad hoc aliqui ex magnis terre principibus sunt compulsi, quinimmo reges aliqui, multi nobiles et potentes crucis signaculum per Dei gratiam receperunt, prefatum magistrum H'; *MGH Epis. Saec. XIII*, vol. 1, no. 678.

[141] *Annales Marbacenses*, p. 97.

[142] Kluger has argued that Herman's missions to the Lombards bear no relevance for his role as the master of a military order and yet, when seen from the perspective of the preparations for a new crusade, many of his actions can be seen as entirely in accordance with the responsibilities of his post; *Hochmeister Hermann*, p. 164.

[143] Richard of San Germano, *Chronica*, pp. 373–374.

[144] HB, vol. 4, pp. 870–871.

[145] HB, vol. 5, pp. 32–34; HB, vol. 4, pp. 905–913.

[146] 'Quia commune bonum Ecclesie et imperii semper zelatus est hactenus, ad sedem apostolicam destinamus'; HB, vol. 5, pp. 32–34.

[147] 'Qui honorem Ecclesie et imperii diligit et utriusque exaltationi intendit'; HB, vol. 3, pp, 99–102.

Gregory.[148] A further indication of the Order's commitment to the Barons' Crusade can be found in 1235. In this year, the pope received a letter from John of Brienne speaking of the pitiable state of the Latin Empire of Constantinople. In response, Gregory decided to redirect a portion of the forthcoming crusade's strength to the defence of the city.[149] One element of this diversion was the implementation of extraordinary ecclesiastical taxation in Achaia so that the resulting funds could be sent to the defence of Constantinople. One of the three officials appointed to carry out this instruction was the preceptor of the Teutonic Knights in Romania, suggesting the ongoing role of the Order in this crusade.[150] Nevertheless, although Herman worked relentlessly to prevent conflict in the West, his mediation failed and, seemingly because of the war between papacy and Empire, the magnates of Germany did not contribute significantly to the Barons' Crusade.[151] In the Holy Land, the truce between the Ibelin and imperial factions broke down and so, in his last years, much of Herman's peacemaking proved unsuccessful. Nevertheless, his actions do seem to betray his general desire for peace across Christendom for the support of the Crusade.

Herman von Salza

Reviewing the evidence given here, it is clear that Herman was responsible for the considerable expansion of the Teutonic Order in material power, military strength and international prestige. His life is proof that an able and determined master was a crucial element in the success of a military order. Forey, commenting upon the rather limited successes of the Order of St Thomas of Acre, wrote 'it lacked a forceful and influential master'.[152] Under Herman, the Teutonic Knights had no such inhibitor. His conduct seems to have been guided by three overriding imperatives. Firstly, he worked relentlessly to defend Christendom. To this end he appears to have prioritised the Latin East; however, when troops could be spared from the kingdom of Jerusalem, he began wars of expansion in areas where the enemies of Christendom posed an imminent threat to the local Church, in Hungary, Prussia and Livonia. A symptom of this desire to defend such frontier zones can be seen in the charters which detail the concessions of land in these areas. When the Order acquired property in Hungary these lands were defined as 'versus Cumanos', or 'contra Cumanos'.[153] Similarly, in Prussia the brethren's posi-

---

148 See also Pacifico, 'I Teutonici tra papato e impero nel Mediterraneo al tempo di Federico II, 1215–1250', p. 125.
149 Lower, *The Barons' Crusade*, pp. 58–61.
150 *Reg. Grégoire IX*, vol. 2, no. 3408.
151 Lower, *The Barons' Crusade*, p. 41.
152 Forey, 'The Military Order of St Thomas of Acre', p. 503.
153 *Codex Diplomaticus Hungariae: Ecclesiasticus ac Civilis*, ed. G. Fejér, vol. 3 (Budapest, 1829), pp. 106–108, 116–117.

tion was described as 'contra Prutenos'.[154] The acquisition of these regions demonstrates Herman's commitment to the general defence of Christendom.

The second factor was the need to maintain peace among Christian princes and between the empire and the papacy in particular. The threat of war between Frederick II and the Church was a constant danger throughout Herman's life and he spent many years in mediation between these protagonists. Herman was evidently acutely aware that his Order, as a religious and imperial institution, sat uneasily on this political fault-line and was highly dependent upon both for patronage and protection. Furthermore, Herman's advocacy of crusade to the Holy Land and expansion into the Baltic was similarly reliant upon the accord between these powers.

Thirdly, Herman always sought to maximise every opportunity to win material wealth or spiritual benefits for his Order. In his efforts to fulfil these targets, Herman's actions speak of his skill, opportunism and diplomacy. Nevertheless, he was not ubiquitously successful and, as we shall see, the long-term weakness of his policies became apparent very swiftly after his death. Even so, he can still be credited with the transformation of a small-scale military order into a major international religious institution.

---

[154] *PU*, vol. 1.1, nos. 67, 78, 89, 102.

CHAPTER 5

Conrad von Thüringen, the Barons' Crusade and a Change of Policy

In 1238 Herman, now an old man, became ill and travelled to Salerno for his health. He died on 20 March 1239.[1] Shortly after his passing the Teutonic Knights were faced with two major dilemmas. Firstly, with the end of the truce in the Latin East and the final preparations for a new crusade, they were required to render assistance to the Holy Land. At the same time, however, they were locked in conflict with the Rus in Livonia. The Order's new master, therefore, needed to decide how he would divide his institution's material resources. The second problem concerned the ongoing issue of the Order's relative loyalties to the papacy and the empire. This matter rose again to the fore in 1239 when Gregory excommunicated Frederick, provoking a new war between these protagonists. The emperor responded by moving to acquire a stranglehold on the papacy through the submission of the Italian cities.[2] Once again the military orders were faced with a conflict of loyalties. To resolve this question, the Teutonic Order had to look to its new master, Conrad von Thüringen. Conrad's policy was very different from that of his predecessor and he shunned the previous position of diplomatic neutrality for one of allegiance to the empire, with significant consequences for the Holy Land.

Born in 1206, Conrad was the youngest son of Herman, landgrave of Thuringia.[3] After his father's death in 1217, Conrad's older brother Ludwig succeeded to the title. Ludwig died in 1227, shortly after embarking for the Holy Land, leaving a young son to succeed him. Conrad and his brother Henry then became regents for their nephew, who was still a minor. During this regency, the two brothers followed the tradition of their forefathers and became patrons of the Teutonic Knights.[4] A number of documents detailing

---

[1] For details of Herman von Salza's illness and death, see Richard of San Germano, *Chronica*, p. 376.

[2] Van Cleve, *The Emperor Frederick II*, pp. 427–454.

[3] This section has drawn on H. Boockmann, 'Konrad von Thüringen', in *Die Hochmeister des Deutschen Ordens 1190–1994*, QuStDO, 40 (Marburg, 1998), pp. 17–20; *Annales Breves Domus Ordinis Theutonici Marburgensis*, in *MGH SS*, vol. 30, p. 5.

[4] For the pre-history of relations between the landgraves of Thuringia and the Teutonic Order see chapter 1.

grants of property and privileges testify to their interest.[5] Conrad also intervened personally after the death of his sister-in-law Elizabeth to have her hospital foundation in Marburg conferred upon the Teutonic Knights instead of the Hospitallers, specifically against the stipulations of her will. They achieved this arrangement with the assistance of Gregory IX in 1234. Gregory subsequently ordered Elizabeth's canonisation. Given Conrad's close relationship with the Order, it is not surprising that in 1234 he chose to become a brother. A further factor which may have influenced this decision was the encouragement he is said to have received from Gregory IX.[6] It is also possible that this was an act of atonement. Previously, he had sacked and burned a church in the town of Fritzlar and massacred the inhabitants; subsequently, deeply repentant, he had sought absolution from the papacy. He also sought forgiveness from the people of Fritzlar and, dressed only in sackcloth, allowed them to beat him.[7] Conrad's evident consciousness of his own sin may provide another motive for his assumption of a religious life.

Conrad's election as master of the Order was, in many ways, inevitable. He was the most prestigious recruit the Order had ever accepted and his membership was a milestone in its development and prestige.[8] After all, Herman von Salza had been merely the son of a Thuringian *ministerialis* family, whilst Conrad was the son of the landgrave. Not only was Conrad closely connected to the papacy, but he also had strong ties to Frederick. Indeed, Boockman describes his family as among 'the most loyal and powerful allies of Frederick II'.[9] Conrad's brother Ludwig had been one of the few imperial nobles to accompany Frederick on his expedition to the Holy Land, although he died of disease shortly after leaving Italy (see p. 25). Conrad himself was Frederick's second cousin. His association with the Hohenstaufen family would only have been strengthened when, in May 1236, Frederick II travelled to Marburg to be present at the canonisation of Elizabeth.[10] Noblemen from across the empire attended this event and it was conducted with enormous ceremony. Conrad, now a brother of the Teutonic Order, was also present.[11]

Conrad's elevation to the position of master was especially significant because he had not held any important office within the Order previously, suggesting that his election was a result of his previous secular rank rather

5   Charter 1: *Urkundenbuch der Deutschordens-Ballei Hessen*, vol. 1, no. 24; *Regesta Thuringiae*, vol. 3, no. 218. Charter 2: *Regesta Thuringiae*, vol. 3, no. 219.
6   *Liber Cronicorum sive Annalis Erfordensis*, in *MGH SRG*, vol. 42, p. 756; Peter von Dusburg, *Chronicon Terrae Prussie*, p. 199.
7   *Annales Erphordenses Fratrum Praedicatorum*, in *MGH SRG*, vol. 42, p. 94–95; Peter von Dusburg, *Chronicon Terrae Prussie*, p. 198.
8   Boockmann, 'Konrad von Thüringen', pp. 17–20.
9   'Den treuesten und mächtigsten Verbündeten Kaiser Friedrich II'; Boockmann, 'Konrad von Thüringen', p. 20.
10   Abulafia, *Frederick II*, p. 247.
11   *Regesta Thuringiae*, vol. 3, no. 608.

than his work for the Order.[12] By 1239 the Teutonic Knights possessed a highly experienced grand commander and marshal (see Appendices E.1 and E.2) as well as many regional masters who would almost certainly have had a stronger grasp of the Order's organisational and strategic dispositions. Despite this, Conrad's high imperial rank and his previous association with Gregory may well have recommended him to the Order's electors at a time when Gregory and Frederick were at war.

After Conrad's appointment, the Order rapidly altered its political position, jettisoning its former policy of neutrality and adopting a new stance of allegiance to the emperor.[13] This decision, considering the Teutonic Knights' general political priorities, marks a distinct shift in their diplomatic stance. By 1239, the brethren's dependency upon the papacy had not diminished; indeed it was particularly acute because they were reliant upon Gregory to encourage the Dominicans to rally forces for their engagements in Prussia and Livonia.[14] Gregory evidently desired Conrad's support and it is interesting to note that he circulated the rumour at this time that the emperor had poisoned Conrad's brother Ludwig whilst on crusade, perhaps in an attempt to gain the support of Conrad and his brother Henry.[15] Despite this, on 11 June 1239, Gregory wrote a stinging letter to the Teutonic Knights expressing his disbelief that they should be opposing him.[16] In the same letter he stripped the brethren of their many privileges and liberties and threatened them with excommunication.[17] The cause for the pope's ire seems to have been Conrad's attendance at the Diet of Eger.[18] Frederick had summoned this Diet in June 1239 to discuss the political crisis, but was opposed by the papal legate, Albert of Behaim, who threatened to excommunicate anyone who offered support to the emperor. The Diet then began and the imperial princes agreed to make peace with the papacy. They decided to send Conrad as their representative to Rome, but his departure was delayed until April 1240.[19] Although no source actually states that Conrad attended the Diet, the fact that he was chosen as its emissary seems to suggest that he did take part. If this was the case then it would explain why the papacy issued its censure of the Order

---

[12] Boockmann, 'Konrad von Thüringen', p. 20; Arnold, 'Der Deutsche Orden zwischen Kaiser und Papst', p. 63.

[13] Historians have previously reached this conclusion; however they do not seem to find Conrad's political stance so surprising, Arnold, 'Der Deutsche Orden zwischen Kaiser und Papst', p. 63; *AZM*, p. 40.

[14] Maier, *Preaching the Crusades*, pp. 49–52.

[15] Matthew Paris, *Chronica Majora*, vol. 3, pp. 592–593.

[16] Arnold argues that events between the Order, the papacy and the empire did not reach a climax until after Conrad's death; however the letter of 11 June 1239 suggests that the Order fell from papal favour while Conrad was master. Arnold, 'Der Deutsche Orden zwischen Kaiser und Papst', p. 64.

[17] *Reg. Grégoire IX*, vol. 3, no. 4876; *MGH Epis. Saec. XIII*, vol. 1, no. 749.

[18] Van Cleve, *The Emperor Frederick II*, pp. 435.

[19] *Annales Erphordenses Fratrum Praedicatorum*, p. 98; *Cronica Reinhardsbrunnensis*, p. 617; HB, vol. 5, pp. 985–990.

in the same month that the Diet was summoned and also why the Teutonic Knights, like the other participants, were threatened with excommunication.

Conrad's reasons for joining the Diet are not clear; however, there are a number of factors that could provide an explanation. Firstly, his family was evidently closely connected to the Staufen and, although he was now the master of a religious order, such allegiances could not be ignored. His brother Henry attended and it is possible that this either generated or heightened a sense of family obligation.[20] Certainly, Conrad was still conscious of his former secular position and was still described in most correspondence as 'quondam lantgravius'.[21] Of course it is possible that Conrad attended the Diet without realising that such an act would anger the papacy to this extent and then, having been punished, sought to recover his position by acting as a peace emissary to the curia. This rather convoluted hypothesis does cover the facts; however, Conrad cannot be fully defended against allegations of a heightened allegiance to the emperor. Ultimately, Conrad had travelled to Eger and, whilst he may have underestimated the extent of Gregory's fury at this act, he must have known that it would anger the papacy. Furthermore, Conrad's subsequent embassy to the papacy failed to convince Gregory either to make peace or to restore the Order's privileges. Moreover, in the eastern Mediterranean theatre the Order altered its political stance and allied itself overtly to the imperial interest.

The Teutonic Knights in the Eastern Mediterranean, 1239–1243

By 1239, the struggle between the Ibelins and the imperial forces in the Holy Land had remained largely dormant for several years. In this year, however, old wounds reopened with outbreak of war between Frederick and Gregory and the arrival of a new crusade. This section will discuss the effects of the new pro-imperial position under both Conrad and his immediate successors until the fall of Tyre in 1243.[22]

During the Barons' Crusade, the Teutonic Knights seem to have exercised their peculiar talent for earning praise during crushing defeats, just as they did in the Fifth Crusade. On campaign, the brethren made a significant military contribution and they received accolades for their exploits. The most notable of these occurred in the aftermath of the defeat of a large raiding expedition led by Henry, count of Bar, and Amalric, count of Montfort, near Gaza on

---

20 HB, vol. 5, p. 987.
21 *Regesta Thuringiae*, vol. 3, no. 647.
22 There is some debate over whether the city of Tyre was taken in 1242 or 1243. It is not the purpose of this work to attempt to judge the validity of either claim and the year of 1243 will be employed because it is the better known of the two dates. For discussion see P. Jackson, 'The End of Hohenstaufen Rule in Syria', *Bulletin of the Institute of Historical Research*, 59 (1986), pp. 20–36; D. Jacoby, 'The Kingdom of Jerusalem and the Collapse of Hohenstaufen Power in the Levant', *Dumbarton Oaks Papers*, 40 (1986), pp. 83–101.

13 November 1239.[23] This force suffered heavy casualties after becoming trapped in a narrow valley by Egyptian troops. When news of the engagement reached the main encampment, the army prepared itself hurriedly for battle. It is claimed that the Teutonic Knights were the first to ready themselves and that they advanced against the Egyptians, seemingly unsupported, earning the respect of those present.[24]

In the aftermath of this defeat there arose the need to create a new treaty with the neighbouring Muslim powers that would protect the Latin East after the departure of the crusading armies. During the negotiations surrounding this agreement, the political allegiances which had previously divided the Holy Land asserted themselves to create two factions. The Ibelin family and their supporters, including the Templars and many of the magnates of the Latin East, wanted to make a treaty with al-Sālih Ismā'īl of Damascus. The imperial faction, supported by the Hospitallers who had become allies of the emperor by this time, favoured an agreement with al-Sālih Ayyūb of Egypt.[25] This issue split the crusading army and in the resulting confusion the Templars came to an understanding with the Damascenes and the Hospitallers made a truce with the Egyptians.[26] Shortly after the departure of the main crusading forces, a smaller expedition arrived led by Richard, earl of Cornwall. He was an imperial supporter and he later demonstrated his allegiance through the donation of Ascalon to the imperial forces.[27] Frederick II later ceded the city to the Hospitallers for their ongoing support.[28] Given his imperial bias it is not surprising that, after a certain amount of persuasion, Richard of Cornwall also confirmed the imperial forces' truce with Egypt.[29] The Templars responded to this by raiding into Egypt, seemingly in a direct attempt to jeopardise the agreement.[30] The struggle between the Ibelin and imperial factions continued from this point until 1243 when the last remaining imperial garrison was expelled from their stronghold in Tyre. It is significant that shortly after this final defeat the Templars signed a new treaty with Damascus, destroying the Hospitallers' pro-Egyptian policy.[31]

The Teutonic Knights' loyalty to the emperor at this time is demonstrated by their political stance during the formation of the treaties. They are said to

---

[23] Lower, *The Barons' Crusade*, pp. 168–170.
[24] Rothelin, pp. 546–547.
[25] Eracles, pp. 419–420; Sanuto, p. 216; *KSJJC*, pp. 177–179.
[26] Eracles, pp. 416–420; Matthew Paris, *Chronica Majora*, vol. 4, pp. 64–5.
[27] Eracles p. 421. The donation of Ascalon to the imperial forces is suggested by the fact that Frederick subsequently granted control of it to the Hospitallers, *CGJJ*, vol. 2, no. 2301. Note also that Richard was a longstanding imperial supporter and there are examples of the emperor bestowing gifts upon him: see Matthew Paris, *Chronica Majora*, vol. 3, p. 369. He was also present at Frederick's council at Vaucouleurs in June 1237; ibid., vol. 3, p. 393. For subsequent relations, see ibid., vol. 4, pp. 146–7.
[28] *CGJJ*, vol. 2, no. 2301.
[29] Matthew Paris, *Chronica Majora*, vol. 4, p. 139–144. He is also said to have been accompanied in the early stages of the expedition by a Hospitaller prior named Theodoric; ibid., vol. 4, p. 44.
[30] Matthew Paris, *Chronica Majora*, vol. 4, p. 197.
[31] For details of this treaty see Matthew Paris, *Chronica Majora*, vol. 4, p. 289. *KSJJC*, p. 180.

have supported the agreement with Egypt and, in so doing, placed themselves in opposition to the Templars and the Ibelins. This position is indicated both in a letter written in 1244 and by an attack made by the Templars upon the possessions of the Hospitallers and Teutonic Knights in Acre in 1241, specifically in retribution for this treaty. The Teutonic Knights' imperial allegiance is emphasised by Matthew Paris, who claims that this attack was made specifically to spite the emperor.[32] After the imperial defeat of 1243, the Teutonic Order and the Hospitallers counselled against the treaty with Damascus, once again in conformity with imperial policy.[33]

A further indication of their altered loyalties – and incidentally of the comparative strength of the Latin East at this time – is a transaction between the brethren and Philip of Maugustel. Philip was an imperial supporter who had staunchly supported Frederick's interests in the Holy Land and had even been nominated as bailli in the kingdom of Jerusalem by the emperor in 1233.[34] In 1241 he gave the village of Corsy to the brethren, which serves as further proof of their loyalties.[35] A further matter of interest is the location of this village on the south-eastern corner of Lake Tiberias (see appendix B). This seems to suggest that the influence of the kingdom of Jerusalem had recovered sufficiently to encompass this eastern region. Admittedly, it is possible that Corsy was still in Muslim hands, but even if it was, this gift may still represent an expectation that the kingdom of Jerusalem would expand to a point where this village could become profitable.

After the fall of Tyre in 1243, there appear to have been repercussions for the Order's complicity with the defeated imperial party. One element of these took the form of a legal case conducted against the brethren's landholdings. As shown in chapter 2, in 1220 the Order bought a number of estates from Beatrix, daughter of Joscelin III of Courtney.[36] The problem was that Beatrix had been one of two heiresses to this patrimony and, on a thin legal precedent, she had both overridden and sold her sister Agnes's inheritance. In 1226 and 1229, the Order had come to an accommodation with Agnes's son, Jacob of Amigdala, in which a portion of their lands were granted back to him. Even so, Jacob reopened this matter in 1244 and on 7 July he was granted a sizeable parcel of land and also an income from the Order's taxa-

---

32 Matthew Paris, *Chronica Majora*, vol. 4, pp. 167–168. Nicholson has cast doubt on the accuracy of Matthew Paris's account; H. Nicholson, 'Steamy Syrian Scandals: Matthew Paris on the Templars and Hospitallers', *Medieval History*, 2 (1992), p. 75. Despite this, there is apparent confirmation that the Teutonic Order's house *was* attacked by the Templars because the *Continuatio Garstensis* also refers to it; *Continuatio Garstensis*, in *MGH SS*, vol. 9, p. 597. Thus Matthew Paris's evidence, in so far as it relates to the Teutonic Knights, is accepted.

33 Matthew Paris, *Chronica Majora*, vol. 4, pp. 302. Bulst has suggested that the Order supported the Templars during this period, yet the Templars' hostility and the Teutonic Knights' continued support of a treaty with Egypt in 1243 argues against this, M. Bulst, 'Zur Geschichte der Ritterorden und des Königsreichs Jerusalem im 13. Jahrhundert bis zur Schlacht bei La Forbie am 17. Okt. 1244', *Deutsches Archiv für Erforschung des Mittelalters*, 22 (1966), p. 216.

34 Riley-Smith, *Feudal Nobility*, p. 201–203.

35 *TOT*, no. 90.

36 Here I follow Mayer, 'Die Seigneurie de Joscelin und der Deutsche Orden', pp. 192–215.

tion revenues from the port and markets of Acre.[37] Given that Tyre had fallen in July of the previous year, it is possible that Jacob had seen an opportunity in the Order's subsequent political vulnerability.

Relations with the Hospitallers

During the Barons' Crusade a strong association formed between the Teutonic Knights and the Hospitallers. This is significant not merely because it is symptom of their shared imperial loyalties but also because of the formerly turbulent relations between these institutions.

The first disagreement between these establishments began in 1190. At this time, the Hospitallers claimed that they should control the new Teutonic Hospital.[38] The Hospitallers founded this demand on their belief that the Teutonic Hospital was a continuation of the earlier German Hospital in Jerusalem (established c.1118). In 1143 and 1190 the papacy had issued documents which gave the Hospitallers authority over this older institution and therefore they believed that they had rights over the Teutonic Knights.[39] At the time, these demands then forced the Teutonic Order to seek protection from the Templars (see chapter 2). By 1198, the Hospitallers' ire had subsided sufficiently for them to allow the Teutonic Order to use elements of their rule at the time of its militarisation in 1198. Later, both orders supported the Armenians during their long war with Antioch (see chapter 2).[40] It may be that this unity of purpose allowed old grudges to subside and certainly they worked together during the preparations for the Fifth Crusade and Frederick's crusade. A further indication of improved relations occurred in 1208 when Otto, count of Henneburg and a *confrater* of the Hospitallers, made a donation to the Order.[41] In 1220 the Teutonic Knights purchased the Castellum Regis estate from Otto.

During Frederick's crusade the situation changed. The Hospitallers demanded that the pope confirm their perceived entitlement to control the Teutonic Knights. Gregory IX initially agreed to this and issued the requisite document, although there is no evidence to suggest that the Hospitallers were ever able to act upon it.[42] The Hospitallers' motives in making this claim are difficult to distinguish, particularly given the long period of cordial relations between the orders. The sources are not conclusive on this point although the

---

[37] *TOT*, nos. 98–90.
[38] *La Continuation de Guillaume de Tyr*, p. 99.
[39] For the 1143 concession see *CGJJ*, vol. 1, nos. 154–155. For the 1190 concession see *Papsturkunden für Templer und Johanniter: Neue Folge*, ed. R. Hiestand (Göttingen, 1984), no. 101; it was renewed in 1254; *CGJJ*, vol. 2, no. 2674. Forstreuter has cast doubt over the reliability of the latter of these two documents although the veracity of the former is undisputed; Forstreuter, *Der Deutsche Orden am Mittelmeer*, pp. 29–34.
[40] Riley-Smith, 'The Templars and the Teutonic Knights in Cilician Armenia', p. 111.
[41] For Otto's status as a *confrater* see *CGJJ*, vol. 2, no. 1313. For his gift, *TOT*, no. 43.
[42] *CGJJ*, vol. 2, no. 1944.

Annales Marbacenses suggest that the Hospitallers may have been angered because Frederick favoured the advice of Herman von Salza over that of the Hospitaller master.[43] Riley-Smith has speculated that the Hospitallers may have resented the endowments made by Frederick to the Teutonic Knights during his crusade.[44] The Hospitallers may also, in a similar way to the Templars, have been taking advantage of the Order's vulnerability during its period under papal censure. Favreau has advanced the further explanation that Frederick's concession of the Old German Hospital in Jerusalem to the Teutonic Knights in 1229 prompted these demands.[45] Whatever their true motives, the Hospitallers' hostility was not to last and in 1231 the Teutonic Order was asked to act as the intermediary for the return of the Hospitaller lands on Sicily.[46] As Riley-Smith has suggested, the co-operation of the two orders in this agreement appears to indicate that this dispute had ended.[47]

The first evidence for the restoration of relations can be found in April 1239 when the Hospitallers granted the Teutonic Knights a portion of a village named Noie in the kingdom of Jerusalem in return for an annual tribute.[48] Later the following year the Hospitallers promised to protect the Teutonic Knights' village of Arabia, which had been granted to them in 1234, in return for a financial consideration.[49] In 1241 the brethren acted as mediators for the Hospitallers in their dealings with Antioch.[50] As shown above, both institutions also supported the imperial policy in the Holy Land at this time and they were both attacked by the Templars in 1241. Whether it was their shared imperial allegiances or some other factor that provoked this improved relationship is unclear; however, their common loyalties would have played their part. Nevertheless, the Teutonic Knights' relationship with the Hospitallers was complicated by the intervention of the papacy in 1240. In January of this year Gregory strengthened his previous condemnation of June 1239 and commanded once again that the Order should accept the authority of the Hospitallers.[51] In March 1241, the pope, unimpressed by Conrad's embassy on behalf of the imperial princes in April 1240, insisted that the brethren send delegates to Rome to explain why they had not submitted to the Hospitallers.[52] These charters are significant for two reasons. Firstly they demonstrate the continuation of the papacy's wrath. Secondly, they seem at

---

43 *Annales Marbacenses*, p. 93.
44 *KSJJC*, p. 397.
45 Favreau-Lilie, 'L'Ordine Teutonico in Terrasanta (1198–1291)', p. 64; Favreau, *Studien zur Früh-geschichte des Deutschen Ordens*, pp. 89–91.
46 *CGJJ*, vol. 2, no. 1982; HB, vol. 3, pp. 280–282.
47 *KSJJC*, pp. 397–398.
48 Forstreuter, *Der Deutsche Orden am Mittelmeer*, pp. 24–25; *TOT*, no. 87. Charter 1: Prutz, 'Eilf Deutschordensurkunden aus Venedig und Malta', p. 388. Charter 2: *TOT*, no. 87; *CGJJ*, vol. 2, no. 2224.
49 *R. Reg.*, vol.1, no. 1097; *TOT*, no. 89; *CGJJ*, vol. 2. no. 2245.
50 *CGJJ*, vol. 2. no. 2280.
51 *CGJJ*, vol. 2, no. 2247.
52 *CGJJ*, vol. 2, no. 2270.

variance with the Knights' burgeoning relationship with the Hospitallers. It is notable, for example, that Gregory issued his first charter on this issue in 1240, yet in the same year the two orders came to an agreement over the village of Arabia.[53] Similarly the second papal charter was issued in March 1241, yet in November 1241 the Teutonic Knights assisted the Hospitallers in Antioch.[54] There is clearly a disparity here between the growing co-operation between the two orders and the papacy's insistence that the Teutonic Order submit to the Hospitallers.

Forstreuter has interpreted this evidence to suggest that the initiative for these demands of subordination came solely from the papacy and that relations between the Hospitallers and Teutonic Knights remained cordial throughout.[55] Subsequently, Favreau disputed this conclusion by claiming that the evidence was indicative instead of hostile relations between the Orders. She argues that the negotiations over the village of Noie imply that there had been a previous dispute between the institutions and that the agreement over Arabia was similarly hostile. Only in the case of the 1241 dealings in Antioch does she accept that there is evidence of positive relations.[56]

Regarding the village of Noie, Favreau seems to be correct. This document does seem to conclude a previous dispute and, as she noted, this may have resulted from Noie's connection to the Seigneurie of Joscelin.[57] Despite this, the fact that two institutions could agree to a compromise does not imply that they were hostile to one another at the time of the agreement. As for the village of Arabia, the 1240 agreement stipulated that 5,000 bezants would be paid to the Hospitallers by the Teutonic Knights from the income of the village in return for the Hospitallers' support and protection. Superficially, this might possibly imply the existence of hostile negotiations (although a localised dispute does not necessarily suggest generally antagonistic relations); however, a wider appreciation of the context can alter this judgement. The Teutonic Order purchased Arabia from Bertrand Porcelet and Isabella of Bethsan in 1234, during the Ibelin–Lombard war.[58] Isabella was the mother of Amaury Barlais, one of the Five Baillis, and her husband was also an imperial supporter. Consequently, at the close of the civil war, any property negotiations conducted previously by such people could be in jeopardy. The brethren had evidently known, from the first, that there were legal entanglements surrounding this village because they requested an unusual quantity of charters confirming its purchase. These were acquired from Richard Filangieri in

---

[53] *R. Reg.*, vol. 1, no. 1097; *TOT*, no. 89; *CGJJ*, vol. 2, no. 2245.
[54] *CGJJ*, vol. 2, no. 2280.
[55] Forstreuter, *Der Deutsche Orden am Mittelmeer*, pp. 24–25.
[56] Favreau, *Studien zur Frühgeschichte des Deutschen Ordens*, pp. 92–93.
[57] Favreau, *Studien zur Frühgeschichte des Deutschen Ordens*, p. 93.
[58] *TOT*, no. 77.

1234,[59] Frederick II in 1235,[60] John Barlais in 1236[61] and Bohemond IV of Antioch also in 1236.[62] The brethren's ownership of the fief was contested at a later date by Isabella's grandson, Aimery.[63] Given the precarious nature of the Order's hold on Arabia, the purchase of support and protection from the Hospitallers was entirely in accordance with their efforts to secure this acquisition. Moreover, if such an agreement was to function effectively it would require a positive relationship between the two institutions. Consequently, the resolution over Arabia does not imply antipathy; indeed, it implies quite the reverse because the Order needed an ally to help protect its fief. Thus, Favreau's objections can be nuanced or removed, leaving Forstreuter's original argument unaffected. Also the contention that relations between the two orders were positive and that the Hospitallers played no part in Gregory's insistence upon the subordination of the Teutonic Knights can be accepted.[64] If this was the case, then evidently the papacy had not only ceased to protect the Order, but was actually using the Hospitallers' previous demands for jurisdiction as a weapon.

The events of 1239–1243 seem to confirm the wisdom of Herman von Salza's previous policy of neutrality. By supporting the emperor the brethren may have won a new ally in the Hospitallers but they had also incurred the wrath of the Levantine barons, the Templars and the papacy. The loss of Gregory IX's support in 1239 must have been a particularly heavy blow. The brethren required his help not merely to maintain their privileges but also to uphold their interests in Prussia and Livonia. Moreover, the papacy had previously defended the Order against the ambitions and demands of other religious institutions and prelates. After the removal of the brethren's privileged status in 1239, the papacy received letters from many regions including Morea,[65] Trier[66] and Prussia,[67] each making accusations or describing ways in

---

59   *TOT*, no. 78.
60   *TOT*, no. 79.
61   *TOT*, no. 81.
62   *TOT*, no, 82.
63   *TOT*, no. 106; Riley-Smith, *Feudal Nobility*, pp. 188–189.
64   This does not imply that the Hospitallers had forgotten their perceived rights over the Teutonic Knights and in 1258, during a general agreement of co-operation between the three major orders, the Hospitallers ensured that the issue of their authority over the Teutonic Knights was kept separate; Favreau, *Studien zur Frühgeschichte des Deutschen Ordens*, pp. 93–94; Favreau-Lilie, 'L'Ordine Teutonico in Terrasanta (1198–1291)', p. 64. Also, as Favreau has pointed out, in 1254 the papal charter which confirmed the Hospitallers claims over the Teutonic Hospital was renewed (1190 charter, *Papsturkunden für Templer und Johanniter: Neue Folge*, no. 101; 1254 charter: *CGJJ*, vol. 2, no. 2674). Despite this, in 1240 it seems unlikely, given the positive and co-dependent relations existing between the orders, that the Hospitallers would have antagonised the Teutonic Knights at this time. For the 1258 charter see *TOT*, no. 116; *CGJJ*, vol. 2, no. 2902.
65   *Reg. Grégoire IX*, vol. 3, no. 4917. For further discussion of the punishment of the Teutonic Knights at this time see Nicholson, *Templars, Hospitallers and Teutonic Knights*, p. 26.
66   *Urkundenbuch zur Geschichte der, jetzt die Preussischen Regierungsbezirke Coblenz und Trier bildenden Mittelrheinischen Territorien*, ed. L. Eltester, A. Goerz et al., vol. 3 (Koblenz, 1874), no. 672.
67   *PU*, vol. 1.1, no. 134.

which the Order's freedoms had been curbed. When the Teutonic Knights were subsequently restored to favour, the new pope, Innocent IV, was compelled to issue a charter explicitly protecting them from the assaults of the clergy and laity.[68] In these ways, the immense dependency of the brethren upon the papacy and the consequences of abusing its trust were laid bare for a second time. Back in 1239, Conrad may not initially have sought to alienate Gregory, but he had moved the Order into a relationship of greater co-operation with Frederick at a crucial and sensitive time. His subsequent attempts to make peace failed and the transmission of this policy to the Holy Land caused further damage. Conrad died shortly after his embassy on 24 July 1240 with the Teutonic Knights still languishing under apostolic censure. He was buried in Marburg.[69]

---

[68] *TOT*, no. 503. This was a reaffirmation of an earlier grant; *TOT*, no. 379.
[69] Peter von Dusburg, *Chronicon Terrae Prussie*, p. 198; Perlbach, 'Deutsch-Ordens Necrologe', pp. 358–359.

CHAPTER 6

Dependence and Independence

If a kingdom is divided against itself, that kingdom cannot stand.
(Mark 3:24.)

Conrad von Thüringen disturbed the Teutonic Knights' political equilib-rium and began a new phase in their relationship with the papacy and the empire. Conrad's successors continually shifted their stance on this issue, drawing criticism on the brethren from all quarters and exacerbating internal divisions. The turbulence of the Teutonic Knights' relations with Christian rulers was aggravated further in the 1240s by a series of battlefield defeats: in the Latin East against the Egyptians and Khwarazmians, in Prussia and Livonia against the Rus and Pagans and in Poland against the Mongols. These stretched the brethren's resources beyond their capabilities, demonstrating the inherent weakness of their strategic dispositions.

To find the root of the problems faced by the Teutonic Order during this period, it necessary to look back at the policy of Herman von Salza. In *c.*1210, Herman had become master at a fortuitous moment. He had inherited a nucleus of knights who were bound to defend the Holy Land. The Latin East itself was frequently covered by truces. During these periods of peace, Herman had been free to engage his knights in other regions. In 1211, for example, the truce between John of Brienne and the Egyptians permitted Herman to use his troops to develop the Order's interests in Hungary for six years. Having achieved a degree of stability in that region, he and the king of Hungary then participated in the Fifth Crusade. After this expedition, with the establishment of a ten-year treaty, Herman was able to turn his attention to the recruitment of a new crusade for the emperor. During Frederick's ensuing expedition a further ten-year armistice was arranged, which enabled Herman to send contingents to Prussia and later to Livonia, while the Holy Land was secure from external attack. Several historians have noted that, although the Teutonic Knights were granted rights in Prussia in 1220s, Herman waited until 1230 to send his main colonising force.[1] These historians seem correct in their conclusion that Herman wished to dedicate himself to the prepara-

---

[1]   Hubatsch, 'Der Deutsche Orden und die Reichlehnschaft über Cypern', pp. 261, 274; Urban, *The Prussian Crusade*, p. 46.

tions for Frederick's crusade and then to wait for the ensuing peace to launch the Prussian enterprise. The principle of re-deploying an Order's soldiers to other regions during a time of peace was not a new one. In 1205, Innocent III ordered the Castilian branch of the Order of Calatrava to travel to Aragon while Castile was covered by a truce so that their knights might not lie idle.[2] Even so, Herman seems to have implemented this strategy to great effect. This worked very well for the establishment of new territories and helped Herman to employ his knights consistently in the defence of Christendom.

The problem with this policy was that it only worked while the Order possessed the initiative. Herman had been able to decide when he wished to stage his military campaigns in Hungary, Prussia and Livonia because, with the Holy Land covered by a truce, he had been free to use his troops as he wished. Having acquired these new territories, however, the brethren were bound to defend them and could no longer neatly timetable their military activities to coincide with the business of the Latin East. Increasingly, as the Teutonic Knights began to suffer from rebellions and foreign invasions in Prussia and Livonia, they were forced onto the defensive and were often engaged simultaneously on a number of fronts, becoming reactive rather than pro-active. In 1239, for example, they made a major contribution to the Barons' Crusade whilst fighting simultaneously against the Rus in Livonia. Nevertheless, the first serious test for the Order came between 1241 and 1244. In 1241 the Mongols invaded Hungary and Poland where they destroyed the local infrastructure and ruthlessly defeated every army sent against them.[3] Further south, in response to the Mongol invasion, the Prussian master, Poppo von Osterna, is thought to have led a band of knights to support the Christian armies against the Mongols.[4] In Livonia the Order's forces were defeated by Alexander Nevsky at the battle of Lake Pepius 1242.[5] In all cases the Order's forces suffered heavy losses. In the wake of these defeats, the Prussian territories rose in rebellion under their leader Swantopelk.[6] Consequently, by 1242, the Order in the Baltic was in tatters, heavily defeated and fighting for its very existence.

These concerns were only compounded by a further threat to the Holy Land from the Khwarazmians. Before their descent upon Eastern Christendom, the Mongols had conquered the Empire of Khwārazm-shāh in central Asia and compelled the remnants of its people to flee west towards the Levant. This naturally posed a threat to the Latin East and the papacy had been aware

---

[2] *La Documentacion Pontificia Hasta Innocencio III*, ed. D. Mansilla (Rome, 1955), no. 321.
[3] For details of this invasion see J. Chambers, *The Devil's Horsemen: The Mongol Invasion of Europe* (London, 2003).
[4] I. Fonnesberg-Schmidt, *The Popes and the Baltic Crusades: 1147–1254*, The Northern World, 26 (Leiden, 2007), p. 232; K. Militzer, 'Poppo von Osterna', in *Die Hochmeister des Deutschen Ordens 1190–1994*, QuStDO, 40 (Marburg, 1998), pp. 27–29.
[5] *Livländische Reimchronik*, pp. 51–53.
[6] Peter von Dusburg, *Chronicon Terrae Prussie*, p. 66.

of this migration from as early as 1230.[7] The Muslim rulers of the Levant were similarly concerned about the Khwarazmians and the Egyptian sultan, al-Sālih Ayyūb, signed a treaty of co-operation with them.[8] After this alliance, the Khwarazmians invaded Christian territory and sacked Jerusalem on 23 August 1244.[9] They then joined forces with the Egyptian army. In response, the field army of the kingdom of Jerusalem and the soldiers of the sultan of Damascus engaged this force on 17 October 1244 at the battle of La Forbie.[10] The encounter was a crushing defeat for the Christian/Damascene army that was comparable in scale to Hattin in 1187.[11]

The Teutonic Knights incurred enormous casualties at La Forbie, with only three survivors from a total mounted force of 400.[12] When considering such losses it is necessary to stress that the Order would not merely have lost only its brother knights in this encounter but also its turcopoles, mercenaries, *confratres* and infantry along with their arms, camp equipment and horses. Given that the cost of equipping a single Hospitaller knight in the kingdom of Jerusalem in 1262 was deemed to be 2,000 *deniers* of Tours, it might well be imagined how much money would be required to rebuild the Teutonic Order's entire field army.[13] The Templars and Hospitallers suffered similarly heavy casualties.[14] In the aftermath of this battle the Khwarazmians raided throughout the Latin East and besieged Ascalon for over two years.[15] The long recovery of the Holy Land was over and the carefully prepared forces of the Teutonic Knights had been shattered in a single day.

By 1244 – only five years after Herman's death – the Teutonic Knights had suffered comprehensive defeats on three fronts. The retention of their scattered territories had proved onerous indeed and the cost of rebuilding would

---

7   Ross, 'Relations between the Latin East and Western Europe', p. 52.
8   Al-Maqrīzī, *A History of the Ayyūbid Sultans of Egypt*, trans. R. J. C. Broadhurst (Boston, 1980), pp. 272–273.
9   Ibn al-Furāt, *Ayyubids, Mamlukes and Crusaders: Selections from the Tārīkh al-Duwal wa'l-Mulūk*, ed. and trans. U. and M. C. Lyons, intro. J. S. C. Riley-Smith, vol. 2 (Cambridge, 1971), p. 3.
10 For accounts of the capture of Jerusalem see Matthew Paris, *Chronica Majora*, vol. 4, pp. 300–311; Rothelin, pp. 562–563.
11 For accounts of the battle of La Forbie see Matthew Paris, *Chronica Majora*, pp. 301–307, 307–311, 337–344; Eracles, pp. 427–429; Rothelin, p. 564; *Annales Sancti Pantaleonis Coloniensis*, in *MGH SS*, vol. 22, p. 539; Abdul Aziz al-Khowayter, 'A Critical Edition of an Unknown Source for the Life of al-Malik al-Zahir Bairbars', vol. 2 (unpublished PhD thesis, University of London, School of Oriental and African Studies, 1960), p. 317; Al-Maqrīzī, *A History of the Ayyūbid Sultans of Egypt*, p. 275; Salimbene de Adam, *Cronica*, ed. G. Scalia, vol. 1 (Bari, 1966), p. 255.
12 The figure of three survivors can be found in a letter of Frederick II in Matthew Paris, *Chronica Majora*, vol. 4, pp. 301, 337–344; Rothelin, p. 564. For discussion concerning the accuracy of the figure of 400 cavalry, see chapter 8.
13 Selwood, *Knights of the Cloister*, p. 119; *CGJJ*, vol. 3, no. 3039 (p. 49).
14 References to the number of survivors from the Templars and Hospitallers can be found in Salimbene of Adam, *Cronica*, vol. 1, p. 255; Matthew Paris, *Chronica Majora*, vol. 4, pp. 301, 307–311, 337–344; Rothelin, p. 564.
15 Ascalon eventually fell on the 15 October 1247. For accounts of the siege of Ascalon see Ibn al-Furāt, *Ayyubids, Mamlukes and Crusaders*, vol. 1, p. 8; Rothelin, pp. 564–565.

be enormous. Furthermore, faced with defeat in Livonia, rebellion in Prussia and invasion in the Latin East, the brethren's overstretched resources were required on many frontiers. They were committed in all these regions and Herman's policy of operating in one region at a time was no longer viable. Bronstein has demonstrated how the Hospitallers were forced to react to battlefield defeats in the Holy Land, such as at al-Mansūra and La Forbie, with irregular and often sweeping reforms to their properties in Western Christendom. At this point, however, the Teutonic Order needed to respond to multiple defeats almost simultaneously.[16]

The Order's strategic situation was compounded by the continuing struggle between the papacy and the empire. In 1243, while Frederick's forces encircled Rome, Sinibald Fiesco was appointed as Pope Innocent IV.[17] Initially it seemed as though this new appointment might help to create peace between empire and papacy; however, it was not long before the situation deteriorated into war. In 1244 a settlement was agreed between these parties, but it was not to last. In March 1244 Innocent fled from Rome to Genoa and then to France where he excommunicated the emperor for a second time at the council of Lyons in May 1245.[18] At this council, the pope suggested to Landgrave Henry of Thuringia (the brother of Conrad, master of the Teutonic Order) that he should become anti-king and oppose Frederick. After some procrastination Henry accepted this appointment in 1246.[19] The war continued and Henry defeated Frederick II's son, Conrad of Hohenstaufen, in battle, although he died shortly afterwards.[20] Subsequently, William of Holland was appointed as a new anti-king and the struggle for Italy and Germany continued. In 1247 the city of Parma fell to papal forces and Frederick moved quickly against it. Frederick began to besiege the city but was then decisively defeated by a sortie. The war continued until 1249 when Frederick became ill. He died in 1250.

Faced with this variety of challenges, the Order appointed a new leader, Gerhard von Malberg, sometime between late 1240 and early 1241.[21] He was the son of Lord Theodoric of Are and Agnes of Malberg and he had previously been married before he joined the Order. Gerhard had formerly held the post of marshal and is known to have been in the Holy Land in 1240 (see appendix E.1).[22] Given that Conrad von Thüringen spent much of 1239–1240 in Italy, it seems likely that Gerhard had commanded the Order's forces during the

---

16 Bronstein, *The Hospitallers and the Holy Land*, pp. 103–133.
17 Van Cleve, *The Emperor Frederick II*, pp. 455–522.
18 For the council of Lyons see *Decrees of the Ecumenical Councils*, vol. 1, pp. 273–301.
19 Matthew Paris, *Chronica Majora*, vol. 4, p. 544.
20 Matthew Paris, *Chronica Majora*, vol. 4, p. 545.
21 This section has drawn on U. Arnold, 'Gerhard von Malberg', in *Die Hochmeister des Deutschen Ordens 1190–1994*, QuStDO, 40 (Marburg, 1998), pp. 22–23.
22 *TOT*, no. 89.

Barons' Crusade because, according to the Teutonic Knights' statutes, it was the marshal's role to lead the Order's host while the master was absent.[23]

Shortly after Gerhard's election, he moved to end the rift between the Order and the papacy. With the defeat of the Order's forces on multiple battlefields, this was certainly not the time for controversy with Rome. Fortunately for Gerhard, these invasions and rebellions also threatened the papacy and so it was in both their interests to make peace.[24] Accordingly, at the behest of the emperor, Gerhard travelled to Rome to congratulate Innocent on his appointment.[25] In the autumn of 1243, Gerhard restored relations with the papacy and on 1 October he took an oath of loyalty which was rewarded symbolically with a ring.[26] One week earlier Innocent had authorised the Dominicans to preach a new crusade through the papal bull *Qui iustis causis* for the support of the brethren in the Baltic.[27] From this point, many of the Order's privileges were restored and a number of new powers were conferred.[28]

Militzer has claimed that Gerhard 'tried to change the Order's policy in siding with the pope more strongly than before'.[29] Although Gerhard undoubtedly sought reconciliation with Innocent IV, it seems likely that his actions were driven more by a pragmatic desire to make peace and protect his Order's territories in Prussia and Livonia than any wish to take sides in the war between empire and papacy. Certainly, the brethren made sure that they remained in favour with the emperor. As shown above, it was upon Frederick's orders that Gerhard went to the papacy in 1243.[30] In the same year Frederick's son, Conrad, issued a series of charters that confirmed the Order's privileges.[31] Also, Gerhard supported imperial policy in the Holy Land in 1243 by advocating the retention of the kingdom of Jerusalem's treaty with Egypt (see chapter 5). Given the exigencies of the time, Gerhard's diplomatic efforts make perfect sense and would have helped to consolidate the Order's position in the face of external threats.[32]

Gerhard's new policy was cut short in 1244 when he was forced to abdicate and transfer to the Templars. The overt reason for this act was said to have been his personal debts.[33] This conclusion has been disputed by Militzer who has claimed that the cause was his 'friendly relationship with the pope'.[34]

---

23 *SDO*, p. 103.

24 Peter von Dusburg, *Chronicon Terrae Prussie*, p. 67.

25 HB, vol. 6, pp. 104–105; *CDOT*, no. 110.

26 See *PU*, vol. 1.1, no. 147. There is a possible reference to this ring in the *Livländische Reimchronik* (p. 100) which speaks of the master passing on a ring to the next master.

27 *PU*, vol. 1.1, no. 146; Fonnesberg-Schmidt, *The Popes and the Baltic Crusades*, pp. 225–226.

28 For examples see *PU*, vol. 1.1, nos. 142–144, 148–152, 154–157; *TOT*, nos. 470–480.

29 Militzer, 'From the Holy Land to Prussia', p. 73. Houben similarly describes Gerhard as 'antistaufischen'; H. Houben, 'Die Landkomture der Deutschordensballei Apulien', *Sacra Militia: Rivista di storia degli ordini militari* 4 (2001), p. 124.

30 Richard of San Germano, *Chronica*, p. 382; HB, vol. 6, pp. 104–105; *CDOT*, no. 110.

31 *TOT*, nos. 93–97.

32 Arnold, 'Gerhard von Malberg', p. 22.

33 *TOT*, nos. 484–486; *AZM*, p. 41.

34 Militzer, 'From the Holy Land to Prussia', p. 73.

However, Militzer's arguments are challenged by the above evidence. Moreover, there is considerable evidence to support the original contention that he resigned through financial difficulties. Firstly, the sum he owed was of such magnitude that a papal charter was necessary to free the brethren from the amount outstanding.[35] The Order was also forced to pay an additional 400 marks to cover some of the loans and there are references to the brethren being compelled to sell property in Germany to cover other repayments.[36] Gerhard was certainly not the first master of a military order to resign through financial difficulties. In 1170 Gilbert of Assailly, master of the Hospitallers, abdicated seemingly because of the debts he had incurred during the invasion of Egypt in 1169 by Amalric I (king of Jerusalem, 1163–1174), although admittedly Gilbert's debts were institutional not personal.[37] Militzer has accused Gerhard of weakness of character, yet, given the constraints of contemporary events, it seems more likely that he acted with prudence and some foresight in his attempt to reconcile the Order with the papacy. He cannot, however, be excused from the repercussions of his personal finances.[38]

In 1244 Gerhard's successor, Heinrich von Hohenlohe, redrew the Order's political stance by returning to a position of allegiance to Frederick II and alienating Pope Innocent IV. Heinrich was the son of a noble family that was first documented in the twelfth century. He is thought to have been born between 1195 and 1200 and to have joined the Order in 1219, along with his brothers Andreas and Frederick.[39] Initially he was placed in charge of the commandery at Mergentheim and he became the German master in 1232 (see appendix C).[40] The origins of Heinrich's imperial loyalties have been traced by Militzer who argues that he 'was a member of a Frankish family traditionally friendly to the Hohenstaufen'.[41] After his election in Acre in 1244, Heinrich travelled to the West and represented Frederick II at the council of Lyons in 1245, where he attempted to regain the emperor's lost interests in the Holy Land.[42] Given that Frederick was excommunicated at Lyons, this action would have implicated Heinrich with the imperial party in the subsequent war. The emperor rewarded the Order's loyalty with patronage

---

[35] *TOT*, no. 486.

[36] *TOT*, no. 486. *CDOT*, no. 121.

[37] William of Tyre, *Chronicon*, vol. 2, pp. 917–918; Burgtorf, *The Central Convent of Hospitallers and Templars*, pp. 65–74.

[38] *AZM*, p. 41.

[39] This section has drawn on Arnold, 'Heinrich von Hohenlohe', pp. 24–26.

[40] Heinrich was German master between 1232 and 1242. There is some discussion as to whether there were periods when he was sent to perform other duties, see Arnold, 'Heinrich von Hohenlohe', p. 24; K. Militzer, *Die Entstehung der Deutschordensballeien im Deutschen Reich*, QuStDO, 16 (Bonn, 1970), pp. 44–49.

[41] Militzer, 'From the Holy Land to Prussia', p. 73. An example of the relationship between the Hohenlohe family and Frederick II can be found in the grant made to Conrad von Hohenlohe of income from the tax returns of Acre during Frederick's crusade in the Latin East; *R. Reg.*, vol. 1, no. 1008; *AOL*, vol. 2, pp. 166–167 (documents).

[42] *Cronica de Mailros*, p. 174; *AZM*, p. 42; HB, vol. 6, pp. 266–267.

and issued several vitally important documents concerning its position in Prussia.[43]

Innocent evidently wished to censure the brethren for their actions but his reprimands took a very different form from Gregory IX's previous denunciations in 1239 and 1240. The invasions of 1241 and the defeat at La Forbie in 1244 had subtly changed the relationship between the papacy and the Teutonic Order. Where previously the Order had been highly dependent upon Rome, by 1245 this relationship had changed to one approaching co-dependence. In the Baltic theatre, Innocent needed to prepare for a second Mongol onslaught and his fears of invasion were only confirmed by the reports of the emissaries he sent to the Mongol leaders. These agents revealed the scale of the Mongol war-machine and the suitability of their migratory culture for large-scale invasion and occupation.[44] The kingdoms of Poland and Hungary – devastated in 1241 – were in no position to resist a second incursion and, therefore, the Teutonic Knights were one of the few coherent political powers in that region which could offer a defence. In short, Innocent needed them. Symptoms of the papacy's reliance on the Teutonic Knights can be found in Innocent's request that they warn him of any Mongol advance.[45] The Order was also given the authority to offer an indulgence (on the same level as the indulgence offered to pilgrims to Jerusalem) for troops who were prepared to fight against the Mongols.[46]

In the Mediterranean theatre, Innocent needed to rally the defenders of the Holy Land to resist the incursions of the Khwarazmians (who in 1247 were still besieging Ascalon) and to rebuild the Latin East. Such a recovery would require every able-bodied man in the kingdom of Jerusalem. Innocent was clearly aware that levels of manpower in this area were falling because in January 1247 he referred to the flood of refugees leaving the Levantine littoral.[47] In such a predicament, Innocent was in no position to reprimand the Teutonic Knights for their imperial allegiances with the brusque reprimands employed by Gregory IX because their compliance was essential in the defence of Christendom. Consequently, he could not remove their privileges or order their subordination because such an act would seriously weaken the Order at the very moment when their full strength was required. Nevertheless, the brethren had still defied the papacy and castigation was evidently deemed necessary. As a result, Innocent tailored his punishment to reflect this altered relationship. Rather than chastising the Order openly, Innocent appears to have threatened them with retribution should their actions become hostile. To this end, in Germany and Lombardy, papal legates were granted

---

[43] HB, vol. 6, pp. 303–306.

[44] Salimbene de Adam, *Cronica*, vol. 1, pp. 298–299, 580–581.

[45] *CDOT*, no. 125.

[46] *Bullarium Franciscanum*, ed. F. H. Sbaraleae, vol. 1 (Rome, 1759), p. 724.

[47] *The Cartulary of the Cathedral of Holy Wisdom of Nicosia*, ed. N. Coureas and C. Schabel, Cyprus Research Centre Texts and Studies in the History of Cyprus, 25 (Nicosia, 1997), no. 24.

the power to remove the Order's privileges and liberties should they deem it necessary.[48] Urban has suggested that, in the Baltic, the appointment of Albert Suerbeer to the archbishopric of Prussia in 1246 was a papal attempt to impose control upon the brethren.[49] Only in the Holy Land were the brethren punished directly through the Templars. Even so, Innocent ordered that only a few brothers should be disciplined, perhaps to ensure that they would be chastened, not weakened.[50] Through these devices, Innocent imitated his predecessor Gregory IX in so far as he used the removal of privileges and the agency of the other military orders to enforce his will. Unlike Gregory IX, however, Innocent tailored these tools to become 'Swords of Damocles' rather than straightforward reprimands. By these means, he may have hoped to curb the Order's imperial loyalties without reducing either its ability or its willingness to protect Christendom.

Perhaps as a result of these inducements Heinrich reversed his policy in *c*.1247 to support the papacy.[51] This change of loyalties is indicated by the use of the Teutonic Knights as emissaries between Innocent IV and the anti-king, Henry of Thuringia.[52] The pope also asked the brethren to hold their fortifications against Frederick.[53] After Henry of Thuringia's death in 1247, the Order received patronage from the second anti-king, William of Holland.[54] The papacy also issued privileges for the brethren in 1247, which exempted them from aspects of secular justice and protected their landholdings.[55] In the Holy Land, the three main military orders were instructed to eject Frederick's supporter Thomas, count of Acerra.[56] These actions effectively demonstrate that the brethren had once again become partisans of the papacy, yet this new policy served merely to attract the opprobrium of the emperor.

Having heard of the brethren's altered loyalties, Frederick acted swiftly and ordered the confiscation of their lands in Sicily and Apulia.[57] These

---

48 *MGH Epis. Saec. XIII*, vol. 2, no. 303; *Reg. Innocent IV*, vol. 1, no. 3006. Notably, on the same day Innocent also granted authority to these same legates to offer remission of sins for those soldiers who were prepared to fight against Frederick; *Reg. Innocent IV*, vol. 1, no. 3002. There are several subsequent charters renewing and confirming the Order's privileges specifically in Germany which may reflect the return of privileges removed by the papal legate; see *TOT*, nos. 522, 528.

49 W. Urban, *The Baltic Crusade* (Dekalb, IL, 1975), pp. 178–179.

50 Innocent IV, 'Lettere Secretae D'Innocenzo IV e altri documenti in una raccolta inedita del sec. XIII', in *Miscellanea Francescana*, vol. 55 (Rome, 1955), no. 246.

51 The timing of this change in policy is difficult to define because there is conflicting evidence about the Order's loyalties during the years 1246–1248. Arnold is correct when he argues that this was a 'confused time' (*wirre Zeit*), Arnold, 'Der Deutsche Orden zwischen Kaiser und Papst', p. 65.

52 *Reg. Innocent IV*, vol. 1, no. 2941.

53 *Reg. Innocent IV*, vol. 1, no. 3289.

54 26 January 1248: *Oorkondenboek van het Sticht Utrecht*, vol. 2, no. 1158; 11 December 1248: *CDOT*, no, 130; 16 April 1249: *Regesta Imperii V*, vol. 1, no. 4974.

55 *TOT*, nos. 510–511.

56 *CGJJ*, vol. 2, no. 2470; *Reg. Innocent IV*, vol. 1, no. 4103; *MGH Epis. Saec. XIII*, vol. 2, no. 564.

57 *Historia Diplomatica Regni Siciliae: Inde ab anno 1250 ad annum 1266*, ed. B. Capasso (Naples,

estates represented a considerable proportion of the Knights' material wealth and were also a vital link in their supply route to the Holy Land (see chapter 10). It is interesting to note that Frederick had employed the same punishment against the Templars and Hospitallers in 1230, suggesting that this was his standard reprimand for a rebellious military order.[58] Although it is unclear whether Frederick's orders were fully executed, the brethren seem to have been in sufficient financial difficulty by 1247 for Innocent to issue a number of documents preventing magnates from taking revenge upon them for defaulting upon their debts.[59] The result was that by 1249 the Teutonic Order was suffering imperial censure, defeat in the Holy Land, bankruptcy and the prospect of a second Mongol invasion.

The Development of Internal Factions and the Crusade of Louis IX

As pressure grew upon the Order to support either the papacy or the empire, it seems that internal factions began to develop. Perhaps an early sign of such divisions can be seen in the Templar attack on the Order in Acre in 1241.[60] According to Matthew Paris, this assault was launched because of the Order's imperial sympathies and yet the Templars are said to have spared a number of brethren whom they considered to be their allies. Since the Templars were papal supporters, their treatment of different groups of Teutonic Knights in different ways may indicate that there were already split allegiances within the Order. Other historians have noted further instances where such divisions were evident. Militzer, for example, has suggested that the appointment of the Order's German master in the mid-1240s became a point of contention as each faction sought to appoint their own candidate. He also argues that it was the weakening of the Order's Staufen party in the mid-1240s which caused the Order to align itself with the papacy.[61] It has been argued above that these political realignments were the result of external factors; however, it is also possible that such internal issues played their part. Certainly, the Teutonic Order was not the only religious institution to face internal disputes over this issue. Even in the Dominican Order, generally a staunch supporter of the papacy, dissenting voices were heard during the 1240s with one member writing an inflammatory work entitled *De correctione ecclesiae epistola*.[62]

1874), no. 19. For discussion of Frederick's motives for this confiscation see M. Hellmann 'König Manfred von Sizilien und der Deutsche Orden', in *Acht Jahrhunderte Deutscher Orden in Einzeldarstellungen*, QuStDO, 1 (Bad Godesberg, 1967), pp. 67–70. Toomaspoeg has indicated that there is not much evidence for these confiscations actually taking place; *Les Teutoniques en Sicilie*, p. 53.

58 Matthew Paris, *Chronica Majora*, vol. 3, pp. 154–155.
59 *TOT*, nos. 517–518; Toomaspoeg, *Les Teutoniques en Sicilie*, p. 53.
60 Matthew Paris, *Chronica Majora*, vol. 4, pp. 167–168.
61 *AZM*, p. 42.
62 Maier, *Preaching the Crusades*, p. 72.

Perhaps as a consequence of the fractured state of the Order, the brethren became estranged from Innocent IV in 1249, who armed papal legates in Italy and Sardinia with powers to strip them of their privileges.[63] Given that the Knights had already infuriated Frederick, these events show that by this time they had alienated both the papacy and the empire and were divided amongst themselves. Forstreuter has characterised these events as follows, 'The Teutonic Order was no monolithic block. The war of the world-shattering powers of this time sucked the Order into a whirlpool and threatened disintegration.'[64]

The greatest expression of this infighting occurred in the years after the death of Heinrich von Hohenlohe (15 July 1249) when the Order became divided between two masters.[65] The first of these masters to appear in the sources was Poppo von Osterna, who was elected in *c.*1252.[66] The evidence for the second comes from a document issued in Venice in 1253 by Wilhelm von Urenbach, who claimed to be the *magister generalis* of the Teutonic Order.[67] He was accompanied by the castellan of Montfort, the marshal and the commander of Koblenz. With two men acting as master at the same time, it is reasonable to conclude that an open rift had developed within the Order. Nevertheless, the 1253 document for Wilhelm von Urenbach is the only source which mentions his assumption of this title. It is not clear therefore when he first aspired to this position and it is possible that he had been pursuing this objective for many years.[68] Certainly, the possibility has been raised that the Order first became divided between Wilhelm and a further master called Gunther von Wüllersleben after the death of Heinrich von Hohenlohe.[69] The only evidence for this master is an entry in a fourteenth-century necrology which mentions only that there was a master called Gunther who succeeded Heinrich and that he died on 4 May.[70] It does not specify that this 'Gunther'

---

63 Italy: *Reg. Innocent IV*, vol. 2, no. 4711; *MGH Epis. Saec. XIII*, vol. 2, no. 680, p. 499; Sardinia: *Reg. Innocent IV*, vol. 2, no. 4747.

64 'Der Deutsche Orden war kein monolithischer Block. Der Kampf der weltbewegenden Mächte jener Zeit hat auch ihn in den Strudel gerissen und mit Absplitterung bedroht'; Forstreuter, *Der Deutsche Orden am Mittelmeer*, p. 210.

65 For Heinrich von Hohenlohe's death see *HU*, vol. 1, no. 236.70, p. 154.

66 It is not known exactly when Poppo became master. The first reference to him in this new capacity occurs on 6 July 1253; *R. Reg.*, vol. 1, no. 1206. It is possible that he was elected at the 1252 general chapter on 14 September, although it is equally possible that he was appointed at some point in 1253; Perlbach, 'Deutsch-Ordens Necrologe', p. 364.

67 Forstreuter has dated this charter, which claims to have been issued in 1223, to 1253. He argues that the date must have been 1253 because the document refers to the division of Samland which took place in this year; Forstreuter, *Der Deutsche Orden am Mittelmeer*, pp. 207–209. This argument is accepted. *Liv., Est. und Kurländisches Urkundenbuch* (Abt. 1), vol. 1 (Aalen, 1967), no. 224.

68 Arnold, 'Der Deutsche Orden zwischen Kaiser und Papst', pp. 66–67.

69 For discussion see K. Militzer, 'Günther von Wüllersleben', in *Die Hochmeister des Deutschen Ordens 1190–1994*, QuStDO, 40 (Marburg, 1998), pp. 26–27; Militzer, 'From the Holy Land to Prussia', pp. 73–74; *AZM*, pp. 42–43.

70 He is known to have been the successor to Heinrich because he is listed as the eighth master while Heinrich was the seventh; Perlbach, 'Deutsch-Ordens Necrologe', p. 364.

was Gunther von Wüllersleben, nor does it give further details about his life. As a result, the events of this leadership contest are obscured by the paucity of material, but it is still clear that at some point between 1249 and 1253 the order *did* become divided. The reasons for this infighting are not specified; however, it seems almost inevitable that it was connected in some way to the question of the Order's loyalties to the papacy and the empire. Even if these disputes began after Frederick's death in 1250 it is possible that the bitterness which this issue had provoked persisted.

The effects of both these internal divisions and the ongoing wars in Prussia and Livonia were felt during the crusade of Louis IX to the Holy Land when the Order found itself internally divided and unable to recover from battle-field losses. In 1244 Louis IX took the cross and on 25 August 1248 his forces departed from Aigues-Mortes.[71] Although Louis had almost certainly taken his oath before hearing news of La Forbie, his arrival in the Holy Land was timely and it was hoped that he could restore the lost lands.[72] The Teutonic Knights, Templars and Hospitallers joined the royal army shortly after its arrival on Cyprus.[73] On 5 June 1249 the combined force landed at Damietta, which fell almost immediately. The three military orders were then granted property in the city.[74] In the subsequent campaign along the Nile the army was heavily defeated at the town of al-Mansūra on 8 February 1250 and Louis was captured soon afterwards. The Order played its part in this battle and, like the Templars and Hospitallers, suffered heavy casualties.[75] In a letter to King Alfonso of Castile, Peter of Koblenz,[76] marshal of the Order, described the defeat as follows:

> Then the commanding king set out with us and with other Christians to a place which is called al-Mansūra, where the Saracens, besetting us with a large army, finally captured the king and killed by the sword or captured all the Christians who were with him. Whereby we lost both horses and

---

71 Here I follow Richard, *The Crusades*, pp. 338–354.

72 The most detailed source for the Teutonic Knights' role in this venture can be found in a letter written by the marshal of the Order to Alfonso of Castile in c.1254. This letter was one of appeal and thus it is possible that it may have exaggerated elements of the Order's role yet it remains the most comprehensive account of their actions. For a transcription see García, 'Alfonso X, la Orden Teutónica y Tierra Santa', pp. 489–509. For the manuscript see 'Carta de la Orden Teutónica a Alfonso X'; García, 'Alfonso X and the Teutonic Order', pp. 319–327.

73 'Carta de la Orden Teutónica a Alfonso X'; *Les Gestes des Chiprois*, p. 741.

74 Rothelin, p. 594.

75 Rothelin, p. 601; Matthew Paris, *Chronica Majora*, vol. 5, p. 158.

76 Peter wrote or countersigned a number of letters on behalf of the Order to the west. Although he is not mentioned before Louis's crusade he swiftly developed his status in the Order and in 1253 he became the castellan of Montfort. *R. Reg.*, vol. 1, no. 1206. Later he became marshal and deputy master. 'Carta de la Orden Teutónica a Alfonso X'; *Annales de Burton*, in *Annales Monastici*, ed. H. R. Luard, RS, 36, vol. 1 (London, 1864), p. 368. Peter is mentioned again in 1261 when he countersigned a charter to John of Ibelin though no rank is accorded to him, even though it is specified for others. The transaction on this occasion was conducted by Grand Commander Hartmann von Heldrungen; see *R. Reg.*, vol. 1, no. 1309.

arms with all the other things we had in that place since all our brothers had been captured or killed.[77]

After his release, Louis remained in the East where he rebuilt the fortifications of Acre, Jaffa, Sidon and Caesarea. He sailed for France on 24 April 1254. The Teutonic Knights had earned praise for their role in this campaign but they had also suffered a second crushing defeat in the eastern Mediterranean in only six years.

Symptoms of the Order's institutional weakness and its heavy commitments in the Baltic became apparent in the Levant during the latter stages of this campaign. In his letter to Alfonso of Castile, Peter of Koblenz described the pitiable condition of the Order and the general weakness of the Latin East. He mentioned that the brethren had not received aid from their commanders in the West for a long time and gave two major reasons.[78] Firstly, he stated that the wars between the papacy and the empire had prevented supplies from reaching the Holy Land from Germany. Secondly, he claimed that those resources which were available were scarcely sufficient to maintain the Order's interests in Livonia and Prussia and, by implication, could not be spared. From this it can be seen that wars of the Baltic had begun to consume supplies that were needed in the Holy Land whilst the disputes of the empire and the papacy were inhibiting the flow of those materials which were available. Admittedly Peter may have over-emphasised the weakness of the Order to encourage Alfonso to render aid; however, all the issues he described chime well with the wider concerns and disputes which have been described thus far.[79]

It seems likely that the effects of the Teutonic Knights' internal disputes were also felt during this campaign, with the movement of their major officers away from the Levantine battlefront. Firstly, the grand commander, Eberhard of Saone, travelled to Livonia in 1250 both to deputise for the regional master, who had fallen ill, and to impose the rights of the Levantine branch of the Order upon its commanders in the Baltic (see below).[80] Secondly, by late 1253 one of the rival masters, Wilhelm von Urenbach, was in Venice along with Helm, his castellan of Montfort, and Herman, his marshal.[81] The other master, Poppo von Osterna, also came to the West in 1253, although it would seem that he left behind his castellan of Montfort, Peter of Koblenz, appar-

---

[77] 'Inde prefactus rex nobis cum et cum aliis Christianis ad locum qui Munzinra dicitur est profectus, ubi nos cum valido exercitu obsidentis (obsidentes) tandem regem ceperunt et christianos omnes qui secum aderant vel occiderunt in ore gladii vel ceperunt. Ubi nos et equos et arma cum omnibus aliis quae habebamus ibidem amisimus captis est omnibus nostris fratribus vel occissis'; This transcription was taken from García, 'Alfonso X, la Orden Teutónica y Tierra Santa', p. 508; 'Carta de la Orden Teutónica a Alfonso X'.

[78] 'Carta de la Orden Teutónica a Alfonso X'.

[79] García, 'Alfonso X and the Teutonic Order', p. 326.

[80] *Annales Erphordenses Fratrum Praedicatorum*, p. 109; *Livländische Reimchronik*, pp. 82–84. For further details on Eberhard see appendix E.2.

[81] *Liv., Est. und Kurländisches Urkundenbuch*, vol. 1, no. 224.

ently as his deputy.[82] Peter became marshal at some point between 1253 and 1254 (see appendix E.1), presumably to fulfil this role. With the movement of so many officers to the West and only a recently appointed marshal to act as deputy, the needs of the Holy Land had seemingly been put to one side as the major players competed for control over the Order as a whole. Reviewing this evidence, it is clear that by late 1253 the Order's Levantine branch had been left defeated, divided, penniless and isolated.

German Pilgrimage to the Holy Land

A further consequence of this turbulent period, which had a long-term effect upon the Holy Land, was the re-direction of German pilgrims away from the Mediterranean and towards the Baltic. After the first Mongol invasion in 1241, the papacy and the Teutonic Knights worked together to rebuild the defences of Western Christendom against any further attack. The first priority was to regain control over their territories in Prussia and Livonia and by 1250 they had begun to make significant headway on this matter. In this year the ruler of Lithuania accepted baptism and in the previous year the Order had negotiated the treaty of Christburg, which effectively ended the rebellion in Prussia. They also made significant territorial gains in Semgallia, Kurland and Samland. Partly for these reasons, the year 1254 has been presented as a high-point in the Order's history in the Baltic.[83]

The papacy had offered its support through a series of charters which authorised preaching for the recruitment of crusading forces against the pagans and the Mongols.[84] Innocent IV also granted the Order the ability to offer secular knights who were prepared to fight against the Mongols the same privileges as those who travelled to the Holy Land.[85] Innocent's successor, Alexander IV, continued this trend and named the Order as the leader of the crusade against the Mongols. He also encouraged them to form defensive alliances with other realms against the possibility of an invasion.[86] In these ways the brethren became the papacy's shield against eastern incursions, yet this policy was to have a deleterious effect upon the Holy Land because, through strengthening Prussia and Livonia, the papacy began to channel German pilgrim forces away from the Mediterranean.

The Baltic region had been a crusading theatre for many years before the arrival of the Teutonic Knights, yet it had generally been of secondary importance to the Holy Land. In 1147 Bernard of Clairvaux, with the support of Pope Eugenius III, allowed several lords in Saxony who had refused to travel

---

[82] Poppo von Osterna was in Germany by late 1253, see Militzer, 'Poppo von Osterna', p. 29.
[83] Urban, *The Baltic Crusade*, p. 192.
[84] For examples, see *PU*, vol. 1.1, nos. 146, 148; vol. 1.2. nos. 2, 3, 7, 12, 23, 59, 61, 83, 110, 113; *Liv., Est. und Kurländisches Urkundenbuch*, vol. 1, no. 268.
[85] *Bullarium Franciscanum Romanorum Pontificum*, vol. 1, p. 724. For Innocent's support see Fonnesberg-Schmidt, *The Popes and the Baltic Crusades*, p. 225.
[86] *Regesta Imperii V*, vol. 2, no. 9223; Potthast, vol. 2, no. 17729.

to the Holy Land to launch a crusade against neighbouring pagan tribes.[87] In 1204 Innocent III encouraged the archbishop of Bremen to recruit troops for an expedition to Livonia, but only if those men could not travel to the Holy Land.[88] Similarly, in 1217 Bishop Christian of Prussia was granted the ability to recruit men to fight in Prussia, provided that they had not already promised to travel to the Latin East.[89] Consequently, crusading had been authorised in these regions but generally for troops who either could not or would not go to the Levant. This trend began to change during the thirteenth century and Fonnesberg-Schmidt has argued that 'from Pope Honorius III's pontificate onwards, however, the papal line was consistent and the Baltic campaigns were recognised as being on a par with the crusades undertaken in the East'.[90]

During Gregory IX's pontificate the Order began to colonise Prussia and Livonia and the papacy supported these endeavours by encouraging imperial noblemen whose predecessors had fought in the Holy Land to set out instead for Prussia. In 1234, for example, Gregory wrote to Frederick, duke of Austria, describing his predecessors' crusading exploits in the Mediterranean and suggesting that he follow their example by fighting against the pagans in the Baltic.[91] From this point the dukes of Austria remained committed to the Baltic crusades and did not return to the Levant. Many further examples can be found for this redirection, including the archbishops of Mainz, who had been present during Henry VI's crusade to the Latin East but were asked in 1245 to support the Order in Prussia.[92] A number of further secular nobles whose predecessors had fought in the Holy Land similarly began to travel instead to the Baltic. These included the landgraves of Thuringia,[93] the margraves of Brandenburg,[94] the margraves of Meissen[95] and the lords of Schwarzburg.[96] Additionally, Prussian and Livonian chronicles record the frequent arrival of smaller bands of pilgrims from across Germany.[97]

A number of further papal charters encouraged this change. In 1245, the Teutonic Knights were given the ability to recruit crusaders for Prussia for an unlimited period, representing what Riley-Smith labels a 'perpetual

---

[87] Phillips, 'Papacy, Empire and the Second Crusade', p. 7.
[88] *Liv., Est. und Kurländisches Urkundenbuch*, vol. 1, no. 14.
[89] *RHP*, vol. 1, no. 389.
[90] Fonnesberg-Schmidt, *The Popes and the Baltic Crusades*, p. 249.
[91] *MGH Epis. Saec. XIII*, vol. 1, no. 596. Appeals were subsequently made to the duke of Austria in 1244. The dukes of Austria went on crusade shortly afterwards to the Baltic see *Reg. Innocent IV*, vol. 1, no. 711; Peter von Dusburg, *Chronicon Terrae Prussie*, pp. 76, 81, 90–91.
[92] *De Primordiis Ordinis Theutonici Narratio*, p. 223; *PU*, vol. 1.1, no. 168.
[93] In 1265 (admittedly, after a change of dynasty); Peter von Dusburg, *Chronicon Terrae Prussie*, p. 113.
[94] In 1251, 1255 and 1266; Peter von Dusburg, *Chronicon Terrae Prussie*, pp. 88, 94, 113.
[95] In 1234; Peter von Dusburg, *Chronicon Terrae Prussie*, p. 59.
[96] In 1252; Peter von Dusburg, *Chronicon Terrae Prussie*, p. 88.
[97] Peter von Dusburg, *Chronicon Terrae Prussie*, pp. 63–64, 69, 76, 81, 83, 85, 88, 94, 100, 113

crusade'.[98] In the same year Innocent IV permitted the Order to end the custom whereby newly admitted brethren were required to travel initially to the Holy Land.[99] In 1245 Innocent IV permitted preaching for campaigns in Prussia and Livonia to continue in the wake of La Forbie, even during the preparations for the crusade of St Louis.[100] In 1257 Alexander IV allowed the Order to absolve individuals from their vow to visit Jerusalem in return for a cash payment of 500 marks, to be used to support their work in Prussia.[101] Consequently, by the 1250s many imperial noblemen who might otherwise have travelled to the Holy Land had embarked instead for the Baltic. In this way, so far from rendering aid to the Holy Land, the Order was actually complicit in the redirection of major crusading families away from the Mediterranean.

To assess the impact of this re-orientation upon the Levant it is useful to compare the events of the 1250s to the period after the battle of Hattin. In the decades after 1187 the kingdom of Jerusalem achieved a partial recovery and regained many of its former territories. This was facilitated by the large number of crusading armies that had travelled to the Levant. Many of these forces had been raised by German rulers, including the armies recruited by Frederick I, Henry VI and Frederick II. By contrast, in the aftermath of La Forbie in 1244 and al-Mansūra in 1250, no significant aid was forthcoming from Germany. Crusading continued to be popular in Germany; however, many noble dynasties had turned their attention towards the pagans in the Baltic. Other families became involved in the wars between the papacy and Frederick II's heirs. The exact extent to which this trend played a part in the downward spiral of the Latin East is unknown; however, the dwindling of this major source of aid must have had an effect. It is perhaps significant that several modern historians and also Peter von Dusburg saw the 1250s as a turning point in the fortunes of the Christian Levant. He wrote, 'In the year of our lord 1250 it began to perceptibly fail.'[102]

Admittedly, the papacy's advocacy of the crusade to the Baltic was not consistent. Where Innocent IV and Alexander IV had shown considerable support for expeditions to this frontier, later pontiffs had different priorities. In 1261, for example, when Urban IV, formerly patriarch of Jerusalem, replaced Alexander IV, formerly bishop of Ostia, crusading policy changed dramatically. Urban announced a new crusade to the Holy Land the following year and preaching began across Germany.[103] This caused controversy because complaints were received that preachers were attempting to persuade

---

98   Riley-Smith, *The Crusades*, p. 197; Fonnesberg-Schmidt, *The Popes and the Baltic Crusades*, p. 228; *PU*, vol. 1.1, no. 168.
99   *TOT*, no. 470.
100 *PU*, vol. 1.1, no. 169; *Liv., Est. und Kurländisches Urkundenbuch*, vol. 1, no. 187.
101 *PU*, vol. 1.2, no. 25.
102 'Anno domini MCCL incepit sensibiliter deficere'; Peter von Dusburg, *Chronicon Terrae Prussie*, p. 207.
103 Maier, *Preaching the Crusades*, p. 80.

pilgrims to turn away from the Baltic and travel instead to the Holy Land. This scenario seems to have occurred with sufficient frequency for the papacy to issue letters forbidding the practice in 1263 and 1265.[104] Even so, Urban IV did not ignore the needs of the Baltic and a number of charters were issued to support the Teutonic Knights in this region.[105] Papal policy appears to have changed once again under Pope Clement IV who legitimised wider preaching for the support of the Baltic.[106] Overall, it seems that although most pontiffs considered both the wars of the Baltic and those of the Holy Land to be essential, their perception of the relative importance of these frontiers fluctuated considerably. The personal background of each pope and the exigencies of the time seem to have merged to cause the papacy's strategy to vary with each new election. Despite this, one conclusion is clear – after the pontificate of Gregory IX no major German crusading army would ever again travel to the Latin East.

The Recovery of the Order in the Holy Land

Despite the diplomatic and military failings of the 1240s, by the mid-1250s the Teutonic Order's position in the Holy Land began to improve. By this time, the Prussian rebellion had been suppressed and the situation in Livonia was relatively stable. Although German pilgrimage to the Holy Land continued to decline throughout this period, the Teutonic Order was able to restore and even to extend its position in the Levant.

Between 1244 and 1260, the Teutonic Knights had been forced to rebuild their field force in this region on two occasions: after the battles of La Forbie and al-Mansūra. After La Forbie, the sources agree that there were only three survivors from the Order's contingent, yet in 1249 Heinrich von Hohenlohe evidently gathered sufficient troops to deploy a major force to assist Louis's Crusade. This is known through a statement of losses made by the marshal, Peter of Koblenz, concerning the Nile campaign: 'We who remained, after 12 companies had been lost together with the better accoutrements which we had in the renowned parts of Syria, returned destitute and unarmed all the way to Acre.'[107] Although we have no further information detailing the size or composition of these companies, this evidence still implies that the brethren had deployed a major force, demonstrating that they had rebuilt at least a measure of their military strength by 1249. Bronstein has noted similar patterns of recovery for the Hospitallers and the Templars.[108] Of

---

[104] *PU*, vol. 1.2, nos. 198, 214, 239.
[105] *PU*, vol. 1.2, nos. 201, 202.
[106] *PU*, vol. 1.2, no. 237.
[107] 'Perditis duodecem manibus melioribus rebus quas habebamus in partibus Syriae honoratis, nos qui residui fuimus usque Acrem nudi pervenimus et inermes.' This transcription is taken from García 'Alfonso X, la Orden Teutónica y Tierra Santa', p. 508. This in turn was taken from 'Carta de la Orden Teutónica a Alfonso X'. A minor alteration has been made to the punctuation of this transcription.
[108] Bronstein, *The Hospitallers and the Holy Land*, pp. 23–24; Barber, *The New Knighthood*, p. 232.

course the fact that the Teutonic Knights' host was destroyed during Louis' crusade demonstrates not only that they had a field force to lose but also that it would need to be rebuilt for a second time. After this defeat, many years passed before the Order received reinforcements in the Holy Land. Poppo von Osterna (master, *c.*1252–1256) pointedly ignored the needs of the brethren in the Levant (Poppo's attitude will be explored in greater detail in the next chapter) and so it was left to his successor Anno von Sangershausen (master, 1256–1273) to restore the Order's military strength in this area. The conditions for such a recovery were enabled by events which took place in both the eastern and the western Mediterranean.

In the Latin East, the political situation improved through the establishment of peace treaties with the neighbouring Muslim rulers. In 1254 Louis IX created a treaty with Damascus and in 1255 a further treaty, countersigned by the Teutonic Knights, was made with the Egyptians for ten years, although Jaffa was expressly excluded from this peace.[109] This treaty was subsequently broken by Christian and then Egyptian raiding parties, although it was reconfirmed in the following year.[110] In this way, the direct threat to the Latin East by neighbouring Muslim rulers was temporarily reduced.

A few years before these treaties, the political situation in Western Christendom altered dramatically with the death of Frederick II. His passing effectively released the Teutonic Knights from their long dependency on imperial favour. Frederick's sons continued to struggle against the papacy; however, the Order was largely able to distance itself from these later conflicts. Commenting on this, Militzer argues that 'the supporters of the Hohenstaufen family [within the Order] lost their backing after the death of Frederick in 1250'.[111] Furthermore, during his final days, Frederick decided to restore the brethren's confiscated properties in Sicily and Apulia. His sons, Manfred and Conrad, then confirmed the Order's possession of many of their former rights and privileges in 1251.[112] The return of these territories and privileges reopened the Order's lines of communication through Italy and Sicily, easing the flow of resources to the Holy Land. Accordingly, the Order was no longer politically exposed between the papacy and the empire and, although it remained reliant upon the papacy, even this relationship (see above) increasingly bore the hallmarks of co-dependency.

The Order's newfound political freedom soon found expression during the violent disputes in the city of Acre, which are commonly referred to as the 'War of St Sabas'. The main protagonists in this conflict were the Italian communes which were locked in a struggle for supremacy in this city. This

---

[109]   Rothelin, p. 630.

[110]   Rothelin, pp. 630–633.

[111]   Militzer, 'From the Holy Land to Prussia', p. 74; Arnold, 'Der Deutsche Orden zwischen Kaiser und Papst', p. 66.

[112]   April 1251: *Regesta Imperii V*, vol. 1, no. 4542; 5 May 1251: *Historia Diplomatica Regni Siciliae*, no. 19; 7 October 1251: ibid., no. 34. See Hellmann, 'König Manfred von Sizilien und der Deutsche Orden', pp. 67–72.

controversy lasted for many years although the main engagements occurred between 1256 and 1261.[113] During this civil unrest an attempt was made to change the governance of the kingdom of Jerusalem. Previously, the kingdom had technically been governed by a series of regents, appointed in the early years by Frederick and later by the rulers of Cyprus. This arrangement persisted throughout the reigns of Frederick's son and grandson, Conrad and Conradin (neither of whom travelled to the Latin East).[114] By this time, the magnates in the Holy Land had arranged that no ruler could receive the kingdom unless he came to the East in person and they informed Conrad of their decision.[115] In 1258, during the civil unrest in Acre, the prince of Antioch took advantage of Conradin's continued absence to appoint his infant nephew, Hugh II of Cyprus, as regent.[116] Furthermore, he insisted that the nobles of the land should pay homage to Hugh, which was a direct infringement of Conradin's rights as monarch.[117] The Venetians and Pisans agreed to this and swore allegiance to the boy. The Genoese and Spanish refused.[118] The prince of Antioch responded by hiring troops to harass the Genoese.[119] In 1258 there was a major sea battle in which the Genoese were defeated by the Venetians.[120] This battle settled the dispute, although military engagements between the Italian cities continued into the 1260s.

The Hospitallers and Templars took differing stances in this conflict. The Hospitallers, with a history of close relations with the Hohenstaufen, refused to pay homage to Hugh II.[121] By contrast, the Templars agreed to support the child. Significantly, the Teutonic Knights chose to side with Hugh and the Templars against Conradin.[122] This action represented an open rejection of their affiliation to the imperial family.[123] Such an overt act reflects both the Order's desire to rid itself of its Hohenstaufen allegiance and – more importantly – its ability to do so. The brethren may have adopted this stance because of their firm friendship with Alexander IV, whose representative also supported Hugh at this time. As shown above, Alexander had offered considerable support for the crusade in the Baltic and consequently it is not surprising that this co-operation extended to the Latin East.[124] In 1256,

---

113 Rothelin, pp. 633–635.
114 Although Conrad technically came of age in 1243, Frederick continued to assume many of the rights of kingship and even to refer to himself as king of Jerusalem; see Riley-Smith, *Feudal Nobility*, p. 209.
115 Riley-Smith, *Feudal Nobility*, pp. 210–211.
116 Rothelin, pp. 633–635; Eracles, pp. 443–444.
117 Rothelin, pp. 633–635.
118 Rothelin, pp. 633–635.
119 Rothelin, pp. 633–635.
120 Eracles, p. 443.
121 Rothelin, pp. 633–635. For discussion of the Hospitallers' general loyalty to the Hohenstaufen see *KSJJC*, p. 191.
122 Rothelin, pp. 633–635.
123 Sterns, 'The Teutonic Knights in the Crusader States', p. 372; Houben, 'I Cavalieri Teutonici nel Mediterraneo Orientale (secoli XII–XV)', p. 58.
124 See *TOT*, nos. 536–576 for a sample. *PU*, vol. 1.2, nos. 3, 59.

Alexander sent the new patriarch of Jerusalem, James Pantaleon, to Acre. He was also appointed as a papal legate and Alexander commanded that the military orders should accord to him the dignity of this rank.[125] In the disputes surrounding the War of St Sabas, the patriarch, like the Teutonic Order, is said to have sided with the Venetians and Hugh II against Conradin.[126] It is perfectly possible that the Order's close relationship with the pope and his representatives defined its stance during this crisis.[127]

With the return of their Apulian and Sicilian territories and their new-found freedom from imperial dependency, the Teutonic Knights were able to regain much of their former strength in the eastern Mediterranean. This seems to have occurred after the election of the former Livonian master, Anno von Sangershausen, as master in 1256.[128] Within a few weeks of his election Anno embarked for the Holy Land and arrived around Christmas 1256. He brought financial assistance and possibly a fresh draft of troops. Considering that by this time the Order needed to rebuild its military strength after the defeats of Louis' crusade, it seems indicative of the scale of reinforcement which Anno brought to the Holy Land that he did not merely consolidate, but actually extended, the Order's military commitments in the Latin East. During his visit from 1256 to 1261, Anno made a number of purchases of land from the secular nobility, many of whom could no longer afford to maintain their position in the East. Julian of Sidon, in particular, was prepared to sell what remained of his estates on the Levantine mainland.[129] The lordship of Sidon had suffered from a number of raids in 1249 and 1253 and these losses may

---

125   *Reg. Alexandre IV*, vol. 1, no. 1161. *CGJJ*, vol. 2, no. 2806.

126   Hamilton, *The Latin Church in the Crusader States*, p. 268.

127   Incidentally, it is possible that the Order's close relationship with patriarch at this time may have provoked the anger of the bishop of Acre. Hamilton has shown that the patriarch and bishop of Acre became involved in a serious dispute in these years which escalated to a point where the Alexander IV was forced to prevent the bishop of Acre from placing the patriarch under sentence of excommunication; Hamilton, *The Latin Church in the Crusader States*, p. 268. It seems suggestive that during this controversy the bishop of Acre provoked two further disputes simultaneously with the Hospitallers and the Teutonic Order ostensibly over two separate matters. It seems likely therefore that the Order's support of the patriarch was itself the cause of the further disputes between these institutions and the bishop of Acre. The bishop of Acre's dispute with the Teutonic Order is described in *TOT*, no. 112. For a detailed discussion of this document see R. Ellenblum, *Frankish Rural Settlement in the Latin Kingdom of Jerusalem* (Cambridge, 1998), pp. 145–156. The bishop of Acre's dispute with the Order over taxation is all the more remarkable given that the pope had explicitly protected the brethren's taxation obligations to the church in the Levant only a year previously (before the newly appointed bishop of Acre's arrival in the Holy Land). See *TOT*, no. 534; *CGJJ*, vol. 2, no. 2865.

128   *Livländische Reimchronik*, pp. 99–100; Perlbach, 'Deutsch-Ordens Necrologe', p. 367.

129   The brethren had long preserved a strong relationship with the lords of Sidon. This appears to have begun during the Fifth Crusade when Herman von Salza fought alongside Balian of Sidon. Balian subsequently confirmed several of Herman's charters in 1220 including the purchase of Castellum Regis and another document regarding the division of plunder taken at the siege of Damietta; *TOT*, nos. 53, 55. He later witnessed several further charters concerning the Order in both the Holy Land and Italy; *TOT*, nos. 56–60. Both Balian and Herman were present in 1225 at the marriage of Frederick and Isabella; see Ross, 'Relations between the Latin East and Western Europe', p. 126. Subsequently, during the early stages of Frederick's crusade to the Holy Land, Balian granted the Order property in the vicinity of Sidon; see *TOT*, no. 62. It was also Balian

have been compounded by Julian's gambling.[130] In this deteriorating situation, Julian felt compelled to sell his properties to the military orders. Accordingly, in 1254, the Hospitallers purchased Casal Robert in the vicinity of Mount Tabor for 24,000 bezants.[131] In 1260, the Mongols attacked Sidon, destroying the town and forcing the people to flee to the sea-castle. After this invasion, the Templars purchased the remainder of the lordship of Sidon and the fortress of Beaufort.[132] Anno similarly used this opportunity to acquire further territories and bought a large number of villages from Julian of Sidon as well as from his constable, John le Tor, and local landowner, Andrew of Shuf. These had a price of 33,500 bezants along with a number of smaller annual stipends.[133] Julian also gave the Order a number of further properties including the fortress, the Cave of Tyron.[134]

Anno and subsequently the grand commander, Hartmann von Heldrungen, also rented or purchased properties from John of Ibelin. In 1261, Hartmann purchased lands in the mountains above Beirut near the river Damor from John for 5,000 bezants. This sum was to be paid according to the weight measure used in Acre.[135] These lands were the fief of Toron Ahmud, which Tibble has identified as, 'a hitherto unknown independent or semi-independent lordship on the north-eastern borders of the Lordship of Beirut'.[136] A number of further agreements were finalised of which arguably the most important was arranged in 1256 when Anno leased the Casal Imbert estate for ten years from John of Ibelin for 13,000 bezants per annum (see appendix B).[137] This rent was subsequently reduced to 11,000 bezants in 1261 and it is interesting to note that this later agreement stipulated that it need not be paid if the city of Acre should fall.[138] Seemingly the condition of this estate and the general situation in the Latin East had deteriorated in the intervening years. Consequently, Anno's ability and readiness to make purchases of this size suggest the scale of the support he had brought to the Latin East. Before 1256 the Order had been dangerously weakened through neglect and defeat. Within months of Anno's arrival, however, the situation had evidently improved so

who accompanied Herman to conclude Frederick's treaty with the sultan; see HB, vol. 3, pp. 102–110.

130 *Les Gestes des Chiprois*, p. 752; Eracles, p. 440; Bronstein, *The Hospitallers and the Holy Land*, pp. 56–57. This section has drawn on Riley-Smith, *Feudal Nobility*, p. 30; S. Tibble, *Monarchy and Lordships in the Latin Kingdom of Jerusalem: 1099–1291* (Oxford, 1989), pp. 173–175; Hilsch, 'Der Deutsche Ritterorden im Südlichen Libanon', pp. 176–177.

131 Bronstein, *The Hospitallers and the Holy Land*, pp. 56–57.

132 Barber, *The New Knighthood*, p. 168.

133 *TOT*, nos. 109, 114, 118. For discussion of Andrew of Shuf see Tibble, *Monarchy and Lordships*, p. 55.

134 *TOT*, no. 110. Marshall believes that Tyron had already fallen to the Muslim forces in 1253 and therefore the Order would have had to retake this strongpoint before they could claim it; see *Warfare in the Latin East*, p. 96.

135 *TOT*, no. 122.

136 *TOT*, no. 120, 122; Tibble, *Monarchy and Lordships*, pp. 60–63.

137 *TOT*, nos. 113, 115, 118; *R. Reg.*, vol. 1, no. 1250. For further discussion of these themes see Richard, *The Latin Kingdom of Jerusalem*, vol. 2, p. 374.

138 *TOT*, no. 121; Tibble, *Monarchy and Lordships*, p. 80.

dramatically that they felt able to purchase additional frontier properties.[139] The quantity of aid that Anno had brought with him must have been sufficient to rebuild the Order's primary host and garrisons, carry out any repairs to the Order's infrastructure and purchase and administer new properties. In general, Anno's visit should be viewed as a major re-investment by the Teutonic Knights in their properties in the Holy Land.

Anno consolidated the Order's position further in 1258 when he signed a major and unprecedented treaty with the Templars and Hospitallers. The three military orders swore to work together to protect the East and they negotiated a system whereby their disputes could be resolved through arbitration rather than military action.[140] This agreement seems to have been a response to both their ongoing internal quarrels and the general need to secure the Latin East against invasion.[141] A number of historians have commented on a clause in this treaty which stipulated that the Templars, Teutonic Knights and Hospitallers should render aid to one another at times of crisis in the county of Tripoli and the principality of Antioch. Part of this clause was a statement stipulating that while the Templars and Hospitallers were expected to render this aid at their own expense, the Teutonic Knights' expenses were to be covered by the Order which summoned them. This distinction between institutions has been interpreted as an indication of the Teutonic Knights' poverty at this time. Yet this conclusion is disputed by the evidence which demonstrates Anno's investment in the Levantine branch of the Order at this time.[142] A possible alternative interpretation may be that the Order had very few properties in either Tripoli or Antioch and therefore, although the brethren might frequently expect to be called upon by the Templars and Hospitallers to render assistance, it would never require aid itself. As a result, given this imbalance, it was only reasonable that their expenses should be covered.

Conclusion

These were difficult years for the Teutonic Order when it suffered a series of reverses which were almost decisive. The ongoing disputes between the papacy and the empire divided the brethren internally whilst a series of battlefield defeats and rebellions threatened their frontier territories. In the event, all these regions weathered the storm; however, the Order which survived was a divided institution. Furthermore, the brethren had played their part in the redirection of German crusaders away from the Holy Land and towards

---

[139] Tibble, *Monarchy and Lordships*, p. 62.

[140] *TOT*, no. 116; *CGJJ*, vol. 2, no. 2902; *R. Reg.*, vol. 1, no. 1269. For discussion see *KSJJC*, pp. 447–450.

[141] Different historians have stressed different factors for this agreement; see Bronstein, *The Hospitallers and the Holy Land*, p. 31; Barber, *The New Knighthood*, p. 155.

[142] For discussion of this theme see *KSJJC*, p. 448; Favreau-Lilie, 'L'Ordine Teutonico in Terrasanta (1198–1291)', pp. 66–67.

the Baltic at a time when every defender was needed in the eastern Mediterranean. This was a vital factor in the long-term decline of the Latin East. By 1258, Anno von Sangershausen had rebuilt the Teutonic Knights' position and even extended it through a series of purchases. Nevertheless, the fact that so many nobles were prepared to sell their lands on the Levantine littoral is in itself an indication that many had lost hope in the survival of the Latin East.

CHAPTER 7

The Division of Resources between the Holy Land and the Baltic

> Accordingly you hold certain fortifications and castles in the lands over-
> seas and on this side of the sea, for the honour of God and the sacred
> Roman Church, just as we hear, which not solely the pagans but also other
> numerous reprehensible and evil men struggle to take away from you
> with violence.   (Pope Alexander IV, 1258)[1]

By 1258 the Teutonic Knights had performed a strong recovery both in the Baltic and in the Holy Land, yet the Order which emerged from these crises had changed significantly in character. Where previously the brethren had been split by their relative loyalties to the papacy and the empire, they were now divided between the ongoing needs of the eastern Mediterranean, Prussia and Livonia.[2] As threats arose on all these frontiers they were constantly forced to address their priorities and to determine how their resources should be divided. This question would only have been complicated by the disparate fortunes of these regions. In both areas the brethren's position was endangered by a number of foes. Nevertheless, during the second half of the thirteenth century, while the Latin East fell into a decline which ended in the final collapse of the kingdom of Jerusalem, the Order's commanders in the Baltic overcame the Prussian rebellions and expanded their control.

Reviewing these trends, historians have frequently attempted to identify the moment at which the brethren moved the focus of their attention away from the Latin East and towards the Baltic. Some historians have claimed that the needs of Prussia and Livonia became the priority as early as the 1230s.[3] Others have suggested later dates or identified different turning points.[4] Subsequently, a number of historians, such as Favreau-Lilie, emphasised the Teutonic Knights' ongoing commitment to the Holy Land and have shown that they continued to purchase property in the eastern Mediterranean even

---

[1] 'Sane munitiones et castra quedam ad honorem dei et sancte Romane ecclesie, sicut accepimus, tenetis in transmarinis et cismarinis partibus, que non solum pagani, sed etiam alii quamplures homines reprobi et perversi auferre vobis per violentiam moliuntur'; *PU*, vol. 1.2, no. 42.
[2] *AZM*, p. 44.
[3] Hubatsch, 'Der Deutsche Orden und die Reichlehnschaft über Cypern', p. 276.
[4] Bulst, 'Zur Geschichte der Ritterorden und des Königsreichs Jerusalem', p. 218.

after the fall of the Order's fortress of Montfort in 1271.[5] The spiritual importance of the Levant has also been stressed. In an attempt to reconcile these
factors, historians have generally emphasised the significance of both frontiers.[6] For example, Forstreuter has argued:

> It is probably fair to say that, for the German Order, the territorial focus
> of power already moved towards the north-east, to the Baltic, soon after
> 1230. The spiritual focus, however, remained in Palestine, where the main
> house of the order stood.[7]

Perhaps one of the reasons why opinions on this subject are so diverse is that
there is no letter, charter or chronicle which makes a definitive statement
on this question and a case can be made for the importance of both areas.
On the one hand, the possession of Prussia and Livonia granted political
independence, military and financial strength, an outlet for the crusading
aspirations of the German nobility and the opportunity to aid in the expansion of Christendom. On the other hand, the defence of the Holy Land was
the institution's founding purpose. This section will discuss the way in which
the Order divided its resources during this period by reviewing the actions of
the individual masters.

Expansion in Livonia or the Defence of the Holy Land?

In 1250 the Order was on the offensive in the Baltic and yet its forces in the
Latin East had just been defeated in Egypt with King Louis. At this time,
Eberhard of Saone, grand commander of the order, who had been present in
Egypt, travelled through Germany to Livonia spreading news of the disaster
of al-Mansūra. He is reported to have estimated the losses incurred on this
campaign at 36,000 fatalities, with a further 15,000 captured. Even though
these figures are almost certainly exaggerated, they represent a recognition
of the scale of the Christian defeat.[8]

Given firstly that the Latin East was in peril, secondly that Prussia and
Livonia were relatively stable and thirdly that the Order's commanders in

---

5   M. Favreau-Lilie, 'The Teutonic Knights in Acre after the Fall of Montfort (1271): Some Reflec-
    tions', in *Outremer: Studies in the History of the Crusading Kingdom of Jerusalem*, ed. B. Z.
    Kedar, H. E. Mayer and R. C. Smail (Jerusalem, 1982), p. 272; Favreau-Lilie, 'L'Ordine Teutonico
    in Terrasanta (1198–1291)', p. 68; Militzer, 'From the Holy Land to Prussia', pp. 76–79.
6   Urban, *The Teutonic Knights*, p. 29. U. Arnold, 'Akkon-Venedig-Marienburg: Der Deutsche
    Orden vom Mittelmeer zum Ostseeraum', in *Acri 1291: La fine della presenza degli ordini mili-
    tari in Terra Santa e i nuovi orientamenti nel XIV secolo*, ed. F. Tommasi (Perugia, 1996), p. 71.
7   'Man darf wohl sagen, daß schon bald nach 1230 der territoriale, machtmäßige Schwerpunkt des
    Deutschen Ordens sich nach Nordosten, an die Ostsee, verschob. Der ideelle Schwerpunkt aber
    blieb in Palästina, wo das Haupthaus des Ordens stand'; Forstreuter, *Der Deutsche Orden am
    Mittelmeer*, p. 189.
8   *Annales Erphordenses Fratrum Praedicatorum*, p. 109.

Western Christendom were aware of these facts, it might be thought that the brethren would have exerted themselves to reinforce the Latin East; yet they did not. Instead, Eberhard, who was also the acting master of Livonia, raised a large force in Riga and launched an offensive campaign of expansion in Livonia in 1252.[9] In 1254 a further expedition took place in Prussia.[10] In this same year the Order's marshal in the Holy Land wrote to the king of Castile – four years after the news of al-Mansūra had reached the West – complaining that he had received no reinforcements from the Western commanderies.[11] It appears that the Order's weakness in the Levant was well known because on 26 June 1254 the archbishop of Trier wrote to the preceptor of the commandery in Koblenz to express his concern at the condition of the Order in the eastern Mediterranean and he declared a wish to send supplies thither.[12] Despite this, as we have seen, it was only two and a half years later that the new master, Anno von Sangershausen, travelled to the kingdom of Jerusalem with reinforcements. As a result it had taken a total of almost seven years and the appointment of a new master for significant aid to reach the Holy Land, while the Order had waged major expansionist wars in both Livonia and Prussia. From these factors, it seems that (at this time at least) the ambitions of the Prussian and Livonian branches of the Order had been prioritised over the needs of the Holy Land.

Although the reasons for this prioritisation are not given, there are two factors which may explain this trend. The first concerns the character of Master Poppo von Osterna, who was appointed *c*.1252 and was therefore in command of the Order for much of this period. After his election in Acre, Poppo travelled almost immediately to the Baltic and did not return.[13] In view of Poppo's prior service, his prioritisation of the needs of Prussia and Livonia is not remarkable. In 1241 he was appointed as Prussian master and is thought to have led a group of brethren to meet the Mongol invasion into Hungary and Poland. After this action he was stripped of his position although he was reappointed in 1244 after the outbreak of the Prussian revolt. He then led multiple expeditions to quell the rebellion with the assistance of crusaders and the Order's troops. Consequently, Poppo's entire career before his election seems to have been focused upon the needs of the Baltic.

A further motive may be found in the competition between the Holy Land and Prussia at this time. When Eberhard of Saone travelled north from the Levant, he delivered a charter to the Order's northern commanders in 1251. This document attempted to stamp the authority of the Levantine chapter over the Order's Western provinces including Prussia and Livonia (the chapter was the main council of leading brethren in the Order's headquarters). It contained

9   *Livländische Reimchronik*, pp. 83–84.
10 Peter von Dusburg, *Chronicon Terrae Prussie*, pp. 90–91.
11 'Carta de la Orden Teutónica a Alfonso X.'
12 *Urkundenbuch der Deutschordens-Ballei Hessen*, vol. 1, no. 124.
13 This section has drawn on Militzer, 'Poppo von Osterna', pp. 27–29.

a list of new regulations for these officers including demands that all brethren swear loyalty to the master and chapter, that no provincial master create new regulations for the Order without the approval of the same and that each year every commander send progress reports to the Holy Land.[14] Around this time, it is believed, a regulation was added to the order's statutes which curbed the freedom of the master by insisting that he should not leave the Holy Land without the consent of the chapter.[15] Returning to the motives of Poppo von Osterna, who was elected in *c*.1252, it is plausible that he viewed the actions of the chapter in the Holy Land as a threat both to his authority and to his Baltic ambitions. Consequently, his concentration on Prussia and Livonia and his neglect of the Holy Land may demonstrate a desire to emphasise his own authority against that of the chapter by keeping the latter weakened through a lack of resources. Several historians have argued that this was a period when the Order became divided between the Baltic and the Holy Land.[16] Certainly, under Poppo von Osterna, there is evidence that this occurred, at least in the short term. In 1256, however, Poppo's policies came abruptly to an end when he resigned in Rome, possibly against his will, and Anno von Sangershausen was elected in his place.[17] Perhaps aware of the acute neglect of the Holy Land, Anno embarked for the eastern Mediterranean within weeks of his election.

Mongols and Mamluks and the Policy of Anno von Sangershausen

In 1260, a Mongol army under Hülegü, Īlkhān of Persia, stood poised on the borders of the Latin East. The Khwarazmians had been only the bow-wave ahead of the Mongol invasion into the Levant and many powers in the eastern Mediterranean had already submitted to Mongol dominance. The Seljuks of Anatolia were defeated at Köse Dagh in 1243 and their lands became a protectorate.[18] In 1247, Hetoum I, king of Armenia, swore allegiance to the Mongols.[19] In 1256, Hülegü led the Mongol offensive which destroyed the Assassins' Persian strongholds and in 1258 he captured Baghdad, marking

---

[14] *PU*, vol. 1.1, no. 251.

[15] *SDO*, pp. 99–100; *AZM*, p. 44; Sterns, 'The Statutes of the Teutonic Knights', pp. 46–47. For further discussion of this clause see Forstreuter, *Der Deutsche Orden am Mittelmeer*, p. 192; Sterns, 'The Teutonic Knights in the Crusader States', p. 375.

[16] *AZM*, pp. 44–45.

[17] *Livländische Reimchronik*, pp. 99–100; Militzer, 'Poppo von Osterna', p. 29.

[18] Al-Maqrīzī, *A History of the Ayyūbid Sultans of Egypt*, p. 271.

[19] For the Armenian mission to the Mongols see Grigor of Akanc, '*History of the Nation of Archers (The Mongols)* by Grigor of Akanc hitherto ascribed to Malak'ia The Monk: The Armenian text edited with an English translation and notes', ed. and trans. R. P. Blake and R. N. Frye, *Harvard Journal of Asiatic Studies*, vol. 12 (1949), p. 297; Bar Hebraeus, *Chronography*, vol. 1, p. 418. For discussion of this subject see T. S. R. Boase, *The Cilician Kingdom of Armenia* (Edinburgh, 1978) 25–29.

an end to the Abbāsid Caliphate.[20] The following year the Mongols attacked Damascus; Al-Nāsir Yūsuf (ruler of Damascus and Aleppo) was overthrown and his retreating army disintegrated.[21] Some historians have argued that the defenders of the Latin East may have considered the Mongols to be a source of potential aid. This argument has been convincingly overturned by Jackson who has demonstrated that the growing Mongol influence posed a direct threat to the Holy Land.[22]

At the same time, a second power developed in the Levant. During Louis IX's campaign, the Egyptian sultan, al-Sālih Ayyūb, died in camp outside al-Mansūra.[23] His successor, al-Mu'azzam Tūrān-Shāh, was then murdered by one of his Mamluk bodyguards called Baybars. With the death of al-Mu'azzam Tūrān-Shāh, the Mamluks increasingly began to assert themselves and to vie with one another for command. Eventually, a faction led by Qutuz rose to the fore and he was named Sultan in 1259. These were the beginnings of the Mamluk empire, which became a major force in the Middle East and posed a second threat to the Latin East.

In 1260 the leaders of the kingdom of Jerusalem assembled in Acre to discuss the threat of invasion.[24] At this time it was the Mongols who seemed to pose the most imminent danger.[25] These magnates had learned that the Egyptians, under Qutuz, had decided to confront the Mongols and they needed to decide whether they would send aid in support of his expedition. Admittedly it is not clear whether the Egyptians had actually asked for help or this council simply discussed the possibility of sending auxiliaries on their own initiative, but either way it is certain that the rulers of the kingdom of Jerusalem agreed not to commit their troops.[26]

This conclusion was reached apparently in response to advice given by Anno von Sangershausen.[27] Certainly, the magnates of the kingdom of Jerusalem had good reason to pay close attention to the advice of the Teutonic Knights. The brethren had encountered the Mongols in 1241 and in 1260 they were recognised as the leader of the crusade in Prussia against the Mongols.[28] It also is not surprising that Anno advised that the kingdom should not make war on the Mongols; having formerly been the master of Livonia, he would

---

[20] Grigor of Akanc, *History of the Nation of Archers*, p. 333; Bar Hebraeus, *Chronography*, vol. 1, pp. 429–431; Matthew Paris, *Chronica Majora*, vol. 5, p. 655; Holt, *The Age of the Crusades*, p. 87.

[21] Bar Hebraeus, *Chronography*, vol. 1, pp. 435–437; Grigor of Akanc, *History of the Nation of Archers*, p. 349; Rothelin, pp. 635–636.

[22] P. Jackson, 'The Crisis in the Holy Land in 1260', *English Historical Review*, 95(1980), *passim*.

[23] This section has been drawn from Holt, *The Age of the Crusades*, pp. 82–87.

[24] Rothelin, p. 637.

[25] This brief account of the Mongol advance into the Levant has drawn extensively upon the work of R. Amitai-Preiss, *Mongols and Mamluks: The Mamluk-Ilkhānid War 1260–1281*, Cambridge Studies in Islamic Civilisation (Cambridge, 1996), pp. 8–48; Jackson, 'Crisis in the Holy Land', p. 511.

[26] For the sources that shape this discussion see Rothelin, p. 637; *Les Gestes des Chiprois*, p. 753.

[27] Rothelin, p. 637.

[28] *Regesta Imperii V*, vol. 2, no. 9223; *PU*, vol. 1.2, no. 99.

have been aware of the havoc wrought by the invasion of 1241. Furthermore, in his former role, he had also received the large number of letters from Innocent IV and Alexander IV which constantly emphasised the danger posed by them. The Rothelin continuation of William of Tyre's chronicle claims that Anno's advice was offered out of distrust of the Muslims and it is possible that this factor may also have played its part.[29] Shortly after these discussions, the magnates of Jerusalem wrote to the West explaining the immediacy of their danger and requesting the swift despatch of reinforcements.[30] They emphasised the enormous threat posed by the Mongols and the weakness of their own defences. This letter stated that a Hospitaller had been sent to France, a Templar to Spain and a Teutonic Knight to Germany to gather troops. Given their perilous position, it might be expected that the Teutonic Knights would have despatched all their available forces to the eastern Mediterranean, but they were faced by a second crisis.

In 1259 the Samogithians invaded and routed the forces of the Livonian Master, Burchard of Hornhausen, at Schoten with the loss of thirty-three brother knights. The Order suffered a further defeat at Durben with the loss of 150 knights.[31] These battles signalled the beginning of a second rebellion in Prussia that would take over two decades to subdue. In the first months of these uprisings, losses among the Teutonic Knights were enormous. The papacy's estimate of the Order's total losses among brother knights in this region rose dramatically from 500 in 1257 to 1,000 in 1261.[32] As a result, even though the Mongols posed a threat to Syria, the Order also needed to respond fast to this northern rebellion.

It might seem, therefore, that the brethren were faced with wars in two theatres; however, initially this proved not to be the case. At first, Anno remained in the Latin East, presumably to see how events would develop after the Egyptian campaign against the Mongols. This confrontation was resolved on 3 September 1260, when the Mamluks defeated the Mongols at the battle of Ayn Jālūt. Shortly after this encounter the Mamluks retook Damascus and then Aleppo.[33] The Egyptian victory had been enabled in part by the withdrawal of Hülegü, a few weeks before the battle, with the bulk of

---

[29] Rothelin, p. 637. Some historians have suggested that the Order saw the wisdom in the Armenian policy of siding with the Mongols: Runciman, *History of the Crusade*, vol. 3, pp. 311–312; Mayer, *The Crusades*, p. 277; Hilsch, 'Der Deutsche Ritterorden im Südlichen Libanon', pp. 177–186. Despite this, it is unlikely that the Order would have seriously perceived the Mongols to be anything other than enemies after the 1241 invasion into Western Christendom.

[30] 'Lettre des chrétiens de Terre-Sainte à Charles d'Anjou (22 avril 1260)', *Revue de L'Orient Latin*, 2 (1894), pp. 211–215. The master of the Templars also wrote on this matter to the West see *Annales de Burton*, pp. 491–495.

[31] Peter von Dusburg, *Chronicon Terrae Prussie*, p. 96.

[32] *PU*, vol. 1.2, nos. 29, 142.

[33] For the battle of Ayn Jālūt and the subsequent expulsion of the Mongols from Damascus and Aleppo see *Les Gestes des Chiprois*, pp. 754–755; Rothelin, pp. 637–638; Bar Hebraeus, *Chronography*, vol. 1, pp. 437–438; Sanuto, p. 221. For discussion of this battle see J. Masson Smith, 'Ayn Jālūt: Mamluk Success or Mongol Failure?' *Harvard Journal of Asiatic Studies*, 44 (1984), pp. 307–345; Amitai-Preiss, *Mongols and Mamluks*, pp. 39–45.

his troops. This movement had been provoked by news of the death of the Great Khan, Möngke. Hülegü had left behind only a comparatively small garrison in the Levant under his general Ket-Buqa.[34] The Mamluk victory over Ket-Buqa granted some respite to the kingdom of Jerusalem from the threat posed by the Mongols and, with the exception of a raid against Sidon, it escaped unscathed.[35] After Ayn Jālūt it seemed for a time that there was an opportunity for expansion and in February 1261 the kingdom of Jerusalem launched a major raid against neighbouring Turcoman tribes.[36] At this time, Anno, presumably comforted by the belief that the Latin East was relatively secure and mindful of the need to address the rebellion in Prussia, returned to the West (see appendix A).

Shortly after Anno's departure, the situation in the East deteriorated sharply. The raid in 1261 was heavily defeated and, having united Damascus, Aleppo and Egypt, the Mamluks came to pose a major threat. At Ayn Jālūt, the Mamluk forces had been led by Sultan Qutuz, but he was assassinated a few days later by Baybars.[37] Baybars quickly assumed control of Mamluk Egypt and Syria, and over the following years he launched a series of heavy raids against the Latin East.[38] These began in 1261 with a venture against Antioch.[39] In 1262 Baybars besieged Antioch and the city was saved only by the arrival of a relief force from Armenia, which was supported by Mongol forces.[40] In 1263 there was a raid against Acre that was repeated in 1267.[41] In 1265 Caesarea and Arsuf fell.[42] In 1266 Mamluk troops captured the Teutonic Knights' Armenian fortress of Amudain during a further raid against Cilician Armenia.[43] In this same year the Teutonic Order was also heavily defeated whilst raiding Mamluk territory and their lands around Montfort were despoiled.[44] In 1268 Antioch fell along with the city of Jaffa and the

---

[34] The departure of Hülegü with the bulk of his troops can be found in *Les Gestes des Chiprois*, p. 751; Amitai-Preiss, *Mongols and Mamluks*, pp. 28–35.

[35] The Mongols attacked Sidon but were unable to capture the sea castle, see Sanuto, p. 221; *Les Gestes des Chiprois*, p. 752.

[36] Eracles, p. 445.

[37] Rothelin, pp. 638–639.

[38] For the development of Mamluk military power and a more detailed study of these events see Amitai-Preiss, *Mongols and Mamluks*, pp. 71–77.

[39] Ibn al-Furāt, *Ayyubids, Mamlukes and Crusaders*, vol. 2, p. 43; Al-Khowayter, 'A Critical Edition, vol. 2, p. 401.

[40] Ibn al-Furāt, *Ayyubids, Mamlukes and Crusaders*, vol. 2, p. 50; *Les Gestes des Chiprois*, p. 755

[41] Ibn al-Furāt, *Ayyubids, Mamlukes and Crusaders*, vol. 2, p. 57; *Les Gestes des Chiprois*, pp. 756, 766–767.

[42] Eracles, p. 450; Ibn al-Furāt, *Ayyubids, Mamlukes and Crusaders*, vol. 2, p. 77; *Les Gestes des Chiprois*, pp. 758–759; al-Khowayter, 'A Critical Edition', vol. 2, p. 555.

[43] For details of the raid see *Les Gestes des Chiprois*, p. 766; Eracles, p. 455. For the fall of Amudain see Ibn al-Furāt, *Ayyubids, Mamlukes and Crusaders*, vol. 2, p. 99; A. D. Stewart, *The Armenian Kingdom and the Mamluks: War and Diplomacy during the Reigns of Het'um II: 1289–1307*, The Medieval Mediterranean, 34 (Leiden, 200), pp. 48–49; Forstreuter, *Der Deutsche Orden am Mittelmeer*, p. 64.

[44] Eracles, p. 455; *Les Gestes des Chiprois*, p. 766; Ibn al-Furāt, *Ayyubids, Mamlukes and Crusaders*, vol. 2, p. 87; al-Khowayter, 'A Critical Edition', vol. 2, p. 586.

castle of Beaufort.[45] In 1271, the Teutonic Knights' fortress of Montfort was taken after the seizure of Crac des Chevaliers, Chastel Blanc and Gibelcar.[46] The reduction of the kingdom of Jerusalem was therefore swift and decisive with the destruction of major fortifications and cities.

In 1267, with the Prussian rebellion still raging, Anno von Sangershausen travelled back to the Latin East, presumably in response to the defeats of 1266. His arrival demonstrates that, for him at least, the Holy Land was important enough to require his personal attention even when Prussia was threatened. Despite this, his presence availed little and he was in Armenia when Montfort fell.[47] Within months of the fall of the fortress, Anno departed for the West and did not return.

It appears that the fall of Montfort was a turning point in the policy of the Teutonic Knights. It is significant that shortly after the loss of the stronghold, Anno created a new castle named Montfort in Prussia. Peter von Dusburg reports that:

> Brother Anno the General Master of the Order of the house of the Teutonic Knights commanded to the master and brothers of Prussia, that they build a castle on the borders of Kulm and Pomerania ... calling it Starkenburg that is called Montfort in Latin.[48]

This is a fascinating event and feels highly symbolic of Anno's policy. It demonstrates how important Montfort had been to the Order and yet it also seems to stand as testimony to Anno's belief that the Latin East would not recover sufficiently to effect its restoration. It is also noticeable that after this time, the Order's masters increasingly spent the bulk of their time in Prussia and Germany and rarely visited the Latin East, perhaps indicating a perception that their future lay in the north rather than the Mediterranean (see appendix A).[49]

A Long-term Solution

After 1271, the Teutonic Knights' policy in the Baltic and the Holy Land appears to have entered a new phase. This section will assess the way in which the brethren approached these regions in the period 1271–1291. If we review the strategy pursued by the Teutonic Knights at this time, there

---

[45] Eracles, p. 456; *Les Gestes des Chiprois*, pp. 771–772.
[46] Eracles, p. 460; *Les Gestes des Chiprois*, pp. 777–778; Sanuto, p. 224.
[47] *Les Gestes des Chiprois*, p. 840.
[48] 'Frater Anno magister generalis ordinis domus Theutonice mandavit magistro et fratribus de Prussia, ut castrum in terminis Colmensis et Pomesaniensis ... vocans ipsum Starkenbergk quod latine dicitur fortis mons'; Peter von Dusburg, *Chronicon Terrae Prussie*, p. 123.
[49] This trend has also been identified in Forstreuter, *Der Deutsche Orden am Mittelmeer*, p. 191–192; *AZM*, p. 134.

seems to be a major disparity between their actions and their objectives. On the one hand, the brethren seem to have increasingly prioritised the affairs of the Baltic. The masters spent the vast majority of their time in this area and rarely travelled to the eastern Mediterranean or even to Italy. In this northern region the Order waged repeated campaigns and employed numerous pilgrim forces even after the suppression of the Prussian rebellion. On the other hand, despite the seeming neglect of the Holy Land, the Order continued both to maintain its military forces in Acre and to invest financially in property. In 1273, the Order began to purchase property in the Montmusard district of Acre, presumably to accommodate the officials and brethren who had been displaced by the fall of Montfort.[50] Furthermore, there is no mention of any complaint from the chapter in the kingdom of Jerusalem which contrasts strongly with the state of affairs in the 1230s.

This scenario creates a problem because it poses the question of where the priorities of the Teutonic Knights lay and, by extension, how the Baltic and the Holy Land fitted into their overall strategy. This is thought to have been a period of division, where rival factions strove to advocate the importance of either the Holy Land or the Baltic. Militzer and Arnold have shown that one party under Conrad von Feuchtwangen, the German master, believed that the Order should prioritise the wars of Prussia and Livonia, whilst the master, Burchard von Schwanden (master, 1283–1290), sought a wider commitment to the Holy Land.[51] They then argue that, with the resignation of Burchard in 1290, Conrad's faction gained the supremacy and turned increasingly towards the Baltic.

This study does not dispute this conclusion; however, there seems to have been a further factor. In many ways, the situation of the Teutonic Order in Prussia and Livonia was comparable to that of the Iberian peninsula between the eleventh and thirteenth centuries. During the preparations for the First Crusade, with the Christian defenders of Iberia pressed against the Pyrenees by the Muslim forces, the pope insisted that the Spanish lords should not travel to the Holy Land.[52] The defensive needs of the Iberian peninsula could not be overlooked and thus, for much of the twelfth century, the Spanish contribution to the eastern Mediterranean was comparatively low. In the thirteenth century, however, after the battle of Las Navas de Tolosa on 16 July 1212, Muslim power in this region was greatly diminished and Islamic territory eventually became confined to the southern province of Granada. With

---

50 Favreau-Lilie, 'The Teutonic Knights in Acre after the Fall of Montfort', pp. 282–284; Forstreuter, *Der Deutsche Orden am Mittelmeer*, p. 50.

51 *AZM*, pp. 147–165; U. Arnold, 'Deutschmeister Konrad von Feuchtwangen und die "preußische Partei" im Deutschen Orden am Ende des 13. und zu Beginn des 14. Jahrhunderts', in *Aspekte der Geschichte. Festschrift für Peter Gerrit Thielen* (Göttingen, 1990), pp. 33–34; Forstreuter, *Der Deutsche Orden am Mittelmeer*, p. 53; U. Niess, 'Konrad von Feuchtwangen', in *Die Hochmeister des Deutschen Ordens 1190–1994*, QuStDO, 40 (Marburg, 1998), pp. 41–42.

52 *Papsturkunden in Spanien: vorarbeiten zur Hispania Pontificia: Katalanien*, ed. P. Kehr (Berlin, 1926), no. 23.

the reduction of the local threat from Islam, the Spanish rulers were able to turn their attention increasingly towards the eastern Mediterranean and they participated in expeditions such as the Barons' Crusade. Accordingly, the consolidation of power in this region created an opportunity for a greater commitment to the Holy Land.

In many ways the wars of the Baltic appear to have followed a similar pattern. During the second Prussian rebellion the Teutonic Order was fully committed to the suppression of the pagan tribes and, as shown above, the pope encouraged and supported such campaigns. By the late 1280s, the brethren had begun to regain control and it appears that this was the moment of choice. For the first time in over two decades of rebellion the initiative had returned to the Order and this situation seems to have posed a problem, presenting the brethren with the opportunity either to expand into realms such as Lithuania or to send further resources to the Holy Land. Little evidence remains for the Knights' ideas and strategies at this time. Despite this, it seems that, possibly since the 1270s, the Order considered a long-term strategy in which the wars of Prussia and Livonia were prioritised so that, with the establishment of peace, greater force could be brought to bear on the Holy Land.

This contention will begin with some contextual analysis. Firstly, there seems to have been a general belief at this time that the wars of Western Christendom should be resolved as a prelude to a wider commitment to the eastern Mediterranean. This theory, as Schein has demonstrated, was linked to the growing idea that a new policy was needed for the defence of the Holy Land.[53] On this point, she argues that, 'They justified the *crux cismarina* by insisting that it was an essential prelude to the *crux transmarina*'.[54] The crusade against Sicily in the 1280s and 1290s, for example, was explained as a prerequisite for the conquest of the Holy Land. Schein has also demonstrated that similar ideas were present in the correspondence of a Bohemian bishop named Bruno of Olmütz.[55] In 1273 Gregory X asked Bruno for advice concerning a new policy towards the defence of the Latin East.[56] In his reply, Bruno outlined the problems of Western Christendom's eastern borders, citing the threat of heretics, pagans, Mongols and civil disorder. Furthermore, he emphasised that these dangers were to the direct detriment of the Latin East because they occupied the soldiers of these regions, who might otherwise have been able to fight in the Holy Land. In his second letter he wrote, 'Accordingly they are unfit to defend Christianity in our regions or to

---

[53] This section has drawn on S. Schein, Fideles Crucis: *The Papacy, the West, and the Recovery of the Holy Land, 1274–1314* (Oxford, 1998), pp. 15–19.

[54] Schein, Fideles Crucis, p. 64.

[55] Schein, Fideles Crucis, pp. 23, 64.

[56] C. Höfler, 'Analecten zur Geschichte Deutschlands und Italiens: Bericht des Bruno von Olmütz an Papst Gregor X', *Abhandlungen der Historische Klasse der Bayerische Akademie der Wissenschaffen* (1846), p. 20; *Codex Diplomaticus et Epistolaris Regni Bohemiae*, vol. 5, no. 1555.

repulse the defeats in the lands overseas.'[57] Bruno's basic point seems to have been that the wars on these borders should be resolved first so that greater emphasis could be placed on the needs of the Holy Land.[58]

The significance of Bruno's ideas for the Teutonic Knights lies in his close affiliation with the Order. Bruno was a committed crusader who travelled twice on expeditions to support the brethren in the Baltic in 1254–1255 and 1267–1268.[59] During the former of these campaigns his diplomatic skills averted a potential disaster when he ended an argument between the army's Austrian and Saxon troops.[60] In 1251 he helped to broker an agreement between the Order and the archbishops of Livonia and Prussia.[61] Within Bohemia itself, as Kouřil has demonstrated, Bruno was instrumental in the development of its local commanderies, advocating the order's material and political advancement.[62] So it can be seen that Bruno was closely linked to the Teutonic Order. The circulation of ideas such as these in political circles connected to the Teutonic Knights raises the possibility that the brethren considered a similar strategy whereby the consolidation of Prussia and Livonia should be sought as a prelude to a greater commitment to the Holy Land. Admittedly, this hypothesis cannot be proved definitively; however, it does chime well with their actions. Certainly, during the Second Prussian rebellion, there is very little evidence of reinforcements being sent to the Holy Land, whilst after the rebellion, considerable efforts were made to send resources to the Levant. The renewal of the Order's interventions in the Latin East occurred in 1290 when Master Burchard von Schwanden led a contingent of forty brother knights and allegedly around 400 soldiers to the Holy Land.[63] This was a sizeable force, comparable to the companies of the more important nobles who travelled to the East. Furthermore, the *Ottokars Österreichische Reimchronik*

---

57 'Unde ad christianitatem in nostris partibus defendendam vel ad dampna transmaritimarum partium propulsanda inhabiles sunt'; *PU*, vol. 1.2, no. 315.

58 Admittedly, these letters do not seem to have been written purely in response to Gregory's request for advice, but also to support the candidature of the king of Bohemia for the imperial throne. P. A., Throop, *Criticism of the Crusade: A Study of Public Opinion and Crusade Propaganda* (Amsterdam, 1940), pp. 105–110. Despite this, it does not follow that the context or policy he described was either inaccurate or inappropriate. Christendom's eastern borders *were* in turmoil and Bruno's argument that these disturbances necessarily disrupted the quantity of aid that could be sent to the Holy Land is entirely plausible, just as his implicit claim that the establishment of peace in these regions could enable the departure of pilgrim forces is similarly convincing.

59 Bruno held this office from 1245 to 1281. For a detailed description of the relationship between Bruno and the Order, which this paragraph has drawn on, see M. Kouřil, 'Der Olmützer Bischof Bruno von Schauenburg und der Deutsche Orden', in *Acht Jahrhunderte Deutscher Orden in Einzeldarstellungen*, QuStDO, 1 (Bad Godesberg, 1967), pp. 143–151.

60 Peter von Dusburg, *Chronicon Terrae Prussie*, pp. 90–91.

61 *PU*, vol. 1.1, no. 244; *TOT*, no. 208.

62 Kouřil, 'Der Olmützer Bischof Bruno von Schauenburg', pp. 143–151.

63 Nicolaus von Jeroschin, *Di Kronike von Pruzinlant*, p. 513; *AZM*, pp. 46, 151. Burchard von Schwanden (master 1283–1290) was born around 1245 and was the son of Rudolf of Schwanden and his wife Elizabeth. He became a brother of the Order in 1268 and the commander of Thuringia-Sachsen in *c.*1277. He was subsequently appointed as the commander of Hessen before his elevation to the position of master. K. Militzer, 'Burchard von Schwanden', in *Die Hochmeister des Deutschen Ordens 1190–1994*, QuStDO, 40 (Marburg, 1998), pp. 38–39.

interestingly mentions that the Prussian master sent 700 soldiers to Acre at this time.[64] This force demonstrates that after the Second Prussian rebellion the Order turned its attention decisively towards the Holy Land.

Burchard also made provision for the despatch of greater financial support. In 1290 he arranged with Pope Nicolas IV that no papal taxation would be levied upon the financial assistance – one third of all annual income from all the Order's lands *citra mare* (presumably including Prussia and Livonia) – despatched to the Holy Land.[65] This 'third' was comparable to the 'responsions' of the Templars and Hospitallers. Regarding responsions, the charter in question does seem to imply that the Order had made such payments previously, although it is difficult to determine when they were implemented. The sources contain no further reference to any responsions collected by the Order for the Holy Land. It is possible that such a system had been established (in theory) for some time but if this was the case then, given the immense costs associated with the colonisation and defence of the Baltic, it is hard to believe that it would have been regularly enforced. Notably, as shown above, there were moments, such as in 1254, when the Order's Levantine branch complained that it had received no help at all from Western Christendom.[66] In these years at least it seems that no responsions were paid. Given that Burchard and Pope Nicolas specifically alluded to the Order's duty to pay its responsions in the charter of 1290, it is possible that this document served as a restatement of the Order's responsibility to implement this system in full. There were problems with Burchard's plans, however. Firstly, throughout this period, as shown above, he was opposed by Conrad von Feuchtwangen, who denied him his assistance and sought to concentrate on the wars of Prussia and Livonia.[67] Furthermore, Burchard's expedition to Acre was a failure and he appears to have made himself deeply unpopular with the local magnates; he resigned his office within weeks of his arrival.[68] A third of the Order's income may have been briefly sent to the Holy Land; however, the brethren's commitment to this region dropped dramatically after the collapse of the kingdom of Jerusalem in 1291.

In summary, although his plans were unsuccessful, it appears that Burchard *did* use the opportunity created by the suppression of the Prussian revolt to instigate a major re-entry into the Holy Land. To this end he marshalled his Order's financial and military resources and began to despatch them to the East. Burchard's arrangement with the pope that taxation should be removed from the monies despatched annually suggests that this was planned to be part of a long-term commitment to the Latin East. Nevertheless, Burchard's resignation in 1290 and the fall of Acre in 1291 evidently ended this process

---

[64] *Ottokars Österreichische Reimchronik*, in *MGH SVL*, vol. 5.1, p. 635. For discussion of this source see Nicholson, *Love, War and the Grail*, p. 80.

[65] *TOT*, no. 665.

[66] Carta de la Orden Teutónica a Alfonso X.'

[67] *AZM*, p. 152.

[68] *Les Gestes des Chiprois*, p. 807.

abruptly. Whether elements of the Teutonic Order had always seen the suppression of the Prussian rebellion as a prerequisite for a new intervention in the eastern Mediterranean is unclear; however, such a scheme would tally well with contemporary attitudes towards the crusade and the ideas of men closely associated with the Order.

CHAPTER 8

The Politics of the Levant

By 1258, the Teutonic Order had become one of the foremost defenders of the Latin East. Under Herman von Salza, the Order's prominence had been derived partially from his personal diplomatic credentials. By this time, however, the brethren's military and material power alone ensured their influence and, although never as important as the Hospitallers and Templars, they possessed significant political power. The previous chapters have discussed the Teutonic Knights' wider policy between the Latin East and the Baltic; this section will examine their role in the governance of the kingdom of Jerusalem in the years after 1258.

After Frederick II's death, the Hohenstaufen territories began to fall apart. By 1267, two of Frederick's successors had assumed the title of king of Jerusalem, Conrad until 1254 and then Conradin until 1267, although neither of them ever travelled to the Latin East to enforce their rights. In 1267, however, the Hohenstaufen family's claims to the Latin East were finally expunged when Pope Clement IV (pope, 1265–1268) stripped Conradin of this throne.[1] Even though it had been many years since these titular rulers had exerted any form of control in the region, this act allowed other contenders to make a bid for the crown of Jerusalem. The first was Hugh of Antioch-Lusignan, bailli of the kingdom and king of Cyprus (1267–1284), who claimed the regency in 1267 and took power the following year. He was duly crowned in Tyre.[2] His candidature was then contested by Maria (granddaughter of Isabella of Jerusalem and great-granddaughter of King Amalric I).[3] Maria claimed the throne in the Latin East, but her demands were rejected and she fled to Rome where in 1277 she sold her right to the kingship to Charles of Anjou, king of Sicily.[4] Meanwhile, in the Levant, Hugh encountered resistance from a party led by the Templars and in 1276 he returned to Cyprus asserting that it was

---

[1] This section has drawn extensively on Riley-Smith, *Feudal Nobility*, pp. 199–228; Salimbene de Adam, *Cronica*, vol. 2, p. 692.

[2] *Les Gestes des Chiprois*, pp. 772–773; Sanuto, p. 223.

[3] For a genealogical table that displays the relationship between these two protagonists see Riley-Smith, *Feudal Nobility*, p. 325.

[4] *Les Gestes des Chiprois*, pp. 773–783. For discussion see J. Dunbabin, *Charles of Anjou: Power, Kingship and State-Making in Thirteenth-Century Europe* (Harlow, 1998), pp. 96–97.

impossible to rule with their interference.[5] The following September, Charles of Anjou's representative, Roger of San Severino, arrived in Acre where he successfully secured his master's purchased right to the throne.[6] Over subsequent years the disputes between the Angevin bailli and the Antioch-Lusignan family continued although they were finally resolved after Charles's death in 1286 when Hugh's descendent Henry II, king of Cyprus (1285–1324), took power in Acre and was crowned king of Jerusalem.

Between the Rulers of Cyprus and the Angevins

In some ways the controversy between the Antioch-Lusignan family and Charles of Anjou resembled the Ibelin–Lombard war. It was a situation where one powerful external ruler attempted to impose his influence upon the Latin East against the wishes of a local faction. Furthermore, the nobility and institutions of the East were faced again with a question of loyalties. As before, there were a number of conflicting pressures upon the Teutonic Knights, although these seem to have been solved (once again) through a policy of neutrality. At this time, the Teutonic Knights' resources were stretched to capacity between the Baltic and the Holy Land. Their estates in the Holy Land were in decline and their fortresses of Amudain and Montfort fell in 1266 and 1271 respectively. As the master rarely visited the Levant, the policy of the brethren in the Holy Land was implemented almost exclusively by the master's deputy (see chapter 10). In these circumstances it was hardly in their interests to involve themselves with a further internal conflict within the kingdom of Jerusalem.

Despite this, both the Angevin and Cypriot parties had a claim to the Knights' loyalties. On the one hand, Charles of Anjou received support from the pope and controlled Sicily and Apulia.[7] The Order needed his protection to safeguard their estates in that region and their lines of communication. Certainly the Hospitallers saw the importance of this factor and they signed a treaty with Charles in 1262 concerning their property in Provence and Forcalquier, swearing homage and military service in exchange for protection and taxation exemptions.[8] In the Holy Land itself, the Hospitallers appear to have adopted a more circumspect position by accepting whichever ruler happened to be in power.[9] The Templars, perhaps perceiving an opportunity in the link between the Angevin empire and the kingdom of Jerusalem, supported Charles and became what Barber has described as 'an integral

---

5 *Les Gestes des Chiprois*, p. 783; Eracles, p. 474. The date given in *Les Gestes des Chiprois* is 1278; however Riley-Smith has shown that it was in fact 1276; *Feudal Nobility*, p. 308.

6 *Les Gestes des Chiprois*, p. 783; Sanuto, p. 227.

7 Toomaspoeg has shown that the Order's policy enabled it to sustain its position under Charles; *Les Teutoniques en Sicilie*, pp. 62–63.

8 Bronstein, *The Hospitallers and the Holy Land*, p. 96.

9 *KSJJC*, pp. 187–189. Riley-Smith argues that they were primarily Lusignan supporters but did not resist the Angevins and were prepared to render some aid to them.

part of the structure of power which Charles had been erecting for himself in the Mediterranean'.[10] On the other hand, Hugh of Antioch-Lusignan was the king of Cyprus, where all three orders held property, and until 1276 he was the effective ruler in Acre.

The Teutonic Knights seem to have adopted a similar stance to the Hospitallers in the Holy Land and accepted the governance of either faction. Accordingly, after Hugh's coronation, both military orders were ready to offer some support to him. In 1272, for example, they agreed to travel to Cyprus to help negotiate a dispute between Hugh and his barons concerning their responsibility to defend the mainland.[11] In 1276, when Hugh departed from Acre claiming that interference from the Templars made it impossible to rule, both these orders tried to convince him to remain.[12] In these ways both the Hospitallers and Teutonic Knights worked with Hugh to maintain the governance of the kingdom of Jerusalem.

Nevertheless, after Charles of Anjou's assumption of power in 1277 the Teutonic Knights were equally prepared to co-operate with his representative, Roger of San Severino. The first indication of positive relations between these two can be found in a letter issued in 1277, which mentioned that Roger had issued a licence to the Order for the shipment of wheat into the port of Acre.[13] Such permits were vital for the maintenance of the brethren's position in Outremer. The following year, a representative of the Order worked with Roger in an attempt to resolve a dispute between the bishop of Tripoli, the Templars and the prince of Antioch.[14] Additionally, in 1283 all three military orders co-operated with Roger's deputy, Odo, to create a treaty between the kingdom of Jerusalem and the Mamluk Sultan Qalāwūn that was designed to ensure peace for almost eleven years.[15]

When the balance of power turned, once again, in favour of the Cypriot rulers, the Teutonic Knights again altered their position. This occurred after Charles of Anjou's death in 1286 and with the arrival of Henry of Antioch-Lusignan. At this time, the Teutonic Knights and the Hospitallers worked to prevent any violence in Acre and they arranged the bloodless evacuation of the Angevin bailli.[16] In summary, during this period, the Teutonic Knights appear to have followed the biblical command 'there is no authority but by the act of God, and the existing authorities are instituted by him'.[17] They seem to have adopted a pragmatic stance and accepted both the Cypriot claimants to

---

[10] Barber, *The New Knighthood*, p. 169.
[11] Eracles, p. 463.
[12] Eracles, p. 474. Sanuto, p. 226.
[13] *I Registri della Cancelleria Angioina*, ed. R. Filangieri, vol. 19 (Naples, 1964), p. 39.
[14] *R. Reg.*, vol. 1, no. 1424.
[15] *R. Reg.*, vol. 1, no. 1450. See also *Early Mamluk Diplomacy (1260–1290): Treaties of Baybars and Qalāwūn with Christian Rulers*, ed. and trans. P. M. Holt, Islamic History and Civilisation, 12 (Leiden, 1995), pp. 69–91.
[16] *R. Reg.*, vol. 1, no. 1466; *Les Gestes des Chiprois*, p. 793.
[17] Romans 13.1.

the throne and Charles's representatives, depending upon whichever faction was in the ascendancy.

The prudent conduct of the brethren during this turbulent period certainly seems to have effectively safeguarded their interests. Even so, a second and stronger motive can be inferred from their actions. It seems significant that, although the Order was prepared to support both the Angevins and the Cypriots, the tasks in which they offered such assistance were almost exclusively focused upon the prevention of civil disorder and the protection of the Latin East. Accordingly, as shown above, the brethren's co-operation with both these factions was evinced through undertakings such as internal negotiations (1272, 1276, 1278 and 1286) and treaties with the Muslims (1283), rather than any actions which might suggest a particular political partisanship. Furthermore, both the Hospitallers and Teutonic Knights were active participants in many of the raiding expeditions against the Mamluks throughout this period (see chapter 9), thus providing further proof that their interests lay in the wider concerns of the Latin East.

Increasing Papal Intervention in the Holy Land

The Order may have distanced itself from the disputes over the throne, yet there was a further transition of power within the kingdom of Jerusalem at this time in which the brethren were complicit. Under the leadership of popes such as Urban IV (pope, 1261–1264) and Gregory X (pope, 1271–1276) the papacy became increasingly preoccupied with the future of the Latin East and began to pursue an interventionist policy in the eastern Mediterranean through the office of the patriarch. This factor has been commented upon by several historians who have shown how the papacy mustered military forces for dispatch to the East, gained closer control over ecclesiastical appointments and even granted trading privileges in the kingdom of Jerusalem to French and Italian mercantile communities in Western Christendom.[18] More pertinent to this study were the papacy's efforts to draw the military orders firmly under the control of the patriarch.

The patriarch's authority over the military orders had frequently been a point of contention in Outremer. Previously, the Templars, Hospitallers and Teutonic Knights had received exemptions from the authority of all prelates, including the patriarch, with the sole exception of the pope. As a result, the only way that the patriarch could exert power over an order was through the pope himself. The Teutonic Order's first major privilege on this matter,

---

[18] For examples of the papacy mustering military forces for the Latin East see *Les Gestes des Chiprois*, p. 101; Sanuto, p. 227. This section has drawn on S. Schein, 'The Patriarchs of Jerusalem in the Late Thirteenth Century: *Seignors Espiritueles et Temporeles*', in *Outremer: Studies in the History of the Crusading Kingdom of Jerusalem*, ed. B. Z. Kedar (Jerusalem, 1982), pp. 297–305; Riley-Smith, *Feudal Nobility*, p. 213; Mayer, *The Crusades*, p. 272.

granted in 1218, forbade prelates from placing the brethren under sentence of excommunication.[19] They were also prevented from extorting taxation from the Order in 1221.[20] More significantly, in the same year the Order was also explicitly granted the same exemptions from Church authority as the Templars and Hospitallers.[21]

Armed with these privileges, all three military orders had, at some time, become involved in disputes with the ecclesiastical hierarchies of the Latin East. The Hospitallers came into conflict with the patriarch in 1154 when the brothers were accused of a number of abuses including a violent attack upon the Church of the Holy Sepulchre. Unable to discipline the Order personally, Patriarch Fulcher of Angoulême (patriarch, 1145–1157) appealed to Rome but his case was rejected.[22] In 1196, the Templars became involved in a quarrel over tithes with the Church authorities.[23] Several further disputes developed over subsequent decades. The Teutonic Knights, by contrast, initially attracted the praise of James of Vitry (bishop of Acre, 1216–1228), who mentioned the Order's readiness to serve the patriarch.[24] Despite this, problems did occur in 1228–1229 and 1239–1241 when the brethren were perceived to be in conflict with Rome, and punishments were meted out against them through the office of the patriarch.[25] Consequently, all the military orders had a rather chequered history of relations with this official.

By the late 1250s the Baltic wars had brought the Teutonic Knights into close co-operation with Rome. The papacy had proved a willing and efficacious advocate of the crusades in the north and the suppression of the Second Prussian uprising, which began in 1260, was contingent upon the recruitment of pilgrim forces, sanctioned and encouraged by the papacy. In the Holy Land, this partnership can be found in operation once again, although the relationship demanded of the Teutonic Knights in this region was one of obedience rather than collaboration. Increasingly, the papacy sought to impose its will on the Order through the office of the patriarch. In 1256, for example, Pope Alexander IV instructed the three main military orders to assist patriarch James Pantaleon during the war of St Sabas.[26] As shown above (chapter 7), this command may explain the political stance taken by both the Teutonic Knights and the Hospitallers during this crisis. In later

[19] This charter was issued on 1 October 1218; *TOT*, no. 305. For later confirmations see *TOT*, nos. 418, 441, 447, 461, 462, 474, 480, 490, 504, 507, 571, 576, 599, 628, 641, *CDOT*, no. 260.
[20] Issued on 19 January 1221; *TOT*, no. 332. For later confirmations see *TOT*, nos. 425, 473, 514, 519.
[21] Issued on 9 January 1221; *TOT*, no. 309. For later confirmations see *TOT*, nos. 373, 416, 545, 551, 553, 555, 556, 557 and *R. Reg.*, vol. 1, nos. 1415, 1417.
[22] William of Tyre, *Chronicon*, vol. 2, pp. 812–814; *KSJJC*, pp. 398–400.
[23] Hamilton, *The Latin Church in the Crusader States*, p. 288.
[24] James of Vitry, *Historia Hierosolimitani*, p. 1085.
[25] HB, vol. 3, pp. 102–110.
[26] *CGJJ*, vol. 2, no. 2806.

years the papacy developed the powers of the patriarch significantly.[27] Firstly, the papacy began to routinely appoint each patriarch as a papal legate.[28] Also, in 1262 the Order of St Lazarus was placed directly under the authority of this prelate.[29] In 1274 Gregory X enabled the patriarch to strip the military orders of their privileges should they fail to offer him their support.[30] This dispensation partially nullified the Orders' exemptions from the authority of bishops and gave the patriarch the means to control and censure a disobedient order. In 1288 Patriarch Nicholas of Hanapes (patriarch, 1288–1291) acquired the power to excommunicate disobedient orders or even to place them under interdict.[31] This trend of transferring power away from the orders has been commented upon by Schein, who has also shown how the papacy 'ceased to grant the orders responsibility of deciding how papal subsidies to the Latin East were to be spent'.[32] In these ways, the orders were effectively leashed to the office of the patriarch. The papacy coupled these powers of censure with the ability to strengthen and support the military orders. In 1277 several of the Teutonic Knights' privileges were renewed by Patriarch Thomas Agni of Lentino (patriarch of Jerusalem, 1272–1277) in Acre.[33] Formerly the privileges of the Order, in so far as they pertained to the Holy Land, had been renewed by the papacy, not by a local prelate. Now the patriarch also had this right.

Despite this uneven relationship, the patriarch and the Teutonic Knights frequently worked in close co-operation to consolidate the defences of the Latin East. This can be seen particularly in their attempts to resolve the ongoing differences between the Italian cities. The War of St Sabas did not end the rivalry between Venice, Pisa and Genoa and in 1261, during a subsequent dispute, the patriarch and military orders tried to negotiate a long-term solution.[34] Similarly in 1277 the military orders and the papal legate helped to arrange the return of Venetian trading privileges in Tyre. These rights had been removed after a failed attack made by the soldiers of Venice upon the city in 1264.[35] The overall guidance of the papacy/patriarch in such disputes

---

27 Hamilton, *The Latin Church in the Crusader States*, p. 273; Schein, 'The Patriarchs of Jerusalem', *passim*.
28 Schein, 'The Patriarchs of Jerusalem', p. 298.
29 D. Marcombe, *Leper Knights: The Order of St Lazarus of Jerusalem in England, c.1150–1544* (Woodbridge, 2003), p. 15. M. Barber, 'The Order of Saint Lazarus and the Crusades', *Catholic Historical Review*, 80 (1994), p. 452.
30 *Reg. Grégoire X*, no. 551.
31 *Reg. Nicolas IV*, vol. 1, no. 225.
32 Schein, 'The Patriarchs of Jerusalem', p. 301. This occurred even though in 1256 the Order had been released from paying the expenses of a papal legate, *TOT*, no. 535.
33 *R.. Reg*, vol. 1, no. 1414; *CDOT*, no. 257; *R. Reg.*, vol. 1, no. 1416.
34 *R. Reg.*, vol. 1, no. 1298; *Urkunden zur Älteren Handels – und Staatsgeschichte der Republik Venedig mit Besonderer Beziehung auf Byzanz und die Levante*, ed. G. Tafel and G. Thomas, vol. 3 (Amsterdam, 1964), no. 346.
35 For the Venetian attack upon Tyre see *Les Gestes des Chiprois*, p. 757; Eracles, p. 447. For the return of the Venetian privileges see *R. Reg.*, vol. 1, no. 1413; *Urkunden zur Älteren Handels – und Staatsgeschichte der Republik Venedig*, vol. 3, no. 369.

is particularly clear in the events which followed the death of Bohemond VII of Antioch-Tripoli in 1287. In 1288 the throne of Antioch-Tripoli became contested between Lucy, sister of Bohemond VII, and the men of Tripoli, who were supported by the Genoese. The papacy responded to this crisis by ordering the three military orders to support Lucy and accordingly they travelled north from Acre.[36] The readiness of the military orders, or at least the Hospitallers, to enforce such papal instructions is revealed in *Les Gestes des Chiprois* which states that Lucy had been told to expect the support of the Hospitallers at Tripoli.[37] Perhaps in an attempt to ensure that the three institutions pursued this policy, the patriarch was given the power to excommunicate a military order in this year.[38] These examples demonstrate, therefore, the military orders' co-operation with the patriarch, but also highlight that it was not a relationship of equals.

A further example of this collaboration can be found in the parliaments of the kingdom of Jerusalem and more particularly in the despatch of appeals to the West. The magnates of the kingdom convened frequently in parliaments, also called *curia generalis*, to discuss affairs of state. Riley-Smith has shown that these usually concerned 'the choice of consorts for queens, relations with the Muslims and the need to appeal to the West'.[39] The Teutonic Knights were regularly present at these meetings and their views were evidently well respected. For example, during the parliament of 1260, Anno von Sangershausen offered the advice which shaped the policy of the nobility towards the battle of Ayn Jālūt (see above). The brethren are also known to have been present during the treaties made with the Muslims in 1255[40] and 1283.[41]

In the latter half of the thirteenth century, as the need for outside support grew, these parliaments were often convened to summon aid from the West. During the assembly in 1260, the proximity of the threat posed by the Mongols compelled the magnates of Outremer to seek support from the rulers of Western Christendom. Among those who issued the ensuing letter of appeal were the Teutonic Knights and the patriarch of Jerusalem.[42] In subsequent years, the patriarch and the Order, along with the secular and ecclesiastical elite of the kingdom of Jerusalem, issued many further appeals to Western rulers including Henry III of England in 1263, Pope Urban IV in 1263 and King Rudolph I of Germany in 1285.[43] After the preparation of such appeal letters, there were times when Teutonic Knights were then employed

---

[36] *Reg. Nicolas IV*, no. 6985; *Les Gestes des Chiprois*, p. 801.

[37] *Les Gestes des Chiprois*, p. 801.

[38] *Reg. Nicolas IV*, no. 225.

[39] Riley-Smith, *The Feudal Nobility*, p. 195.

[40] Rothelin, p. 630.

[41] *R. Reg.*, vol. 1, no. 1450. See also *Early Mamluk Diplomacy*, pp. 69–91.

[42] *Annales de Burton*, pp. 491–495; 'Lettre des chrétiens de Terre-Sainte à Charles d'Anjou', p. 212; *R. Reg.*, vol. 2, no. 1291. For discussion of these and many other appeals see Ross, 'Relations between the Latin East and Western Europe', *passim*.

[43] (letter to Henry III) *CGJJ*, vol. 3, no. 3059; (letter to king of France referencing an earlier letter to Urban) *Reg. Urbain IV*, vol. 2, no. 344; (letter to King Rudolph) *PL*, vol. 98, cols. 820B–821B.

to convey them to the West and in 1260, presumably on the initiative of Anno von Sangershausen, a Teutonic Knight was sent from Acre to Germany to gather aid.[44]

After an envoy's arrival in Western Christendom, the military Orders were often required to support the agents and preachers who were sent out to rally the requested support. In 1263, for example, Pope Urban IV instructed the prelates of the Church and the commanders of the military orders to assist an embassy sent to German-speaking lands and to Hungary to promote the affairs of the Holy Land.[45] Similar requests were made in April and October of the same year and also in January 1264 regarding embassies to northern France, England and Scotland.[46] At the same time, Urban specifically demanded that the Teutonic Order support his preparations for a new crusade.[47] Seemingly in response to this request, William of Sesso, an official in Bologna, then relayed these instructions in a letter that referred to agents of the Teutonic Order who had been sent to recruit forces for the Holy Land.[48] These examples demonstrate how the brethren's Western properties could be used as a communications network for the purposes of recruitment. In these ways, the papacy, patriarch and military orders each used their resources in conjunction to support the defence of the Latin East.

Although the papacy was deeply concerned with the fate of Latin Syria and used the military orders to implement its policies in this theatre, there were times when it was prepared to subordinate both this imperative and the Orders' resources to achieve other objectives. This can be seen clearly in the collection and allocation of papal taxation during this period. The resources necessary to fund the papacy's crusading ambitions were gathered largely through taxation on the Church as a whole. Previously, during the preparations for ventures such as the Fifth Crusade and the first crusade of Louis IX, the Teutonic Knights, along with the Templars and Hospitallers, had been exempt from payment of such taxes.[49] In 1264 however, the situation changed and a papal tax of one tenth of all ecclesiastical revenues was exacted for three years upon the entire Church, including these three institutions, to support Charles of Anjou's ambitions in Sicily.[50] This levy caused

Rudolph had expressed an interest in travelling to the Holy Land in 1274 at the council of Lyons. See, Sanuto, p. 225.

[44] *Annales de Burton*, p. 493.

[45] For the mission to Germany see *CGJJ*, vol. 3, no. 3057. For the mission to Hungary see Potthast, vol. 2, no. 18663.

[46] For the embassy to France see *CGJJ*, vol. 3, no. 3060. For the embassy to England see *Reg. Urbain IV*, vol. 2, no. 472. For the embassy to Scotland see *Reg. Urbain IV*, vol. 4, no. 2975.

[47] *CGJJ*, vol. 3, no, 3097.

[48] Prutz, 'Eilf Deutschordensurkunden', pp. 388–389.

[49] For the Teutonic Knights' previous exemptions from crusading taxation see *TOT*, nos. 332, 345, 425, 473, 514, 519. These charters include demands that the Order should not be forcibly compelled to pay these taxes by other churchmen.

[50] Bronstein, The Hospitallers and the Holy Land, p. 96; N. Housley, *The Italian Crusades: The Papal–Angevin Alliance and the Crusades against Christian Lay Powers, 1254–1343* (Oxford, 1982), pp. 216–217.

outrage because it drew resources away from the Holy Land. The Hospitallers even took the extreme step of refusing to pay.[51] In 1265 the Teutonic Knights, along with the other military orders, were briefly exempted, but the same levy was re-imposed by the end of the year and then continued to be demanded from the Teutonic Order throughout its duration.[52] Admittedly in 1266 the papacy freed the Teutonic Knights from all taxation required by a papal legate for three years; however, this charter did not specifically refer to the tenth and further evidence suggests that it continued to be collected.[53] In 1274 papal attention returned to the Holy Land and a six-year tax was imposed at the Second Council of Lyons from which the military orders were spared.[54] Priorities changed once again in 1283, 1284 and 1289 when the papal tenth was levied upon the military orders to finance wars in the Iberian peninsula and Sicily.[55] In 1296 the Teutonic Knights were exempted entirely from this tax, but this was a little late to be of use to the Holy Land.[56] As a result, although the papacy provided significant aid to the Levant during this period, there were occasions when it diverted both its own resources and even those of the military orders away from the Levant to support other policies. Consequently, the partnership between the Teutonic Knights and the papacy was both unequal in its nature and inconsistent in the aid it rendered to the east.

Relations between the Military Orders

During the decline and fall of the kingdom of Jerusalem many contemporaries sought to provide explanations for the military reverses suffered by the Christian forces. Among the most popular targets of such condemnation were the military orders. The *Eberhardi Archidiaconi Ratisponensis Annales*, written around the turn of the fourteenth century, makes the following statement:

> The city of Acre, which alone the Christians possessed in the Holy Land, was besieged by the sultan of Babylon, and having been attacked without intermission for forty days and nights it was captured, and in that place many thousands of Christians were captured and killed, others fled, however, by ship. And accordingly it was the opinion of many that if the brothers of the military orders in that place, namely those of the Hospital, the Temple and the Teutonic Knights, along with the other people [therein] had worked together, the city would not have been captured.[57]

---

[51] Bronstein, *The Hospitallers and the Holy Land*, p. 96.
[52] *Reg. Clément IV*, vol. 1, nos. 69, 121, 300; *CGJJ*, vol. 3, no. 3122.
[53] *TOT*, no. 643.
[54] *CGJJ*, vol. 3, no. 3543; *Decrees of the Ecumenical Councils*, vol. 1, p. 310.
[55] *Reg. Martin IV*, nos. 457, 583; *Reg. Nicolas IV*, no. 1142; Housley, *Italian Crusades*, p. 215.
[56] Housley, *Italian Crusades*, p. 215.
[57] Civitas Akaron, quam solum habebant christiani in terra sancta, obsessa est per soldanem Babylonem, et per 40 dies et noctes sine intermissione inpugnata capta est, et ibidem multa christian-

Similarly, Menko, abbot of Werum in Frisia,[58] commented upon the condition of the Holy Land in the 1270s, stating:

> The Lands Overseas have not been worthy to receive such a helper and protector on account of their own civil discords because not only the Genoese, who, coming from the city of Genoa and inhabiting the city of Acre were at discord with the Pisans from the city of Pisa but also those who are called the knights of God, namely from the Hospital of St John and the Teutonic House and also the Templars, are not observing the obligations of charity in accordance with the requirements of monastic life and the name that is knights of God, but are fighting amongst themselves.[59]

These contemporary criticisms find their echo in modern literature and Mayer, describing the period 1254–1291, has argued that 'relations between the military orders were just as bad as were all relations between the evenly matched powers in the Holy Land'.[60]

Certainly, there is evidence which suggests that disputes did occur between these institutions. In 1273, for example, Pope Gregory X referred to their many quarrels and ordered them to solve these disputes peacefully because they threatened the stability of the Latin East.[61] Even Peter von Dusburg, a Teutonic Knight himself, explained the fall of Acre as the result of internal disputes within the kingdom, although he blamed the leading magnates of the kingdom rather than the military orders.[62]

Despite the conclusions of these modern and contemporary commentators, other historians, such as Riley-Smith, have argued that 'the history of Latin Syria shows that for most of the time they [the military orders] co-operated on campaign and in council as reconciliators and negotiators'.[63] Furthermore, the conclusions drawn in preceding sections have demonstrated that, during the controversies over the throne of Jerusalem and between the Italian cities, the primary role of the Teutonic Knights and Hospitallers was one of mediation and consolidation.

With regard to the Teutonic Knights in particular, these accusations seem

orum milia et capta sunt et occisa; aliqua autem per navigium fugierunt. Et quia multorum erat opinio, quod si fratres domorum ibidem, scilicet Hospitalis, Templi et Teutonicorum, et reliquus populus omnino concordasset, civitas capta non fuisset'; *Eberhardi Archidiaconi Ratisponensis Annales*, in *MGH SS*, vol. 17, p. 594.

58 Nicholson, *Templars, Hospitallers and Teutonic Knights*, p. 44.
59 'Transmarini non fuerunt digni talem recipere coadiutorem et defensorem propter suas civiles discordias, quia non solum Ianuenses, qui de Ianua civitate venientes Akon civitatem inhabitabant, et Pisani de Pisa civitate invicem discordaverunt, sed etiam illi qui dicuntur milites Dei, videlicet de Hospitali sancti Iohannis et de domo Teutonica nec non et Templarii, debitam caritatem secundum exigentiam religionis et nomen, dicuntur milites Dei, non observant, sed invicem sibi inimicantur'; *Menkonis Chronicon*, in *MGH SS*, vol. 23, p. 555. For further examples and discussion of this subject see Forey, *The Military Orders*, pp. 208–210.
60 Mayer, *The Crusades*, p. 277.
61 Prutz, 'Eilf Deutschordensurkunden', p. 391.
62 Peter von Dusburg, *Chronicon Terrae Prussie*, p. 208.
63 *KSJJC*, p. 151.

particularly unfounded because not only did they aid in the resolution of the wider disputes in Outremer, but they also played a vital part in the settlement of those disagreements which did occur between the other military orders. For instance, after the 1258 agreement between the three orders, the Templars and Hospitallers appear to have sought to resolve their differences over their landed property. In May 1262 the two orders reached an accord over the division of villages in the lordship of Sidon and in the same year they concluded a further agreement over the mills of Doc and Ricordane.[64] As Riley-Smith has shown, these property negotiations were resolved by recourse to the 1258 treaty (see chapter 6), which stipulated that should a point of contention develop between two orders, they could appeal to the third for adjudication.[65] Accordingly, it was Hartmann von Heldrungen, grand commander of the Teutonic Order, who acted as one of the principal arbitrators (see appendix E.2). In this way, the three orders had managed to solve these quarrels in accordance with their prior agreement, but notably it was the Teutonic Order which had acted as the peacemaker. The brethren also helped to settle further controversies between either the Templars or the Hospitallers and a secular power. As discussed, the Hospitallers and Teutonic Knights attempted to resolve the ongoing disputes between the Templars and Hugh of Antioch-Lusignan over the throne of Jerusalem.[66] In 1265, Ernest of Wulfen, grand commander of the Teutonic Order, witnessed an agreement between Hugh Revel, master of the Hospitallers, and the bishop of Hebron concerning the village of Naria.[67] In 1278, Hartmann von Heldrungen, now master of the Order, was present when the Angevin bailli tried to manage a quarrel between the prince of Antioch, the Templars and the bishop of Tripoli.[68] Reviewing the actions of the Teutonic Order during this period, it appears that their actions, as Riley-Smith has argued for the military orders as a whole, were generally characterised by negotiation and the establishment of accord. Moreover, if the Latin East came to be policed by the military orders, then it seems that the military orders came to be policed by the Teutonic Knights.

Admittedly, between 1260 and 1291, the Teutonic Knights were themselves involved in several small-scale property disputes, such as an ongoing argument with the bishop of Hebron over a house in the Montmusard district of Acre.[69] Also, the Order's quarrels with the Amigdala family persisted into the 1280s. Even so, these controversies were localised, confined to judicature and hardly posed a serious threat to the security of the Latin

---

[64] For these disputes see *KSJJC*, pp. 449–450. See also the following charters: *CGJJ*, vol. 3, nos. 3026, 3028, 2029, 2044, 3045.

[65] *KSJJC*, p. 449.

[66] See above, p. 132.

[67] *CGJJ*, vol. 3, no. 3120; *R. Reg.*, vol. 1, no. 1337. For further details on Ernest see appendix E.2.

[68] *R. Reg.*, vol. 1, no. 1424. For background on Hartmann see Arnold, 'Hartmann von Heldrungen', pp. 36–38.

[69] *TOT*, no. 126; *R. Reg.*, vol. 1, no. 1390.

East.[70] Furthermore, the Teutonic Knights' earlier quarrels with the Templars over the white mantles, and with the Hospitallers over the question of subordination, either did not emerge or did not prevent the Orders from working in co-operation.[71] Consequently, such matters hardly outweigh the brethren's contributions to the prevention of discord.

To conclude, the contention that antipathy between the military orders in the last decades of the Latin East was a critical factor which provoked the fall of the Latin East is challenged by the evidence shown above and indeed by much of the material discussed in this chapter as a whole. For the Templars and Hospitallers such allegations of infighting seem to be largely unfounded, while for the Teutonic Knights there is still less evidence to support such a conclusion. Indeed their ongoing commitment to the establishment of internal stability argues quite the reverse.

The Fall of Acre 1291

Whatever assistance Western Christendom had rendered to the east it had not been enough and in 1291 the Teutonic Knights found themselves arrayed on the battlements of Acre, awaiting the attack that would end the kingdom of Jerusalem. There are many sources for the final collapse of the kingdom and in almost every case they describe the valour of the Teutonic Knights.[72] After the arrival of the king of Cyprus, at the outset of the siege, a rota system was implemented to provide guards for the walls of the city. The Teutonic Knights, led by Henry of Boland, preceptor of Sicily and deputy to the master, along with the crusaders who had travelled to Acre from Prussia in 1290, stood their shift with the troops of the king of Cyprus.[73] After the Mamluks gained entrance to the city, according to the account of Master Thadeus, written in Messina in 1291, the Teutonic Knights' house in Acre came under attack.[74] The brethren are reported to have defeated the first Muslim assault upon the building, but to have been unable to resist the second. Both the account of Master Thadeus and that of Ludolph von Suchem claim that they did not

---

[70] Favreau, 'Die Kreuzfahrerherrschaft Scandalion (Iskanderūne)', pp 18–29.
[71] It is worth noting, however, that the Hospitallers did refer to their perceived rights over the Teutonic Order in the 1258 agreement. *KSJJC*, p. 447. *TOT*, no. 116.
[72] The following sources describe the role of the Teutonic Knights in the fall of Acre: Thadeus of Naples, *Ystoria de Desolatione et Conculcatione Civitatis Acconensis et Tocius Terre Sancte*, in *The Fall of Acre: 1291*, ed. R. Huygens, Continuatio Mediaeualis, Corpus Christianorum: Continuatio Mediaeualis 202 (Turnhout, 2004), p. 119–121; *Excidii Aconis Gestorum Collectio*, in ibid., p. 69; Ludolph von Suchem, *Itinere Terrae Sanctae*, Bibliothek des Literarischen Vereins in Stuttgart, 25 (Stuttgart, 1851), p. 44; Abū l-Mahāsin, *Arab Historians of the Crusades*, p. 348; 'Iohannis Abbatis Victoriensis', p. 261; *Ottokars Österreichische Reimchronik*, pp. 642, 689.
[73] *Excidii Aconis Gestorum Collectio*', p. 62; 'Iohannis Abbatis Victoriensis', p. 261; Perlbach, 'Deutsch-Ordens Necrologe', p. 364. Arnold has suggested that it might have been Burchard von Schwanden who appointed Henry as deputy in 1290, Arnold, 'Akkon-Venedig-Marienburg: Der Deutsche Orden vom Mittelmeer zum Ostseeraum', p. 72.
[74] Thadeus of Naples, *Ystoria*, p. 120.

surrender but were killed to the last man.[75] The chronicle of Abū l-Mahāsin gives a slightly different account and suggests that the Order retreated into the Templar castle and withstood the Muslim assaults for two days before asking for amnesty.[76] It is possible that the forces of the Teutonic Knights were divided between these two buildings and met correspondingly different fates.

The fall of Acre in 1291 did not end the brethren's interventions in the Mediterranean and several historians have commented upon the fact that, after 1291, the Order's headquarters moved first to Venice and only later to Marburg, suggesting that the brothers wished to preserve a foothold in this region.[77] They also continued to maintain a force on Cyprus and there are documents which mention the presence of the Order's officials on the isle in 1300.[78] Harunia in Armenia also remained in their possession after the fall of Acre and it seems perfectly plausible that the Teutonic Knights, like the Hospitallers, retained a contingent in this kingdom.[79] They were also included in the many plans for the recapture of the Holy Land.[80] Nevertheless, after 1291 the eastern Mediterranean became a theatre of decidedly secondary importance in comparison to Prussia and Livonia. A symbol of this trend can be seen in a fictional account of the fall of Acre. According to *Ottokars Österreichische Reimchronik* the master of the Teutonic Order, during his escape from the burning city, promised that he would seek vengeance for this defeat. He stated that the target of his revenge, however, would be the pagans in Prussia, not the Mamluks in the Holy Land.[81]

---

[75] Ludolph von Suchem, *Itinere Terrae Sanctae*, p. 44; Thadeus of Naples, *Ystoria*, p. 120.

[76] Abū l-Mahāsin, *Arab Historians of the Crusades*, p. 348.

[77] Forstreuter, *Der Deutsche Orden am Mittelmeer*, p. 193; Militzer, 'From the Holy Land to Prussia', pp. 80–81; Forey, *The Military Orders*, p. 222.

[78] *Notai Genovesi in Oltremare atti Rogati a Cipro da Lamberto di Sambuceto: 3 luglio 1300–3 agosto 1301*, ed. V. Polonio, Collana Storica di Fonti e Studi 31 (Genoa, 1982), no. 140. I would like to thank Dr Paul Crawford for drawing my attention to this document.

[79] Forstreuter, *Der Deutsche Orden am Mittelmeer*, p. 65.

[80] *Chronica Minor Minoritae Erphordensis: Continuatio VII*, in *MGH SRG*, vol. 42, p. 704; Schein, *Fideles Crucis*, pp. 102–107, 220–233.

[81] *Ottokars Österreichische Reimchronik*, pp. 689–690; Arnold, 'Deutschmeister Konrad von Feuchtwangen', pp. 22–23.

CHAPTER 9

The Military Organisation
of the Teutonic Knights in the Holy Land

The Statutes of the Teutonic Order

I now turn to the internal and constitutional framework which enabled the Teutonic Knights to carry out their diplomatic, charitable and military functions. To begin discussion on this subject it is necessary firstly to examine the history and composition of the Order's statutes. These regulations were intended to be the blueprint for the institution's structure and they defined the responsibilities of the major officers. The first surviving version has been dated to *c.*1264 and comprises three main parts (the rule, laws and customs) as well as the subsidiary sections (the prologue, vigils, calendar, Easter tables and genuflections).[1]

The first reference to these statutes can be found in accounts of the Order's militarisation in 1198 when it was granted elements of the Hospitaller and Templar rule. Hospitaller statutes covering the care of the sick and the support of the poor were spliced with Templar regulations concerning clerics, soldiers and other brethren to create a hybrid which drew upon the strengths of both institutions.[2] As Sterns has shown, over time the Teutonic Knights began to edit and adapt these regulations and in 1244 Innocent IV granted his permission for them to remove clauses which were of no further use to them.[3] In *c.*1251 Eberhard of Saone delivered a list of new instructions to the Order's commanders in Elbing. These demands not only attempted to develop the existing regulations but mentioned, for the first time, the three major subsections: the rule, laws and customs.[4] These statutes were transmitted to the brethren through a weekly public recital. According to the charter delivered by Eberhard of Saone, one paragraph of the rule, laws and customs was to

---

[1] Sterns, 'The Statutes of the Teutonic Knights', p. 48.
[2] *De Primordiis Ordinis Theutonici Narratio*, p. 225. This section has drawn on Sterns, 'The Statutes of the Teutonic Knights', pp. 43–59.
[3] *TOT*, no. 470; Sterns, 'The Statutes of the Teutonic Knights', p. 44. Some of the later influences on the Teutonic Order's statutes and liturgy came from other orders such as the Dominicans, see C. Dondi, *The Liturgy or the Canons Regular of the Holy Sepulchre of Jerusalem*, Bibliotheca Victorina, 16 (Turnhout, 2004), p. 34; Sterns, 'The Statutes of the Teutonic Knights', pp. 61–142.
[4] *PU*, vol. 1.1, no. 251; Sterns, 'The Statutes of the Teutonic Knights', p. 46.

be read out to the brethren every Sunday.[5] Subsequently, the Order arranged that the rule should be recited in its entirety at special occasions such as Christmas, Easter and the meeting of the general chapter.[6] Every house of the Order was expected to hold a copy of the 'rule' and 'laws' sections of the statutes and literate brethren were given the opportunity to study them.[7] To ensure uniformity, the statutes emphasise the need for scribes to copy them correctly.[8] With regard to the *c.*1264 edition of the rule, Militzer seems correct to argue that it is still a hybrid of the rules of the Templars and Hospitallers although there were a number of elements drawn from other institutions and some innovations.[9] I will not attempt here a comprehensive examination of the influences which shaped these statutes, but will rather explore their application in the brethren's actions in both the Latin East and Western Christendom.[10]

These statutes appear to have been highly regarded by the papacy because in 1236 Pope Gregory IX confirmed a decision made by the bishop of Winchester and the patriarch of Jerusalem that the English Order of St Thomas of Acre should be militarised and live in conformity with the rule of the Teutonic Order.[11] This event is significant because it suggests that the Knights' rule was considered to be the most appropriate for adaptation to the needs of a new military order in the Holy Land. As Forey has argued, the formation of the Teutonic Knights' rule from the combined strengths of the Hospitaller and Templar rule would have made it suitable for employment in a medical order wishing to adopt a military role.[12]

The Office of the Marshal and the Teutonic Order's field force

Like the other major military orders, the Teutonic Knights were a tightly cohesive and powerful fighting force. Their troops were among the elite of the Christian army and they occasionally helped to form its vanguard.[13] On campaign, their warriors were organised according to the statutes.[14] These stipulated that the marshal should take charge of most battlefield matters and be supported by the other major officers.[15] His responsibilities pertained

---

[5] *PU*, vol. 1.1, no. 251; Sterns, 'The Statutes of the Teutonic Knights', p. 46; *SDO*, p. 74.
[6] *SDO*, p. 134.
[7] *SDO*, p. 71.
[8] *SDO*, p. 74.
[9] *AZM*, p. 131.
[10] For discussion of these themes see *AZM*, pp. 115–144; Sterns, 'The Statutes of the Teutonic Knights', pp. 41–153.
[11] *Reg. Grégoire IX*, vol. 2, no. 2944.
[12] Forey, 'The Military Order of St Thomas of Acre', pp. 487–488.
[13] Forey, *The Military Orders*, pp. 88–89. For a list of marshals see appendix E.1.
[14] For further discussion on the military statutes of the rule see Sterns, 'The Teutonic Knights in the Crusader States', pp. 334–339.
[15] *SDO*, pp. 103–104.

to all matters concerning military personnel and equipment.[16] As Militzer has shown, the regulations concerning the office of the marshal were drawn from the rule of the Templars.[17] In battle, if the master was present then the marshal was expected to wait for his command before commencing with an attack, although he had executive control over all other military affairs.[18] If the master was absent the marshal assumed full responsibility. In practice, reviewing the military campaigns of this period, it appears that the master rarely participated in military undertakings in the eastern Mediterranean. For example, during the campaigns of 1239 (the Barons' Crusade), 1244 (La Forbie) and 1253–1254 (the latter part of Louis's Crusade), the master was absent and responsibility devolved instead on the marshals: Gerhard von Malberg, Werner of Merenberg and Peter of Koblenz respectively (see appendix E.1). The marshal was also evidently permitted to command the Order's forces on raiding expeditions because during the Fifth Crusade this officer, probably Ludwig of Hörselgau, along with the grand commander and a contingent of brethren, were defeated during such an operation in the Nile delta.[19]

Under the marshal's direct command was a field force composed of a number of different formations. Firstly, the Order was led by a command group. This consisted firstly of the master, when present, who was entitled to between four and five horses. He was supplied with an escort of four turcopoles in time of war and two brother knights as companions as well as a number of non-military personnel.[20] The marshal was entitled to a body-guard of two brother knights and two turcopoles, who were responsible for the standard.[21] He was also accompanied by the crier, who relayed all the marshal's commands to the troops.[22] The other officers, including the grand commander, drapier, vice-marshal and vice-commander, would also have joined this group.

Beneath this central command unit there was a series of contingents. Firstly, there were the brother knights. These represented the core of the host and each man was allotted four horses apiece when sufficient animals were available.[23] It was from the ranks of these men that the masters of the Order were drawn after 1216.[24] Brother knights were generally of knightly, noble

---

[16] *SDO*, p. 103.
[17] *AZM*, p. 122.
[18] *SDO*, p. 105.
[19] Oliveri Scholastici, *Historia Damiatina*, p. 252. Ludwig is likely to have been marshal at this time because he is mentioned as marshal in 1215.
[20] *SDO*, pp. 98–99. This was a smaller wartime command group than that of the Templar master who was permitted to employ up to ten brother knights as companions in battle. *La Règle du Temple*, ed. H. de Curzon (Paris, 1886), p. 86. For the relative sizes of the entourage of the masters of the military orders see Burgtorf, *The Central Convent of Hospitallers and Templars*, p. 215.
[21] *SDO*, p. 103.
[22] *SDO*, p. 114.
[23] *SDO*, p. 110.
[24] *TOT*, no. 303; *AZM*, p. 53.

or at least *ministerialis* origin, although this did not become a fixed requirement until the end of the thirteenth century.[25] Each brother knight could be
supported by an esquire who was allotted to him by the master of esquires
while on campaign.[26] Esquires seem to have been paid retainers and it was
the master of esquires' role to manage their wages. The status of the master
of esquires is unclear; however, it is possible that, like this officer's opposite
number in the Hospitallers, he was a sergeant brother.[27]

A second contingent was made up of turcopoles. Turcopoles were light
cavalry who fought in the Levantine manner and were often recruited from
Syrian and Armenian Christians. They were part of the armed host of all the
major military orders in the eastern Mediterranean. They acted as scouts and
skirmishers for the military orders and formed the vanguard or rearguard of
their forces.[28] These men fought under the command of the turcopolier and
under their own standard. The turcopolier was an innovation of the Templars
which the Teutonic Order replicated.[29] He was subordinate to the marshal
and was elected by both the marshal and the master.[30] He was also responsible for 'the brothers who are not knights'.[31] Sterns has suggested that these
included the Teutonic Order's sergeants and certainly this was the arrangement for the Templars.[32] Sergeants were later known as 'grey mantles' and,
according to Militzer, were often drawn from burgher or farming families,
occupying a lower social standing than brother knights.[33] Barber has shown
that Templar sergeants 'appear to have been more racially mixed than the
knights' and included Armenians and Syrians. They could also be armed in
the eastern fashion.[34] The sources for the Teutonic Knights do not name any
individual sergeant brothers in the Levant or list their armaments, but if they
were recruited from these ethnic groups then it might explain why they were
deployed under the authority of the turcopolier.

The weapons used by all the brother knights could vary considerably. Unlike
the Templars' rule, the statutes of the Teutonic Knights were not prescriptive

---

[25] *SDO*, p. 136. Incidentally, when the law was passed that recruits had to be of knightly origin,
it was accepted that this prerequisite could be waived by the command of the master. This was
already a practice in the Templar order possibly even before 1190, *La Règle du Temple*, p. 234.

[26] *SDO*, p. 109–110. For discussion on this passage see Sterns, 'The Statutes of the Teutonic
Knights', p. 308.

[27] *KSJJC*, p. 285.

[28] For discussion see Marshall, *Warfare in the Latin East*, pp. 58–60. *SDO*, p. 111.

[29] *La Règle du Temple*, p. 90. The first mention of a Hospitaller turcopolier occurs in 1248 and he
is later mentioned in the statutes in 1303, *CGJJ*, vol. 4, no. 4612; Burgtorf, *The Central Convent
of Hospitallers and Templars*, p. 103.

[30] *SDO*, p. 111.

[31] *SDO*, p. 111.

[32] Sterns, 'The Statutes of the Teutonic Knights', p. 310; *La Règle du Temple*, p. 90.

[33] This was apparently the case in Western Christendom so it was probably also true in the eastern
Mediterranean; see *AZM*, pp. 68–70. For discussion of recruitment patterns, see Forey, *The Mili-
tary Orders*, 134–135; A. J. Forey, 'Recruitment to the Military Orders: Twelfth to Mid-fourteenth
Centuries', *Viator*, 17 (1986), pp. 139–171.

[34] Barber, *The New Knighthood*, p. 191; Burgtorf, *The Central Convent of Hospitallers and Templars*,
p. 37.

and allowed the brethren to arm themselves in the manner most appropriate to local conditions. This was presumably a reflection of the differing demands of campaigning in the Baltic and the Levant.[35] Although the statutes permitted this diversity of weaponry, all the members of the Order were expected to refrain from adorning their weapons, armour or equestrian harness with gold, silver or bright colours. This emphasis on a lack of adornment was stressed in *c*.1130 by Bernard of Clairvaux in *De laude novae militiae* in respect of the Templars. The Teutonic Knights, as inheritors of the Templars' rule and vocation, naturally pursued the same policy.[36] Over time, the brethren deviated further from the strictures of the Templar statutes regarding weaponry and in 1244 they were granted the right to place a cover over their lance tips by Innocent IV, which the Templar rule prohibited.[37]

In the Templar Order, responsibility for ensuring that the brethren were dressed correctly fell to the drapier.[38] When a man joined this order it was the drapier's responsibility to take all his fine clothes and jewellery.[39] It seems likely, although it is not specified in the statutes, that his opposite number in the Teutonic Order performed a similar function. Even so, the drapier's primary role was to maintain and store the brothers' clothes and armour and in this capacity he was subject to the authority of the marshal.[40] The drapier could also give old garments to the marshal and grand commander to be distributed to the Order's servants.[41] In areas which were not visited by the drapier (i.e. areas outside the Holy Land) it seems that the local brethren were expected to buy their own clothes, but not to use cloth which had been dyed any colour other than those which the Order regularly employed.[42] Like the grand commander and marshal, the appointment of the drapier required the mutual agreement of the master and chapter.[43] Two lesser officials who performed similar auxiliary roles were the brother saddler and the brother in charge of the small smithy. These men manufactured or repaired the leather

---

[35] *SDO*, pp. 46–47; *La Règle du Temple*, pp. 109–111.

[36] Bernard of Clairvaux, *Liber ad milites templi de laude novae militiae*, in *Sancti Bernardi Opera*, ed. J. Leclercq and H. M. Rochais, vol. 3 (Rome, 1963), pp. 213–239.

[37] *TOT*, no. 470.

[38] *La Règle du Temple*, pp. 29–30. The first drapier mentioned in the records of the Teutonic Order is one Conrad in 1229, *R. Reg.*, vol. 1, no. 1002. The first mention of a drapier in the Hospitaller Order occurs in the statutes of 1204–1206 and in the Templar Order in 1135–1147; Burgtorf, *The Central Convent of Hospitallers and Templars*, p. 105. Subsequently, the following Teutonic Order drapiers are mentioned in the Holy Land: Peter (1240), Ludwig (1244), Almaric of Würzburg (1253), Gunter (1261), Nicholas (1272), Henry of Boland (1280): *TOT*, no. 89; *R. Reg.*, vol. 1, nos. 1120, 1206, 1309, 1384, 1435.

[39] *La Règle du Temple*, p. 106.

[40] *SDO*, p. 104. In the Templar Order this officer was bound to support the Commander of the Kingdom of Jerusalem; however the Teutonic Order did not have this position. *La Règle du Temple*, p. 94; *AZM*, p. 118.

[41] *SDO*, p. 108.

[42] *SDO*, p. 137.

[43] *SDO*, p. 97. This was also the case in the Templars, *La Règle du Temple*, p. 80; *AZM*, p. 118.

or metal items (such as stirrups, spurs and reins, etc.), which were required for the Order's horses.[44]

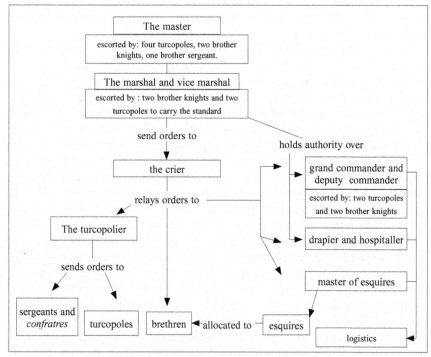

Figure 1: The military command structure of the Order.

In battle the statutes defined the conduct of the Teutonic Knights' troops depending upon whether they were in offensive or defensive situations. In the former scenario, after the decision had been taken to attack, the command was relayed to the rank and file by the marshal through the crier. The attack would then be executed with the standard bearer riding at the fore. No brother was allowed to ride ahead of the standard bearer.[45] This stipulation was presumably designed to prevent impetuous knights from charging ahead of the main force. To make a mounted charge fully effective it was necessary to maintain close formation and strict discipline. All three of the major military orders had stipulations in their statutes concerning these considerations.[46] In defensive scenarios, if the Order's encampment was assaulted, the military personnel were expected to defend themselves if they were attacked person-

---

[44] *SDO*, p. 110.

[45] *SDO*, pp. 116–117.

[46] Marshall, *Warfare in the Latin East*, pp. 158–163; M. Bennett, '*La Règle du Temple* as a Military Manual or How to Deliver a Cavalry Charge', in *The Rule of the Templars*, ed. J. M. Upton-Ward, Studies in the History of Medieval Religion, 4 (Woodbridge, 2005), pp. 175–188.

ally, whilst all non-engaged combatants were required to assemble around the standard before moving to relieve the portions of the camp that were under attack.[47] Whilst under arms the brothers were expected to remain as silent as possible and tightly arrayed.[48] They were not allowed to water their horses unless instructed to do so.[49]

In the earlier part of the thirteenth century, the Order's military exploits generally took place during the large crusading expeditions. As the century progressed, particularly after the defeat of La Forbie, the pattern of warfare began to change. Increasingly, as the Christian territories were forced onto the defensive, they generally conducted offensive warfare through *chevauchées* rather than seeking territorial expansion.[50] The Teutonic Knights participated in several such expeditions, providing sufficient manpower to be counted alongside the foremost participants. They are known to have been active in the raids of 1266[51] and 1271.[52] They were also among the knights who in 1269 attempted, albeit unsuccessfully, to rescue a raiding expedition led by Robert of Creseques and Oliver of Termes, which had been attacked by Mamluk forces on its return journey to Acre.[53] The Teutonic Knights were evidently valued for their martial qualities and this was demonstrated by their presence in the vanguard of the army during the raid of 1266.[54] This role was generally performed by the Templars and Hospitallers because they were known to be amongst the steadiest troops in the Latin East.[55] The presence of the Teutonic Knights in this formation is therefore an indication of their ability. Despite this, there was always a danger that should the vanguard become separated from the main army, the gap created could be exploited by an enemy. This happened previously to the army of King Louis VII in January 1148 in Asia Minor.[56] It also occurred during the 1266 raiding expedition when the vanguard was ambushed. There are reports of high casualties amongst the Hospitallers and Teutonic Knights in this encounter[57] and a papal charter was issued in the following year which specifically enjoined prelates to send aid to the Teutonic Order because of its losses.[58] It may also be significant that Anno von Sangershausen returned to the Holy Land within two years of this defeat after a long absence (see appendix A).

[47] *SDO*, p. 112.
[48] *SDO*, p. 112.
[49] *SDO*, p. 112.
[50] For discussion of raiding activity in the Latin East at this time see Marshall, *Warfare in the Latin East*, pp. 183–209.
[51] Eracles, p. 455; *Les Gestes des Chiprois*, p. 766; *Chroniques de Chypre d'Amadi et de Strambaldi*, vol. 1, p. 208.
[52] *Annales de Terre Sainte*, in *AOL*, vol. 2 (1884), p. 454 (documents); Sanuto, p. 224.
[53] Eracles, p. 458.
[54] Eracles, p. 455.
[55] Forey, *The Military Orders*, pp. 88–89.
[56] Odo of Deuil, De Profectione Ludovici VII in Orientem: *The Journey of Louis VII to the East*, ed. and trans. V. G. Berry (New York, 1948), pp. 114–118.
[57] Eracles, p. 455; *TOT*, no. 647; *Les Gestes des Chiprois*, p. 766.
[58] *TOT*, no. 647.

A further military function performed by the Order was one of hostage negotiation. The *Meklenburgisches Urkundenbuch* gives a detailed account of the attempt made to ransom Henry, duke of Mecklenburg. Henry had arrived in the Holy Land in June 1272 and tried to visit Jerusalem in secret but was captured soon afterwards.[59] On 10 December 1287, Henry's wife Anastasia deposited the sum of 2,000 silver marks with the Teutonic Order so that they might secure the release of her husband.[60] The authorities in Lübeck, where the business was transacted, confirmed the financial transfer three days later.[61] A messenger must have travelled to the Holy Land because on 14 August 1289 Wirichus of Homberg, grand commander of the Order, replied to the officials in Lübeck, informing them that he had not been able to secure Henry's release and suggesting that Henry's return could only be brought about by divine providence.[62] He arranged for the return of the 2,000 marks of silver to Anastasia with no charge levied for the expenses incurred by the brethren.[63] On 19 December 1289, Henry's son replied to this letter and gave the Teutonic Order a number of valuable possessions that the duke had taken on crusade and which the Order had tried to restore to him. Henry's son did impose the condition that these goods should be returned in the event of his father's release.[64] He also confirmed the recovery of this money.[65] Henry was subsequently released in 1298 (although it is not known how this was brought about). These transactions demonstrate the Order's role as ransom agents for pilgrims of some consequence. Additionally these events provide an unusually complete account of the precise administrative procedure employed for the return of captives in the Holy Land.

The Size of the Teutonic Order's Field Army in the Levant

Historians have tended to be rather dismissive of the size of the Teutonic Qrder in the Levant. Prawer, comparing them to the Templars and Hospitallers, wrote, 'smaller and poorer than their comrades-in-arms, the Teutonic Knights never played as important a part in the history of the kingdom.'[66] Riley-Smith, when discussing the 1258 agreement between the three major orders, wrote 'The Teutonic Knights were, of course, the poorest of the orders in Syria.'[67] It

---

[59] Urban, *The Baltic Crusade*, pp. 224, 256; R. Röhricht, *Die Deutschen im Heiligen Lande* (Innsbruck, 1894), pp. 128–129.
[60] *Meklenburgisches Urkundenbuch*, vol. 3 (Schwerin, 1865), no. 1934.
[61] *Meklenburgisches Urkundenbuch*, vol. 3, no. 1935.
[62] For further details of Wirichus see appendix E.2.
[63] *Meklenburgisches Urkundenbuch*, vol. 3, no. 2030.
[64] *Meklenburgisches Urkundenbuch*, vol. 3, no. 2042.
[65] *Meklenburgisches Urkundenbuch*, vol. 3, nos. 2043, 2057, 2059.
[66] J. Prawer, *The Crusaders' Kingdom: European Colonialism in the Middle Ages*, 2nd edn (London, 2001), p. 275.
[67] *KSJJC*, p. 448.

is not the purpose of this work to fully contradict these statements about the size and importance of the Teutonic Knights. They were indeed less wealthy and less powerful than the Templars and Hospitallers in the Latin East. Even so, when reading statements of this kind, it is too easy to interpret them as implying that the Order was a negligible force. The difficulty when assessing the size of the Teutonic Knights' field force in the Latin East, relative to the Templars and Hospitallers, is the lack of quantitative evidence – there are only two references which supply figures for the total force which the Order could deploy during any single engagement.[68] The first of these can be found in the chronicle of Peter von Dusburg, which mentioned that in *c*.1210 the Order could deploy only ten brother knights.[69] Naturally, the Order was at an early stage in its development at this time and this figure tallies well with other circumstantial evidence.

The second piece of evidence, which can be found in Salimbene of Adam's chronicle, is a transcription of a letter written by Robert, patriarch of Jerusalem, which details the Christian defeat at La Forbie in 1244 and gives specific figures for the battlefield losses of the military orders. The size of the Teutonic Order's force is described as follows: 'From the house of the Germans none survived except for three brothers, all the others were killed, some 400 from the same house.'[70] This figure has been accepted by several historians, such as Richard and Jotischky, who have interpreted it to mean 400 brother knights.[71] This has been rejected by Riley-Smith who claims that 'it is very unlikely that the Teutonic Knights could raise 300 [400] brethren-at-arms'.[72] Riley-Smith's argument seems to be sensible because 400 knights would have given the Order a greater field force than that of either the Templars or Hospitallers, who could generally muster around 300 knights apiece.[73] These older orders had both the military power to conduct independent campaigns in the Levant and a wider support network in Western Christendom, which concentrated its efforts almost solely upon the Latin East. Given that the Teutonic Order had neither such power nor such focused support this conclusion is accepted.

---

68 Militzer has drawn a similar conclusion; see *AZM*, pp. 387–393. Despite this, Militzer has estimated that there was a total of 400 knightly brethren in the Holy Land in *c*.1250 and an overall total of 1,800 brothers who served in Palestine up to 1309. These numbers seem too high.

69 'Posset habere in armis paratos decem fratres milites et non plures'; Peter von Dusburg, *Chronicon Terrae Prussie*, p. 31. This force is comparable to the knight service drawn from the Ibelin estate in *c*.1185–1186, John of Ibelin, *Le Livre des Assises*, pp. 607–610.

70 'De domo Alemannorum non remanserunt nisi tres fratres, alii omnes occisi sunt, videlicet CCCC de eadem domo'; Salimbene of Adam, vol. 1, p. 255. A transcript of this same letter can be found in Alberti Milioli Notarii Regini, *Liber de Temporibus et Aetatibus et Cronica Imperatorum*, p. 516. This second source however has been partially derived from Salimbene's chronicle.

71 J. Richard, *Saint Louis: Crusader King of France*, trans. J. Birrell, ed. S. Lloyd (Cambridge, 1983), p. 97; A. Jotischky, *Crusading and the Crusader States* (Harlow, 2004), p. 231.

72 Riley-Smith actually gives the figure of 300 knights; however this would appear to be a typing error because the chronicle of Salimbene of Adam, to which he is referring, states 400. J. S. C. Riley-Smith in Ibn al-Furāt, *Ayyubids, Mamluks and Crusaders*, vol. 1 (Cambridge, 1971), p. 173.

73 Forey, *The Military Orders*, p. 79; Prawer, *The Crusaders' Kingdom*, p. 261.

A different interpretation has been offered by Forey who suggests that the figure of 400 did not refer solely to brother knights but also to secular troops affiliated to the Order.[74] This idea opens a new approach to this piece of evidence. Notably, within this letter, the patriarch gave two figures for each of the contingents of the Templars and Hospitallers. The Templars are said to have deployed 312 *fratres milites* and 324 turcopoles, whilst the Hospitallers supplied 325 *fratres milites* and 200 turcopoles.[75] For the Teutonic Knights, the patriarch gives only one number for their total field force. It may be the case, therefore, that this figure referred collectively to knights, turcopoles, *confratres* and mercenaries. This interpretation feels more realistic because it suggests that the Teutonic Order possessed a total force of 400 troops compared to a total Hospitaller contingent of 525 and a Templar force of 626.

Certainly the evidence of this letter should not be lightly laid aside; Patriarch Robert of Jerusalem was an influential man who played a leading role in the events of 1244. He was present in Jerusalem when it fell and he is reported to have proclaimed the decision to march out against the Khwarazmians.[76] He was also present at the battle.[77] As such it is likely that he was aware of the size of the military orders' contingents. Nevertheless, Riley-Smith has made further criticisms of the figures given in this letter, including the stated losses incurred by the Cypriot and Antiochene contingents (300 knights apiece) which he claimed were 'obviously exaggerated'.[78] These statistics certainly do seem to be unduly high and this naturally casts doubt on the other data in this letter. Despite this, some of the other numbers can be verified from other sources. For instance, the claim that there were three survivors from the Teutonic House is replicated in a separate contemporary letter written by the patriarch, and also in two further accounts.[79] Admittedly these separate accounts do not state the size of the Teutonic Order's main host, although the fact that some of the letter's statistics can be found elsewhere speaks in favour of its general reliability.

To test further the veracity of the claim that the Order deployed 400 horsemen, a piece of qualitative evidence will now be reviewed. During the Barons' Crusade, five years before La Forbie, a contingent of the army decided to advance towards Egypt. At Gaza, a column led by a number of French lords detached itself to embark upon a raiding expedition. This force of around 600 knights was eventually trapped and forced to flee by the Egyptian army.[80] The main body of the Christian army then became aware of this disaster and hurried to support the refugees who were fleeing from the Muslim onslaught. The first to arrive at the battlefield were the Teutonic Knights who advanced

74 Forey, *The Military Orders*, p. 79; See also *AZM*, p. 390.
75 Salimbene of Adam, vol. 1, p. 255.
76 Matthew Paris, *Chronica Majora*, vol. 4, pp. 307–311.
77 Hamilton, *The Latin Church in the Crusader States*, p. 264.
78 Riley-Smith in Ibn al-Furāt, *Ayyubids, Mamluks and Crusaders*, p. 173.
79 Matthew Paris, *Chronica Majora*, vol. 4, pp. 301, 342; Rothelin, p. 564.
80 Rothelin, pp. 538–547.

unaided against the oncoming Egyptian army.[81] This 'powerful contingent' (grant route) alone is said to have been sufficient to deter the advancing Muslim army and even to have cut down a number of the Muslim vanguard.[82] Given that the Egyptian army had already destroyed a force of 600 knights, it is implausible that the Teutonic Order could have acted in this way without a sizeable field force.[83] They must have possessed sufficient cavalry to face down the oncoming Muslim forces. In these circumstances a force of around 400 horsemen would probably have been the minimum necessary to achieve this feat. To conclude, although it is impossible to state with any degree of certainty the precise size of the force which the Teutonic Knights were able to commit to the defence of the East, the figure of 400 horsemen at La Forbie chimes well with the available evidence.

The Strongholds of the Teutonic Order in the Eastern Mediterranean

The Teutonic Order possessed a number of fortresses in the Latin East including Amudain and Harunia in Armenia and Montfort, the Cave of Tyron and Castellum Regis in the kingdom of Jerusalem. The Order also possessed lesser castles including the fortification on the road connecting Acre and Castellum Regis called Jiddin.[84] Although it has been shown above that the Teutonic Order could deploy a considerable field force, its contributions to the defence of strongpoints in the Latin East were, in relation to the Templars and Hospitallers, proportionally far lower. By way of comparison, Forey has demonstrated that the Hospitallers alone are known to have held 'at one time or another some fifty-six strongholds'.[85]

Strongholds represented a serious commitment of time and resources and certainly it took a considerable length of time and much assistance for the Teutonic Order to build its fortress of Montfort.[86] Such undertakings were extremely expensive and the Templar fortress at Safad is said to have cost 1,100,000 Saracen bezants.[87] Montfort similarly required enormous investment although there is no statement concerning the overall cost of the project. The

---

81 Rothelin, pp. 546–547.
82 'Grant route'; Rothelin, p. 547.
83 The figure of 600 knights can be found in Rothelin, p. 539.
84 D. Pringle, A. Petersen, M. Dow et al., 'Qal'at Jiddin: A Castle of the Crusader and Ottoman Periods in Galilee', *Levant*, 26 (1994), pp. 135–166.
85 Forey, *The Military Orders*, p. 59.
86 For a selection of archaeological and general discussion of Montfort see E. W. G. Masterman, 'A Visit to the Ruined Castles of the Teutonic Knights', *Palestine Exploration Fund: Quarterly Statement* (London, 1919), pp. 71–75; Pringle, 'A Thirteenth Century Hall at Montfort Castle in Western Galilee', pp. 52–81; M. Benevisti, *The Crusaders' Fortress of Montfort* (Jerusalem, 1982), *passim*; H. Kennedy, *Crusader Castles* (Cambridge, 2001), pp. 129–131; Hubatsch, 'Montfort und die Bildung des Deutschordensstates im Heiligen Lande', pp. 161–199.
87 R. B. C. Huygens, 'Un Nouveau texte de traité "De constructione castri Saphet"' *Studi Medievali* ser. 3, 6 (1965), p. 384.

building work began in 1226 and continued with the assistance of crusaders from Frederick II's expedition.[88] In 1228, Bohemond IV of Antioch contributed funds for the construction and in 1230 Gregory IX granted remission of one seventh of penance for those pilgrims who helped in its construction.[89] Further riches were conferred upon the Order for the purchase of the lands surrounding the castle by the duke of Austria and Frederick II.[90] In 1229 Frederick ensured in his treaty with the Egyptian Sultan that the construction of the fortress could continue during the peace.[91] The employment of crusaders to build fortifications such as Montfort was typical of this period and during the Fifth Crusade, the Barons' Crusade and Louis IX's expedition, pilgrims helped to build fortifications and enhance city defences.[92] In 1245, when Pope Innocent IV confirmed a series of privileges that had been confiscated by Gregory IX, he acknowledged the completion of Montfort.[93] Given that this act occurred after the Order's return to favour, it is likely that the castle was finished either at this time or while the brethren were perceived to be in opposition to the papacy, between 1239 and 1243.[94]

In 1271 Montfort fell to the Mamluk forces. The siege began on 5 June and Muslim sources report that it started with an arrow and catapult barrage. On 11 June, Baybars ordered that the walls should be undermined and offered 1,000 dirghāms for every stone removed.[95] Plate 3 shows the channel quarried out by Baybars' troops beneath the fortress during this mining attempt. Given that the outer bailey then fell on 12 June and the garrison surrendered on the same day, it is remarkable how much progress these miners had been able to make in a single day of excavation. The Teutonic Knights were then allowed to evacuate the fortress and return to Acre under escort.[96] On 4 July 1271, Baybars ordered the castle to be destroyed.[97]

---

[88] D. Pringle, *Secular Buildings in the Crusader Kingdom of Jerusalem: An Archaeological Gazetteer* (Cambridge, 1997), p. 75. Various dates are given for the beginning of the construction of Montfort: (1226) Filippo da Novara, *Guerra di Federico II*, p. 78; (1229) HB, vol. 3, p. 92; (1226) 'Table Chronologique de Héthoum Comte de Gor'igos', *RHC. Arm.*, vol. 1, p. 485; Sanuto, p. 211; (1229) Matthew Paris, *Chronica Majora*, vol. 3, p. 175. This matter has been discussed in detail by Kluger who has examined the possibility that the brethren began to build Montfort on land that did not belong to the order; see Kluger, *Hochmeister Hermann*, pp. 74–76. Kluger argues (p. 77) that the construction of the fortress began in the first half of 1226 and I accept his conclusion.

[89] *TOT*, nos, 64, 72.

[90] *TOT*, no. 63; Oliveri Scholastici, *Historia Damiatina*, p. 207. The importance of the duke of Austria's grant was emphasised by Gregory IX, *TOT*, no. 72.

[91] HB, vol. 3, pp. 92.

[92] See Richard, *The Crusades*, p. 353; Powell, *Anatomy of a Crusade*, p. 133.

[93] For the text of this document see Forstreuter, *Der Deutsche Orden am Mittelmeer*, p. 232.

[94] For discussion of the completion date of Montfort see Hubatsch, 'Montfort und die Bildung des Deutschordensstates im Heiligen Lande', p. 187.

[95] This chronology is based on the following sources: Al-Khowayter, 'A Critical Edition, vol. 2, p. 756 and *Annales de Terre Sainte*, p. 455.

[96] Al-Khowayter, 'A Critical Edition, vol. 2, p. 756.

[97] The best account of the fall of the castle is Al-Khowayter, 'A Critical Edition, vol. 2, pp. 756–757.

Plate 2. Montfort © A. Morton

Plate 3. The Mamluk mine © N. Morton

One of the most significant aspects of the fall of Montfort is the fact that the fortress fell after only seven days.[98] This was extremely brief in comparison to the sieges of other castles in this period. Forey has noted that Hugh Revel, master of the Hospitallers, wrote 'disdainfully' that Safad fell in 1268 after a siege of only sixteen days; Montfort fell in under half the time.[99] The most natural explanation for the brevity of the Teutonic Knights' resistance can be found in the building itself because Montfort, as a fortification, was not as defensible as the other great fortresses of the Latin East such as Crac and Safad. Furthermore, Boas has demonstrated that there are weaknesses to Montfort's geographical location. Montfort is located on a spur of land which is formed from the confluence of Wadi Keziv and a secondary wadi. It is protected on three sides by steep slopes which descend to the valley floor and can only be approached with ease from the east along the spur. On this side, however, there are two rock-cut moats. The defensive flaw lies in the fact that the spur itself is not sufficiently distant from the valley's southern slopes to be out of range of war machines. Boas has discovered mangonel balls in this area which suggests that the fortress was bombarded from this location.[100] Despite such geographical weaknesses, there may still be a longer answer to the swift fall of Montfort.[101]

Even though there were many Levantine fortresses that were stronger than Montfort, its fortifications were far from negligible and in 1260 it was described in the Rothelin continuation as one of the ten strongest castles in the Latin East. In March of that year, Thomas Bérard, master of the Templars, listed Montfort among the handful of castles that were strong enough to resist the Mongols.[102] Montfort had also defended itself against an attack led by Badr al-Dīn al-Aidamurī and Badr al-Dīn Baisarī in 1266, although this may only have been a raiding expedition.[103] The brevity of the fortress' resistance in 1271 therefore warrants further examination. In the years before 1271, Montfort's position had become increasingly precarious. It had already been raided in 1266 and possibly before in 1263.[104] In 1268 Hugh of Antioch-

---

[98]   *Annales de Terre Sainte*, p. 455.

[99]   Forey, *The Military Orders*, p. 75.

[100] A. J. Boas, *Archaeology of the Military Orders: A Survey of the Urban Centres, Rural Settlement and Castles of the Military Orders in the Latin East c.1120–1291* (London, 2006), pp. 126–127.

[101] For discussion of Montfort as a military building see Forey, *The Military Orders*, p. 63; Kennedy, *Crusader Castles*, p. 129.

[102] The reference in Rothelin to the castles of the military orders does not name Montfort explicitly but states that there was one castle held by the Teutonic Knights that was deemed sufficiently strong to withstand the Mongols. Given that Montfort was the only major castle held by the brethren in the kingdom of Jerusalem, it is the only possible candidate, Rothelin, p. 636; *Annales de Burton*, p. 493.

[103] Ibn al-Furāt, *Ayyubids, Mamlukes and Crusaders*, vol. 2, p. 87; Sanuto, p. 222; Al-Khowayter, 'A Critical Edition, vol. 2, p. 586.

[104] There is said to have been a raid in 1263 against the lands of the military orders in the vicinity of Acre. Given the proximity of the Montfort estate to this city it seems possible that the lands of the Teutonic Knights were raided in this year; see *Annales Sancti Rudberti Salisburgenses*, p. 796. The probability of this is increased by the existence of a charter in 1264 forbidding the Order from levying taxation for the reconstruction of its buildings and fortifications see *TOT*, no.

Lusignan and Sultan Baybars discussed a possible treaty in which, among other clauses, the bulk of the villages attached to the Montfort estate would be relinquished to the Muslims.[105] This treaty, as Holt has demonstrated, was not ratified due to objections to several clauses; nevertheless it appears that the estate had fallen into poor condition because in 1270 the Hospitallers allowed the Teutonic Knights to grow crops in their lands around Manueth specifically to help supply the Montfort estate.[106] From this evidence it can be seen that, although in 1271 Montfort itself remained intact, the estate it was supposed to protect was in tatters.

A further factor of note is that four fortresses fell in 1271, of which Montfort was the last to be besieged. Chastel Blanc, the first to capitulate, offered sufficient resistance to Baybars for him to be compelled to leave a blockading force to complete its capture. Crac des Chevaliers surrendered after a siege of five weeks and one day.[107] Gibelcar then fell in under two weeks and finally Montfort in only seven days.[108] It can be seen therefore that there was a trend of diminishing resistance in the defence of these strongpoints, which suggests that as defeat was added to defeat, the sheer futility of resistance became apparent. In summary, from these facts we can build an image of a fortress whose lands had been pillaged for many years to a point where the retention of the stronghold was already in question, with a garrison that was only sustained through support from the Hospitallers. By June 1271 three other castles had already fallen and it seems plausible that these combined factors may have had a cumulative effect upon the morale of the defenders, providing an explanation for the swift fall of the fortress.

634. For the raid of 1266 see Sanuto, p. 222; Ibn al-Furāt, *Ayyubids, Mamlukes and Crusaders*, vol. 2, p. 87; Al-Khowayter, 'A Critical Edition, vol. 2, p. 586.
[105] *Early Mamluk Diplomacy*, pp. 16–17.
[106] *CGJJ*, vol. 3, no. 3400; *Early Mamluk Diplomacy*, pp. 16–17.
[107] 3 March–8 April; Boas, *Archaeology of the Military Orders*, p. 131.
[108] For data concerning the speed with which castles fell during this period see Marshall, *Warfare in the Latin East*, pp. 244–245.

CHAPTER 10

Control, Co-ordination and Supply

The diplomatic and military roles of the Teutonic Knights in the Baltic and the Holy Land required an international administrative support network in Western Christendom. In their early years, the brethren received gifts of money and property from both pilgrims and secular and ecclesiastical patrons from Western Christendom. Over time, as the lands granted to the Order multiplied, they began to be grouped by area into administrative units or commanderies. These were then gathered into provincial or national districts under the authority of a local commander or *Landkomtur*, in much the same way as the Templars and Hospitallers.[1] The commanders of the most important territories (Germany, Prussia and Livonia) were then raised above the other regional officers with a change in their title from *Landkomtur* to *Landmeister* (although this distinction was not made in the statutes). Each of the territories was exploited to produce resources from agriculture, taxation, donations or raw materials which could then be channelled to support the Order's medical and military commitments. Subsequent growth in these provinces was achieved with further benefactions and also through the purchase or exchange of property. This chapter discusses how the Teutonic Knights' administrative structure developed to facilitate the collection and movement of resources to the Latin East and how these goods were, in turn, utilised upon arrival. It will also show how the institution was administered and governed in the Latin East and how well the brethren adapted their statutes to reflect their expanding commitments in Prussia and Livonia.

The Master

The highest official of the Teutonic Order was its master. The master was ultimately responsible for the institution as a whole and held executive power over its provinces and personnel. When present at military engagements it was the master's prerogative to command an attack and theoretically in other matters he also could dispense with any of the stipulations of the statutes except

---

[1]   The provincial administration system in the West became more complex as the Order developed; for discussion see *AZM*, p. 168.

for his fundamental vows of poverty, chastity and obedience.[2] At the time of its establishment, as *De Primordiis Ordinis Theutonici Narratio* reports, the Teutonic hospital was led by a priest called Sibrand.[3] In later years, a number of other leaders – Gerhard, prior Heinrich, Ulric and preceptor Heinrich – are mentioned.[4] In 1196, Pope Celestine III granted the brethren the right to appoint their own master.[5] Ironically, two years later at the Order's militarisation, the brothers do not seem to have exercised this right because their new master, Henry Walpot, was selected by the Templars. There was no suggestion, however, that this act was resented.[6]

Over time the election of a master became a complex affair because it was necessary to ensure that a candidate was chosen who would be acceptable to the various interest groups within the institution. When the master became aware that he was dying he was required to appoint a brother who would act as his deputy and to give this man the seal of the Order.[7] This practice may have been acquired from the Hospitallers.[8] This deputy then needed to assemble the provincial governors of the Order, including those of Germany, Austria, Armenia, Prussia and Livonia. When these officers had congregated, the deputy appointed a brother knight to act as the 'commander of the election'.[9] This brother was expected to select a total of thirteen brethren to form a chapter, consisting of one priest, eight knights and four others (believed to be sergeants).[10] The chapter then chose the new master. These elections often took place in the Holy Land, although this was not apparently a legal necessity because, according to the *Livländische Reimchronik*,

---

2 *SDO*, pp. 55–56, 105.
3 *TOT*, no. 25. This paragraph has drawn extensively upon Arnold, 'Entstehung und Frühzeit des Deutschen Ordens', pp. 85–94.
4 Arnold lists them as follows: Sibrand (1190), Gerhard (1192), Heinrich, prior (1193–1194), Ulrich (1195) Heinrich, preceptor (1196); 'Entstehung und Frühzeit des Deutschen Ordens', pp. 85–94. For Arnold's diagram of these masters see p. 94. Subsequent masters were Herman Walpot (died on 5 November although the year is not known), Otto von Kerpen (died on 7 February 1209) and Herman Bart (died 3 June 1209/1210). For evidence of these later masters see Perlbach, 'Deutsch-Ordens Necrologe', pp. 358–361; Peter von Dusburg, *Chronicon Terrae Prussie*, p. 30; *TOT*, no. 43.
5 *TOT*, no. 296.
6 *De primordiis Ordinis Theutonici narratio*, p. 225.
7 *SDO*, p. 90.
8 The Teutonic Order seems to have followed precisely the same process as the Hospitallers although it is notable that the Hospitaller statutes do not include this procedure until the Statutes of Margat in 1204–1206. The brethren would not therefore have acquired these regulations when they were granted the Hospitaller rule at their militarisation in 1198. Perhaps this procedure was employed informally before this time or perhaps the brethren adopted it after 1206 in imitation of the Hospitallers, *CGJJ*, vol. 2, no. 1193 (p. 35); *KSJJC*, p. 275. In the Templar Order this deputy was always the marshal. The Teutonic Rule is not prescriptive, *La Règle du Temple*, pp. 142–143.
9 *SDO*, pp. 92–94. The appointment of this official appears to have been drawn from the Templars; see *La Règle du Temple*, p. 145.
10 *AZM*, p. 69. Militzer claims that the fact that there was only one priest at the election of the master in comparison to eight brother knights is a reflection of the dominance of the latter of these two groups, *AZM*, p. 53–54. Barber has shown that in the Order of the Templars the priest was present to symbolise Christ and it seems likely that this was also the case in the Teutonic Order, *La Règle du Temple*, p. 147; Barber, *The New Knighthood*, p. 185.

Anno von Sangershausen's election in Rome was in conformity with the customs of the Order.[11] Despite this, the statutes seem to suggest that this event should take place in a single location, almost certainly the Holy Land, because they speak of the logistical difficulties involved in the attendance of the commander of Livonia.[12] If it was theoretically possible to elect the master in any location – even in Livonia itself – then it would not have been presumed that this official would have endured the most arduous journey.

To be eligible for the master's position a candidate had to be a *militaris et religiosa persona*. This was stated explicitly by Honorius III in 1216.[13] This stipulation is interesting because it suggests that, even at this early stage, the military side of the Order was deemed to be superior to the medical.[14] Significantly, the Hospitallers did not institute this rule until 1262.[15] Of the brother knights who were chosen for this role, it can be seen in appendix C that masters had held a range of offices previously, including command of regions such as Germany, Prussia or Livonia.

Linked to these considerations, perhaps the greatest challenge was to ensure that the electors would choose a master who would protect the interests of the Order. The Templar rule, for example, emphasised that a master should be chosen who would support the Holy Land. The Hospitallers impressed the need for a new master to care for the poor.[16] The Teutonic Order's statutes stipulated that the electors should be drawn from as many different provinces as possible so that a master could be selected who would be acceptable to all.[17] For an international organisation, the wisdom of this clause is natural; however, for the Teutonic Order it seems to have been a point of particular significance. Where in the Templar and Hospitaller rules only the Levantine commanders were obliged to attend the election, in the Teutonic Order all the regional commanders including those of Prussia and Livonia were required to be present.[18] From this it can be seen that the Teutonic Knights placed greater emphasis on acquiring the consent of their Western commanderies in their choice of a master. On one level this clause seems to be simply a reflection of the immense importance of Germany, Prussia and Livonia in the management of the Order. It may also reflect a desire to prevent rifts forming within the institution as a result of the election process. We have already seen (p. 105 above) that after the death of Heinrich von Hohenlohe (15 July 1249) two rival masters were appointed.[19] We have also seen that the Teutonic Knights were frequently divided in their policy between their interests in the Baltic

---

[11] *Livländische Reimchronik*, pp. 99–100.
[12] *SDO*, pp. 91–92.
[13] *SDO*, pp. 90–93; *TOT*, no. 303.
[14] *AZM*, p. 53.
[15] *CGJJ*, vol. 3, no. 3039 (p. 46); *KSSJC*, p. 275.
[16] *La Règle du Temple*, pp. 142–152; *CGJJ*, vol. 2, no. 1193.
[17] *La Règle du Temple*, p. 145; *SDO*, pp. 92–94.
[18] *SDO*, p. 91; *La Règle du Temple*, p. 143; *CGJJ*, vol. 2, no. 1193 (p. 35).
[19] Perlbach, 'Deutsch-Ordens Necrologe', p. 359.

and the Holy Land and at other times by their loyalties to the papacy and the empire. The choice of master was a critical factor for the stability of the Order and it may have been hoped that such a clause would encourage consensus and prevent the election process being hijacked by any particular party. After his election, the master was endowed with the ring, which had been originally given to Gerhard von Malberg in 1243 by Innocent IV.[20]

In political terms, the master was the head of the Order, but he was subject to a number of formal and informal restrictions. The influence of secular rulers and the papacy upon his decision-making has already been discussed extensively so this section will be concerned solely with internal matters. When assessing the position of the master a contradiction becomes apparent. According to the statutes, he could, theoretically, override any of the Order's regulations except for his monastic vows.[21] In other sections of the statutes, however, regulations existed which curbed his authority or compelled him to consult other officials. If the master wanted to lend money, for example, he could only hand over a maximum of 100 bezants on his own authority.[22] If he wished to lend up to 500 bezants he was expected to discuss the case with ten brethren.[23] If he wished to send a brother away from the Holy Land, he was required to seek the approval of the other office holders.[24] For more important matters, such as the purchase or sale of land, the reception of new brethren or the appointment of officials, the approval of the chapter had to be sought.[25] The Teutonic Order's chapter, like that of the Hospitallers, was a gathering of the wisest and most influential brethren and its meetings were held in the Order's headquarters in the Holy Land.[26] Consequently, the master was simultaneously bound to seek consultation and allowed to dispense with these regulations and act unilaterally. A possible explanation could be that this enabling clause was intended to be used in times of emergency or on occasions when the master was not able to seek consultation. If this was the case, however, it was not stated explicitly and presumably there was still scope for the abuse of this power.

What these regulations may reflect is the tension which seems to have existed between the master and the chapter over the control of the Order. These disputes seem to have occurred largely as a result of their differing interests. On the one hand, the chapter met in the Levant and was composed of local brethren, who naturally emphasised the interests of the Holy Land. On the other, the master had the interests of the entire Order to consider,

---

20 See *PU*, vol. 1.1, no. 147. There is a possible reference to this ring in the *Livländische Reim-chronik* (p. 100) which speaks of the master passing on a ring to the next master. It would make sense if this were the same ring given by the pope.

21 *SDO*, pp. 55–56, 105.

22 This was only half the amount that the master of the Temple could lend; *La Règle du Temple*, pp. 77–78; *SDO*, pp. 49, 98.

23 *SDO*, p. 98.

24 *SDO*, p. 101.

25 *SDO*, pp. 49, 97.

26 *SDO*, p. 49; H. Nicholson, *The Knights Hospitaller* (Woodbridge, 2001), p. 69.

including those of Prussia and Livonia. Evidence of the chapter's attempts to wrest control over the master – and therefore over the Order as a whole – can be found clearly in the document sent by the chapter to Elbing in 1251. Shortly before this, the Teutonic Knights had suffered major losses during the defeat of the crusade of Louis IX. The chapter then appointed Eberhard of Saone, grand commander, as temporary master of Prussia and Livonia and sent him to meet the brethren in the Baltic. Eberhard travelled north spreading word of the defeat at al-Mansūra and delivered a letter in Elbing which imposed a series of new regulations upon the brethren.[27] The purpose of this document appears to have been to curb the powers of the master and those of the provincial masters and to centralise authority upon the chapter in the Holy Land (for the precise stipulations outlined in this document, see chapter 7).[28] If successful, the chapter would have had greater power to draw the Order's combined resources towards the Latin East. *Prima facie* the chapter had chosen a good time for their demands because at this point the Order was divided between two masters. The chapter might have hoped therefore that, with the institution in chaos, it could impose its will.

If this was the case then it would not have been the first time that a chapter had sought to take advantage of a moment of weakness to increase its powers. A similar scenario occurred in the Hospitaller Order during the resignation of Gilbert of Assailly in 1170.[29] At this time, embarrassed by defeat and debt, Gilbert resigned without consulting the chapter. The chapter then insisted that he could not step down without its consent and that of the papacy. It then demanded that before Gilbert could resume his office, he had to accept a number of limitations on his powers. These included stipulations that he and future masters would not embark upon new endeavours or acquire frontier castles without the chapter's approval. Gilbert refused these terms and resigned for a second time. This incident provides a further example of how the chapter in a military order could exploit a leadership crisis to enhance its power. Despite this, it appears that the plans of the Teutonic Order's chapter in 1251 were resisted after the election of Poppo von Osterna in *c.*1252. As shown in chapter 7, Poppo seems to have emphasised his supremacy over the Levantine chapter by depriving the Holy Land of resources and committing the Order's troops instead to the war in the Baltic. This would certainly have played upon the Achilles' heel of the chapter, which was both weakened by defeat and perennially reliant upon overseas supply. It seems that Poppo's demonstration of power decided the matter because very few of the regulations imposed in 1251 were committed to the *c.*1264 version of the statues. Further attempts to restrict the master's authority can also be found in this version; for example, there is a regulation that the master should not leave the

---

[27] *Annales Erphordenses Fratrum Praedicatorum*, p. 109.
[28] *PU*, vol. 1.1, no. 251; Militzer, 'From the Holy Land to Prussia', p. 73.
[29] *KSJJC*, pp. 61–63, 292–293; Burgtorf, *The Central Convent of the Hospitallers and Templars*, pp. 65–74.

Holy Land without the agreement of the chapter.[30] Subsequently, this stipulation was developed further and the chapter was given the power to decide whether the master's absence was necessary and also to set a deadline for his return. In theory, should the master fail to return within an allocated time period then the chapter was entitled to take action against him.[31]

Consequently, it can be seen that there were occasions when the chapter attempted to impose its control over the master. On the whole these episodes seem to have been driven by a desire to emphasise the importance of the Holy Land and the authority of the chapter. The master, by contrast, could not afford to focus exclusively on the Latin East and spent much of his time in Western Christendom; naturally the affairs of Prussia and Livonia also required attention. Furthermore the brutal actions of Poppo von Osterna seem to demonstrate that however much the chapter may have wished to control the master, its powers could pose little threat to a masterful leader who could dispense with such regulations and was in a position to control the flow of resources to the eastern Mediterranean.

The General Chapter

On 14 September of every year, the Teutonic Order was expected to meet in a council named the general chapter.[32] The main purpose of this meeting was to discuss the condition of the institution and to review appointments. In theory every official, except the master, was expected to surrender his office, which would then either be reconfirmed to the existing incumbent or given to another brother. Each outgoing officer was expected to render an account of his post and its financial condition whilst each incoming incumbent was required to write explicitly on the situation of his new post.[33] The meeting itself was attended by the brethren and senior officers of the Order. According to the statutes, the commanders of Cyprus and Armenia were required to be present whilst the attendance of other provincial officers was optional, suggesting that *theoretically* the general chapter was supposed to be held in the Holy Land.[34] In practice, however, as Militzer has shown, the general chapter assembled in a variety of locations, commonly in Germany.[35] It might be thought that the chapter would have resisted the organisation of a general chapter outside the Holy Land because it would have less influence over the proceedings. Certainly, in the Hospitaller Order, when the master

---

[30] *SDO*, pp. 99–100.
[31] *SDO*, p. 135.
[32] *SDO*, p. 102.
[33] *SDO*, pp. 102–103.
[34] *SDO*, p. 102.
[35] *AZM*, pp. 134–135. This was also the case for the Templars who also held general chapter meetings outside the Levant, see H. Nicholson, *The Knights Templar: A New History* (Stroud, 2004), p. 116.

William of Villaret proposed to hold a general chapter in Avignon in 1300, the chapter insisted that it should be held at the Order's headquarters in Cyprus and nowhere else.[36] William acceded to this request. The chapter in the Teutonic Order, however, is not recorded as having resisted this practice. In addition to the central general chapter, each provincial commander was similarly required to convene a local general chapter at which all his subordinate officers would be appointed.[37]

The Senior Officials of the Order

The master was supported by the marshal and the grand commander. These officials held executive control over the military and administrative wings of the Order.[38] The marshal, as shown above, was the Order's military commander in the Latin East and held sweeping powers over the Order's Levantine arms and soldiers.[39] The first marshal is mentioned in a charter composed in 1208 in Acre.[40] Like the Templars and Hospitallers, the marshal was primarily concerned with the Order's defensive responsibilities in the Holy Land; however, unlike these older institutions, the Teutonic Knights also appointed marshals in Livonia and Prussia where heavy military obligations necessitated such appointments. Ironically, although the marshal in the Holy Land was the main marshal, the forces at his disposal were considerably smaller than those of either of the lesser marshals in Prussia and Livonia. Despite this, although the statutes of the Order describe the duties of the Levantine marshal in detail, the marshals in the Baltic are not mentioned.

The grand commander's office was concerned with shipping, the grain supply, workshops, slaves, the treasury and the management of the Order's properties.[41] Although many of the grand commander's duties were administrative he could also be called upon to perform a military role. As Riley-Smith has said with regard to the Hospitallers, 'it would be wrong, however, to regard the grand commander only as a civil administrator'.[42] The grand commander of the Teutonic Order deputised for the marshal if he was absent and there were a number of occasions when the grand commander is known to have participated in military expeditions.[43] In 1220, the preceptor of the Order was captured during a raiding expedition in the Nile delta.[44] On

---

[36] A. J. Forey, 'Constitutional Conflict and Change in the Hospital of St John during the Twelfth and Thirteenth Centuries', *Journal of Ecclesiastical History*, 33 (1982), p. 21; Burgtorf, *The Central Convent of Hospitallers and Templars*, pp. 115–116, 158–161.
[37] *SDO*, pp. 96–97.
[38] For a list of grand commanders, see appendix E.2.
[39] *SDO*, p. 103.
[40] *TOT*, no. 43; *AZM*, p. 117. For a list of marshals, see appendix E.1.
[41] *SDO*, p. 106.
[42] *KSJJC*, p. 306.
[43] *SDO*, pp. 103–104.
[44] Oliveri Scholastici, *Historia Damiatina*, p. 252.

19 October 1244 the grand commander, Conrad of Nassau, was killed at La Forbie.[45] Eberhard of Saone seems to have participated in Louis IX's crusade and he was subsequently sent to deputise for the Livonian master; during which appointment he led a number of military campaigns.[46]

The grand commander was supported in his role by the treasurer who received the income and rents payable to the Order (see below) as well as making payments on the brethren's behalf. The treasurer was specifically accountable for his actions and had to report to the master every month.[47] The grand commander's deputy was the vice-commander, an office which first appeared in the Teutonic Order under the title minor preceptor in 1230.[48] This position did not exist in the Templar Order and first appeared in Hospitaller documents in 1235.[49] Whether the earlier reference to this official in the Teutonic Order suggests that this post was an innovation is unclear. The incumbent was responsible for matters pertaining to the tradesmen of the Order, the grain supply and the workshops.[50]

Alongside these high officials there were a number of further commanders who managed the Order's commanderies outside the kingdom of Jerusalem. These included the masters of Prussia, Livonia and Germany and the commanders of Austria, Apulia, Achaia and Armenia. They were each appointed by the master and chapter and in theory held their offices for one year, although in practice they generally held their position for far longer.[51] In the Templar and Hospitaller orders these officials were responsible for the collection and transportation of resources from their designated region to the Latin East and, in some cases, for the provision of auxiliary forces for local rulers, for example in the wars against the Moors in Spain.[52] The Teutonic Order was slightly different. Like the Templars and Hospitallers it had commanderies in areas such as Germany, Apulia, Sicily, etc. which produced resources; however, it also possessed two large quasi-independent dominions in Prussia and Livonia. The regional masters in these areas could each dispose of military and financial resources that were greater than anything which could be mustered by the master in the Latin East and this disparity increased as the thirteenth century developed. They also received supplies from other regions in much the same way as the Order in the Holy Land did. Admittedly these officials were not completely independent of central authority and the master frequently travelled to these regions or sent instructions from Acre. Nevertheless there must have been many important

---

[45] Matthew Paris, *Chronica Majora*, vol. 4, p. 339.
[46] See chapter 7.
[47] *SDO*, pp. 107–109.
[48] *TOT*, no. 74.
[49] *KSJJC*, p. 308; *CGJJ*, vol. 2, no. 2126; *AZM*, p. 121.
[50] *SDO*, p. 108.
[51] *SDO*, p. 97.
[52] A. J. Forey, 'The Military Orders and the Spanish Reconquest in the Twelfth and Thirteenth Centuries', *Traditio*, 40 (1984), pp. 197–234.

decisions, driven by necessity or expediency, that were taken unilaterally by these governors.[53] Comparing the material power of the Prussian and Livonian masters against the theoretical authority of the headquarters in the Holy Land, it appears that there was a power structure based on three key officials in the internal administration of the Teutonic Order (indeed when the great strength of the Order's German master is considered this could rise to four). This created a very different hierarchy from those of the other major orders. In the Templar and Hospitaller institutions the regional commanders were satellites in orbit around the governing administration in the Holy Land. In 1113, for example, the Hospitaller Order's branches in Western Christendom were placed explicitly under the control of its headquarters in the Holy Land.[54] In the Teutonic Order, the Holy Land was merely one of three nuclei which attracted the resources generated in more peaceful regions and, although the Holy Land was the theoretical centre, in practice the masters of Prussia and Livonia were quasi-rulers of their own territories and possessed far greater practical power. The importance of these officials is demonstrated by the fact that several masters, including Poppo von Osterna, Anno von Sangershausen and Conrad von Feuchtwangen had formerly occupied these positions (see appendix C). In practice, therefore, the Teutonic Order, pre-1291, was an institution divided between a small number of geographically dispersed but highly powerful officials and the master of the Order was required to work with officials who possessed theoretical power that was only slightly lower than his own and practical power that could be considerably greater.

Partly because of the importance of the Livonian and Prussian branches of the Order, the masters of the Teutonic Order spent the greater part of their time in Western Christendom – even though this was discouraged by the statutes – and this required them to appoint a deputy in the Latin East.[55] Burgtorf has shown that the Templar and Hospitaller masters between 1120 and 1310 spent 17.6 per cent and 19.6 per cent of their time respectively outside the Levant, but these absences included spells in Muslim captivity and crusading in Egypt.[56] Although a lack of data makes it difficult to generate a percentage for the time spent abroad by Teutonic Knights' masters, it would have been many times more than that of their opposite numbers in the Templars and Hospitallers; a brief glance at appendix A will confirm this pattern.

For the Templars and Hospitallers there was a greater need to plan for contingencies such as the death of a master in battle (e.g., Bernard of Tremelay at Ascalon in 1153,[57] Roger of Moulins at Cresson in 1187,[58] William of Chartres in 1219,[59] Armand de Périgord at La Forbie in 1244) or

---

[53] *Urkundenbuch der Deutschordensballei Thüringen*, nos. 395, 396.
[54] *CGJJ*, vol. 1, no. 30.
[55] *SDO*, pp. 99–100.
[56] Burgtorf, *The Central Convent of Hospitallers and Templars*, p. 243.
[57] William of Tyre, *Chronicon*, vol. 2, pp. 798–799; Barber, *The New Knighthood*, pp. 74–75.
[58] *KSJJC*, p. 106.
[59] Burgtorf, *The Central Convent of Hospitallers and Templars*, p. 122.

his long-term captivity (e.g., Bertrand of Blancfort in 1157,[60] Odo of Saint-Armand in 1179, William of Châteauneuf in 1244–1250).[61] These problems were not so important for the Teutonic Knights because none of their masters was killed in battle in the thirteenth century and only one was briefly held in captivity (Herman von Salza during the Fifth Crusade). Their greatest concern was the master's absence from the Holy Land.[62]

Consequently, it was necessary for the Teutonic Order to appoint a capable long-term deputy in the Latin East. For the Templar and Hospitaller Orders in the thirteenth century, this was generally a grand commander.[63] The Teutonic Order's statutes recommended the grand commander as deputy, but permitted the master and chapter to choose any other brother should they wish it.[64] While acting in this capacity, a deputy was allowed to fly the master's standard and, on campaign, to use his tent. He could also utilise the master's privileges in relation to the reception of guests and visitors. He could not, however, wear the master's armour or sit at his place at table.[65] Throughout Herman von Salza's period in office, Brother Haymo and Grand Commander Luttold deputised for him in the kingdom of Jerusalem during his frequent absences (see chapter 4). These men appear to have exercised a number of powers including the right to receive and buy property. Examples of this can be seen in 1234 when Luttold purchased the village of Arabia from Bertrand Porcelet and in 1239 when he obtained a number of vineyards from the abbot of St Mary of the Latins in Jerusalem.[66] Luttold also obtained confirmations for his purchase of the property in 1234 from Richard Filangieri, suggesting that he was able to liaise with important political figures at this time.[67] The last known reference to Luttold can be found in 1246.[68] While Conrad von Thüringen was master, the marshal, Gerhard von Malberg, acted as deputy and he seems to have led the Order's forces during the Barons' Crusade.[69] Subsequently, during Louis's crusade, Peter of Koblenz became deputy and in this capacity he countersigned a letter of appeal written to Henry III of England.[70] It is possible, given that the master, marshal, grand commander and castellan of Montfort were all absent from the Holy Land at some point during this expedition (see chapter 6), that he acted initially in this capacity without having held any previous office. Despite this, by 1254, he had

---

60 William of Tyre, *Chronicon*, vol. 2, p. 831; Barber, *The New Knighthood*, p. 95.
61 After this event the Hospitallers introduced a procedure to adopt in case the master should be held captive, *CGJJ*, vol. 3, no. 3039 (p. 45).
62 Herman von Salza was briefly held captive during the Fifth Crusade; see chapter 2 and appendix C.
63 *La Règle du Temple*, pp. 86–87; *AZM*, p. 120; *KSJJC*, p. 305.
64 *SDO*, pp. 106–107.
65 *SDO*, pp. 107–108.
66 *TOT*, nos. 77, 88.
67 *TOT*, nos. 77, 88.
68 'Le Reliquie dell'Archivio dell'Ordine Teutonico in Venezia', p. 1431.
69 *R. Reg.*, vol. 1, no, 1097; *TOT*, no. 89; *CGJJ*, vol. 2, no. 2245.
70 *Foedera, Conventiones*, vol. 1, p. 308.

become marshal. Even greater powers appear to have been exerted later by Grand Commander Hartmann von Heldrungen, who deputised for Anno von Sangershausen during the 1260s and 1270s. At this time he and the marshal helped to negotiate compromises between the Templars and Hospitallers (see chapter 8). In 1272, Hartmann travelled to Cyprus, along with the Templar master and the Hospitaller marshal, to mediate between the king of Cyprus and his barons.[71] In 1283, the marshal, Conrad of Sulmeys, represented the Order during the peace negotiations between the kingdom of Jerusalem and Sultan Qalāwūn.[72] Consequently, the deputies of the master in the Holy Land, like the regional commanders in Livonia and Prussia, appear to have acted with considerable autonomy, to a point where they were able to shape their Order's policy in these areas. The final deputy described by the sources was Henry of Boland. Henry was the commander in Sicily and was also the former drapier; he died in command of the Order's forces during the fall of Acre.[73]

The 'Headquarters' of the Teutonic Order 1190–1291

Given the frequent absences of the master, the relative independence of Prussia and Livonia, the impotence of the chapter, the general decline of the Holy Land and the frequent convocation of general chapters in Germany, it is something of a misnomer to discuss the Order's headquarters in the Latin East.[74] Despite this, the statutes do mention an *obersten hûs* and realistically this building would probably have been the seat of executive power at least over the Teutonic Knights' properties in the eastern Mediterranean.[75] Historians have tended to argue that the Order's headquarters would have been first in Acre and then, after its construction, in the fortress of Montfort. After Montfort's fall in 1271, it would have returned to Acre.[76] This view has been challenged by Militzer, who has argued that during the period when Montfort was under the brethren's control the responsibilities of the Order's headquarters were performed jointly in a 'Haupthaus Akkon-Montfort' (although

---

[71] Eracles, p. 463.
[72] *R. Reg.*, vol. 1, no. 1450; *Early Mamluk Diplomacy*, pp. 69–91. Forstreuter (*Der Deutsche Orden am Mittelmeer*, pp. 192–193) believes that the marshal only became deputy master in 1240 (Gerhard von Malberg); however, it seems that both Peter (in 1254) and Conrad von Sulmeys (in 1283) also held this position.
[73] For Henry's former position as drapier see *R. Reg.*, vol. 1, no. 1435. For his role in the siege of Acre see Perlbach, 'Deutsch-Ordens Necrologe', p. 364.
[74] *AZM*, p. 134.
[75] *SDO*, p. 32.
[76] Sterns, 'The Teutonic Knights in the Crusader States', p. 327; Hubatsch, 'Der Deutsche Orden und die Reichlehnschaft über Cypern', p. 280; Hamilton, *The Latin Church in the Crusader States*, p. 273. Favreau-Lilie similarly argues that Montfort performed many of the roles of a headquarters; 'L'Ordine Teutonico in Terrasanta (1198–1291)', pp. 67–68. See also Arnold, 'Entstehung und Frühzeit des Deutschen Ordens', p. 104; Forstreuter, *Der Deutsche Orden am Mittelmeer*, pp. 189–190; Prutz, *Die Besitzungen des Deutschen Ordens*, p. 45.

with most functions performed in Acre).[77] Many of Militzer's arguments are extremely valid; however, his conclusions can be developed further to demonstrate that it was Acre alone which was always the headquarters. To emphasise the advantages of a headquarters in Acre, Militzer highlights its position as capital city, the fact that the Hospitallers and Templars had their headquarters there and its importance as a port.[78] He has also drawn attention to a document issued by Pope Honorius III in 1216, which described Acre as the seat of the master and the chapter. This was confirmed in 1220, 1227, 1259 and 1262.[79] Furthermore, with regard to the main hospital of the Order, the Teutonic Order's statutes stipulate: 'In the main house or where the master with the counsel of the chapter decides, there [should] be a hospital at all times.'[80] The Order's major hospital was in Acre rather than Montfort and thus this stipulation, in addition to a further clause which concerns the provision of doctors at the headquarters, demonstrates that the headquarters was Acre.[81] Certainly every document which was witnessed by the Order's hospitaller and which gives its place of issue was signed in Acre.[82] Despite these arguments, Militzer still suggests that Montfort did carry out some of the tasks of a headquarters.

The first piece of evidence he refers to concerns the position of the castellan of Montfort. This official, unlike any other castellan, could only be appointed with the combined consent of the chapter and master, seemingly in the general chapter.[83] The fact that such importance was attached to this appointment has been taken as an indication of Montfort's primacy in comparison to other fortresses. Despite this, there is nothing remarkable about this stipulation. It should be noted that all the Teutonic Knights' other major castellans were located in the Order's provinces and were under the authority of a local master. The appointment of these castellans was therefore the responsibility of the provincial masters and such decisions would have taken place in a local general chapter held in a commandery nearby.[84] Montfort, however, was the only major fortress of the Teutonic Order which lay in the kingdom of Jerusalem and therefore its castellan fell under the direct responsibility of

---

[77] *AZM*, p. 134. Burgtorf has commented that 'it is doubtful that the Teutonic Knights ever moved theirs [headquarters] to Montfort/Starkenburg'. Burgtorf, *The Central Convent of the Hospitallers and Templars*, p. 94.

[78] *AZM*, pp. 133–134.

[79] *AZM*, p. 132; *TOT*, no. 303, 306, 424, 607, 623.

[80] 'In dem obersten hûs, oder dâ der meister mit dem capitele ze râte wirdet, spitâle habe zu allen cîten', *SDO*, p. 31. Translation taken from Sterns, 'The Statutes of the Teutonic Knights', p. 209. This was also the case in the Hospitaller rule; see Nicholson, *The Knights Hospitaller*, p. 68.

[81] *AZM*, p. 133; *SDO*, p. 32. For further discussion see Forstreuter, *Der Deutsche Orden am Mittelmeer*, p. 190.

[82] September 1208: Henry *custos infirmorum*, *R. Reg.*, vol. 1, no. 828. April 1228: Henry *hospitalarius*, *TOT*, no. 63. 7 July 1244: Conrad *hospitalarius*, *R. Reg.*, vol. 1, no. 1120. 6 June 1253: Conrad of Minerla *hospitalarius*, *R. Reg.*, vol. 1, no. 1206. 1 July 1277: Albert *hospitalarius*, *R. Reg.*, vol. 1, no. 1413.

[83] *SDO*, p. 97; *AZM*, pp. 132–133; Forstreuter, *Der Deutsche Orden am Mittelmeer*, p. 190.

[84] *SDO*, p. 96–97.

the chapter and headquarters, not of a provincial commander.[85] This official, therefore, had to be chosen by the chapter directly. It seems that this simple distinction was the reason for the apparent prominence of the castellan of Montfort. Furthermore, it should also be noted that in the Hospitaller Order the castellans of Margat and Crac were accorded a special level of seniority in some clauses of their statutes, even though neither of their castles was the headquarters of their Order.[86] Indeed, Burgtorf has indicated that the castellans of Margat and Crac were superior to the commanders of Armenia and Cyprus or any of the Western provinces.[87] The pre-eminence of a particular castellan within a military order does not necessary imply that the stronghold in his charge was the institutional headquarters.

A further matter concerns the position of the Order's central treasury, which Militzer suggests could have been in Montfort.[88] If true, this might provide some evidence that the castle fulfilled a function of a headquarters. This study will argue, by contrast, that the Order followed a similar pattern to the Hospitallers in the division of its wealth, with a major treasury in Acre and smaller reserves in other regions and fortresses.

It is clear that the treasurer conducted much of his business in Acre. Table 1 details the rents paid by the Order to various noblemen and their place of payment.

Table 1: Annual rents of the Teutonic Order

Date of initiation	Day of annual payment	Nature and amount of payment	Place of payment	Reference
1236	14 September (Feast of the Exaltation of the Cross)	Rent for several villages of 40 gold bezants	Acre	*TOT*, no. 84
1239	1 March	Rent for land in mountains above Acre of 20 bezants	Acre	*TOT*, no. 86
1257	Three payments per year in February, June and October	Rent for property in Acre. Total per annum is 309 bezants	Acre	*TOT*, no. 113.
1257	2 February	1 bezant to the church in Acre	Acre	*TOT*, no. 112.

[85] The Cave of Tyron was in the kingdom of Jerusalem and it did belong, in theory, to the Teutonic Order; however, it is possible that the Order was never able to enforce its claims to this fortress and thereby appoint a castellan. Also Castellum Regis was in the kingdom of Jerusalem but, given its proximity to Montfort, it is likely that it was controlled by the same official. Certainly, no mention is ever made to the castellan of Castellum Regis.

[86] *CGJJ*, vol. 3, no. 3317.

[87] J. Burgtorf, 'The Military Orders in the Crusader Principality of Antioch', in *East and West in the Medieval Eastern Mediterranean I: Antioch from the Byzantine Reconquest until the End of the Crusader Principality*, ed. K. Ciggaar and M. Metcalf (Leuven, 2006), pp. 222, 226; Burgtorf, *The Central Convent of Hospitallers and Templars*, p. 52; *CGJJ*, vol. 2, no. 2213 (p. 553).

[88] *AZM*, pp. 132–134.

Secondly, although there is evidence for a treasury at Montfort, this does not imply that it was the main treasury of the headquarters. In 1249, for example, a charter which details the sale of a number of villages to the Order by John of Caesarea for 4,000 bezants specifies that this money should be paid to him from either Montfort or Acre, suggesting that there was a treasury at both locations.[89] It was customary for castles which were at the centre of a great estate to keep a financial reserve. Many historians and archaeologists have commented on Montfort's role as an estate centre and certainly a brief glance at the map at appendix B will confirm that it was ideally situated for such a function.[90] The military orders held a number of such estates in the eastern Mediterranean and many of these possessed a treasury. In the Hospitaller Order, for example, the castle of Margat had its own treasury, demonstrating that such a financial function could simply be a response to the demands of local administration.[91] Thus while Montfort may have been a treasury for the Order, this does not provide evidence that it was the 'head-quarters' and there are good grounds to suggest that it was solely Acre which performed this function.

Synthesis

Regarding the statutes of the Teutonic Order in general, one conclusion is particularly apparent: Prussia and Livonia are barely mentioned. At the time of its militarisation in 1198 the Teutonic Order inherited a rule that was derived from those of the Hospitallers and Templars. Both these institutions were arranged so that their resources and authority could be focused on the Holy Land and this was reflected in their rule and wider statutes. In these knightly orders, the master's authority was shared with that of the chapter and general chapter and, in theory, all three of these bodies were expected to work together for the good of the Holy Land. The provincial commanders were each in orbit around this single central point. The Teutonic Knights were granted the same rule and at first, given that their early campaigns (1198–1210) were solely in the eastern Mediterranean, this structure would have been appropriate. After 1210, Herman von Salza began to use resources to fight wars of expansion and conquest along Western Christendom's eastern borders. By the 1230s, therefore, the brethren were deeply engaged in Prussia, Livonia and the Holy Land, and by the 1240s they were fighting simply to hold these frontiers. Given that the Teutonic Knights had acquired major responsibilities on so many fronts one would expect that their statutes would have been modified to reflect this changing condition. To a limited extent this is true. For

---

[89] *TOT*, no. 100.
[90] See A. J. Boas, *Crusader Archaeology: The Material Culture of the Latin East* (London, 1999), p. 109; Forey, *The Military Orders*, p. 63; Kennedy, *Crusader Castles*, p. 129.
[91] *CGJJ*, vol. 3, no. 3844.

example, the statutes permit the brethren to use different weapons on different frontiers, demonstrating an awareness of the varying military demands of each region.[92] The rule also mentions briefly the importance of the Livonian master, a reflection of the growing independence of this province.[93] Despite this, when reading the statutes, it is clear that the regulations still define an Order that is centred upon the Holy Land. They describe only the roles of the Levantine office holders (the grand commander, marshal, drapier, etc.) and outline only the administrative layout of the Latin East. They stipulate that the master was expected to remain in the East and that the general chapter and the election of the master were supposed to occur there.

More importantly, no special regulations are given for the administration of Prussia and Livonia, regions which, by the 1240s, were beginning to acquire the trappings of independent countries. For example, the Livonian marshal (an office that by 1264 had been in existence for over two decades) is not mentioned. Clearly the exclusion of such provincial officers from the statutes of the military orders was not customary and the Templar statutes mention that there were marshals in provinces such as Antioch and Tripoli.[94] No mention is made in the Teutonic Order's statues of the need to acquire a financial framework in Prussia and Livonia that could deal, for example, with the payment and provision of armies that by the late thirteenth century could number many thousands. No reference is given to the reception of pilgrims or the way in which the provincial masters of Prussia and Livonia should liaise, as they did, with the papacy or secular rulers. No framework is established for the co-ordination of campaigns between the Holy Land and the Baltic. No distinction is made between a *Landkomtur* and a *Landmeister*. Overall, the statutes mention Livonia and Prussia on only three occasions (in comparison, Armenia receives four references). In conclusion, the statutes of the Order essentially treat the Teutonic Order as if it was an institution that was still centred upon the Holy Land. Little recognition is given either to the needs or the growing importance of Prussia and Livonia. The masters of these provinces, despite their enormous power, were theoretically accorded only the limited power of any other provincial commander such as those of Austria, Armenia or even Romania.

Even so, the form taken by the statutes is not particularly surprising given its provenance. The statutes were written in the Holy Land, probably under the supervision of the chapter of the Order. As shown above, the chapter believed that the Order *should* focus upon the Holy Land, just as the master *should* remain there and the institution's provinces overseas *should* be centred upon their authority. It seems likely, therefore, that the statutes of the Order in their 1264 edition are a better representation of what the chapter believed

---

[92] *SDO*, pp. 46–47.
[93] *SDO*, p. 91.
[94] Burgtorf, *The Central Convent of Hospitallers and Templars*, p. 105; *La Règle du Temple*, pp. 90–91, 103.

the Order *should* be rather than what it actually was. Certainly the examples given above demonstrate that they bore little relation to the realities of the Order's role in Prussia and Livonia just as their stipulations concerning the master were routinely ignored. Regarding the value of the statutes, it seems that they were probably accurate with regard to the infrastructure of the Order in the Holy Land and probably for the daily life of the brethren. From a power and authority perspective, they may be more reliable if approached as a manifesto of the chapter rather than a true depiction of the Order's condition.

Communication and Rural Administration in the Levant

The Teutonic Knights possessed two major blocks of landholdings in Outremer. Firstly, in Armenia they owned two estates which were centred on the fortresses of Amudain and Harunia. Little is known about communication between these estates and there are only two documented journeys made by members of the Order to this region: the first by Herman von Salza in 1211 and the second by Anno von Sangershausen in 1271.[95] There is more evidence for communication within the Order's estate in the Galilean hills to the north of Acre. This estate centred on Montfort and was serviced by a road which travelled north-east from Acre. This castle and the brethren's palace in Acre administered the Order's properties in the Holy Land. Accordingly, the transport of materials from Acre to Montfort was a crucial consideration because a fortress of that size would have needed a secure supply line. Notably, in 1257 there was a disagreement between the Order and the bishop of Acre which concerned, among other matters, the tithes levied on transportation between Castellum Regis (three miles away from Montfort) and Acre, a vitally important route.[96]

The road from Castellum Regis to Acre was reasonably straight, passing through the village of Tersyha, where it met the road which connected Toron to Acre and thence through the villages of Amca and Habelye. Seemingly for the defence of this route the Teutonic Knights built the fort of Jiddin, which is perhaps comparable to the forts constructed by the Templars and Hospitallers to protect the roads to Jerusalem.[97] Little documentary evidence survives for this building and there are only fleeting references to its existence.[98] Jiddin has been thoroughly examined by Pringle who argues that it was built by

---

[95] For Herman's visit see Wilbrand of Oldenburg, *Peregrinatores*, pp. 163–174. For Anno's visit see *Les Gestes des Chiprois*, p. 840.
[96] *TOT*, no. 112.
[97] Pringle et al., 'Qal'at Jiddin', pp. 135–166.
[98] Burchard of Mount Sion, 'Descriptio Terrae Sanctae', in *Itinera Hierosolymitana Crucesignatorum*, ed. S. de Sandoli, Studium Biblicum Franciscanum: Collectio Maior, 24, vol. 4 (Jerusalem, 1984), p. 142.

the Order after 1220 and was lost between 1268 and 1271.[99] He states that Jiddin 'occupies a rocky ridge on the north side of the Wadi Jiddin, which forms a natural route of penetration north-east into the mountains from Amqa (Amca) on the edge of the coastal plain'.[100]

Much of the rural administration devolved upon the grand commander. This official was responsible for matters such as workshops, pack animals, grain and wagons.[101] He seems to have been primarily located in Acre and to have concerned himself with the affairs of the kingdom of Jerusalem. Below the grand commander, there were lesser officials who supported his office directly (discussed above) and also a number local administrators who managed the individual estates. For example, to the north of Montfort, the Order briefly acquired a geographically distinct group of properties which it purchased from Julian of Sidon between 1256 and 1261 (see chapter 6 and appendix B). Although the 1264 statutes of the Order do not stipulate which officer administered this region there is a single reference in 1258 to one Gautier who was 'le commandeor des freres des Alemans de Seete'.[102] It is likely that this official was appointed to govern these landholdings. Concerning the management of the Montfort estate the statutes are similarly silent; however, it is possible that this area was under the authority of a local administrator and, at least partially, the castellan of Montfort. By way of comparison, in the Templar Order's provinces, the local commander was required to supply any castellan with essential resources including troops, wheat and metal, but the castellan was expected to provide all the remaining materials himself.[103] If we apply this model to the Teutonic Order then it may be that the grand commander was similarly expected to provide such goods for the castellan of Montfort (this would certainly explain his stated responsibility for grain, wagons and pack animals).[104] By return the castellan of Montfort may have been accountable for all the local resources and this would explain why the grand commander is so rarely recorded in Montfort.

Below these commanders were a number of scribes who carried out much of the routine work of the Order. Riley-Smith has demonstrated how lords in the Holy Land tended to adopt existing institutions for the collection of taxation, employing local agents to act as intermediaries between them and their vassals.[105] It seems that the Teutonic Knights followed this procedure and the Order's charters mention several scribes. In 1273, there is a reference to a

99 Pringle, *Secular Buildings*, pp. 80–82. For further discussion that supports the assertion that the Teutonic Order built this fortification see Pringle et al., 'Qal'at Jiddin', pp. 135–166.
100 Pringle et al., 'Qal'at Jiddin', p. 135.
101 *SDO*, p. 106.
102 *TOT*, no. 115 at p. 97.
103 *La Règle du Temple*, p. 103.
104 *SDO*, p. 106.
105 Riley-Smith, *The Feudal Nobility*, pp. 53–54.

scribe, Brahim (Ibrāhīm).[106] There are also two references to a scribe named Georgius in 1273 and 1280, who was identified as a scribe of the treasurer.[107] It is likely that these men were either native Christians or Muslims and a further reference to similar officials can be found in the statutes, which state that the master's entourage should include a 'heathen scribe'.[108]

The estates themselves produced several crops and trade-goods and the Teutonic Knights possessed a considerable number of villages both in the kingdom of Jerusalem and in Armenia. Their largest concentration of land was in the hills of Galilee to the north of Acre and this area is said to have been highly productive. Sanuto claimed that 'it abounds with fruit and all good things.'[109] The products of these estates are shown in appendix D.

In villages such as Noie, tenants grew luxury foods such as sugar. Sugar was used in the Order's hospital and this is reflected in a stipulation of the Order's rule which emphasises the care with which sugar should be used as a medicine.[110] Before the Order began to produce sugar of its own, King Aimery granted the brethren a regular supply in 1193, specifically for medical purposes.[111] In 1999–2000 an archaeological excavation was carried out in Acre in the area where the Teutonic Order is believed to have possessed its major properties and this uncovered a large number of sugar moulds, reinforcing the suggestion that sugar was used in the hospital.[112] Aside from its medical applications it is also possible that, like the Hospitallers and Templars, sugar was produced in bulk for export to Western Christendom where it could have been sold for a great price.[113]

Urban Income

In addition to the revenue gathered from agriculture and leasing/renting properties, the Order also drew an important income from the shipping and market taxes of the port of Acre, known respectively as *cathena* and *fundaq*.[114] In

---

106   *R. Reg.*, vol. 1, no. 1399. For further discussion see Houben, 'I Cavalieri Teutonici nel Mediterraneo Orientale (secoli XII–XV)', pp. 61–64; B. Z. Kedar, 'The Subjected Muslims of the Frankish Levant', in *Muslims under Latin Rule*, ed. J. M. Powell (Princeton, 1990), p. 157.

107   *R. Reg.*, vol. 1, nos. 1399, 1435. Houben has suggested that there might be a further piece of evidence pertaining to the scribes of the Order on Cyprus. This contention is based on an inscription to one 'Yorge, lescrivan des Alemans' (George, scribe of the Germans). Whether these 'Germans' were actually Teutonic Knights, however, is not known; 'Intercultural Communication', p. 155. C. Enlart, 'Deux inscriptions françaises trouvées à Chypre', *Syria: Revue d'art oriental d'archéologie*, 8 (1927), p. 236.

108   'Heidenisschen schribere'; *SDO*, p. 98.

109   'Habundat fructibus et omnibus bonis'; Sanuto, p. 249. For further discussion of the products of the Order's Levantine estates see Prutz, *Die Besitzungen des Deutschen Ordens*, pp. 58–75.

110   *SDO*, p. 66.

111   *TOT*, no. 34.

112   Boas, *Archaeology of the Military Orders*, pp. 61–62, 94.

113   Bronstein, *The Hospitallers and the Holy Land*, pp. 19, 53–54.

114   J. S. C. Riley-Smith, 'Government in Latin Syria and the Commercial Privileges of Foreign

1220, when the Order purchased the properties and rights of Otto, count of Henneburg, it acquired an income of 2266.66 bezants from this source.[115] This was ceded immediately to John of Brienne. In 1228 revenue from this source was granted again with a concession of 100 bezants per annum by the prince of Antioch.[116] During Frederick's crusade, the Order gained a further annuity of 13,400 bezants from *cathena* and *fundaq* in Acre. Of this, 6,400 bezants per annum was acquired in exchange for property in Italy.[117] The remaining income of 7,000 bezants per annum was given as compensation for Frederick's failure to endow the Order with the estate of Toron (see chapter 4).[118] The total net income was therefore 13,500 bezants per annum. This was reduced in 1244 when the Order ceded half the 7,000 bezants per annum to Jacob of Amigdala although this still left the Order with an annual income of 10,000 bezants.[119]

To give some idea of the scale of this income it is instructive to see how many knights this sum could support on an annual basis. The problem with such a task is that the income necessary to support a knight, as Riley-Smith has shown, grew dramatically from roughly 300 bezants per annum, as stated by the *Livre au Roi* in 1200, to around 1,000 bezants per annum by the 1260s.[120] Given that the Teutonic Order acquired the bulk of this income in 1229, it would be useful to establish what the salary of a knight was in 1229 so that the value of this income, at the time of its acquisition, can be understood. There is a document, issued in 1229 by Frederick II to Conrad von Hohenlohe (brother of Heinrich von Hohenlohe), which provides some illumination on this subject. This charter conferred an income of 6,000 bezants per annum upon Conrad from *cathena* and *fundaq* in exchange for his own service and that of nine further *milites*.[121] To frame some idea of the cost of retaining a single *miles* from this document, it is not possible to simply divide the total income equally between Conrad and his nine *milites* because Conrad would presumably have claimed a higher proportion of this income than a single member of his retinue. Despite this, it seems fair to suggest

Merchants', in *Relations Between East and West in the Middle Ages*, ed. D. Baker (Edinburgh, 1973), pp. 112–117.

[115] *TOT*, no. 53.

[116] *TOT*, no. 64.

[117] For the grant of 6,400 bezants in annual income see *TOT*, no. 68; HB. vol. 3, pp. 122–123. Mayer seems to feel that this income was sold almost immediately in a property exchange with the Amigdala family in 1229. Despite this it seems that only the sum of 6,400 bezants was paid to this family for these properties not the annuity itself; HB, vol. 3, pp. 117–119; Mayer, 'Die Seigneurie de Joscelin und der Deutsche Orden', pp. 207–208. For the transfer of property to Frederick in exchange, see *TOT*, no. 153; HB, vol. 3, pp. 129–130. It is possible that some of this income was not actually within Frederick's gift because the *Chronica Majora* contains a reference to the Canons of the Holy Cross being deprived of their income from the port of Acre; vol. 3, p. 185.

[118] *TOT*, no. 66; HB, vol. 3. pp. 123–125.

[119] *TOT*, no. 98.

[120] Riley-Smith, *Feudal Nobility*, p. 10.

[121] *AOL*, vol. 2, pp. 166–167 (documents).

that this document presupposed that a knight would require an income of perhaps between 400 and 600 bezants at this time. Relating these figures back to the Order's income of 13,500 bezants, it is estimated accordingly that this revenue alone could have provided payment for around twenty-seven knights.[122] Consequently, it can be seen that this was a vital source of income.

Supply from Overseas

The Teutonic Knights' considerable properties in the Holy Land would have provided them with a proportion of the income and resources necessary to fulfil their military and medical undertakings; this income was then supplemented with goods and funds received from their overseas estates. Such lands were a great boon to all the major orders because they could provide a steady stream of weapons, recruits, money and foodstuffs to the eastern Mediterranean. Malcolm Barber, in his study on the Templars, has written: 'without an extensive network of support in the West, the Templars would have vanished with the first major defeat they suffered.'[123] Having transported such resources to the Latin East they could then use them to fund military endeavours, build fortifications, recover from battlefield losses and provide services for pilgrims. For the Templars and Hospitallers, the primary purpose of their Western estates was to provide aid for their commanders in the Holy Land. Admittedly, a measure of their income may have been used locally in the defence of frontier regions such as Spain; however, their role in these areas was auxiliary and never competed with their commitment to the eastern Mediterranean. In these orders, the commanderies in Western Christendom were required to send one third of their total revenue to the Latin East. These funds were known as 'responsions'. The statutes of the Hospitaller Order, for example, frequently make reference to these monies and special statutes were created for their reception as well as further stipulations for commanders who defaulted in these payments.[124] Forey has suggested that similar payments were drawn from the Teutonic Order's Western estates for employment in the Latin East.[125] In theory this may have been true although only one document in 1290 mentions levies comparable to such responsions. It is far more likely that in practice the Order's revenues from Western Christendom were divided instead between the Holy Land and the Baltic. As shown above, the

---

[122] This sum has been calculated by dividing the Order's total income (13,500) by the estimated annual wage of a *miles* taken from the charter issued to Conrad von Hohenlohe. (It was suggested above that this income could be between 400 and 600 bezants. A middle figure of 500 has been used in this calculation.) Thus, 13,500/500=27. For further discussion of the Order's Levantine income see Prutz, *Die Besitzungen des Deutschen Ordens*, pp. 58–75. For other sums on the *milites* who could be retained on this income and other sources of revenue from the lordship of Toron, see Mayer, 'Die Seigneurie de Joscelin und der Deutsche Orden', p. 213.

[123] Barber, *The New Knighthood*, p. 230; Barber, 'Supplying the Crusader States', pp. 314–326.

[124] *CGJJ*, vol. 3, no. 4549; *CGJJ*, vol. 3, no. 3039.

[125] Forey, *The Military Orders*, p. 128.

Teutonic Order frequently sent supplies to Prussia and Livonia both to fund colonisation activities and to maintain their holdings. Indeed, the brethren only survived the Prussian rebellions of the thirteenth century with consistent reinforcement.

Those resources which were designated for the use of the Teutonic Order in the Holy Land were conveyed to the east through a highly developed administrative system. Initially, the Order's producer regions in France, Germany or Italy supplied surpluses in both resources and cash. These materials were then conveyed either by cart or by coastal shipping to the major ports in Italy or Sicily for transportation to the Holy Land.[126] The main harbours used by the Teutonic Order were located in Apulia and Sicily and included Barletta, Brindisi and Bari. Each of these cities was a major terminus for the Levantine trade and all were similarly employed by the Templars and Hospitallers.[127] According to contemporary legal practice each ship was required to obtain the requisite export licence from the authorities and a number of these concerning the Teutonic Order have survived from the reign of Charles of Anjou.[128] These charters generally give Apulia as the point of departure although some do specify an individual port such as Barletta or Manfredonia.[129]

Around these ports, the Order developed the infrastructure that could facilitate and supplement the flow of resources to the Holy Land. These facilities can be broken into three main categories. Firstly, throughout this period, the Order was granted property within the ports themselves and in the surrounding countryside. In the environs of Brindisi, for example, the brethren acquired from Emperor Henry VI an estate which was situated between this city and Oria.[130] In 1215 Frederick II gave the Order a house in the port with an adjoining bathhouse.[131] Lanfrancus of Bogossa, in his last testimony, granted further lands and houses.[132] The Order also owned agricultural land around Bari as well as further property inland such as the Church of S. Paraseeves in Venosa.[133] Other documents suggest that the brethren held a stake in the salt industry in Cannae in Apulia, to the north-west of Bari. Their interests here appear to have begun during the reign of Frederick II, but were lost soon after the 1245 Council of Lyons – presumably through the

---

[126] Toomaspoeg, *Les Teutoniques en Sicilie*, pp. 42–64.
[127] For discussion of the military orders' supply lines see J. H. Pryor, '*In Subsidium Terrae Sanctae*: Exports of Foodstuffs and War Materials from the Kingdom of Sicily to the Kingdom of Jerusalem, 1265–1284', *Asian and African Studies*, 22 (1988), pp. 127–146.
[128] *I Registri della Cancelleria Angioina*, vol. 1, p. 295; ibid., vol. 3, p. 192; ibid., vol. 7, p. 200; ibid., vol. 15, pp. 36–37.
[129] *I Registri della Cancelleria Angioina*, vol. 1, p. 295; ibid., vol. 3, p. 192; ibid., vol. 15, pp. 36–37.
[130] *Regesta Imperii IV*, vol. 3, no. 727. Confirmed by Frederick II, *Regesta Imperii V*, vol. 1, no. 1194.
[131] *TOT*, no. 145; *CDOT*, no. 18.
[132] *TOT*, no. 147.
[133] *I Registri della Cancelleria Angioina*, vol. 4, p. 154.

disfavour of Frederick II (see chapter 6). They were subsequently reinstated by Charles of Anjou.[134] Many of the Order's further acquisitions in these and other maritime cities can be found listed in imperial charters issued in February 1217 and April 1221.[135]

The produce of their agricultural land and industries would have provided the Order with resources and revenue that could be despatched to the kingdom of Jerusalem with far greater ease than supplies generated in Germany. Urban property would have provided space for administration, storage and accommodation. In the early years, it seems that the brethren attempted to consolidate their resources around the eastern Mediterranean by conducting a number of property exchanges in which more distant properties were replaced with lands and incomes that were closer to the Holy Land. In 1216, for example, the brethren arranged that Frederick II should take possession of some property in Germany in return for an income from the taxation receipts of Brindisi.[136] In 1229, the Teutonic Knights granted Frederick property in Apulia in exchange for a sizable annual revenue from the port of Acre.[137] In these ways, before their colonisation of Prussia and Livonia, the brethren went to some trouble to draw their resources into closer orbit around the Holy Land.

In addition to landed wealth in Apulia and Sicily, the Order also benefited from income from the harbour tolls of Italian ports. These were granted by Frederick II to the Order between 1217 and 1238 and consisted of a number of annual stipends payable in ounces of gold or silver. In 1217, for example, he endowed the brethren with 200 ounces of silver every year from the port of Messina.[138] Over subsequent years further concessions were made, generally to provide clothing for the Order and to support the poor.[139] Table 2 shows all the grants of this kind.

With this additional income, the Order had a constant supply of precious metal that would have been ideal for transportation because it would not have been bulky and would not necessarily have needed to be exchanged for local currency.[140] Problems with currency exchange had occurred on many occasions previously when Western money needed to be exchanged for Eastern coinage. A notable example of this occurred during the Second Crusade when

---

[134] *I Registri della Cancelleria Angioina*, vol. 2, p. 278. Toomaspoeg, *Les Teutoniques en Sicilie*, p. 63.

[135] February 1217: *Regesta Imperii V*, vol. 1, no. 897; HB, vol. 1, pp. 917–920; April 1221: *TOT*, no. 149.

[136] *Regesta Imperii V*, vol. 1, no. 887; *AZM*, p. 32.

[137] HB, vol. 3, pp. 129–130.

[138] *CDOT*, no. 28.

[139] *CDOT*, no. 28.

[140] See A. Murray, 'Money and Logistics in the Forces of the First Crusade: Coinage, Bullion, Service and Supply: 1096–1099', in *Logistics of Warfare in the Age of the Crusades*, ed. J. Pryor (Aldershot, 2006), p. 229–250.

the Greek moneychangers took advantage of the crusading forces by offering a low rate of exchange.[141]

Table 2. Grants to the order

City	Amount of revenue (per year)	Increase 1	Increase 2
Bari	150 ounces of gold[1] (1221)		
Brindisi	150 ounces of gold[2] (1216)	200 ounces of gold[3] (1221 confirmed 1222)[4]	350 ounces of gold[5] (1238)
Messina (Sicily)	200 ounces of silver[6] (1217)		
Total annual income	300 ounces of gold 200 ounces of silver	350 ounces of gold 200 ounces of silver	500 ounces of gold 200 ounces of silver[7]

[1] *TOT*, no. 149.
[2] *Regesta Imperii V*, vol. 1, no. 887, confirmed in 1218, *MGH Epis. Saec. XIII*, vol. 1, no. 40.
[3] HB, vol. 2, p. 224; *TOT*, no. 150.
[4] *TOT*, no. 151; Potthast, vol. 1, no. 6815.
[5] *Regesta Imperii V*, vol. 1, no. 2361.
[6] *TOT*, no. 146; *CDOT*, no. 28; HB, vol. 1, pp. 510–511, confirmed in 1218, *MGH Epis. Saec. XIII*, vol. 1, no. 41.
[7] For discussion of these tolls, see Toomaspoeg, *Les Teutoniques en Sicilie*, pp. 45–48.

A further way in which the Teutonic Knights' supply lines were supported in these maritime cities was in the removal of the taxes levied upon ships and cargoes. As early as 1197 they were not required to pay tax on cargoes between Messina and Reggio.[142] In 1217, the brethren were accorded the same privileges as the Hospitallers in Sicily and Apulia.[143] In 1221, Frederick freed the Order from all taxation whether on land or by sea throughout the empire.[144] Overall, these privileges would naturally have reduced the Order's outgoing payments and maximised the amount they could send to the East.

These factors demonstrate the immense importance of the Apulian cities as links in the Order's supply chain to the Holy Land. They were placed under the authority of the preceptor of Apulia and this officer was first mentioned in 1225.[145] Naturally, given the significance of these harbours, it was imperative to remain in favour with the local ruler. For much of this period these ports were controlled by the Hohenstaufen family, who were generally active supporters of the Teutonic Knights (see chapters 1–4). Indeed, as shown above, Henry VI and Frederick II were responsible for much of the Order's material development in these regions. Despite this, in the late 1240s Frederick confiscated the brethren's Italian and Sicilian properties, placing a stranglehold on their supply lines. Even though these landholdings were returned by Frederick's sons in 1251, it seems significant that, as late as 1254, the Order's marshal

[141] Odo of Deuil, *De Profectione Ludovici VII*, p. 40.
[142] *Regesta Imperii IV*, vol. 3, no. 709.
[143] *Regesta Imperii V*, vol. 1, no. 911.
[144] *TOT*, no. 256.
[145] Houben, 'Die Landkomture der Deutschordensballei Apulien', p. 117.

in Acre claimed that he had still not received any supplies from overseas.[146] Admittedly all the lines of communication were not entirely blocked at this time and in *c*.1253 a charter written in Venice by Wilhelm von Urenbach suggests that this port, which was not aligned with Frederick's policies, was still open to the Order.[147] Furthermore, in 1250 Eberhard of Saone travelled successfully from Egypt to Livonia through Germany.[148] After the return of the Order's properties by Frederick's son Manfred, the brethren were allowed to continue to use the Apulian ports until his death in 1266.[149] They do not seem to have been particularly affected by Charles's subsequent assumption of power and there is no record of any controversies or confiscations, although concern for the retention of their Apulian and Sicilian properties may have encouraged them to offer their support to Charles's representatives in the kingdom of Jerusalem.[150]

The Teutonic Knights' relationship with the Venetians is particularly interesting. This association can probably be dated back to around 1220 when the Order acquired the Castellum Regis estate. In a document, compiled in 1243, the Venetians referred to a number of villages owned by the brethren including Tayeretrane and Maron (see appendix B). The Venetians apparently owned one third of both these villages, yet this fact is not mentioned in the documents which describe the Order's acquisition of these settlements in 1220.[151] Presumably some form of *modus vivendi* was reached between the Venetian officials and the Order. In later years the bond between Venice and the Teutonic Knights became particularly apparent. During the war of St Sabas, for example, both parties supported the election of Hugh II as regent and the brethren are said to have sided with the Venetians in their disputes with the other Italian cities.[152] The Order also participated in the negotiations between the Venetians, Pisans and Genoese in 1261 and again in 1277, when they helped to arrange the return of Venetian privileges in Tyre.[153] Furthermore, the Order relied upon Venice as a supply port.[154] After the fall of Acre in 1291, the Teutonic Knights – alone of the military orders – transferred their headquarters to Venice. In these ways, the ongoing relationship between Venice and the Order can be seen in their mutual support during the late thirteenth century.

---

[146] April 1251: *Regesta Imperii V*, vol. 1, no. 4542; 5 May 1251: *Historia Diplomatica Regni Siciliae*, no. 19; 7 October 1251: *Historia Diplomatica Regni Siciliae*, no. 34; letter *c*.1254: 'Carta de la Orden Teutónica a Alfonso X'.

[147] *Liv., Est. und Kurländisches Urkundenbuch*, vol. 1, no. 224. See above, pp. 105–107.

[148] *Annales Erphordenses Fratrum Praedicatorum*, p. 109.

[149] *Historia Diplomatica Regni Siciliae*, no. 19.

[150] Hellmann, 'König Manfred von Sizilien und der Deutsche Orden', p. 72; Toomaspoeg, *Les Teutoniques en Sicilie*, p. 62.

[151] *Urkunden zur Älteren Handels – und Staatsgeschichte der Republik Venedig*, vol. 2, pp. 373–376.

[152] Rothelin, pp. 633–635.

[153] *R. Reg.*, vol. 1, nos. 1298, 1413.

[154] *I Registri della Cancelleria Angioina*, vol. 19, p. 39.

Having amassed these resources in Italy, the brethren then shipped them to the Holy Land. They owned several ships and, although few details survive concerning the nature of these vessels, there are many references to their presence across the eastern Mediterranean.[155] The customary route for such vessels lay between the Apulian ports and Acre and this is reflected in the shipping licences.[156] According to these official documents, the primary material transported by the Order was grain.[157] Several shipments of this kind were recorded during the 1260s and 1270s and it is likely that the Order became increasingly dependent upon grain imports as its landholdings in the Latin East dwindled.[158] The reception of grain was the responsibility of the vice commander although overall control was exercised by the grand commander.[159] In addition to these foodstuffs, there is also a reference to a shipment of horses that was licensed in 1276. According to the export permit, the Order was allowed to transport twelve warhorses, twelve riding horses and a quantity of mules.[160] This charter demonstrates that the brethren, in the same way as both the Templars and Hospitallers, exported horses for the use of its brothers and servants. Horses were an extremely valuable commodity for the conduct of war in the Latin East and various sources reflect their importance. The letter issued by the Order's marshal in 1254, in the wake of Louis IX's failed Egyptian campaign, draws particular reference to the need to provide remounts for the Teutonic Knights' depleted military force.[161]

Once these goods had arrived in the Holy Land, Charles of Anjou required various parties to take responsibility for their disembarkation in Acre. In 1277, for example, Patriarch Thomas was required explicitly to write to Charles to confirm that each shipment of foodstuffs had arrived and been unloaded in Acre.[162] The Teutonic Knights themselves were required to witness bills of unloading for goods transported to the Holy Land by the other orders.[163] Charles's reasons for this process are not given, although it is possible that he wanted to ensure that cargoes were not being sold to the Muslims. Trading

---

155 For references to the ships of the Order in Italian ports, see *I Registri della Cancelleria Angioina*, vol. 19, p. 39; in Cyprus: *Notai Genovesi in Oltremare atti Rogati a Cipro da Lamberto di Sambuceto: 3 luglio–3 agosto 1301*, no. 140; off the Egyptian coast: Oliveri Scholastici, *Historia Damiatina*, pp. 253; off the Levantine coast and in the port of Acre: Eracles, p. 386; *Les Gestes des Chiprois*, p. 700.

156 *I Registri della Cancelleria Angioina*, vol. 1, p. 295; ibid., vol. 3, p. 192; ibid., vol. 7, p. 200; ibid., vol. 15, pp. 36–37.

157 *I Registri della Cancelleria Angioina*, vol. 1, p. 295; ibid., vol. 13, p. 34; ibid., vol. 15, pp. 36–37.

158 *I Registri della Cancelleria Angioina*, vol. 1, p. 295; ibid., vol. 13, p. 34; ibid., vol. 7, p. 200; ibid., vol. 15, p. 36; Favreau-Lilie, 'L'Ordine Teutonico in Terrasanta (1198–1291)', p. 69.

159 *SDO*, pp. 106, 108–109.

160 *I Registri della Cancelleria Angioina*, vol. 13, p. 34.

161 'Carta de la Orden Teutónica a Alfonso X'

162 *I Registri della Cancelleria Angioina*, vol. 15, pp. 36–37.

163 For discussion of this procedure, see Pryor, '*In Subsidium Terrae Sanctae*', p. 129. For examples see *I Registri della Cancelleria Angioina*, vol. 1, pp. 293, 295, ibid., vol. 3, pp. 189, 239.

with the Muslims, particularly of arms and timber, was a frequent practice at this time that was condemned repeatedly by the papacy.[164]

With these details it is possible to sketch a case study for a typical shipment from Apulia to Acre. We shall take as our example the abovementioned shipment of horses and mules in 1276. These animals would have been gathered in Apulia where an export licence was obtained. They were then shipped to Acre where they would have been met by the grand commander, John of Westfalia. The deputy commander would have overseen the disembarkation and then the marshal, possibly Conrad of Sulmeys, would have taken responsibility for the warhorses and horses[165] while the grand commander would probably have taken responsibility for the mules. Although the marshal was empowered to distribute mules, the grand commander was accountable for the Order's pack animals so it appears that their role was shared in this regard.[166] Technically the master, Hartmann von Heldrungen, could then have selected whichever animals he might have wanted for his own use, although he was absent at this time.[167]

Through these administrative structures, the Order assembled resources from both the Levant and Western Christendom to support its work in the Holy Land. It seems that over time the Order would have become more reliant on overseas supply as its landholdings in the Latin East fell to the Mamluks. The pressure this put on the Order's resources would only have been exacerbated by the growing demands of the Prussian and Livonian fronts, which were similarly engaged during this period. It can be conjectured that the rising inability of the Order in the Holy Land to support itself would have supplied further arguments to those within the Order who demanded a concentration of effort in the Baltic.

---

[164] For papal prohibitions against trading with Muslims, see: Third Lateran Council 1179: *Decrees of the Ecumenical Councils*, vol. 1, p. 223; Fourth Lateran Council 1215: ibid., vol. 1, p. 270; First Council of Lyons 1245: ibid., vol. 1, p. 300; Second Council of Lyons 1274: ibid., vol. 1, p. 311.

[165] *SDO*, p. 106.

[166] *SDO*, p. 106.

[167] *SDO*, p. 106. Similarly with the Templars, *La Règle du Temple*, pp. 92–93.

Conclusion

Herman von Salza cast a long shadow over the history and development of the Teutonic Knights. In 1291, and possibly beyond, the Teutonic Order was still very much the institution he had created. Many twentieth-century works discuss his life and these tend to lavish praise upon his character and achievements. Wojtecki describes him as *'epochmachenden'* (epoch-making), Urban as 'brilliant', Arnold as 'one of the famous diplomatists of the thirteenth century', Militzer as 'one of the most important politicians of his generation'.[1] In some ways this study has followed a similar pattern, although the affairs of the Holy Land are more conducive to a discussion of the problems he resolved rather than the victories he gained. Despite this, Herman was a man like any other and the flaws in his policies seem to have appeared shortly after his death.

When Herman took control of the Order, it was an institution which had been built upon four vital cornerstones: the support of pilgrims and noblemen from across Germany, the patronage of the German emperors (both Hohenstaufen and Welf), the approval of the papacy and the encouragement of the magnates of the Latin East. In time, Herman built upon all four of these areas of patronage to create an order which was at the heart of imperial, papal and Levantine politics and which could offer comprehensive assistance to pilgrims travelling to the Holy Land. Herman was not merely an efficient continuator of his Order's previous policies and, using the lengthy truces in the Holy Land, he embarked on new campaigns in Hungary, Prussia and Livonia. Through these opportunistic endeavours, it seems that Herman may have envisaged a future for his Order in which it would form a wall all the way down Christendom's eastern borders. Although Herman's policies were not uniformly successful, he clearly had an eye for ability and he surrounded himself with commanders who could undertake such ambitious schemes. Herman's opportunism, however, was also his weakness and there were three major flaws to his policies. Firstly, by drawing himself assertively into the centre of imperial and papal politics, he placed the Order between two institutions whose previous history was characterised more by conflict than accord. In time the Order's bonds to the emperor and papacy became a noose from which it was fortunate to survive. Secondly, Herman may have acquired a territorial stake in the border regions of the eastern Mediterranean, Prussia and Livonia but, in doing so, he stretched the Order's military and financial resources to their extreme. Thirdly, Herman paid little attention to the forma-

---

[1] Wojtecki, 'Der Deutsche Orden unter Friedrich II', p. 219; Urban, *The Teutonic Knights*, p. 23; *AZM*, p. 31; Arnold, 'Eight Hundred Years of the Teutonic Order', p. 224.

tion of a structure of governance (and its codification in the Order's statutes) that would reflect either the brethren's present or its future needs. Indeed, Herman's style of governance gives the clear impression that his authority was based more on his own personality than on the more consensual style of governance typical of other military orders. In these ways, Herman created an organisation that was overstretched, vulnerable to the machinations of its patrons and prone to internal divisions. The consequences of these weaknesses were felt in the decades after his death when his successors were forced to wrestle with his legacy. In time the papal–imperial conflict split the Order's loose organisational structure into two embittered factions, just as the brethren's overstretched military resources struggled to accommodate the losses incurred by the battlefield defeats at La Forbie in 1244, Lake Pepius in 1242 and during the first Prussian insurrection of 1242. Indeed, after Herman's death, it seems that it was not until the early years of Anno von Sangershausen's rule that a measure of consolidation was achieved, although this in turn was shattered for a second time with the outbreak of a new Prussian rebellion and the invasions of the Mamluks. Consequently, to paraphrase Kipling, Herman may have made a heap of all his winnings and risked them all on one turn of pitch-and-toss, but it was for his successors to lose and rebuild them again with worn out tools.[2] Of these successors, Anno von Sangershausen and Hartmann von Heldrungen appear to have been important in restoring a measure of internal stability to the Order, particularly at a time when it faced extensive military commitments. It is even possible, given the divided condition of the Order at the end of Poppo von Osterna's governance, that these masters prevented the complete disintegration of the Order.

The Teutonic Knights were unlike the Templars and Hospitallers. These older orders stood like solid, but eroding, bulwarks in the defence of the Holy Land. By contrast, as the thirteenth century progressed, the level of aid offered by the Teutonic Order to the Latin East seems to have fluctuated depending upon events in the Baltic and the character of each master (see chapter 7). Like the papacy, the Order had other interests that occasionally had to take precedence over the Holy Land. Accordingly, there were times when the Order despatched significant aid to the eastern Mediterranean (in 1256 under Anno von Sangershausen and in 1290 with Burchard von Schwanden) but there were also moments when the Levant was seriously, even purposefully, neglected (under Poppo von Osterna between 1253 and 1256). An element in this ongoing struggle for resources between the Baltic and Holy Land was the controversy between the Order's chapter and its northern commanders. Reviewing the *c.*1264 version of the statutes, it is remarkable just how little the needs and administration of Prussia and Livonia are reflected and the whole document seems to work on the presupposition that the Order was still focused almost exclusively upon the Holy

---

2   Rudyard Kipling, 'If', *Rudyard Kipling's Verse*, vol. 3 (London, 1919), p. 108.

Land. Accordingly, the statutes themselves appear to have become a pawn in the disputes of these disparate frontiers.

Those resources which were sent to the Latin East were gathered first in Italy and then shipped to Acre. The Order, like the Latin East as a whole, was reliant on overseas supply for the retention of its foothold in the Levant. Given the importance of this logistical umbilical cord, it was an ongoing imperative for the brethren to remain on good terms with the Italian cities and the rulers of southern Italy. The structure of the Order's supply system seems to have developed organically, with the appointment of new officials when the need arose. Many of these seem to have been modelled on officers in the Hospitaller and the Templar orders, which provided the initial blueprint for the Order. Although the Teutonic Knights adopted many of the systems of these older institutions, relations between these Orders were frequently turbulent. Particularly in the first half of the thirteenth century, both the Hospitallers and Templars attempted to impose their will upon the Order. It is likely that they were aware both of the advantages of yoking the energetic and rapidly growing German institution to their own position, whilst equally conscious of the inherent dangers of permitting the development of an independent Order that could rival their power. In the event, these interventions served to provoke hostility between the Orders, which was only put aside when the Christian position in the Levant began to decline.

In the Holy Land, the Order does appear to have made many positive contributions. It was frequently the arbitrator of disputes and managed to remain neutral in many of the self-destructive conflicts that riddled the Latin East. As the thirteenth century progressed, the Teutonic Knights, like the Hospitallers, appear to have focused increasingly upon the fundamental need to consolidate all the remaining resources of the kingdom of Jerusalem to offer the best defence possible. From a crusading perspective, the brethren's contributions to the eastern Mediterranean were more varied. The Order itself was the product of two major German crusades organised by Frederick I and Henry VI, which first created and then militarised the Order. In later years, Herman von Salza played a vital role in the recruitment, preparation and negotiations necessary to lay the foundations for Frederick II's crusade and later the Barons' Crusade. During the ensuing campaigns the Order generally contributed a strong military force. They seem to have offered significant support to the Fifth Crusade, the Barons' Crusade and Louis IX's first crusade. The fact that the Order was able to make a reasonable contribution to this last expedition is all the more remarkable because simultaneously it was divided internally, was involved in the subjugation of a rebellion in Prussia and had lost its Levantine field force at La Forbie only a few years previously. Nevertheless, from a Latin Eastern perspective, the value of these actions would have been counterbalanced by the Order's role in the diversion of German crusading resources away from the Latin East and towards the Baltic.

A further vital issue for the history of the Order in the Holy Land was its commitment to the Hohenstaufen dynasty. It has been shown how, under

Herman von Salza, the Order grew in material strength through the support of Frederick and his satellites, just as it acquired ecclesiastical privileges and aid from the papacy. Historians have generally become preoccupied with the Order's relative allegiance to either side and yet this approach seems to be misleading. Firstly, it is vital to recognise how dependent the Teutonic Knights under Herman von Salza were upon both the pontiff and the emperor. These men each had the power to elevate or damage the Order and their wishes could not be ignored. As a result, Herman could neither choose freely between these patrons during periods when they were at war, nor ignore their demands. Although he attempted to plot a safe and neutral course between these two masters, his personal ambitions lay elsewhere. Herman's life appears to have been devoted to the defence of Christendom and the expansion of his Order's role therein. Although he frequently mediated between his two great benefactors, these negotiations were generally intended to encourage them to turn their attention to the crusades. Furthermore, Herman's relentless desire to increase his institution's role in Prussia, Hungary, Livonia and the Holy Land demonstrates both his priorities and his objectives. As a result, it is the contention of this work that Herman's relationship to both the papacy and the empire was not founded upon a desire to become a partisan of either side but was an attempt to encourage and enable these patrons both to endow his Order and to commit their resources to the defence of Christendom. After Herman's death, his successors generally proved either unable or unwilling to pursue this diplomatic course and they began to take sides. With the appointment of each new master, the pendulum of the Order's allegiances swung dramatically, provoking censure and reproof from both the pontiff and the emperor. In 1250, the Order was finally freed from its conflict of loyalties when Frederick II died.

To conclude, the thirteenth century was a period of rapid development for the Teutonic Order which was masterminded by the opportunistic but over-ambitious Herman. During this time the Order became a major contributor to the defence and expansion of Christendom and provided a significant, if fluctuating, level of financial and military assistance to the Holy Land. In this region the Order seems to have been a stabilising influence even though it could do little to prevent the final collapse of the kingdom of Jerusalem in 1291. The Order's Mediterranean politics were not confined to the strategies of the Hohenstaufen family and its readiness to render aid to the German emperors was almost solely reliant on their willingness to render constructive assistance to the Latin East. As for Herman himself, despite his flaws, his actions did ensure that by 1240 (a mere fifty years after its establishment) the Teutonic Order was a major military order of comparable significance to either the Templars or the Hospitallers.

Appendices

Appendix A The Location of the Masters, 1210–1291

Date	Master	Location	Known deputy in Levant	Source
14 Feb. 1211	Herman von Salza	Acre		*TOT*, no. 45.
Dec. 1211	Herman von Salza	Acre–Armenia–Cyprus (Herman accompanied Wilbrand on his diplomatic mission)		Wilbrand of Oldenburg, *Peregrinatores*, p. 177.
9 April 1215	Herman von Salza	Acre		*TOT*, no. 48.
19 Dec. 1216	Herman von Salza	Rome		*TOT*, no. 303.
17 Feb. 1217	Herman von Salza	Acre		Eracles, p. 323.
17 Feb. 1217	Herman von Salza	Ulm		HB, vol. 1, pp. 917–920.
Sept. 1217	Herman von Salza	Cyprus		*R. Reg.*, vol. 1, no. 900.
Before May 1218		Atlīt		Eracles, p. 325.
May 1218	Herman von Salza	Embarked from Acre for Egypt		*Chronica Majora*, vol. 3, p. 35.
June 1218	Herman von Salza	Damietta		*R. Reg.*, vol. 1, no. 911.
1219 (early)	Herman von Salza	Damietta		Eracles, p. 342.
11 Nov. 1219	Herman von Salza	Damietta		*R. Reg.*, vol. 1, no. 925.
*c.*15 Nov. 1219	Herman von Salza	Damietta		*R. Reg.*, vol. 1, no. 926.
1 March 1220	Herman von Salza	Damietta		*R. Reg.*, vol. 1, no. 930.
30 May 1220	Herman von Salza	Acre		*TOT*, nos. 52–3.
4 Oct. 1220	Herman von Salza	Sent to the papacy		HB, vol. 1, p. 863.
25 Nov. 1220	Herman von Salza	Near Montemalo		HB, vol. 2, pp. 40–41.
March 1221	Herman von Salza	In Egypt		*TOT*, no. 55.
Aug.–Sept. 1221	Herman von Salza	A hostage in Egypt		Oliveri Scholastici, *Historia Damiatina*, p. 276.
1221 (post Sept.)	Herman von Salza	Sent to Damietta		Oliveri Scholastici, *Historia Damiatina*, p. 277.
1221	Herman von Salza	Travelled to Puille, to the emperor, and from there to the papacy		Eracles, p. 352–355. For discussion on the timing of Herman's journey see Kluger, *Hochmeister Hermann*, pp. 33–34.

5 Feb. 1222	Herman von Salza	Possibly in Foggia because emperor responds to a request from him.	*Regesta Imperii V*, vol. 1, no. 1372.
22 Nov. 1222	Herman von Salza	Near Joham	HB, vol. 2, pp. 272–274.
20 Dec. 1222	Herman von Salza	Near Prechinam	HB, vol. 2, pp. 283–284.
Jan. 1223	Herman von Salza	Capua	HB, vol. 2, pp. 294–296.
19 March 1223	Herman von Salza	Sorae	HB, vol. 2, pp. 349–351.
21 Sept. 1223	Herman von Salza	Nordhausen	*Urkundenbuch des Klosters Walkenried*, ed. J. Dolle (Hanover, 2002), no. 124.
Feb. 1224	Herman von Salza	Catania	HB, vol. 2, pp. 398–400.
March 1224	Herman von Salza	Sent from Catania to Germany	HB, vol. 2, pp. 409–413.
30 April 1224	Herman von Salza	Mention of a petition made by Herman in the papal curia so he was probably in Rome around this time	*TOT*, no. 164.
May 1224	Herman von Salza	Frankfurt	*Chronica Regia Coloniensis*, p. 253.
July 1224	Herman von Salza	Northern Germany	*Diplomatarium Danicum* (Raekke 1), pp. 24–28.
Aug. 1224	Herman von Salza	Dannenburg	*Chronica Regia Coloniensis*, p. 254.
March 1225	Herman von Salza	Palermo	HB, vol. 2, pp. 473–475.
June 1225	Herman von Salza	Foggia	HB, vol. 2, pp. 489–494.
28 July 1225	Herman von Salza	St Germain	HB, vol. 2, pp. 503–505.
Sept. 1225	Herman von Salza	Halle	*Regesta Thuringiae*, vol. 2, no. 2230.
Jan. 1226	Herman von Salza	Near San Chirico	HB, vol. 2, pp. 528–531
March 1226	Herman von Salza	Peschiera del Garda	HB, vol. 2, pp. 543–548.
May 1226	Herman von Salza	Parma	HB, vol. 2, pp. 586–588.
2 June 1226	Herman von Salza	Mantua	*Urkundenbuch der Deutschordensballei Thüringen*, no. 40.
June 1226	Herman von Salza	Fidenza	HB, vol. 2, pp. 625–629.
July 1226	Herman von Salza	Sarrezzano	HB, vol. 2, pp. 667–671.
Aug. 1226	Herman von Salza	San Miniato	*Regesta Imperii V*, vol. 1, no. 1670.

17 Nov. 1226	Herman von Salza	Foggia (Sent to the Papacy)		HB, vol. 2, pp. 691–692.
11 Jan. 1227	Herman von Salza	Sent to Germany		*RHP*, vol. 2, no. 6156
15 March 1227	Herman von Salza	Würzburg		HB, vol. 2, pp. 908–909.
1227	Herman von Salza	Herman was sent to the papacy around this time		Richard of San Germano, *Chronica*, in *MGH SS*, vol. 19, p. 347
July 1227	Herman von Salza	Anagni		*TOT*, no. 424.
Sept. 1227	Herman von Salza	Near Otranto		HB, vol. 3, pp. 21–23.
Oct. 1227	Herman von Salza	Acre		*Chronica Majora*, vol. 3, pp. 127–129.
7 Sept. 1228	Herman von Salza	Acre		*Chronica Majora*, vol. 3, pp. 159–160.
15 Sept.1228	Herman von Salza	Acre		*Regesta Imperii V*, vol. 1, no. 1734.
12 March 1229	Herman von Salza	Near Jaffa		HB, vol. 3, pp. 90–93.
21 March 1229	Herman von Salza	Near Jaffa		HB, vol. 3, pp. 99–102.
Oct. 1229	Herman von Salza	St Germain		Richard of San Germano, *Chronica*, p. 357.
Nov. 1229	Herman von Salza	He came from the pope to Aquinum and from there to St Germain		Richard of San Germano, *Chronica*, p. 357.
Jan. 1230	Herman von Salza	Sent to the papacy (he returned quickly to the emperor)		Richard of San Germano, *Chronica*, p. 358.
c. March 1230	Herman von Salza	Sent again to Rome returning in April		Richard of San Germano, *Chronica*, p. 358.
1230		Near Acre	Haymo	*TOT*, nos, 73–74.
Aug. 1230	Herman von Salza	Ceprano		*CDOT*, no. 81.
Aug. 1231	Herman von Salza	Sent to Lombardy		Richard of San Germano, *Chronica*, p. 365.
April 1232	Herman von Salza	Aquileia		HB, vol. 4, pp. 326–328.
10 May 1232	Herman von Salza	Near the port of Naonis		HB, vol. 4, pp. 344–353.
Sept. 1232	Herman von Salza	Near Melfi		*Liv., Est. und Kurländisches Urkundenbuch*, vol. 1, no. 127.
28 Dec. 1232	Herman von Salza	Torun		*CDOT*, no. 87
28 Dec. 1233	Herman von Salza	Torun		*Schlesisches Urkundenbuch*, ed. W. Irgang, vol. 2 (1977), no. 55.
July 1234	Herman von Salza	Rieti		*Regesta Thuringiae*, vol. 3, no. 442.
1234			Luttold	*TOT*, no. 77

Appendices

June 1235	Herman von Salza	Nuremburg		*Nürnberger Urkundenbuch*, no. 272.
Aug. 1235	Herman von Salza	Mainz		*Regesta Thuringiae*, vol. 3, no. 552.
Sept. 1235	Herman von Salza	Hagenau		*HU*, vol. 1, no. 143.
Nov. 1235	Herman von Salza	Augsburg		*TOT*, no. 79.
1235		Acre	Luttold	*TOT*, no. 80.
Jan. 1236		Tripoli	Luttold	*TOT*, no. 82.
April 1236	Herman von Salza	Near Speyer		*Regesta Imperii V*, vol. 1, no. 2152.
May 1236	Herman von Salza	Boppard		*Regesta Imperii V*, vol. 1, no. 2163.
July 1236	Herman von Salza	Near Augsburg		*MGH Leges Const.*, vol. 2, p. 274.
10 Aug. 1236		Acre	Luttold	*TOT*, no. 84.
Jan. 1237	Herman von Salza	Vienna		HB, vol. 5, p. 9.
Feb. 1237	Herman von Salza	Vienna		HB, vol. 5, p. 20.
21 June 1237	Herman von Salza	Würzburg		*Regesta Thuringiae*, vol. 3, no. 685.
Aug. 1237	Herman von Salza	Near Augsburg		*Regesta Imperii V*, vol. 1, no. 2268.
1 Oct. 1237	Herman von Salza	Near Godio		HB, vol. 5, pp. 115–119.
Dec. 1237	Herman von Salza	Lodi		HB, vol. 5, pp. 149–150.
Aug. 1238	Herman von Salza	Salerno		Richard of San Germano, *Chronica*, p. 376.
April 1239			Luttold	*R. Reg.*, vol. 1, no. 1090.
7 May 1240	Conrad von Thüringen	Mergentheim		*Urkundenbuch der Deutschordensballei Thüringen*, no. 75.
1240		In the house of the Hospitallers	Gerhard von Malberg (marshal)	*TOT*, no. 89.
Dec. 1241		Tyre	Luttold	*TOT*, no. 90.
7 July 1244	Heinrich von Hohenlohe	Acre		*TOT*, nos. 98–99.
1245	Heinrich von Hohenlohe	Council of Lyons		*Chronica de Mailros*, p. 174.
June 1245	Heinrich von Hohenlohe	Verona		*HU*, vol. 1, no. 236.45
10 April 1246	Heinrich von Hohenlohe	Elbing		*HU*, vol. 1, no. 236.55.
19 April 1246	Heinrich von Hohenlohe	Orlow		*HU*, vol. 1, no. 236.56.
13 Oct. 1246	Heinrich von Hohenlohe	Vienna		*HU*, vol. 1, no. 236.58.
March 1247	Heinrich von Hohenlohe	Esslingen		*HU*, vol. 1, no. 236.62.
8 Aug. 1247	Heinrich von Hohenlohe	Lyon		*HU*, vol. 1, no. 236.64.

13 June 1248	Heinrich von Hohenlohe	Mergentheim		*HU*, vol. 1, no. 236.67.
1249			Eberhard of Saone (grand commander)	*TOT*, no. 100
c.5 May 1253	Wilhelm von Urenbach	Venice		*Liv., Est. und Kurländisches Urkundenbuch*, vol. 1, no. 224.
6 June 1253	Poppo von Osterna	Acre		*R. Reg.*, vol. 1, no. 1206.
26 Sept. 1253	Poppo von Osterna	Acre		*TOT*, no. 104.
10 March 1254	Poppo von Osterna	Elbing		*PU*, vol. 1.1, no. 283.
1254			Peter (marshal)	*Foedera, Conventiones*, vol. 1, p. 308.
13 Sept. 1254	Poppo von Osterna	Bohemia		*PU*, vol. 1.1, no. 294.
28 Dec. 1254	Poppo von Osterna	Inowraclaw		*PU*, vol. 1.1, no. 303.
10 Feb. 1255	Poppo von Osterna	Hohensalza		*Schlesisches Urkundenbuch*, vol. 3, no. 146.
20 Sept. 1255	Poppo von Osterna	Memel		*PU*, vol. 1.1, no. 323.
1255		Holy Land	Peter of Koblenz	*Annales de Burton*, p. 368.
1256			Eberhard of Saone	'Le Reliquie dell'Archivio dell'Ordine Teutonico in Venezia', p. 1436.
1256	Poppo von Osterna	Rome		*Livländische Reimchronik*, pp. 99–100.
1256	Anno von Sangershausen	Rome		*Livländische Reimchronik*, pp. 99–100.
4 Jan. 1257	Anno von Sangershausen	Sidon		*TOT*, nos 108, 110.
10 Jan. 1257	Anno von Sangershausen			*TOT*, no. 111.
Sept. 1257	Anno von Sangershausen	Acre		*R. Reg.*, vol. 1, no. 1260.
1 Nov. 1257	Anno von Sangershausen	Acre		*R. Reg.*, vol. 1, no. 1262.
20 March 1258	Anno von Sangershausen	Acre		*R. Reg.*, vol. 1, no. 1265.
9 Oct. 1258	Anno von Sangershausen	Acre		*TOT*, no. 116.
1260	Anno von Sangershausen	Acre		Rothelin, p. 637.
22 April 1260	Anno von Sangershausen	Acre		*R. Reg.*, vol. 2, no. 1291

March 1261	Anno von Sangershausen	Acre		*R. Reg.*, vol. 1, no. 1300.
16 Oct. 1262	Anno von Sangershausen	Saxony		*Urkundenbuch der Deutschordensballei Thüringen*, no. 166.
Nov. 1261		Acre	Hartmann von Heldrungen	*TOT*, nos. 119, 120, 121.
24 Jan. 1263	Anno von Sangershausen	Elbing		*PU*, vol. 1.2, no. 179.
10 Feb. 1263	Anno von Sangershausen	Torun		*PU*, vol. 1.2, no. 183.
28 March 1263	Anno von Sangershausen	Torun		*PU*, vol. 1.2, no. 194.
16 Sept. 1263			Hartmann von Heldrungen	'Le Reliquie dell'Archivio dell'Ordine Teutonico in Venezia', p. 1441.
12 Feb. 1264	Anno von Sangershausen	Torun		*PU*, vol. 1.2, no. 219.
21 Jan. 1265	Anno von Sangershausen	Altenburg		*Urkundenbuch der Deutschordensballei Thüringen*, no. 181.
27 July 1265	Anno von Sangershausen	Germany		*Urkundenbuch der Deutschordensballei Thüringen*, no. 188.
March 1266	Anno von Sangershausen	Torun		*PU*, vol. 1.2, no. 254.
29 June 1266	Anno von Sangershausen	Grieffsstedt		*PU*, vol. 1.2, no. 256.
Sept. 1266	Anno von Sangershausen	Altenburg		*Altenburger Urkundenbuch: 976–1350*, ed. H. Patze (Jena, 1955), no. 203
1266	Anno von Sangershausen	Altenburg		*Urkundenbuch der Deutschordensballei Thüringen*, no. 197.
27 May 1267	Anno von Sangershausen	Acre		*R. Reg.*, vol. 1, no. 1348.
1270	Anno von Sangershausen	Holy Land		*R. Reg.*, vol. 2, no. 1374C.
15 June 1271	Anno von Sangershausen	Armenia		*Les Gestes des Chiprois*, p. 840.
29 Dec. 1271/2	Anno von Sangershausen	Hosterlitz		*Urkundenbuch der Deutschordensballei Thüringen*, no. 233.
16 Sept. 1272	Anno von Sangershausen	Kl. Vargula		*Urkundenbuch der Deutschordensballei Thüringen*, no. 244.
21 Jan. 1273	Anno von Sangershausen	Sachsenhausen		*Codex Diplomaticus Nassoicus: Nassauisches Urkundenbuch*, ed. K. Menzel and W. Sauer, vol. 2 (1969, Aalen), no. 836.

8 July 1273	Anno von Sangershausen	Anno died on this day.		Perlbach, 'Deutsch-Ordens Necrologe', p. 358.
23 July 1278	Hartmann von Heldrungen	Report stipulating that the master had previously helped to resolve a dispute in county of Tripoli.		*R. Reg.*, vol. 1, no. 1424.
13 Nov. 1278	Hartmann von Heldrungen	Dresden		*Urkundenbuch der Deutschordensballei Thüringen*, no. 299.
25 July 1279	Hartmann von Heldrungen	Plauen		*Urkundenbuch der Deutschordensballei Thüringen*, no. 312.
31 Aug. 1279	Hartmann von Heldrungen	Plauen		*Urkundenbuch der Deutschordensballei Thüringen*, no. 314.
28 Dec. 1279	Hartmann von Heldrungen	Plauen		*Urkundenbuch der Deutschordensballei Thüringen*, no. 320.
Around 1279–80	Hartmann von Heldrungen	In Marburg and later in Germany		*Livländische Reimchronik*, pp. 202–203.
25 April 1280	Hartmann von Heldrungen	Mörle		*Hessisches Urkundenbuch*, vol. 2 (Osnabrück, 1965), no. 590.
7 Dec. 1281	Hartmann von Heldrungen	Germany		*Urkundenbuch der Deutschordensballei Thüringen*, no. 348.
19 Aug. 1282	Hartmann von Heldrungen	His death at Acre and the election of a new master		*Livländische Reimchronik*, p. 223.
1283			Conrad of Sulmeys (marshal)	*R. Reg.*, vol. 1, no. 1450.
2 Sept. 1284/5	Burchard von Schwanden	Acre		*Urkundenbuch der Deutschordensballei Thüringen*, nos. 395–396.
27 June 1286	Burchard von Schwanden	Acre		*R. Reg.*, vol. 1, no. 1466.
1286	Burchard von Schwanden	Acre		*Les Gestes des Chiprois*, p. 793.
21 March 1287	Burchard von Schwanden	Wurzburg		*Nürnberger Urkundenbuch*, no. 747.
12 May 1287	Burchard von Schwanden	Frankfurt		*Nürnberger Urkundenbuch*, no. 750.
18 May 1287	Burchard von Schwanden	Frankfurt		'Urkundenbuch der Deutschordensballei Hessen', no. 475.
2 Feb. 1288	Burchard von Schwanden	Elbing		*PU*, vol. 2, no. 523.
9 May 1288	Burchard von Schwanden	Frankfurt		*Urkundenbuch der Deutschordensballei Thüringen*, no. 446.

Summer 1288	Burchard von Schwanden	In Prussia going to Livonia	*Livländische Reimchronik*, p. 247.
7 Feb. 1289	Burchard von Schwanden	Rome	*PU*, vol. 2, no. 533.
2 March 1289	Burchard von Schwanden	Erfurt	'Urkundenbuch der Deutschordensballei Hessen', no. 500.
23 Dec. 1289	Burchard von Schwanden	Erfurt	*Meklenburgensis*, vol. 3, no. 2043.
28 Jan. 1290	Burchard von Schwanden	Erfurt	*Urkundenbuch der Deutschordensballei Thüringen*, no. 476.
2 March 1290	Burchard von Schwanden	Erfurt	'Urkundenbuch der Deutschordensballei Hessen', no. 508.
1290	Burchard von Schwanden	Acre	Nicolaus von Jeroschin, *Di Kronike von Pruzinlant*, p. 513.

Appendix B Rural properties of the Teutonic Order[1]

1 Messerephe	30 Zoenite	59 Bikicin (Bequicin)
2 Quatranye	31 Beletim (Beletini)	60 Bennuefe (Bennouthe)
3 Cabra	32 Scebeique	61 Elgabetye
4 Quiebre	33 Jashon	62 Ethchit
5 Noie	34 Corsy	63 Bether (Besser)
6 Lemezera	35 Cassie	64 Moreste
7 Ghabecie	36 Samohete	65 Elmunzura
8 Amca	37 Berzey	66 Ouzelle
9 Arabia	38 Geelin	67 Haynhamer
10 Aguille (Aguilla)	39 Danehyle	68 Elchoreibe (Houreybe)
11 Achara	40 Tayerebika	69 Delbon
12 Arket	41 Raheb	70 Mahasser le grant
13 Clil	42 Fasoce	71 Niha
14 Gez	43 Tayeretrane	72 Sarsorith (sarsouris)
15 Habelye	44 Fennes	73 Elmecheirfe
16 Busenen	45 Roeis	74 Elmizraa
17 Gelon	46 Horfeis	75 Elmohtara
18 Meblie	47 Gabatye	76 Baadran
19 Mergecolon	48 Fierge	77 La Judede (Gerderde)
20 Lebeyne	49 Deleha	78 La Fornie
21 Haseinie	50 Elmuchetne	79 Befedin
22 Nef	51 Eschemacha	80 Batun
23 Seisor	52 Hazibe	81 Le Barouc
24 Beitegen	53 Kanzirie	82 La Foraidis
25 Zechanim	54 Gezin	83 Bahaclin
26 Acref	55 Haddous	84 Zambacquie
27 Carphasonie	56 Toura	85 Cafernebrach
28 Tersyha	57 Benemssin	86 Deir Zekarim
29 Tarphile	58 Kaytule	87 La Mougarie

[1]   This map was created using the following sources. Pringle, *The Churches of the Crusader Kingdom of Jerusalem*, vol. 2, pp. 418–427. Hilsch, 'Der Deutsche Ritterorden im Südlichen Libanon', p. 180. Favreau, 'Die Kreuzfahrerherrschaft Scandalion (Iskanderūne)', p. 21. *Atlas of the Crusades*, ed. J. S. C. Riley-Smith (New York, 1981), p. 102.

88 Boocosta
89 Deir Bebe
90 Deir Elchamar
91 Cafar-facouh
92 Dardorith
93 Daircossa
94 Le Haddis (Haddris)
95 Haynzehalta
96 Queffra
97 Boussaih
98 Bossonaih le haut

99 Esfif (Eissif)
100 Le Doeyir
101 Corratye
102 Cuneyesce
103 Bemmorhei
104 La Orhanie
105 Ezsaronie
106 Caffar
107 Ebbrih
108 Bahnayl
109 Haynouzeih

110 Beddei
111 Schuff
112 Sapheth lo Cathemon
113 Serouh (Serohu)
114 Missop
115 Cafresi
116 La Loaize
117 Iubie
118 Maron

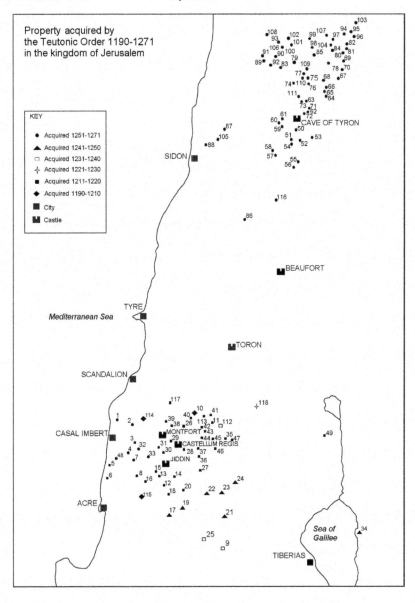

Property acquired by
the Teutonic Order 1190-1271
in the kingdom of Jerusalem

KEY

● Acquired 1251-1271
▲ Acquired 1241-1250
□ Acquired 1231-1240
✛ Acquired 1221-1230
■ Acquired 1211-1220
◆ Acquired 1190-1210
■ City
▥ Castle

Appendix C Masters of the Order, 1210–1296[1]

Name	Period in office	Reason for leaving office	Previous rank in Order
Herman von Salza	1209/1210– 20 March 1239	Died of illness	Not known
Conrad von Thüringen	After 1239–24 July 1240	Died of illness	Conrad is not known to have held any previous office in the Order
Gerhard von Malberg	After 24 July 1240– shortly before 7 July 1244	Resigned and transferred to the Hospitallers	Marshal
Heinrich von Hohenlohe	Some time before 7 July 1244–15 July 1249	Died	German master until 1242
Gunther (von Wüllersleben?)[2]	After 15 July 1249 – 3/4 May 1252	Died	Uncertain, possibly commander of Apulia
Poppo von Osterna	After 3/4 May 1252–1256	Resigned	Poppo had formerly been the Prussian master but whether he held this position when he was elected as master is unknown
Anno von Sangershausen	1256–8 July 1273	Died	Master of Livonia
Hartmann von Heldrungen	After 8 July 1273–19 August 1283	Died	Grand commander
Burchard von Schwanden	After 19 August 1283–1290	Resigned and transferred to the Hospitallers	Commander of Hessen
Conrad von Feuchtwangen	1291–July 1296	Died	Conrad had formerly been the master of Prussia and Livonia, however, before his election he was German master

[1] Much of the data here has been drawn from *Die Hochmeister des Deutschen Ordens 1190–1994*, QuStDO, 40 (Marburg, 1998).
[2] See Chapter 6.

Appendix D The Crops and Agricultural Infrastructure of the Order

The table below should not be treated as an exhaustive inventory of the Order's agricultural assets. The presence of several industries is known largely through the presence of the agricultural buildings such as mills or olive presses that serviced them. These buildings were valuable and therefore feature within charters detailing landholdings. Consequently those agricultural industries that did not require machinery or buildings of this nature may appear under-represented.

Crops/Industries of the Teutonic Order in the Holy Land

Crop/Industry	Year of acquisition	Location	Date when property/industry raided or lost	Reference for acquisition of privilege or property
Barley	Not known	Not specified		*TOT*, no. 112.
Beans	Not known	Not specified		*TOT*, no. 112.
Chick-peas	Not known	Not specified		*TOT*, no. 112.
Corn	Not known	Not specified		*TOT*, no. 112.
Fish	Not known	Not specified		*TOT*, no. 112.
Fruit	1220	Castellum Regis	1266 raided 1271 lost. The fruit produced in Castellum Regis is referred to in the account of Burchard of Mount Sion, 'Descriptio Terrae Sanctae', p. 142.	*TOT*, no. 53
Lentils	Not known	Not specified		*TOT*, no. 112.
Mill	1212	Amudain estate in Armenia	1266	*TOT*, no. 46.
Mill	1228	Principality of Antioch	1268 (at the latest)	*TOT*, no. 61.
Mill	1220	Lands surrounding the village of Tarphile in Castellum Regis estate	1266 raided. 1271 lost. Montfort was built near this village and this reference may refer to the mill incorporated within the castle complex. See Pringle, 'A Thirteenth Century Hall', pp. 68–75.	*TOT*, no. 53.
Mill	1220	Castellum Regis	1266 raided 1271 lost. Evidence for this mill is in *TOT*, no. 128.	*TOT*, no. 53.
Mills	1236	City of Harunia	Not known. Mills mentioned in charter.	*TOT*, no. 83
Mills	1257	The Estate of the Shuf	Possibly raided by Mongols in 1260. Mills mentioned in charter.	*TOT*, nos. 108, 111, 117.
Mill	1236	Village of Chacorim in Harunia estate	Not known	*TOT*, no. 83
Mill	1258	Village of Cafar-facouh in the Shuf		*TOT*, no. 114

Commodity	Date	Location	Fate	Notes	Reference
Millet	Not known	Not specified			*TOT*, no. 112.
Oats	Not known	Not specified			*TOT*, no. 112.
Olives	1220	Village of Clil in Castellum Regis estate	1266 raided 1271 lost	The presence of an olive press has been demonstrated in archaeological evidence, see, Pringle, *Secular Buildings*, p. 34.	*TOT*, no. 53.
Olives	1220	Village of Danehyle in Castellum Regis estates	1266 raided 1271 lost	Presence of olive press demonstrated in archaeological evidence: see Pringle, *Secular Buildings*, p. 47.	*TOT*, no. 53.
Olives	1220	Village of Raheb in Castellum Regis estate	1266 raided 1271 lost	Presence of olive press demonstrated in archaeological evidence: see Pringle, *Secular Buildings*, pp. 82–83.	*TOT*, no. 53.
Olives	1220	Castellum Regis	1266 raided 1271 lost	Presence of olive press recorded by Ellenblum, *Frankish Rural Settlement*, p. 51.	*TOT*, no. 53.
Quinces	Not known	Not specified			*TOT*, no. 112.
Wool	Not known	Not specified			*TOT*, no. 112.
Sugar	1198	None: royal allowance given daily	Not known		*TOT*, no. 34.
Sugar	1220	Village of Noie half of which was owned by the Order	1266 raided 1271 lost	Presence of sugar industry demonstrated in archaeological evidence; see Pringle, *Secular Buildings*, p. 107. Also *TOT*, no. 87.	*TOT*, no. 53.
Vineyard	1196	Jaffa	1197	It is possible that is was restored after the return of Jaffa in 1204.	*TOT*, no. 32.[1]
Vineyard	Before 1196	Near the Order's house named Scalone			*TOT*, no. 303.
Vineyard	1228	Principality of Antioch	1268 (at the latest)	Gift includes a press presumably either for olives or grapes.	*TOT*, no. 61.
Vineyards	1257	The Estate of the Shuf	Possibly raided by Mongols in 1260	Mills mentioned in charter	*TOT*, no. 117.
Vineyard	1258	Village of Cafar-facouh in the Shuf		In the vicinity of Sidon.	*TOT*, no. 115.
Vineyard	1228	Balian of Sidon		A charter made in 1179 mentions the presence of vineyards. This is supported by a later charter which gives a detailed inventory of the local lands including many vineyards: *TOT*, nos 11, 128] For discussion of the archaeological evidence see, Pringle, *Secular Buildings*, pp. 71–72.	*TOT*, no. 62.
Vineyards	1220	Castellum Regis	1266 raided 1271 lost	Rented by the Order	*TOT*, no. 53
Vineyard	1239				*TOT*, no. 88.
Wheat	1198	None: royal allowance granted yearly	Not known	A measure to be given to the Order annually by King Aimery.	*TOT*, no. 34.

1   This charter was confirmed by Celestine III in 1196. *TOT*, no. 33.

Appendix E.1 Marshals of the Order 1208–1300

Henry
- September 1208, Acre: Witness to the donation of Otto of Henneburg in Acre.[1]

Ludwig of Hörselgau
- Prehistory: Ludwig came from a Thuringian *ministerialis* family.[2]
- 9 April 1215, Acre: Witness to the donation of Matilda, widow of the advocate of Schwarzenburg.[3]
- 1220, Damietta: The marshal was captured at Damietta. It is possible that this was Ludwig.[4]

Gunther
- 20 April 1228, Holy Land: Witness to a property exchange with Jacob of Amigdala.[5]
- October 1230, Holy Land: Witness to charter.[6]

Gerhard von Malberg[7]
- Prehistory: Gerhard was the son of Lord Theodoric of Are and Agnes of Malberg and had previously been married before he joined the Order.
- Gerhard presumably led the Order during the campaign of the Barons' Crusade.
- 1240, in a Hospitaller property: Acting as deputy to the master in the property agreement with the Hospitallers.[8]
- Subsequent history: Gerhard von Malberg was appointed as master of the Teutonic Order between late 1240 and early 1241.

Werner of Merenberg
- 7 July 1244: Signatory to agreement with Jacob of Amigdala.[9]
- 19 October 1244: It is likely that he was killed at La Forbie. As marshal it is almost certain that he was present at the battle and there are said to have been only three survivors who were either sergeants or ordinary brethren.

---

[1] *TOT*, no. 43.
[2] *AZM*, p. 394.
[3] *TOT*, no. 48.
[4] Oliveri Scholastici, *Historia Damiatina*, p. 252.
[5] *TOT*, no. 63.
[6] *TOT*, no. 74.
[7] See Arnold, 'Gerhard von Malberg', pp. 22–23.
[8] *TOT*, no. 89.
[9] *R. Reg.*, vol. 1, no. 1120.

Herman[10]
- *c*.5 May 1253, Venice:[11] Signatory to document issued by Master Wilhelm von Urenbach.[12]

Almaric of Wurzburg
- 6 June 1253, Acre: Almaric was the drapier of the Order but at this time was acting as substitute marshal during property negotiations with the Barlais family.[13]

Peter of Koblenz
- Prehistory: Peter is known to have been the castellan of Montfort in 1253.[14]
- *c*.1254: he issued a letter of appeal to King Alfonso X of Castile from Acre as marshal of the Order.[15]
- 1255: Signatory to letter of appeal to Henry III of England.[16]
- Subsequent history: Peter is mentioned again in 1261 as a witness to a contract involving John of Ibelin but no rank is accorded to him even though it is specified for other signatories.[17]

Conrad of Sulmeys
- Prehistory: Conrad was from a noble family in Hessen and held several positions in Western Christendom before his elevation to the marshal's office.[18]
- 3 June 1283, Holy Land: Conrad, acting as deputy to the master, was a signatory to the treaty with the Sultan of Egypt.[19]
- According to a necrology, Conrad was killed on 25 July (no year given) in company with a number of other brothers. No further details are given.[20]

Henry
- 1300, Cyprus: Signatory to commercial agreement.[21]

10 Marshal Herman seems to have been a supporter of Wilhelm von Urenbach, just as Almaric and possibly Peter may have been appointees of Poppo von Osterna. It is possible that there were moments when these marshals were rivals serving different masters.
11 For discussion of the date of this charter, see above, p. 105.
12 *Liv., Est. und Kurländisches Urkundenbuch*, vol. 1, no. 224.
13 *R. Reg.*, vol. 1, no. 1206.
14 *R. Reg.*, vol. 1, no. 1206.
15 'Carta de la Orden Teutónica a Alfonso X.'
16 *Annales de Burton*, p. 368.
17 *R. Reg.*, vol. 1, no. 1309.
18 *AZM*, p. 395.
19 *R. Reg.*, vol. 1, no. 1450.
20 Perlbach, 'Deutsch-Ordens Necrologe', p. 365.
21 *Notai Genovesi in Oltremare atti Rogati a Cipro da Lamberto di Sambuceto: 3 luglio–3 agosto 1301*, no. 140.

Appendix E.2 Grand Commanders of the Order, 1215–1291

Drabodo of Utinge
- 9 April 1215, Acre: Witness to the donation of Matilda, widow of the advocate of Schwarzenburg.[1]
- 1220, Damietta: The preceptor of the Order was captured at Damietta. It is possible that this was Drabodo.[2]

Luttold
- 1234, Holy Land: Official recipient of the village of Arabia from Isabella of Bethsan and Bertrand Porcelet. He also received a confirmation of this gift issued by Richard Filangieri.[3]
- 1235, Holy Land: Negotiated property with John Griffin.[4]
- January 1236, Tripoli: Received confirmation of gift from Isabella of Bethsan and Bertrand Porcelet.[5]
- 22 January 1236, Holy Land: Received the city of Harunia from the king of Armenia.[6]
- 10 August 1236, Acre: Named as deputy of the master. Luttold represented the Order in its purchase of a village from Beatrice daughter of Gautier Ledur.
- April 1239, Holy Land: Deputy of the master. Received Noie from the Hospitallers.[7]
- December 1241, Tyre: Received a gift of property from Philip of Maugustel.
- 30 April 1242, Acre: Deputy of the master. Arranged a rental agreement over property from the bishop of Acre.

Conrad of Nassau
- 7 June 1244, Acre: Conducted property negotiations with Jacob of Amigdala.[8]
- 11 September, Acre: Signatory to letter of appeal describing the capture of Jerusalem.[9]
- 19 October 1244: It is likely that he was killed at La Forbie. Matthew Paris's chronicle contains a letter from the patriarch of Jerusalem which mentions that a preceptor of the Order was killed during the battle; this may have been him.[10]

---

[1] *TOT*, no. 48.
[2] Oliveri Scholastici, *Historia Damiatina*, p. 252.
[3] *TOT*, nos, 77, 78.
[4] *TOT*, no. 80.
[5] *TOT*, no. 82.
[6] *TOT*, no. 83.
[7] *R Reg*, vol. 1, no. 1090.
[8] *R. Reg.*, vol. 1, no. 1120.
[9] *R. Reg.*, vol. 1, no. 1123.
[10] *Chronica Majora*, vol. 4, p. 339.

Eberhard of Saone and Herman

- 30 April 1249, Holy Land: Eberhard, at that time deputy master, conducted property negotiations with the lord of Caesarea.[11]
- He was sent to be Livonian master for a time and as he travelled north in 1250 for this appointment he spread news of al-Mansūra, which suggests that he had participated in the Nile campaign.[12]
- 6 June 1253, Acre: During Eberhard's time as Livonian master it seems that his position as grand commander was taken by a brother named Herman. Herman is mentioned in a property contract with the Barlais family.[13]
- In 1254 Eberhard resigned his Livonian position and returned to the Holy Land.
- 15 September 1256, Acre: Eberhard represented the Order in a property agreement with John of Ibelin. He deputised for the master at this time.[14]
- September 1257, Acre: Eberhard was signatory to agreement with the bishop of Acre.[15]

Hartmann von Heldrungen

- Hartmann, born *c.*1210, was from a Thuringian noble family. He had formerly been the commander of Sachsen and German Master. He is believed to have become grand commander in 1261.[16]
- November 1261, Holy Land: Engaged in property negotiations with John of Ibelin.[17] He was acting as deputy for the master.
- 31 May 1262, Acre: Helped to solve property disagreements between Hospitallers and Templars.[18] He was acting as deputy for the master.
- 19 December, Acre: Helped to solve property disagreements between Hospitallers and Templars.[19] He was acting as deputy for the master.
- 4 April 1263, Acre: Signatory to letter of appeal.[20]
- June 1263, Holy Land: Agreement with William of Amigdala.[21]
- Hartmann subsequently became master in 1273 aged around 60.

Ernest of Wulfen[22]

- 14 March, 1265: Signatory to agreement between the bishop of Hebron and the Hospitallers.

---

[11] *R. Reg.*, vol. 1, no. 1175.
[12] *Annales Erphordenses Fratrum Praedicatorum*, p. 109.
[13] *R. Reg.*, vol. 1, no. 1206.
[14] *R. Reg.*, vol. 1. no. 1250.
[15] *TOT*, no. 112.
[16] Arnold, 'Hartmann von Heldrungen', pp. 36–38.
[17] *R. Reg.*, vol. 1, nos. 1307–1309.
[18] *R. Reg.*, vol. 1, no. 1318.
[19] *R. Reg.*, vol. 1, no. 1322.
[20] *R. Reg.*, vol. 1, no. 1325.
[21] *R. Reg.*, vol. 1, no. 1327.
[22] In the charter he is simply referred to as Ernest. Röhricht has identified him as Ernest of Wulfen. *R. Reg.*, vol. 1, no. 1337.

- Ernest is mentioned in a necrology of the Order but as the marshal. Whether he ever fulfilled this role is unclear; however, it is stated that he died on 12 April.[23]

Conrad of Anefeld

- 16 February 1272, Acre: In negotiation with Amigdala family.[24]
- 1272, Cyprus: In negotiation between the king of Cyprus and his barons.[25]
- 11 August 1273: Agreement with the bishop of Hebron.[26]
- 1 July 1277: He represented the Order in the vicinity of Acre at negotiations concerning the Italian cities. He is referred to as the former grand commander.[27]

John of Westfalia

- 31 August 1277, Acre: Present when the patriarch of Jerusalem confirmed an ecclesiastical privilege of the Order.[28]
- 13 September 1277 and 19 October 1277, Acre: both same as above.[29]
- 23 April 1280, Acre: Agreement with Amigdala family.[30]

Wirichus of Homberg

- 14 August 1289, Acre: Reporting to the West on negotiations over the ransoming of the Duke of Mecklenburg.[31]
- 14 August 1290: Wirichus died in Acre.[32]

[23] Perlbach, 'Deutsch-Ordens Necrologe', p. 364.
[24] *R. Reg.*, vol. 1, no. 1384.
[25] Eracles, p. 463.
[26] *R. Reg.*, vol. 1, no. 1390.
[27] *R. Reg.*, vol. 1, no. 1413.
[28] *R. Reg.*, vol. 1, no. 1414; *CDOT*, no. 257.
[29] *R. Reg.*, vol. 1, no. 1418; *CDOT*, no. 259.
[30] *R. Reg.*, vol. 1, no. 1435.
[31] *Meklenburgisches Urkundenbuch*, vol. 3, no. 2030.
[32] Perlbach, 'Deutsch-Ordens Necrologe', p. 366.

Bibliography

Manuscript Sources

Madrid, Biblioteca de la Real Academia de la Historia, Colección Salazar: 'Carta de la Orden Teutónica a Alfonso X' (G49, fol. 453, Sig. 9/946. Index Number 33005.)

Primary Material

Abū l-Mahāsin, *Arab Historians of the Crusades*, ed. and trans. F. Gabrieli and E. J. Costello (London, 1984).

Al-Maqrīzī, *A History of the Ayyūbid Sultans of Egypt*, trans. R. J. C. Broadhurst (Boston, 1980).

Alberti Milioli Notarii Regini, *Liber de Temporibus et Aetatibus et Cronica Imperatorum*, in *MGH SS*, vol. 31, pp. 336–668.

Altenburger Urkundenbuch: 976–1350, ed. H. Patze (Jena, 1955).

Analecta Novissima, ed. J. Pitra, 2 vols (Paris, 1885–1888).

Annales Breves Domus Ordinis Theutonici Marburgensis, *MGH SS*, vol. 30, pp. 4–5.

Annales de Burton, in *Annales Monastici*, ed. H. R. Luard, RS, 36, vol. 1 (London, 1864).

Annales Erphordenses Fratrum Praedicatorum, in *MGH SRG*, vol. 42, pp. 72–116.

Annales Marbacenses, *MGH SRG*, vol. 9, pp. 1–103.

Annales Monastici, ed. H. R. Luard, RS, 36, 5 vols (London, 1864–1869).

Annales Sancti Rudberti Salisburgenses, in *MGH SS*, vol. 9, pp. 758–810.

Annales Sancti Pantaleonis Coloniensis, in *MGH SS*, vol. 22, pp. 529–547.

Annales de Terre Sainte, in *AOL*, vol. 2 (1884), pp. 429–461 (documents).

Annali Bolognesi, ed. L. V. Savioli, 3 vols (Bassano, 1784–1795).

Archieven der Ridderlijke Duitsche Orde: Balie van Utrecht, ed. J. J. De Geer, 2 vols (Utrecht, 1871).

Archives de l'Orient Latin, ed. P. Riant, 2 vols (Paris, 1881–1884).

Bar Hebraeus, *The Chronography of Gregory Abû'l Faraj: The Son of Aaron, the Hebrew Physician commonly known as Bar Hebraeus*, trans. E. Wallis Budge, 2 vols (Oxford, 1932).

Bernard of Clairvaux, *Sancti Bernardi Opera*, ed. J. Leclercq and H. M. Rochais, 8 vols (Rome, 1957–1977).

Bullarium Franciscanum, ed. J. H. Sbaraleae, 4 vols (Rome, 1759–1768).

'Bulle des Pabstes Cölestin III für den Deutschen Orden vom 22. December 1196', in *Scriptores Rerum Prussicarum: Des Geschichtsquellen der Preus-*

sischen Vorzeit, ed. T. Hirsch, M. Töppen and E. Strehlke, vol. 1 (Leipzig, 1861), pp. 225–227.

Burchard of Mount Sion, 'Descriptio Terrae Sanctae', in *Itinera Hierosolymitana Crucesignatorum*, ed. S. de Sandoli, Studium Biblicum Franciscanum: Collectio Maior, 24, vol. 4 (Jerusalem, 1984), pp. 119–219.

Calixtus II, *Bullaire*, ed. U. Robert, vol. 2 (Paris, 1891).

Cartulaire Général de l'Ordre des Hospitaliers de S. Jean de Jérusalem: 1100–1310, ed. J. Delaville Le Roulx, 4 vols (Paris, 1894–1905).

The Cartulary of the Cathedral of Holy Wisdom of Nicosia, ed. N. Coureas and C. Schabel, Cyprus Research Centre Texts and Studies in the History of Cyprus, 25 (Nicosia, 1997).

Catalogue d'Actes des Comtes de Brienne: 950–1356, ed. H. d'Arbois de Jubainville (Paris, 1872).

Chartes de la Commanderie de Beauvoir de l'Ordre Teutonique, in *Collection des Principaux Cartulaires du Diocèse de Troyes*, vol. 3 (Paris, 1878).

Codex Diplomaticus Hungariae: Ecclesiasticus ac Civilis, ed. G. Fejér, 5 vols (Budapest, 1829–1830).

Codex Diplomaticus Ordinis Sanctae Mariae Theutonicorum, ed. J. H. Hennes (Mainz, 1845).

Chronica de Mailros, ed. J. Stevenson (Edinburgh, 1835).

Chronica Minor Minoritae Erphordensis: Continuatio VII, in *MGH SRG*, vol. 42, pp. 702–704.

Chronica Regia Coloniensis, in *MGH SRG*, vol. 18, pp. 1–299.

Chronicon Breve Fratris, ut videtur, Ordinis Theutonicorum, *MGH SS*, vol. 24, pp. 151–154.

Chronique D'Ernoul et de Bernard Le Trésorier, trans. M. L. de Mas Latrie (Paris, 1871).

Chroniques de Chypre d'Amadi et de Strambaldi, ed. R. de Mas Latrie, 2 vols (Paris, 1891–1893).

Codex Diplomaticus et Epistolaris Regni Bohemiae, 5 vols (Prague, 1907–1982).

Codex Diplomaticus Nassoicus: Nassauisches Urkundenbuch, ed. K. Menzel and W. Sauer, 3 vols (1969, Aalen).

Codex Diplomaticus Ordinis Sanctae Mariae Theutonicorum, ed. J. H. Hennes (Mainz, 1845).

Codice Diplomatico Brindisino, ed. G. Maria Monti, 2 vols (Trani, 1940–1964).

The Conquest of Jerusalem and the Third Crusade, trans. P. W. Edbury, Crusade Texts in Translation, 1 (Aldershot, 1996).

Continuatio Garstensis, in *MGH SS*, vol. 9, pp. 593–600.

Continuatio Itala, in *MGH SS*, vol. 26, pp. 85–86.

Continuation de Guillaume de Tyr de 1229 à 1261, dite du manuscript de Rothelin, in *RHC. Oc.*, vol. 2, pp. 489–639.

La Continuation de Guillaume de Tyr: 1184–1197, ed. M. R. Morgan (Paris, 1982).

Cronica Reinhardsbrunnensis, in *MGH SS*, vol. 30, pp. 490–656.

Cronica S. Petri Erfordensis Moderna, *MGH SS*, vol. 30, pp. 335–457.

The Crusaders as Conquerors: The Chronicle of Morea, trans. H. Lurier (New York and London, 1964).

Decrees of the Ecumenical Councils, ed. N. P. Tanner, 2 vols (Georgetown, 1990).

De Primordiis Ordinis Theutonici Narratio, in *Scriptores Rerum Prussicarum:*

Bibliography

Des Geschichtsquellen der Preussischen Vorzeit, ed. T. Hirsch, M. Töppen and E. Strehlke, vol. 1 (Leipzig, 1861), pp. 220–225.

Diplomatarium Danicum (Raekke 1), ed. N. Skyum-Nielsen, 7 vols (Copenhagen, 1975–1990).

La Documentacion Pontificia Hasta Innocencio III, ed. D. Mansilla (Rome, 1955).

Early Mamluk Diplomacy (1260–1290): Treaties of Baybars and Qalāwūn with Christian Rulers, ed. and trans. P. M. Holt, Islamic History and Civilisation, 12 (Leiden, 1995).

Eberhardi Archidiaconi Ratisponensis Annales, in *MGH SS*, vol. 17, pp. 591–605.

Eracles, L'Estoire de Eracles Empereur et la Conqueste de la Terre d'Outremer, in *RHC. Oc.*, vol. 2 (Paris, 1859).

Excidii Aconis Gestorum Collectio, in *The Fall of Acre: 1291*, ed. R. Huygens, Corpus Christianorum: Continuatio Mediaeualis, 202 (Turnhout, 2004).

Brother Felix Fabri, *Fratris Felicis Fabri Evanatorium in Terrae Sanctae, Arabiae et Egypti Peregrinationem*, ed. C. D. Hassler, Bibliothek des Literarischen Vereins in Stuttgart, 18, 3 vols (Stuttgart 1843–1849).

Filippo da Novara, *Guerra di Federico II in Oriente (1223–1242)*, ed. S. Melani (Naples, 1994).

Foedera, Conventiones, Litterae et cuiuscunque generis Acta Publica inter reges Angliae et alios quosvis Imperatores, Reges, Pontifices, Principes, vel Communitates, ed. T. Rymer, 4 vols ([place of pub??] 1816–1869).

Gesta Crucigerorum Rhenanorum, in *Quinti Belli Sacri: Scriptores Minores*, ed. R. Röhricht (Geneva, 1879), pp. 29–56.

Gesta Episcoporum Halberstadensium, in *MGH SS*, vol. 23, pp. 73–129.

Les Gestes des Chiprois, in *RHC. Arm.*, vol. 2 (Paris, 1896), pp. 653–871.

Grigor of Akanc, '*History of the Nation of Archers (The Mongols)* by Grigor of Akanc hitherto ascribed to Malak'ia The Monk: The Armenian text edited with an English translation and notes', ed. and trans. R. P. Blake and R. N. Frye, *Harvard Journal of Asiatic Studies*, 12 (1949), pp. 269–399.

Hessisches Urkundenbuch, 3 vols (Osnabrück, 1965).

Historia Diplomatica Friderici Secundi, ed. J. L. A. Huillard-Bréholles, 6 vols (Paris, 1852–1861).

Historia Diplomatica Regni Siciliae: Inde ab anno 1250 ad annum 1266, ed. B. Capasso (Naples, 1874).

Historia de Expeditione Friderici Imperatoris, in *MGH SRGNS*, vol. 5, pp. 1–115.

Historia Ordinis Equitum Teutonicorum: Hospitalis S. Mariae V. Hierosolymitani, ed. R. Duellius (Vienna, 1727).

Hohenlohisches Urkundenbuch, ed. K. Weller, 3 vols (Stuttgart, 1899–1912).

Humbert of Romans, 'De Modo Prompte Cudendi Sermones', in *Maxima Bibliotheca Veterum Patrum*, ed. M. de la Bigne, vol. 25 (Lyon, 1677).

Ibn al-Furāt, *Ayyubids, Mamlukes and Crusaders: Selections from the Tārīkh al-Duwal wa 'l-Mulūk*, ed. and trans. U. and M. C. Lyons, intro. J. S. C. Riley-Smith, 2 vols (Cambridge, 1971).

Innocent IV, 'Lettere Secretae D'Innocenzo IV e altri documenti in una raccolta inedita del sec. XIII', in *Miscellanea Francescana*,ed. G. Abate, vol. 55 (Rome, 1955).

Iohannis Abbatis Victoriensis, *Liber Certarum Historiarum: Liber Secundus*, in *MGH SRG*, vol. 36, pt 1, pp. 211–305.

Bibliography

Itinerarium Peregrinorum et Gesta Regis Ricardi, in *Chronicles and Memorials of the Reign of Richard I*, ed. W. Stubbs, RS, 38, vol. 1 (London, 1864).

Jamal ad-din Muhammed be Salim bin Wasil, *Moufarraj al-Kurub*, ed. H. M. Rabiah and S. Abed ad Fatah Ashour, vol. 4 (Cairo, 1972).

James of Vitry, *Historia Hierosolimitani*, in *Gesta Dei per Francos*, vol. 1 (Hanover, 1611), pp. 1047–1145.

James of Vitry, *The History of Jerusalem*, trans. A. Stewart, Palestine Pilgrims' Text Society 11 (London, 1896).

John of Ibelin, *Le Livre des Assises*, ed. P. W. Edbury, The Medieval Mediterranean, 50 (Boston, 2003).

Die Kreuzfahrt des Landgrafen Ludwigs des Frommen von Thüringen, in *MGH SVL*, vol. 4, pp. 179–308.

'Lettre des chrétiens de Terre-Sainte à Charles d'Anjou (22 avril 1260)', *Revue de L'Orient Latin*, 2 (1894), pp. 206–215.

Liber Cronicorum sive Annalis Erfordensis, in *MGH SRG*, vol. 42, pp. 724–781.

Liv., Est. und Kurländisches Urkundenbuch (Abt.1), 12 vols (Aalen, 1967–1981).

Livländische Reimchronik, ed. L. Mayer (Paderborn, 1876).

Ludolph von Suchem, *Itinere Terrae Sanctae*, Bibliothek des Literarischen Vereins in Stuttgart, 25 (Stuttgart, 1851).

Marino Sanuto, *Liber Secretorum Fidelium Crucis: Super Terre Sancte Recuperatione et Consevatione*, in *Gesta Dei Per Francos*, ed. J. Bongars (Jerusalem, 1972).

Matthew Paris, *Chronica Majora*, ed. H. R. Luard, RS, 57, 7 vols (London, 1872–1883).

Meklenburgisches Urkundenbuch, 4 vols (Schwerin, 1863–1867).

Menkonis Chronicon, in *MGH SS*, vol. 23, pp. 523–561.

Monumenta Historica Hungariae, ed. A. Theiner, 2 vols (Rome, 1859–1860).

Narratio Itineris Navalis ad Terram Sanctam, in *MGH SRGNS*, vol. 5, pp. 179–196.

Nicolaus von Jeroschin, *Di Kronike von Pruzinlant*, in *Scriptores Rerum Prussicarum: Des Geschichtsquellen der Preussischen Vorzeit*, ed. T. Hirsch, M. Töppen and E. Strehlke, vol. 1 (Leipzig, 1861).

Notai Genovesi in Oltremare atti Rogati a Cipro da Lamberto di Sambuceto: 3 luglio 1300–3 agosto 1301, ed. V. Polonio, Collana Storica di Fonti e Studi, 31(Genoa, 1982).

Nürnberger Urkundenbuch, Quellen und Forschungen zur Geschichte der Stadt Nürnberg, 1 (Nuremberg, 1959).

Odo of Deuil, *De Profectione Ludovici VII in Orientem: The Journey of Louis VII to the East*, ed. and trans. V. G. Berry (New York, 1948).

Oliveri Scholastici, *Historia Damiatina*, in *Die Schriften des Kölner Domscholasters, Späteren Bishofs von Paderborn und Kardinal-Bischofs von S. Sabina*, Bibliothek des Litterarischen Vereins in Stuttgart, 202 (Tübingen, 1894).

Oorkondenboek van het Sticht Utrecht: tot 1301, ed. K. Heeringa, 5 vols (The Hague, 1920–1959).

Ortnit und die WolfDietriche, in *Deutsches Heldenbuch*, vol. 4 (Berlin, 1873).

Otto of Freising, *The Deeds of Frederick Barbarossa*, ed. and trans. C. Mierow (Toronto, 1994).

Ottokars Österreichische Reimchronik, in *MGH SVL*, vol. 5.1, pp. 1–720.

Bibliography

Papsturkunden in Spanien: vorarbeiten zur Hispania Pontificia: Katalanien, ed. P. Kehr (Berlin, 1926).

Papsturkunden für Templer und Johanniter, ed. R. Hiestand (Göttingen, 1972).

Papsturkunden für Templer und Johanniter: Neue Folge, ed. R. Hiestand (Göttingen, 1984).

Patrologia Latina, ed. J.-P. Migne, 221 vols (1844–1864).

Peter von Dusburg, *Chronicon Terrae Prussie*, in *Scriptores Rerum Prussicarum: Des Geschichtsquellen der Preussischen Vorzeit*, ed. T. Hirsch, M. Töppen and E. Strehlke, vol. 1 (Leipzig, 1861). [page numbers?]

Pommersches Urkundenbuch, ed. K. Conrad and R. Prümers et al., 11 vols (Cologne, 1970–1990).

Preussisches Urkundenbuch, ed. A. Seraphim, M. Hein, E. Maschke et al., 6 vols (Königsberg, 1961–2000).

Ralph of Diceto, *Radulfi de Diceto Decani Londoniensis Opera Historica*, ed. W. Stubbs, RS, 68, 2 vols (London, 1876).

Regesta Diplomatica necnon Epistolaria Historiae Thuringiae, ed. O. Dobenecker, 3 vols (Jena, 1896–1925).

Regesta Honorii Papae III, ed. P. Pressutti, 2 vols (Hildesheim, New York, 1978).

Regesta Imperii IV: Ältere Staufer, ed. J. F. Böhmer, 3 vols (Cologne, 1972–2001).

Regesta Imperii V: Die Regesten des Kaiserreichs: unter Philipp, Otto IV, Friedrich II, Heinrich (VII), Conrad IV, Heinrich Raspe, Wilhelm und Richard, 1198–1272, ed. J. F. Böhmer, 4 vols (Innsbruck, 1881–1983).

Regesta Regni Hierosolymitani: 1097–1291, ed. R. Rohricht, 2 vols (Innsbruck, 1893. *Additamentum*, 1904).

Die Regester Innocenz' III, ed. O. Hageneder, A. Haidacher, A. Sommerlecher et al., 9 vols (Cologne, 1964–2004).

Les Registres de Alexandre IV, ed. C. Bourel de la Roncière, BEFAR, 3 vols (Paris, 1895–1953).

Les Registres de Clément IV, ed. É. Jordan, BEFAR (Paris, 1893).

Les Registres de Grégoire IX, ed. L. Auvray, BEFAR, 3 vols (Paris, 1896–1908).

Les Registres de Grégoire X, ed. J. Guiraud, BEFAR (Paris, 1892).

Les Registres d'Innocent IV, ed. É. Berger, BEFAR, 4 vols (Paris, 1884–1921).

Les Registres de Martin IV, ed. O. Martin, BEFAR (Paris, 1901).

Les Registres de Nicolas IV, ed. E. Langlois, BEFAR (Paris, 1886–1891).

I Registri della Cancelleria Angioina, ed. R. Filangieri, 47 vols (Naples, 1950–2003).

La Règle du Temple, ed. H. de Curzon (Paris, 1886).

'Le Reliquie dell'Archivio dell'Ordine Teutonico in Venezia', *Atti del Reale Istituto Veneto di Scienze, Lettere ed Arti*, ed. R. Predelli, 64 (1904–1905), pp. 1379–1463.

Richard of San Germano, *Chronica*, in *MGH SS*, vol. 19, pp. 321–384.

Salimbene de Adam, *Cronica*, ed. G. Scalia, 2 vols (Bari, 1966).

Schlesisches Urkundenbuch, ed. W. Irgang, 6 vols (1971–1998).

Die Statuten des Deutschen Ordens nach Ältesten Handschriften, ed. M. Perlbach (Hildesheim, 1975).

Studien zur Geschichte des Fünften Kreuzzuges, ed. R. Röhricht (Innsbruck, 1891).

'Table Chronologique de Héthoum Comte de Gor'igos', *RHC. Arm.*, vol. 1, pp. 471–490.

Bibliography

Tabulae Ordinis Theutonici: Ex Tabularii Regii Berolinensis Codice Potissimum, ed. E. Strelke (Berlin, 1869; reprint ed. H. Mayer, Jerusalem and Toronto, 1975).

Thadeus of Naples, *Ystoria de Desolatione et Conculcatione Civitatis Acconensis et Tocius Terre Sancte*, in *The Fall of Acre: 1291*, ed. R. Huygens, Corpus Christianorum: Continuatio Mediaeualis 202 (Turnhout, 2004).

Tiroler Urkundenbuch, 3 vols (Innsbruck, 1937–1957).

Urkunden zur Älteren Handels- und Staatsgeschichte der Republik Venedig mit Besonderer Beziehung auf Byzanz und die Levante, ed. G. Tafel and G. Thomas, 3 vols (Amsterdam, 1964).

Urkundenbuch der Deutschordens-Ballei Hessen, in *Hessisches Urkundenbuch*, vol. 1 (Osnabrück, 1965).

Urkundenbuch der Deutschordensballei Thüringen, ed. K. H. Lampe (Jena, 1936).

Urkundenbuch zur Geschichte der Babenberger in Österreich, ed. H. Fichtenau and E. Zöllner et al., 4 vols (Vienna, 1950–1997).

Urkundenbuch für die Geschichte des Niederrheins, ed. T. Lacomblet, 4 vols (Aalen, 1960).

Urkundenbuch zur Geschichte der jetzt die Preussischen Regierungsbezirke Coblenz und Trier bildenden Mittelrheinischen Territorien, ed. L. Eltester, A. Goerz et al., 3 vols (Koblenz, 1865–1874).

Urkundenbuch des Klosters Walkenried, ed. J. Dolle (Hanover, 2002).

Wilbrand of Oldenburg, *Peregrinatio*, in *Peregrinatores Medii Aevi Quatuor*, ed. J. C. Laurent (Leipzig, 1864).

William of Tyre, *Chronicon*, ed. R. Huygens, Corpus Christianorum: Continuatio Mediaeualis 63, 2 vols (Turnhout, 1986).

Württembergisches Urkundenbuch, 11 vols (Stuttgart, 1972–1978).

Secondary Sources

Abulafia, D., *Frederick II: A Medieval Emperor* (London, 2002).

Amitai-Preiss, R., *Mongols and Mamluks: The Mamluk-Īlkhānid War 1260–1281*, Cambridge Studies in Islamic Civilisation (Cambridge, 1996).

Angold, M., *The Fourth Crusade: Event and Context* (Harlow, 2003).

Arnold, B., *Princes and Territories in Medieval Germany* (Cambridge, 2003).

Arnold, U., 'Akkon-Venedig-Marienburg: Der Deutsche Orden vom Mittelmeer zum Ostseeraum', in *Acri 1291: La fine della presenza degli ordini militari in Terra Santa e i nuovi orientamenti nel XIV secolo*, ed. F. Tommasi (Perugia, 1996), pp. 69–74.

Arnold, U., 'Der Deutsche Orden zwischen Kaiser und Papst im 13. Jahrhundert', in *Die Ritterordern zwischen geistlicher und weltlicher Macht im Mittelalter*, ed. Z. H. Nowak (Torun, 1990), pp. 57–70.

Arnold, U., 'Deutschmeister Konrad von Feuchtwangen und die "preußische Partei" im Deutschen Orden am Ende des 13. und zu Beginn des 14. Jahrhunderts', in *Aspekte der Geschichte. Festschrift für Peter Gerrit Thielen* ed. U. Arnold ed al. (Göttingen, 1990), pp. 33–34.

Bibliography

Arnold, U., 'Eight Hundred Years of the Teutonic Order', in *MO*, vol. 1, pp. 223–235.

Arnold, U., 'Entstehung und Frühzeit des Deutschen Ordens', in *Die Geistlichen Ritterorden Europas*, ed. J. Fleckenstein and M. Hellman (Sigmaringen, 1980), pp. 81–107.

Arnold, U., 'Gerhard von Malberg', in *Die Hochmeister des Deutschen Ordens 1190–1994*, QuStDO, 40 (Marburg, 1998), pp. 22–23.

Arnold, U., 'Hartmann von Heldrungen', *Die Hochmeister des Deutschen Ordens 1190–1994*, QuStDO, 40 (Marburg, 1998), pp. 36–38.

Arnold, U., 'Heinrich von Hohenlohe', in *Die Hochmeister des Deutschen Ordens 1190–1994*, QuStDO, 40 (Marburg, 1998), pp. 24–26.

Barber, M., *The New Knighthood: A History of the Order of the Temple* (Cambridge, 1995).

Barber, M., 'The Order of Saint Lazarus and the Crusades', *Catholic Historical Review*, 80 (1994), pp. 439–456.

Barber, M., 'Supplying the Crusader States: The Role of the Templars', in *The Horns of Hattin*, ed. B. Z. Kedar (Jerusalem, 1992), pp. 314–326.

Barber, M., *The Two Cities: Medieval Europe 1050–1320* (London, 2000).

Barber, M., and Bate, K. (eds), *The Templars: Selected Sources* (Manchester, 2002).

Bar-Kochva, B., *Judas Maccabaeus: The Jewish Struggle against the Seleucids* (Cambridge, 1989).

Benevisti, M., *The Crusaders' Fortress of Montfort* (Jerusalem, 1982).

Bennett, M., '*La Règle du Temple* as a Military Manual or How to Deliver a Cavalry Charge', in *The Rule of the Templars*, ed. J. M. Upton-Ward, Studies in the History of Medieval Religion, 4 (Woodbridge, 2005), pp. 175–188.

Boas, A. J., *Archaeology of the Military Orders: A Survey of the Urban Centres, Rural Settlement and Castles of the Military Orders in the Latin East c.1120–1291* (London, 2006).

Boas, A. J., *Crusader Archaeology: The Material Culture of the Latin East* (London, 1999).

Boase, T. S. R., *The Cilician Kingdom of Armenia* (Edinburgh, 1978).

Boockmann, H., 'Konrad von Thüringen', in *Die Hochmeister des Deutschen Ordens 1190–1994*, QuStDO, 40 (Marburg, 1998), pp. 17–20.

Bronstein, J., *The Hospitallers and the Holy Land: Financing the Latin East 1187–1274* (Woodbridge, 2005).

Brundage, J. A., *Medieval Canon Law and the Crusader* (Madison, WI, 1969).

Bulst, M., 'Zur Geschichte der Ritterorden und des Königsreichs Jerusalem im 13. Jahrhundert bis zur Schlacht bei La Forbie am 17. Okt. 1244', *Deutsches Archiv für Erforschung des Mittelalters*, 22 (1966), pp. 197–226.

Burgtorf, J., *The Central Convent of Hospitallers and Templars: History, Organisation and Personnel, 1099–1310*, History of Warfare, 50 (Leiden, 2008).

Burgtorf, J., 'The Military Orders in the Crusader Principality of Antioch', in *East and West in the Medieval Eastern Mediterranean I: Antioch from the Byzantine Reconquest until the End of the Crusader Principality*, ed. K. Ciggaar and M. Metcalf (Leuven, 2006), pp. 217–246.

Chambers, J., *The Devil's Horsemen: The Mongol Invasion of Europe* (London, 2003).

Chevalier, M., 'Les Chevaliers teutoniques en Cilicie: "les maccabées" du royaume arménien', *Bizantinistica*, 6 (2004), pp. 137–153.

Cohn, W., *Herman von Salza* (Breslau, 1930).

Coureas, N., *The Latin Church in Cyprus: 1195–1312* (Aldershot, 1997).

Der Nersessian, S., 'The Kingdom of Cilician Armenia', in *HOC*, vol. 2, pp. 630–660.

Dondi, C., *The Liturgy or the Canons Regular of the Holy Sepulchre of Jerusalem*, Bibliotheca Victorina, 16 (Turnhout, 2004).

Dunbabin, J., *Charles of Anjou: Power, Kingship and State-Making in Thirteenth-Century Europe* (Harlow, 1998).

Edbury, P. W., *John of Ibelin and the Kingdom of Jerusalem* (Woodbridge, 1997).

Edgington, S., 'Administrative Regulations for the Hospital of St John in Jerusalem Dating from the 1180s', *Crusades*, 4 (2005), pp. 21–37.

Edwards, R. W., *The Fortifications of Cilician Armenia*, Dumbarton Oaks Studies, 23 (Washington, DC, 1987).

Ellenblum, R., 'Colonization Activities in the Frankish East: The Example of Castellum Regis (Mil'ilya)', *English Historical Review*, 111 (1996), pp. 104–122.

Ellenblum, R., *Frankish Rural Settlement in the Latin Kingdom of Jerusalem* (Cambridge, 1998).

Enlart, C., 'Deux inscriptions françaises trouvées à Chypre', *Syria: Revue d'art oriental d'archéologie*, 8 (1927), pp. 234–238.

Favreau, M., 'Die Kreuzfahrerherrschaft Scandalion (Iskanderūne)', *Zeitschrift des Deutschen Palästina-Vereins*, 93 (1977), pp. 12–29.

Favreau, M., *Studien zur Frühgeschichte des Deutschen Ordens* (Stuttgart, 1974).

Favreau-Lilie, M., 'The German Empire and Palestine: German pilgrimages to Jerusalem between the 12th and 16th century', *Journal of Medieval History*, 21 (1995), pp. 321–341.

Favreau-Lilie, M., 'L'Ordine Teutonico in Terrasanta (1198–1291)', in *L'Ordine Teutonico nel Mediterraneo*, ed. H. Houben (Galatina, 2004), pp. 55–72.

Favreau-Lilie, M., 'The Teutonic Knights in Acre after the Fall of Montfort (1271): Some Reflections', in *Outremer: Studies in the History of the Crusading Kingdom of Jerusalem*, ed. B. Z. Kedar, H. E. Mayer and R. C. Smail (Jerusalem, 1982), pp. 272–284.

Fischer, M., 'Biblical Heroes and the Uses of Literature', in *Crusade and Conversion on the Baltic Frontier: 1150–1500*, ed. A. V. Murray (Aldershot, 2001), pp. 261–275.

Fischer, M., 'The Books of the Maccabees and the Teutonic Order', *Crusades*, 4 (2005), pp. 59–71.

Fonnesberg-Schmidt, I., *The Popes and the Baltic Crusades: 1147–1254*, The Northern World, 26 (Leiden, 2007).

Forey, A. J., 'Constitutional Conflict and Change in the Hospital of St John during the Twelfth and Thirteenth Centuries', *Journal of Ecclesiastical History*, 33 (1982), pp. 15–29.

Forey, A. J., 'The Military Order of St Thomas of Acre', *English Historical Review*, 92 (1977), pp. 481–503.

Forey, A. J., 'The Military Orders and the Spanish Reconquest in the Twelfth and Thirteenth Centuries' *Traditio*, 40 (1984), pp. 197–234.

Forey, A. J., *The Military Orders: From the Twelfth to the Early Fourteenth Centuries* (London, 1992).

Forey, A. J., 'Recruitment to the Military Orders: Twelfth to Mid-fourteenth Centuries', *Viator*, 17 (1986), pp. 139–171.

Forstreuter, K., *Der Deutsche Orden am Mittelmeer*, QuStDO, 2 (Bonn, 1967).

García, J. M. R., 'Alfonso X, la Orden Teutónica y Tierra Santa: una nueva fuente para su estudio', in *Las Órdenes Militares en la Península Ibérica*, ed. R. I. Benito and F. R. Gómez, vol. 1 (Cuenca, 2000), pp. 489–509.

García, J. M. R., 'Alfonso X and the Teutonic Order: An Example of the Role of the International Military Orders in Mid Thirteenth-Century Castile', in *MO*, vol. 2, pp. 319–327.

Gillingham, J., *Richard I* (New Haven, CT, 2002).

Hamilton, B., 'King Consorts of Jerusalem and their Entourages from the West from 1186 to 1250', in idem, *Crusaders, Cathars and the Holy Places* (Aldershot, 1999), pp. 13–24.

Hamilton, B., *The Latin Church in the Crusader States: The Secular Church* (London, 1980).

Harris, J., *Byzantium and the Crusades* (London, 2003).

Hellmann, M., 'König Manfred von Sizilien und der Deutsche Orden', in *Acht Jahrhunderte Deutscher Orden in Einzeldarstellungen*, ed. P. Klemens Wieser QuStDO, 1 (Bad Godesberg, 1967), pp. 65–72.

Hilsch, P., 'Der Deutsche Ritterorden im Südlichen Libanon: Zur Topographie der Kreuzfahrerherrschaften Sidon und Beirut', *Zeitschrift des Deutschen Palästina-Vereins*, 96 (1980), pp. 174–189.

Höfler, C., 'Analecten zur Geschichte Deutschlands und Italiens: Bericht des Bruno von Olmütz an Papst Gregor X', *Abhandlungen der Historische Klasse der Bayerische Akademie der Wissenschaffen* (1846), pp. 1–28.

Holt, P. M., *The Age of the Crusades: The Near East from the Eleventh Century to 1517* (London, 1987).

Houben, H., 'I Cavalieri Teutonici nel Mediterraneo Orientale (secoli XII–XV)', in *I Cavalieri teutonici tra Sicilia e Mediterraneo*, ed. A. Giuffrida, H. Houben and K. Toomaspoeg (Galatina, 2007), pp. 47–90.

Houben, H., 'Intercultural Communication: The Teutonic Knights in Palestine, Armenia and Cyprus', in *Diplomatics in the Eastern Mediterranean: 1000–1500*, ed. A. D. Beihammer, M. G. Parani and C. D. Schabel (Leiden, 2008), pp. 139–157.

Houben, H., 'Die Landkomture der Deutschordensballei Apulien (1225–1474)', *Sacra Militia: Rivista di storia degli ordini militari* 4 (2001), pp. 115–154.

Houben, H., 'Wie und wann kam der Deutsche Orden nach Griechenland?' *Néa 'Ρώμη: Rivista di ricerche bizantinistiche*, 1 (Rome, 2004), pp. 243–253.

Housley, N., *The Italian Crusades: The Papal–Angevin Alliance and the Crusades against Christian Lay Powers, 1254–1343* (Oxford, 1982).

Hubatsch, W., 'Der Deutsche Orden und die Reichlehnschaft über Cypern', *Nachrichten der Akademie der Wissenschaften in Göttingen: Phil.-hist. Klasse* (Göttingen, 1955), pp. 245–306.

Hubatsch, W., 'Montfort und die Bildung des Deutschordensstates im Heiligen Lande', *Nachrichten der Akademie der Wissenschaften in Göttingen: Philologisch-Historische Klasse* (Göttingen, 1966), pp. 161–199.

Huygens, R. B. C., 'Un nouveau texte de traité "De constructione castri Saphet"'
Studi Medievali vol. 6 (1) (1965), pp. 355–387.

Jackson, P., 'The Crisis in the Holy Land in 1260', *English Historical Review*,
95 (1980), pp. 481–513.

Jackson, P., 'The End of Hohenstaufen Rule in Syria', *Bulletin of the Institute of
Historical Research*, 59 (1986), pp. 20–36.

Jacoby, D., 'The Kingdom of Jerusalem and the Collapse of Hohenstaufen Power
in the Levant', *Dumbarton Oaks Papers*, 40 (1986), pp. 83–101.

Johnson, E. N., 'The Crusades of Frederick Barbarossa and Henry VI', in *HOC*,
vol. 2, pp. 87–122.

Jotischky, A., *Crusading and the Crusader States* (Harlow, 2004).

Kedar, B. Z., 'The Subjected Muslims of the Frankish Levant', in *Muslims under
Latin Rule*, ed. J. M. Powell (Princeton, 1990), pp. 135–174.

Kedar, B. Z., 'The *Tractatus de locis et statu sancte terre Ierosolimitane*', in
The Crusades and their Sources: Essays Presented to Bernard Hamilton, ed.
J. France and W. Zajac (Aldershot, 1998).

Kennedy, H., *Crusader Castles* (Cambridge, 2001).

Kluger, H., *Hochmeister Hermann von Salza und Kaiser Friedrich II: Ein Beitrag
zur Frühgeschichte des Deutschen Ordens*, QuStDO, 37 (Marburg, 1987).

Kouřil, M., 'Der Olmützer Bischof Bruno von Schauenburg und der Deutsche
Orden', in *Acht Jahrhunderte Deutscher Orden in Einzeldarstellungen*, ed.
P. Klemens Wieser, QuStDO, 1 (Bad Godesberg, 1967), pp. 143–151.

Krieger, K. F., 'Obligatory Military Service and the Use of Mercenaries in Imperial Military Campaigns under the Hohenstaufen Emperors', in *England and
Germany in the High Middle Ages*, ed. A. Haverkamp and H. Volrath (Oxford,
1996), pp. 151–168.

La Monte, J., *The Wars of Frederick II against the Ibelins in Syria and Cyprus*
(New York, 1936).

Labuda, G., 'Die Urkunden über die Anfänge des Deutschen Ordens im Kulmerland und in Preußen in den Jahren 1226–1243', in *Die Geistlichen Ritterorden Europas*, ed. J. Fleckenstein and M. Hellman (Sigmaringen, 1980), pp.
299–317.

Leeper, A. W. A., *A History of Medieval Austria* (Oxford, 1941).

Lilie, R., *Byzantium and the Crusader States: 1096–1204* (Oxford, 1993).

Lower, M., *The Barons' Crusade: A Call to Arms and its Consequences* (Philadelphia, PA, 2005).

Luttrell, A., 'The Aragonese Crown and the Knights Hospitallers of Rhodes:
1291–1350', *English Historical Review*, 76 (1961), pp. 1–19.

Luttrell, A., 'The Earliest Hospitallers', in *Montjoie: Studies in Crusade History
in Honour of Hans Eberhard Mayer*, ed. B. Z. Kedar, J. Riley-Smith and
R. Hiestand (Aldershot, 1997), pp. 37–54.

Luttrell, A., 'The Earliest Templars', in *Autour de la Première Croisade*, ed.
M. Balard (Paris, 1996), pp. 193–202.

Maier, C. T., *Preaching the Crusades: Mendicant Friars and the Cross in the
Thirteenth Century* (Cambridge, 1998).

Marcombe, D., *Leper Knights: The Order of St Lazarus of Jerusalem in England,
c.1150–1544* (Woodbridge, 2003).

Marshall, C., *Warfare in the Latin East: 1192–1291* (Cambridge, 1994).

Bibliography

Masson Smith, J., 'Ayn Jālūt: Mamluk Success or Mongol Failure?' *Harvard Journal of Asiatic Studies*, 44 (1984), pp. 307–345.

Masterman, E. W. G., 'A Visit to the Ruined Castles of the Teutonic Knights', *Palestine Exploration Fund: Quarterly Statement* (London, 1919), pp. 71–75.

Mayer, H. E., 'Angevins versus Normans: The New Men of King Fulk of Jerusalem', *Proceedings of the American Philosophical Society*, vol. 133 (1989), pp. 1–25.

Mayer, H. E., *The Crusades*, trans. J. Gillingham, 2nd edn (Oxford, 1990).

Mayer, H. E., 'Die Seigneurie de Joscelin und der Deutsche Orden', in *Die Geistlichen Ritterorden Europas* eds J. Fleckenstein, M. Hellman (Sigmaringen, 1980), pp. 171–216.

Militzer, K., 'Burchard von Schwanden', in *Die Hochmeister des Deutschen Ordens 1190–1994*, QuStDO, 40 (Marburg, 1998), pp. 38–41.

Militzer, K., *Die Entstehung der Deutschordensballeien im Deutschen Reich*, QuStDO, 16 (Bonn, 1970).

Militzer, K., 'Günther von Wüllersleben', in *Die Hochmeister des Deutschen Ordens 1190–1994*, QuStDO, 40 (Marburg, 1998), pp. 26–27.

Militzer, K., 'From the Holy Land to Prussia: The Teutonic Knights between Emperors and Popes and their Policies until 1309', in *Mendicants, Military Orders and Regionalism in Medieval Europe*, ed. J. Sarnowsky (Aldershot, 1999), pp. 71–81.

Militzer, K., 'Poppo von Osterna', in *Die Hochmeister des Deutschen Ordens 1190–1994*, QuStDO, 40 (Marburg, 1998), pp. 27–29.

Militzer, K., 'The Role of Hospitals in the Teutonic Order', in *MO*, vol. 2, pp. 51–59.

Militzer, K., *Von Akkon zur Marienburg: Verfassung, Verwaltung und Sozialstruktur des Deutschen Ordens 1190–1309*, QuStDO, 56 (Marburg, 1999).

Mitchell, P., *Medicine in the Crusades: Warfare, Wounds and the Medieval Surgeon* (Cambridge, 2004).

Moore, J. C., *Pope Innocent III (1160/61–1216): To Root Up and to Plant*, The Medieval Mediterranean, 48 (Boston, 2003).

Müller, G., *Jerusalem oder Akkon: Über den Anfang des Deutschen Ordens nach dem gegenwärtigen Stand der Forschung* (Bad Münstereifel, 1989).

Munz, P., *Frederick Barbarossa: A Study in Medieval Politics* (London, 1969).

Murray, A., 'Money and Logistics in the Forces of the First Crusade: Coinage, Bullion, Service and Supply: 1096–1099', in *Logistics of Warfare in the Age of the Crusades*, ed. J. Pryor (Aldershot, 2006), pp. 229–250.

Nicholson, H., *The Knights Hospitaller* (Woodbridge, 2001).

Nicholson, H., *The Knights Templar: A New History* (Stroud, 2004).

Nicholson, H., *Love, War, and the Grail: Templars, Hospitallers and Teutonic Knights in Medieval Epic and Romance 1150–1500* (Boston, 2004).

Nicholson, H., 'Steamy Syrian Scandals: Matthew Paris on the Templars and Hospitallers', *Medieval History*, 2 (1992), pp. 68–85.

Nicholson, H., *Templars, Hospitallers and Teutonic Knights: Images of the Military Orders 1128–1291* (Leicester, 1993).

Niess, U., 'Konrad von Feuchtwangen', in *Die Hochmeister des Deutschen Ordens 1190–1994*, QuStDO, 40 (Marburg, 1998), pp. 41–42.

O'Callaghan, J. F., *Reconquest and Crusade in Medieval Spain* (Philadelphia, PA, 2003).

217

Pacifico, M., 'I Teutonici tra papato e impero nel Mediterraneo al tempo di Federico II, 1215–1250', in *I Cavalieri teutonici tra Sicilia e Mediterraneo*, ed. A. Giuffrida, H. Houben and K, Toomaspoeg, Acta Theutonica, IV (Galatina, 2007), pp. 91–157.

Perlbach, M., 'Deutsch-Ordens Necrologe', *Forschungen zur Deutschen Geschichte*, 17 (1877), pp. 357–371.

Perlbach, M., 'Die Reste des Deutschordensarchives in Venedig', *Altpreussische Monatsschrift*, 19 (1882), pp. 630–650.

Phillips, J., *Defenders of the Holy Land: Relations between the Latin East and the West: 1119–1187* (Oxford, 1996).

Phillips, J., *The Fourth Crusade and the Sack of Constantinople* (London, 2005).

Phillips, J., 'Papacy, Empire and the Second Crusade', in *The Second Crusade: Scope and Consequences*, ed. J. Phillips and M. Hoch (Manchester, 2001), pp. 15–31.

Piana, M., *Burgen und Städte der Kreuzzugszeit* (Petersburg, 2008).

Pósán, L., 'Prussian Missions and the Invitation of the Teutonic Order into Kulmerland', in *The Crusades and the Military Orders: Expanding the Frontiers of Medieval Latin Christianity*, ed. Z. Hunyadi and J. Laszlovsky (Budapest, 2001), pp. 429–448.

Powell, J. M., *Anatomy of a Crusade: 1213–1221* (Philadelphia, PA, 1990).

Powell, J. M., 'Honorius III and the Leadership of the Crusade', *Catholic Historical Review*, 63 (1977), pp. 521–536.

Powell, J. M., 'The Papacy and the Early Franciscans', *Franciscan Studies*, 36 (1976), pp. 248–262.

Powell, J. M., 'Patriarch Gerold and Frederick II: The Matthew Paris Letter', *Journal of Medieval History*, 25 (1999), pp. 19–26.

Prawer, J., *The Crusaders' Kingdom: European Colonialism in the Middle Ages*, 2nd edn (London, 2001).

Prestwich, M., *Edward I* (New Haven, CT, 1997).

Pringle, D., *The Churches of the Crusader Kingdom of Jerusalem*, 3 vols (Cambridge, 1993–2007).

Pringle, D., *Secular Buildings in the Crusader Kingdom of Jerusalem: An Archaeological Gazetteer* (Cambridge, 1997).

Pringle, D., 'A Thirteenth-Century Hall at Montfort Castle in Western Galilee', *Antiquaries Journal*, 66 (1986), pp. 52–81.

Pringle, D., Petersen, A., Dow, M. and Singer, C., 'Qal'at Jiddin: A Castle of the Crusader and Ottoman Periods in Galilee', *Levant*, 26 (1994), pp. 135–166.

Probst, C., *Der Deutsche Orden und sein Medizinalwesen in Preussen: Hospital, Firmarie und Arzt bis 1525*, QuStDO, 29 (Bad Godesberg, 1969).

Prutz, H., *Die Besitzungen des Deutschen Ordens im Heiligen Lande* (Leipzig, 1877).

Prutz, H., 'Eilf Deutschordensurkunden aus Venedig und Malta', *Altpreussische Monatsschrift*, 20 (1883), pp. 385–400.

Pryor, J. H., 'The Crusade of Emperor Frederick II, 1220–29: The Implications of the Maritime Evidence', *American Neptune*, 52 (1992), pp. 113–132.

Pryor, J. H., 'The Naval Architecture of Crusader Transport Ships: A Reconstruction of some Archetypes for Round-hulled Sailing Ships: Part I', *Mariner's Mirror*, 70 (1984), pp. 171–219.

Pryor, J. H., '*In Subsidium Terrae Sanctae*: Exports of Foodstuffs and War

Materials from the Kingdom of Sicily to the Kingdom of Jerusalem, 1265–1284', *Asian and African Studies*, 22 (1988), pp. 127–146.

Pryor, J. H., 'Transportation of Horses by Sea during the Era of the Crusades: Eighth Century to 1285 AD: Part 1: to *c.*1225', *Mariner's Mirror*, 68 (1982), pp. 9–27.

Purkis, W. J., *Crusading Spirituality in the Holy Land and Iberia, c.1095–c.1187* (Woodbridge, 2008).

Reuter, T., 'The "Non-Crusade" of 1149–50', in *The Second Crusade: Scope and Consequences*, ed. J. Phillips and M. Hoch (Manchester, 2001), pp. 150–163.

Richard, J., *The Crusades: 1071–1291* (Cambridge, 2001).

Richard, J., *The Latin Kingdom of Jerusalem*, trans. J. Shirley, ed. R. Vaughan, 2 vols (Amsterdam, 1979).

Richard, J., *Saint Louis: Crusader King of France*, trans. J. Birrell, ed. S. Lloyd (Cambridge, 1983).

Riedmann, J., 'Unbekannte Schreiben Kaiser Friedrichs II. und Konrads IV. In einer Handschrift der Universitäts-bibliothek Innsbruck', ed. J. Fried and R. Schieffer, *Deutsches Archiv für Erforschung des Mittelalters*, 62 (2006), pp. 135–200.

Riley-Smith, J. S. C. (ed.), *Atlas of the Crusades* (New York, 1981).

Riley-Smith, J. S. C., *The Crusades: A History*, 2nd edn (London, 2005).

Riley-Smith, J. S. C., *The Feudal Nobility and the Kingdom of Jerusalem: 1174–1277* (London, 1973).

Riley-Smith, J. S. C., 'Government in Latin Syria and the Commercial Privileges of Foreign Merchants', in *Relations between East and West in the Middle Ages*, ed. D. Baker (Edinburgh, 1973), pp. 109–132.

Riley-Smith, J. S. C., *The Knights of St John in Jerusalem and Cyprus c.1050–1310* (London, 1967).

Riley-Smith, J. S. C., 'The Templars and the Teutonic Knights in Cilician Armenia', in *The Cilician Kingdom of Armenia*, ed. T. S. R. Boase (Edinburgh, 1978), pp. 92–117.

Röhricht, R., *Die Deutschen im Heiligen Lande: 650–1291* (Innsbruck, 1894).

Ross, L., 'Frederick II: Tyrant or Benefactor of the Latin East?' *Al-Masāq*, 15 (2003), pp. 149–159.

Runciman, S., *A History of the Crusades*, 3 vols (Cambridge, 1954).

Schein, S., Fideles Crucis: *The Papacy, the West, and the Recovery of the Holy Land, 1274–1314* (Oxford, 1998).

Schein, S., 'The Patriarchs of Jerusalem in the Late Thirteenth Century: *Seignors Espiritueles et Temporeles*', in *Outremer: Studies in the History of the Crusading Kingdom of Jerusalem*, ed. B. Z. Kedar (Jerusalem, 1982), pp. 297–305.

Selwood, D., *Knights of the Cloister: Templars and Hospitallers in Central-Southern Occitania c.1100–c.1300* (Woodbridge, 1999).

Sterns, I., 'The Teutonic Knights in the Crusader States', in *HOC*, vol. 5, pp. 315–378.

Stewart, A. D., *The Armenian Kingdom and the Mamluks: War and Diplomacy during the Reigns of Het'um II: 1289–1307*, The Medieval Mediterranean, 34 (Leiden, 2001).

Throop, P. A., *Criticism of the Crusade: A Study of Public Opinion and Crusade Propaganda* (Amsterdam, 1940).

Bibliography

Tibble, S., *Monarchy and Lordships in the Latin Kingdom of Jerusalem: 1099–1291* (Oxford, 1989).

Toomaspoeg, K., *Les Teutoniques en Sicilie: 1197–1492* (Rome, 2003).

Tyerman, C., *The Fourth Crusade and the End of Outremer: 1192–1291* (London, 2004).

Tyerman, C., *God's War: A New History of the Crusades* (London, 2006).

Urban, W., *The Baltic Crusade* (Dekalb, IL, 1975).

Urban, W., *The Prussian Crusade* (Lanham, MD, 1980).

Urban, W., *The Teutonic Knights: A Military History* (London, 2003).

Van Cleve, T. C., 'The Crusade of Frederick II', in *HOC*, vol. 2, pp. 429–462.

Van Cleve, T. C., *The Emperor Frederick II of Hohenstaufen: Immutator Mundi* (Oxford, 1972).

Wojtecki, D., 'Der Deutsche Orden unter Friedrich II', in *Probleme um Friedrich II*, ed. J. Fleckenstein, Voträge und Forschungen, XVI (Sigmaringen, 1974), pp. 187–224.

Unpublished Material

al-Khowayter, A. A., 'A Critical Edition of an Unknown Source for the Life of al-Malik al-Zahir Bairbars', edited with introduction, translation and notes (unpublished PhD thesis, London University, School of Oriental and African Studies, 1960).

Riley-Smith, J. S. C., 'The Death and Burial of Latin Christian Pilgrims to Jerusalem and Acre, 1099–1291' (unpublished paper, 2006).

Ross, L., 'Relations between the Latin East and Western Europe', 1187–1291 (unpublished PhD thesis, Royal Holloway University, 2003).

Sterns, I., 'The Statutes of the Teutonic Knights: A Study of Religious Chivalry' (unpublished doctoral thesis, University of Pennsylvania, 1969).

Index

Aachen, 28
Abū l-Mahāsin, 17, 143
Achaia, *see* Teutonic Knights – in Achaia
Acre, 1, 10, 12, 16, 50, 77, 80, 115, 122, 124, 129, 132–133, 136, 138, 141, 150, 155, 174–176, 180, 183–184
   The *cathena* and *fundaq*, 53, 90, 176–177
   The Third Crusade, 10, 14, 55
   The Crusade of Emperor Henry VI, 12
   The Fifth Crusade, 32–33
   The Crusade of Emperor Frederick II and its aftermath, 60, 61, 63, 72–81
   The Crusade of Louis IX, 107
   Teutonic Knights' possessions in, 27, 56, 75, 90, 126, 169–171, 174
   The War of St Sabas, 112–114, 136
   Fall in 1291, 142, 169
Adolf, count of Berg, 37
Agnes, daughter of Joscelin III of Courtney, 90
Agnes, mother of Gerhard von Malberg, 99
Agridi, battle of, 73
Aguille, 27
Aigues-Mortes, 106
Al-Adil, brother of Saladin, 27
Aimery, king of Cyprus and Jerusalem, 13, 17, 27 57, 75, 176
Albert of Behaim, papal legate, 87
Albert of Rizzato, patriarch of Antioch, 80
Albert Suerbeer, archbishop of Prussia, 103
Albert, lord of Tirol, 37
Alexander Nevsky, 97
Aleppo, 122, 123
Alexander IV, pope, 36, 110, 118, 123, 135
Alice of Armenia, 54, 68
Alfonso X, king of Castile, 22, 106–107
Almaric of Wurzburg, marshal of the Teutonic Order, 203
Altenburg, 29
Amalric, king of Jerusalem, 101
Amalric, count of Montfort, 88
Amaury Barlais, 93

Amca, 174
Amudain, castle of the Teutonic Order, 29, 55, 57, 124, 132, 154, 174
Anastasia, wife of Duke Henry of Mecklenburg, 151
Andrew II, king of Hungary, 30, 47–48
Andrew of Shuf, 115
Andronicus Comnenus, 14
Anno von Sangershausen, master of the Teutonic Order, 24, 114–116, 120, 122–124, 137, 150, 161, 167, 169, 174, 186, 199
Movements, 193–195
Antioch, patriarchs of, *see* Albert of Rizzato
Antioch, princes of, *see* Bohemond III, Bohemond IV, Bohemond VII
Antioch, principality of, 56–57, 91, 116, 124, 133, 137, 141
Aquileia, diet of, 79
Arabia, 92–94, 168
Aragon, 97
Armand de Périgord, master of the Templars, 167
Armenia, 91, 121, 124
   The Third Crusade, 10
   Relations with the German Empire, 13
   Relations with the papacy, 56
   Relations with the Templars, 56
   Relations with the Teutonic Knights, 55–59, 174
Ascalon, 89, 98, 102
Asia Minor, 150
Assassins, 121
Atlīt, 33
Audita Tremendi, 11
Ayn Jālūt, battle of, 123–124, 137

Badr al-Dīn al-Aidamurī, 157
Badr al-Dīn Baisarī, 157
Baghdad, 121
Baghras, 56
Baldwin IX, count of Flanders, 69
Bari, 179, 181
Barletta, 179

221

227

Index

Thomas Agni of Lentino, patriarch of
 Jerusalem, 136, 183
Thomas Bérard, master of the Templars,
 157
Thomas of Salerno, 44
Tiberias (lake), 9, 90
Toron, 12, 54, 65, 68, 177
Toron Ahmud, 115
Toron de Saladin, 10
Trier, 94
Tripoli, county of, 49, 116, 137
Troyes, council of, 32
Tuscan League, 26
Tyre, 9, 12, 73, 80, 89, 90, 131

Ulric, leader of the Teutonic Hospital, 160
Urban III, pope, 9
Urban IV, pope, 110, 134, 137

Valdemar, king of Denmark, 45
Venice/Venetians, 105, 107, 113, 136,
 143, 182

Walter of Brabant, pilgrim, 19, 37

Walter IV, count of Brienne, 52
Werner of Merenburg, marshal of the
 Teutonic Order, 146, 202
Werner von Orseln, master of the Teutonic
 Order, 7
Wilbrand of Oldenburg, pilgrim, 29, 30
Wilhelm von Urenbach, master of the
 Teutonic Order, 105, 107, 182
 Movements, 193
William of Chartres, master of the
 Templars, 167
William of Châteauneuf, master of the
 Hospitallers, 168
William, archbishop of Tyre, 32
William of Gurcenich, 37
William, count of Holland, 99, 103
William of Sesso, 138
William of Vilaret, master of the
 Hospitallers, 165
Wirichus of Homberg, grand commander
 of the Teutonic Order, 151, 206
Wolfdietrich, 19

Lightning Source UK Ltd.
Milton Keynes UK
UKOW01f0017050917
308597UK00001B/148/P